Logos and Existence

American University Studies

Series VII
Theology and Religion

Vol. 98

PETER LANG
New York • San Francisco • Bern
Frankfurt am Main • Berlin • Wien • Paris

Donald R. Ferrell

Logos and Existence

The Relationship of Philosophy and Theology in the Thought of Paul Tillich

PETER LANG
New York • San Francisco • Bern
Frankfurt am Main • Berlin • Wien • Paris

Library of Congress Cataloging-in-Publication Data

Ferrell, Donald R.
　　Logos and existence : the relationship of philosophy
and theology in the thought of Paul Tillich / Donald R.
Ferrell.
　　　　p. cm. — (American university studies. Series VII,
Theology and religion ; 98)
　　Includes bibliographical references.
　　1. Tillich, Paul, 1886-1965.　2. Philosophical
theology—History—20th century.　I. Title.　II. Series:
American university studies. Series VII, Theology and
religion ; v. 98.
BX4827.T53F47　　1992　　230'.092—dc20　　90-23371
ISBN 0-8204-1469-7　　　　　　　　　　　　CIP
ISSN 0740-0446

CIP-Titelaufnahme der Deutschen Bibliothek

Ferrell, Donald R.
Logos and existence : the relationship of philosophy and
theology in the thought of Paul Tillich / Donald R.
Ferrell.—New York; Bern; Frankfurt am Main; Paris:
Lang, 1992
　　(American university studies : Ser. 7, Theology and
religion ; Vol. 98)
　　ISBN 0-8204-1469-7
NE: American university studies / 07

© Peter Lang Publishing, Inc., New York 1992

Printed in the United States of America.

Acknowledgments

Excerpts from *A History of Philosophy* by Frederick Copleston. Copyright © 1946 by The Newman Press. Reprinted by permission of Burns & Oates Ltd. and Search Press Ltd.

Excerpts from *A Commentary on Heidegger's Being and Time* by Michael Gelven. Copyright © 1970 by Michael Gelven. Reprinted by permission of Michael Gelven.

Excerpts from *Being and Time* by Martin Heidegger, translated by Macquarrie and Robinson. Copyright © 1962 by SCM Press. Reprinted by permission of HarperCollins Publishers.

Excerpts from *A History of Christian Thought* by Paul Tillich. Copyright © 1968 by Hannah Tillich. Reprinted by permission of HarperCollins Publishers.

Excerpts from *Dynamics of Faith* by Paul Tillich. Copyright © 1957 by Paul Tillich, renewed © 1985 by Hannah Tillich. Reprinted by permission of HarperCollins Publishers.

Excerpts from *What is Religion?* by Paul Tillich. Edited by James Luther Adams. Copyright © 1969 by Hannah Tillich. Reprinted by permission of HarperCollins Publishers.

Excerpts from "Existential Philosophy: Its Historical Meaning" by Paul Tillich. Copyright © 1944 by **The Journal of the History of Ideas**. Reprinted by permission of **The Journal of the History of Ideas**.

permission of Robert C. Solomon, University of Texas, Austin, Texas 78712.

Excerpts from "The Nature of Religious Language" by Paul Tillich. Copyright © 1955 by **The Christian Scholar**. Reprinted by permission of **Soundings**, successor journal to **The Christian Scholar**.

Excerpts from "The Two Types of Philosophy of Religion" by Paul Tillich. Copyright © 1946 by **Union Seminary Quarterly Review**. Reprinted by permission of **Union Seminary Quarterly Review**.

Excerpts from "The Problem of Theological Method" by Paul Tillich. Copyright © 1947 by **The Journal of Religion**. Reprinted by permission of The University of Chicago Press.

Excerpts from *Biblical Religion and the Search for Ultimate Reality* by Paul Tillich. Copyright © 1955 by The University of Chicago Press. Reprinted by permission of The University of Chicago Press.

Excerpts from *The Protestant Era* by Paul Tillich, translated by James Luther Adams. Copyright © 1948 and 1957 by The University of Chicago Press. Reprinted by permission of The University of Chicago Press.

Excerpts from *Systematic Theology*, Volumes I, II, and III by Paul Tillich. Copyright © Volume I 1951, Copyright © Volume II 1957, Copyright © Volume III 1963 by The University of Chicago Press. Reprinted by permission of The University of Chicago Press.

Excerpts from *Gesammelte Werke*, Volumes I, II, III, IV, V, VI by Paul Tillich. Copyright © Volume I 1959, Copyright © Volume II 1962, Copyright © Volume III 1965, Copyright © Volume IV 1961, Copyright © Volume V 1964, Copyright © Volume VI 1963 by Evangelisches Verlags-Werke. Reprinted by permission of Walter de Gruyter & Co.

Table of Contents

Preface

This study of Paul Tillich's thought originated as a PhD dissertation at the Graduate Theological Union, Berkeley, California. The PhD in philosophy of religion and philosophical theology at the Graduate Theological Union, as with other fields of study, is supported by the rich resources of the Graduate Division of the University of California, Berkeley, in this case the Philosophy Department.

My interest in Tillich's thought was first aroused when I was an undergraduate at West Virginia University. Professor William S. Minor, then a faculty member in the Philosophy Department, assigned THE COURAGE TO BE in his Contemporary Philosophy class in which I was enrolled, and I read it with almost total absorption. Little did I know at the time that this was the beginning of an engagement with Tillich's thought that has continued throughout my academic and therapeutic careers.

The significance of Tillich's philosophical theology became more clear to me when I began my theological education at Union Theological Seminary, New York City. It was my privilege to study with the late Dr. Daniel Day Williams, a master theologian and teacher, whose appreciative yet critical understanding of Tillich first led me to begin thinking about Tillich's method of correlation as it came to expression especially in his understanding of the relationship between philosophy and theology.

This deep, yet still largely nascent, interest in Tillich's thought I took with me to the Graduate Theological Union to carry out my work toward the PhD. Becoming immersed, as I did then, in the study of philosophy, on the one hand, and historical and philosophical theology on the other, my sense of Tillich's significance deepened as a result and the project of writing my PhD dissertation on Tillich emerged. I was guided in my own thinking about Tillich,

xii   *Preface*

by the late Dr. Bernard Loomer, who became the chair of my dissertation committee, and Dr. Durwood Foster, who also served on the committee.

It was my good fortune to enroll in the Continental Philosophy course taught by Dr. Hubert Dreyfus in the Philosophy Department at the University of California after I had begun my dissertation research on Tillich's thought. In my encounter with Kierkegaard and Heidegger as they were brilliantly taught and interpreted by Professor Dreyfus I was able to formulate, what in my mind, is one of the central ambiguities in Tillich's thinking, namely his attempt to create a synthesis between philosophy and theology as two distinct, but related forms of thought.

Anyone who reads Professor Dreyfus' long-awaited commentary on Heidegger's BEING AND TIME (Hubert L. Dreyfus, BEING-IN-THE-WORLD: A COMMENTARY ON HEIDEGGER'S BEING AND TIME, DIVISION I, Cambridge, MA: MIT Press, 1991) will see how much my approach to Tillich was shaped by his work on Kierkegaard and Heidegger. I only regret that his book was not available when I wrote my dissertation, and that the manuscript had already gone to press when his book appeared. Having Professor Dreyfus' book available would have helped me sharpen my argument and perhaps to have seen less continuity between Kierkegaard's and Heidegger's solutions to the issues of anxiety, truth and meaning than I saw before having carefully read his book. Certainly the interpretation I make of the thought of Kierkegaard and Heidegger's thought in this regard would have been made in more explicit dialogue with Professor Dreyfus's treatment of these issues had the book been available to me at the time of writing.

It was also my good fortune that Dr. John Coleman Bennett came to join the faculties of Pacific School of Religion and the Graduate Theological Union after retiring as President of Union Theological Seminary. Dr. Bennett not only participated as a member of my dissertation committee in the process of bringing this study to its completed state as a dissertation, but he has played a major role in its coming to publication as a book. I wish to express my gratitude to him for his encouragement and support and the generous sharing of his time and energy in helping to make this publication possible.

This study, by virtue of the academic and scholarly form in which it appears, manifests both the strength and weaknesses of that form. It was my intention when writing it both to carry out a sustained dialogue with Tillich's own texts as well as to discuss the critical assessment of Tillich's thought that had appeared to the time of writing. Hence, there is both ample quotation from Tillich's works as well as extensive discussion of the interpretation of Tillich's thought by others in the footnotes. Such a scholarly format, I understand, is off-putting to many readers; however, I continue to believe such writing has a valuable place within the economy of scholarly discourse.

Perhaps more significant is the critical conclusions to which I have come as to the adequacy of Tillich's synthesis of philosophy and theology. It might be said that the questions I raise about the "classical" character of Tillich's thought have been answered by Langdon Gilkey in his excellent recent study of Tillich's thought (Langdon Gilkey, GILKEY ON TILLICH, New York, The Crossroads Publishing Company, 1990). Gilkey makes the case for the dynamic, historical and dialectical character of Tillich's thought, especially in his daring suggestion that absolute nonbeing (Greek: "ouk on") may in some way "affect" the being of God as being-itself, a conclusion Tillich himself was not able to reach, yet, Gilkey argues, seems implied in his own thinking about being and nonbeing.

While I applaud Professor Gilkey for this imaginative and creative re-visioning of Tillich's thought, it is, in my view, in tension with Tillich's deep commitment to a more classical ontology, a commitment which constitutes in my reading what might be called "the essential Tillich".

Whatever the truth may be in this regard, perhaps the value of the present study may be seen, in part, as offering a contrasting interpretation to Gilkey's, thus sharpening the on-going encounter with Tillich's thought by those who feel, as I do, that his work constitutes a profound achievement in the history of religious and philosophical thinking and is of enduring significance for our present cultural quest for meaning.

There are others who have supported me in bringing this study to publication, whom I would also like to thank. My former wife, Dr. Marcia Freer, to whom I was married during the many years of graduate work and the writing of this study, made it possible for me to continue as a graduate student by putting her own professional development on hold and providing financial support over the course of many "lean" years of my being minimally employed. Fortunately, we were able to correct this situation after I began my teaching career and Marcia was able to finish her own graduate work and become a professor of psychology. However, such sacrifice was costly to her and needs to be acknowledged.

Joanna Luria Mintzer, to whom I am now married, has wholeheartedly endorsed the scholar-theologian in me and has not only graciously made room in our lives together for such work, but has passionately engaged with me in the exploration of questions of meaning that have somehow remained inescapable elements in my life and her's.

Dr. Ann Belford Ulanov, Jungian Analyst and Professor of Psychiatry and Religion at Union Theological Seminary, in my analytic work with her, has kept the question before me of "the courage to be" and what she has called, in her own profound and creative extension of Tillich's thought, "the anxiety of being" (Ann Belford Ulanov, "The Anxiety of Being", THE THOUGHT OF PAUL TILLICH, Adams, Pauck, Shinn editors, New York: Harper & Row, 1985) and in doing so has challenged and nurtured a greater capacity to be within me that has played a significant role in the decision to bring this study to publication.

Dr. Jeffery Utter, Lecturer in Religious Studies, California State University, Northridge, California read parts of the manuscript and has been a critical partner in dialogue regarding Tillich's theology as well as many other theologians and theological questions. I regret that a continent now divides us, making such dialogue more difficult.

Finally, I wish to dedicate this book to my two daughters, Andrea and Ariel. They have both given big chunks of what could have been childhood time with their father so that this study could be completed, and they each, in their own way, have taught me the wonder and mystery of being.

Donald R. Ferrell
Landgrove, Vermont
August 22, 1991

To

Andrea and Ariel

PART ONE

Chapter One

The Method of Analysis

Two of the most striking characteristics of Paul Tillich's thought are its historical continuity and systematic rigor. There is a remarkable continuity running from his earliest published works up to the crowning achievement of his life, the *Systematic Theology*. The motifs in Tillich's thought which have received their final formulation in the *Systematic Theology* are to be found in his earliest reflections and thus reveal a continuous development throughout his career.[1] At the same time the principle of systematic formulation is the overarching methodological style of Tillich's thought. He has consistently defended the unity of knowledge and therefore the legitimacy of the system.

The system has found expression at two important points in Tillich's work. It is seen first in his early attempt to arrange all the sciences within an embracing structure according to the ultimate presuppositions of the total cognitive enterprise and in relation to the varied methodologies and goals of the sciences.[2] One of the distinctive features of Tillich's effort to achieve a system of the sciences is precisely his insistence that the individual sciences cannot be adequately understood without reference to each other and to the "totality of knowledge" in which they stand. Thus the system of the sciences includes the working out of the ultimate principles of thought and reality which inform every cognitive venture. The truth is finally one and hence all the sciences serve "the one truth." They cannot live without a sense of their connection to the whole, and they are not fully intelligible unless they are understood in reference to the whole.[3] It is clear, for Tillich, that the whole of human knowledge must be subjected to organizing principles and that no particular discipline can make claims to have knowledge without reference to the embracing structure (system) which these principles make possible.[4] Thus a unifying philosophy of meaning, which deals both with the nature of thought and the nature of reality, is indispensable for the cognitive enterprise.

The second point in Tillich's thought in which the system finds expression is, of course, his *Systematic Theology*. In comparing these two exercises in system construction one is immediately struck by the following consideration. In the *System of the Sciences* Tillich is concerned not merely to arrange the scientific disciplines in encyclopedic fashion according to their objects and methods. Rather the sciences are expressions of the human spirit and thus must be understood in the context of a total analysis of the structure of reality. This analysis, for Tillich, is at the same time philosophical and theological in that it seeks to place the sciences within a system which lays bare the ultimate presuppositions of thought and being and directs the sciences toward the total structure of truth, thus giving the sciences an ultimate orientation. This means that while theology has its own methods and data, it cannot be merely one science among others and thus it does not find a place in the system of the sciences merely as one other science with its own limited field of knowledge. It is rather "Theonome Systematik."[5] Theology is indeed related to the other sciences, and part of Tillich's concern in constructing the system of the sciences was to "win a place for theology within the totality of human knowledge;"[6] however, it seems clear that the sciences find their place in a system which in *Das System der Wissenschaften* is only partially worked out and which moves in Tillich's later thought in the direction of a theological system in which philosophy and not the sciences plays a major role.[7] It is this larger theological system which finds expression in the *Systematic Theology*.[8]

Tillich has consistently defended the theological system against all his critics. For him the system is the most adequate form of methodological rationality available to the theologian. This means that the rational character of theology demands that its propositions must be stated under the logical canon of consistency, and consistency requires that each proposition be developed in terms of its own implications and in relation to all the other propositions. The system is the organic whole which results in pursuing the principle of consistency to its logical end. Thus as the most adequate form of methodological rationality, Tillich does not see the system as an alien structure imposed upon the "project" (in this case the Christian message) with which one is engaged. He continually distinguishes his understanding of system from the deductive systems of Lullus and Spinoza (ST:1: p. 52) and the "closed" system of Hegel.[9] For Tillich, "the concept of meaning is the concept of system"[10] and thus no fragment of meaning can stand independently of the whole in which it receives its meaning. Every fragment contains an implicit system of meaning to which it is committed if it is to have any meaning at all. Thus, the primitive Christian confession "Jesus Christ is Lord" is a fragment of meaning which can only be fully understood in a total system of meaning. It is the task of theology to create such a system in every generation and in the face of the obvious failure of every system to stand for all time.[11]

The system, then, means for Tillich, in the first place, the attempt to be consistent in one's thought. Consistency within the system itself means that each proposition of the system must be compatible with all the others. Hence while no proposition can be deduced from any other as if there were a formal necessity between them, consistency requires that no proposition contradict any other proposition in the system. In the second place the system means that no proposition can be isolated from the total context of meaning and in its isolated form become the basis of an adequate truth claim.[12] Put more positively this means that each proposition is subject to the determining principles of the system and receives its full meaning only in relation to all the other propositions of the system. Finally, as Tillich says: "The systematic construction has led me to conceive the object of theology in its wholeness, as a *Gestalt* in which many parts and elements are united by determining principles and dynamic interrelations." (ST, III: 3).

The drive toward wholeness of thought is the inner dynamic of the system. However, it should be said immediately that wholeness of thought which the system attempts to achieve does not mean that "everything under the sun" is to be included.[13] The system is not the frantic attempt "to relate every snippet to the whole fabric" for fear that the "universe will fall into pieces unless [the ontologist's] conceptualization constantly fixes everything into place."[14] For Tillich the "ambiguity of life" permeates all of the functions of the human spirit, including the cognitive function, and the system cannot overcome this ambiguity by becoming a cosmic roadmap in which the terrain of the universe is charted for the anxious traveler. Tillich's commitment to wholeness of thought rather grows out of his awareness that thinking is a dialectical process, which, once the finitude of the thinker is acknowledged, is subject only to this limitation and not to arbitrary delimitations of the scope and method of thought. Wholeness means that no implication of thought can be ruled out in advance and that the total structure of experience constitutes the proper object of thought. The system is the attempt to bring ultimate notions and their implications into a coherent whole. Thus, if the system is seen, as I believe Tillich does see it, as a cognitive structure clearly grounded in finitude and the creativity of human thought, then the fears of those who see it as the usurpation of finitude or the distortion of the Christian message are largely unwarranted.

This brief discussion of the place of system in Tillich's work is intended to draw attention to the fact that there is an internal unity within the structure of his thought, which must be fully acknowledged before one can deal adequately with it. The unity of Tillich's thought is represented by the system, and the system is the embodiment of a rational methodology which correlates symbols and concepts and explores as fully as possible their implications within a total vision and in the face of the whole range of human experience and concerns.[15] The conceptual wholeness of Tillich's thought demands, then, that every element must be related to every other element and to the whole in which they stand if it is to be understood.

However, merely by concentrating upon the elements or propositions of the system and asking if they are consistently developed in relation to one another, obviously will not yield an adequate understanding of Tillich. We must attempt to "get to the bottom" of the system, as it were, if we are to understand the details within it (in this case the relationship between philosophy and theology). We must attempt to penetrate to the foundation of Tillich's system, to those foundational notions to which his thought is committed and upon which he has constructed his system. These ultimate notions have both an historical and logical character. In order to avoid confusion, however, we shall turn our attention to their logical character at this point, leaving the question of their relationship to the philosophical and theological traditions in which Tillich stands to be discussed in a general way later.

As was pointed out above, Tillich has made clear that his is not a deductive system. However, we have also seen that Tillich has striven to make his system as consistent and coherent as possible. This means that while there are no self-evident and necessary axioms from which other truths are deduced for Tillich, yet the system embodies a clear logical form. Now, without discussing complex methodological questions at this point, we shall try to characterize the logical form of Tillich's system in a general way. Keeping in mind that while the system with which we are dealing is a theological system whose point of departure is the "theological circle" (ST; 1:8ff) and whose subject matter is thus delimited by that circle, yet Tillich's system, as a construction of thought,[16] shares certain general characteristics with any thought construction.[17]

The logical form of Tillich's system we shall designate, borrowing a term from Frederick Ferré which he has used to define the nature of metaphysics, as that of "conceptual synthesis."[18] By the term conceptual synthesis is meant the fact that Tillich draws together in synthetic form concepts taken from the history of thought which otherwise are *systematically* unrelated to one another. There is no intrinsic relationship, for example, between the concept "being" as it appears in the history of western philosophy and the (again following Ferré) explanatory "model" of Christian thought, "Jesus the Christ."[19] However, Tillich unifies these two concepts (leaving aside the question of their symbolic character for the moment) into a conceptual relationship to one another and reality is given a fundamental interpretation in terms of them.

If we follow Ferré's analysis further, we note that conceptual synthesis selects certain concepts which in relation to the synthesis (system), constitute its "metaphysical facts." Ferré states:

> the "facts" of metaphysics are supremely dependent on the conceptual activity of mind . . . A metaphysical system is a construct of concepts designed to provide coherence for all "the facts" on the basis of a theoretical model drawn from among "the facts." A "metaphysical fact," therefore, is a concept which plays a key role within the system, without which the system would flounder. . . . If this is the case, "metaphysical facts" are always relative to a specific metaphysical system.[20]

There are two aspects of Ferré's account of "metaphysical facts" which seem helpful in delineating the logical form of conceptual synthesis. In the first place, the metaphysical system, while addressing itself to "all the facts" must select from the manifold of facts those concepts upon which the individual system is to be constructed, and these selected "metaphysical facts" will play a logically decisive role in the structure of the system in question. That is to say, the metaphysical facts of the system have a significant logical priority over the content of the system such that "the system would flounder" without them. In the second place, the concepts which are chosen from among the facts as the basis of any given system become relative to that system in the sense that they are not logically inevitable for every thinker who attempts to construct a metaphysical system. Each creative philosopher will select from among the facts (which includes the history of thought) those concepts which seem to him most adequate as basic principles, but he is not required to think in terms of any given conceptuality. Thus, the choice of any particular "metaphysical fact" as a theoretical model represents a creative decision and a risk of the thinker in question.[21]

If we substitute for Ferré's term "metaphysical fact" what we have called the "foundational notions" of the system, then, using Ferré's analysis, we have adequate criteria for determining the role these ultimate notions play within the system. In the first place they have a logical priority over the content of the system in the sense that the system is based upon them and cannot stand without them. They have an internal necessity for the system and hence they cannot be derived from more basic notions. The fact that they are relative to a given system, and "depend for their confirmation upon the adequacy of the system in which they operate,"[22] points to the second important characteristic of the ultimate notions of the system. In being presupposed by the system, the ultimate notions as concepts are not established by formal proof or empirical verification, although both modes of analysis may be relevant to their full explication. The ultimate notions of a system of thought, rather, constitute the foundational principles on the basis of which both formal and empirical analysis proceeds in relation to the given system. As foundational principles, then, the ultimate notions function as "root metaphors" (Pepper), or "coordinating ideas" (Emmet) or "basic proposals" (Christian) or "theoretical models" (Ferré),[23] and as such, rather than having the character of objective validity in the sense that thought can demonstrate their validity apart from the system which they inform, they seem more closely associated with what could be called "faith judgements."[24]

Frank Dilley has put the matter well:

> There is no such thing as a neutral objective proof for metaphysical hypotheses, since the criterion for the truth of a metaphysical description, assuming its internal consistency and comprehensiveness, is its adequacy as a world description. Adequacy, however, is a function of perspective, of one's starting point, of one's basic judgement as to what is metaphysically significant in experience, of one's "faith." Metaphysical descriptions are "confessions" of the nature of things as seen from a particular perspective and are actually tested in terms of an appeal to the nature of things as seen from that perspective; hence there is a degree of circularity in metaphysical argumentation.[25]

Because the ultimate notions of any system are confessional-intuitive or hypothetical in character rather than objectively demonstrable, then it is to be expected that the history of thought will reveal a variety of such ultimate notions, and each set of ultimate notions will contain a relative degree of adequacy to the facts which they describe. However, the criteria by which they are evaluated will not rest upon the simple criteria of truth or falsity, because one cannot say that they are merely true or false. Rather their adequacy must be understood in terms of internal consistency and coherence and externally in relation to all the facts of experience at one's disposal. As metaphysical theories, then, they cannot be judged simply as true or false, but more or less adequate as cognitive descriptions of the "way reality really is."[26]

In terms of the foregoing, then, it should be clear that the only adequate way of understanding a given attempt at conceptual synthesis is to isolate the ultimate notions of the system and to show how they function within the system. It is to this task that we now turn in relation to Tillich's system. It would seem on the basis of the systematic character of Tillich's thought that this method is the most adequate way of understanding and interpreting him. At this point, we are not concerned to raise the question of the adequacy of his system, but merely to delineate the ultimate notions upon which it rests. It should also be understood that, while the idea of the ultimate notions of a system seems clear, there will probably be significant disagreement as to which notions are ultimate for any system. Thus it would seem that the fruitfulness of this method depends largely upon its capacity both to illuminate and to interrogate the structure of Tillich's thought once a given interpreter has decided upon its ultimate notions, rather than achieving universal agreement as to which notions are actually ultimate for Tillich.[27]

Notes

1   There are many examples of the historical continuity of Tillich's thought. (1) His earliest research dealt with the thought of Schelling and Schelling's influence can be seen throughout Tillich's career. (2) Tillich raised the problem of the historicity of Jesus as early as 1911 and the same problem is dealt with again in *ST*, vol 11. Paul Tillich, *On the Boundary* (Charles Scribner's Sons, N.Y., 1966), p. 49ff. (3) Tillich states that in 1904 (Paul Tillich, *A History of Christian Thought*, ed., Carl Braaten (Simon and Schuster, N.Y., 1972), p. 450ff), he formulated a position on the problem of doubt for a meeting of German and Swiss Christian fraternities of which he was a member at the University of Halle. He returned to this problem often throughout his life. Cf. his lecture "Rechtfertigung und Zweifel," *Vorträge der theologischen Konferenz zu Giessen*, No. 39 (1924), pp. 19-34; *The Protestant Era*, tr. James Luther Adams (University of Chicago Press, Chicago, 1948), pp. xiv-xv; *The Dynamics of Faith* (Harper Torchbooks, N.Y., 1957), p. 16ff and the discussion in the *ST*. Many other examples reflect the consistency with which Tillich addressed himself to fundamental problems during his life. They are not intended to suggest that his thought is a mere monolith, however, without internal alterations and development.

2   Paul Tillich, "Das System der Wissenschaften nach Gegenständen und Methoden," *Gasammelte Werke*, (Evangelisches Verlagswerk, Stuttgart, 1959), V.I, pp. 111-293. Tillich divides the sciences according to the following schema: Die Denk-oder Idealwissenschaften: logic and mathematics; Die Seinsoder Realwissenschaften: physical and social sciences; Die Geistes-oder Normwissenschaften: philosophy, art, jurisprudence, political science, and ethics.

3   *Ibid.*, p. 111.

4   Cf. James Luther Adams' very illuminating suggestion that *The System of the Sciences* represents Tillich's drive toward a new theological method. *Paul Tillich's Philosophy of Culture, Science, and Religion* (Harper and Row, N.Y., 1965), p. 116ff.

5   *Gesammelte Werke, op. cit.*, Vol. 1, p. 274 (hereafter GW). We shall discuss the meaning of this definition of theology in more detail in Part Two.

6   *On the Boundary, op. cit.*, p. 55.

7   Cf. Tillich's statement that Theology's relationship to the sciences is based on the philosophical element in both and thus merges in to the question of the relationship of theology and philosophy. *Systematic Theology* (University of Chicago Press, Chicago; Vol. 1:1951; vol. 2:1957; vol. 3:1963), vol. 1, p. 1 (hereafter ST).

8   Perhaps this assertion will become clearer when we discuss Tillich's understanding of theology and philosophy in more detail in Part Two. The point here is that Tillich's attempt to execute a "theology of culture" leads him to formulate ultimate principles which inform the system of the sciences, but these principles are the basis of a system in his later thought of which theology is the center rather than merely one of the disciplines of meaning-determination of *Das System der Wissenschaften.*

9   *A History of Christian Thought, op.cit.,* p. 414. Hegel's decisive error was his claim that his own system had achieved the finality of divine truth (Hubris). It is closed in the sense of "finished." While no system is closed in this sense, each system is closed in the sense that it is a creation of human thought and as such takes on the finality of an individual creation. "Das geisteswissenschaftliche System dagegen ist abgeschlossen, es ist eine *einmalige schopferische Setzung,* die nicht durchbrochen, sondern nur abgelost werden kann. Das echte System ist eine individuelle Schopfung." GW, *op. cit.,* v. 1, pp. 223-24; 243-44.

10   GW, *op. cit.,* p. 223.

11   Paul Tillich, *Biblical Religion & the Search for Ultimate Reality* (University of Chicago Press, 1955), p. 57. Kenneth Hamilton in *The System and the Gospel* (Macmillan Publishing Co., N.Y., 1962) has raised some critical questions regarding Tillich's system. His thesis that the system is incompatible with the Gospel simply begs the question with which Tillich has struggled all his life, viz., the question of the authority of the Christian message. Hamilton fails to understand that the Christian symbols, which are, for Tillich, original expressions of a theonomous situation, do not achieve authority over men apart from their interpretation and that Tillich's system stands in a long history of such interpretation. One could argue that Tillich's own interpretation of the Christian symbols has helped in our present epoch constitute their authority. To argue that the Christian symbols are forced into the meaning of the system is to assume that they have an intrinsic meaning and authority in themselves.

12   Cf. Tillich's critique of Kierkegaard for lacking in his vision of truth an adequate conceptuality and thus isolating the idea of the "God-Man" from its total context of meaning. *A History of Christian Thought, op. cit.,* p. 471.

13   "System stands between summa and essay. The summa deals explicitly with *all actual* and many potential problems. The essay deals explicitly with *one*

actual problem. The system deals with a group of actual problems which demand a solution in a special situation . . . Today a need for systematic form has arisen in view of the chaos of our spiritual life and the impossibility of creating a summa." ST, 1: 59.

14 Harvey Cox, *The Secular City* (Macmillan Company, 1965), p. 66. Cox's *ad hominem* arguments against metaphysics rests upon a personal preference for pragmatism. His case against metaphysics is merely a caricature of metaphysics as such and leaves the critical questions completely untouched.

15 Cf. John Dillenberger, "Paul Tillich: Theologian of Culture" in *Paul Tillich, Retrospect and Prospect* (Abingdon Press, Nashville & N.Y., 1966), pp. 31-41 for an illuminating essay concerning the scope and structure of Tillich's thought.

16 It should be kept in mind that Tillich nowhere identifies his system with reality as such. Hence, the misleading term "system of reality" should be totally avoided. Indeed, as a system of thought, it is a system whose object is reality as it is disclosed under certain conditions, and the question "is reality really like Tillich's says it is?" is always legitimate, but that does not rule out the systematic form as such. As Tillich makes clear, one systematic statement of the nature of reality can only be criticized in terms of another whether implicit or explicit, and thus the system as such is never in question, but rather its adequacy as a statement of reality.

17 Tillich has delineated these characteristics in a general way in his discussion of the rational character of systematic theology. *Ibid.*, p. 53ff.

18 Frederick Ferré, *Language, Logic and God* (Harper & Row, N.Y., 1961), p. 161ff.

19 "There is no logically necessary or deductive step from being to existence or from God to Christ," (ST, 11: 3). There is, of course, an historical relationship between these concepts in that some theologians have employed the conceptuality of being to explicate Christian doctrine, but this is an historical accident, not an intrinsic necessity.

20 Ferré, *op. cit.*, p. 161.

21 "The carrying out of this intention [of preserving the biblical witness] raises for the theologian the question of what language to choose, what concepts to appeal to, in his interpretive enterprise. In solving this problem the theologian accepts an enormous risk . . . It may be that he will choose to work with concepts . . . that turn out to be incompatible with the mentality of his own and later ages. This is the risk Tillich has knowingly accepted. . . . The act of constructing a system is, for this reason, deeply existential." Tom Driver, *Union Seminary Quarterly Review*, vol. xxi, no. 1, Nov. 1965, pp. 31-32.

22 Ferré, *op. cit.*, p. 161.

23 Stephen Pepper, "The Root Metaphor Theory of Metaphysics," *The Journal of Philosophy*, vol. xxxii, no. 14, July, 1935, pp. 365-74; Dorothy Emmet, *The Nature of Metaphysical Thinking* (Macmillan & Co., N.Y., 1961); William Christian, *Meaning and Truth in Religion* (Princeton University Press, Princeton, N.J., 1964); Ferré, *op. cit.* While there are quite different emphases and directions in these views, there seems to be agreement as to the logical character of ultimate presuppositions.

24 Provided, of course, that the notion of faith is not understood in its distorted form as knowledge for which there is a low degree of evidence or a mode of existence for which rational considerations are inappropriate. Cf. Paul Tillich, *The Dynamics of Faith* (*op. cit.*). The judgment in faith as ultimate concern involves a quest for adequate conceptual symbols in which one's ultimate concern is expressed. As Tillich has argued, it is within the structure of ultimate concern that the convergence of faith and knowledge and theology and philosophy is to be found.

25 Frank B. Dilley, *Metaphysics and Religious Language* (Columbia University Press, N.Y. and London, 1964), p. 69. Dilley has attempted to clarify the problem of philosophical disagreement on the basis of the "confessional" character of metaphysics. Philosophers disagree in the first instance because they hold different faiths.

26 There are a number of issues raised here, which cannot be discussed in detail. First, when we say that the ultimate notions of a metaphysical system are neither true nor false, we are using these terms in the strictest philosophical sense as properties of propositions or judgments. The criterion of adequacy is meant to extend beyond the criteria developed for judging propositions either true or false, and to suggest that in this strict sense it is not correct to ask whether a metaphysical theory is true or false. The question is one of adequacy, both formal and empirical. Secondly, it is also maintained that the criterion of adequacy takes us beyond the positivist's attempt to eliminate metaphysics as meaningless use of language, and therefore to a more positive evaluation of the philosophical tradition and the on-going task of metaphysics of understanding the world on the basis of ultimate notions and their generalization. However, what we are seeking here is a theory of metaphysics, a meta-metaphysics, rather than commitment to a particular metaphysical conceptuality.

27 There is disagreement among Tillich's interpreters in regard to construing his system after the model of a metaphysical system. John Herman Randall, Jr., has shown how the role of ontology in Tillich's thought is constructive for his program, and thus sees Tillich's effort as constructive metaphysics, although he notes Tillich's distrust of the word "metaphysics". Cf. John Herman Randall, Jr., *The Theology of Paul Tillich*, ed. Charles W. Kegley and Robert W.

Bretall (Macmillan Co., N.Y., 1952), pp. 132-161. Randall recognizes, however, some difficulty in assessing the role of theology in Tillich's system. (pp. 141; 160-161). David H. Kelsey, on the other hand, has taken a quite different view. He maintains that Tillich is first a confessional church theologian, who uses ontological analysis for purposes of theological argument; however, for Kelsey, it would be inappropriate, on the basis of Tillich's writings on theological method, to construe his theology as a metaphysical system. Cf. David H. Kelsey, *The Fabric of Paul Tillich's Theology* (Yale University Press, New Haven and London, 1967), p. 3. At best ontology is for Tillich, according to Kelsey, "philosophical anthropology" (p. 61). However, Kelsey makes a too sharp distinction between ontological concepts and religious symbols (pp. 51-88) and totally ignores Tillich's emphasis upon the *analogia entis* as the method by which religious symbols can be used. We shall argue that Tillich's attempt to create a theological system in constant correlation with philosophy and the role of ontology in his system warrants the method we are using. We shall return to this problem below.

Chapter Two

The Structure of Tillich's System

The problematic character of the delineation of the ultimate notions in Tillich's thought may be seen if we begin by examining the formal structure of his system. Tillich has attempted to construe method and structure in such a way that structure follows from method and method is carried through in relation to the completed structure. It is necessary, then, that first we look at Tillich's conception of method before proceeding to an analysis of the structure of his system. At this point our analysis of both method and structure will be quite cursory. We shall carry out a more substantive analysis in Part Two.

Tillich designates his method as the "method of correlation" (ST, 1: 59-66). In developing the conceptual meaning of his method, Tillich makes clear that method rests upon a prior knowledge of the system which it builds; however, both method and system are high-level abstractions, derived from the immediate cognitive relationship to the object of theological reflection. In fact,

> in at least one respect the description of a method is a description of a decisive aspect of the object to which it is applied. The cognitive relation itself, quite apart from any special act of cognition, reveals something about the object, as well as about the subject, in the relation (ST 1: 60).

Thus Tillich seems to be in agreement with a long-standing philosophical tradition beginning with Socrates[1] that method and system are ways of making explicit what man in some sense already knows or understands, although for Tillich, knowledge of the object of theology is not given in man's "natural" (existential) state and thus it cannot be evoked through the "maieutic" of philosophical method.[2] Knowledge of God must be given to man from "beyond" in the revelatory experience; however, revelatory knowledge comes as the answer to the question of God which arises out of man's existence. Thus, man's capacity to ask the question of God presupposes his awareness of an original unity with God, which "under the conditions of existence" he no longer experiences. Man, then, has some awareness of God, albeit a negative awareness of his separation from God.[3] Method and structure, therefore, are grounded in this twofold cognitive situation of essential unity with God and existential separation from God (ST, 1: 61).

The method of correlation consists, therefore, of making explicit on the one hand the questions which arise out of the structure of existence, a structure which man already vaguely understands, and on the other systematically formulating the answers given to man's questions on the basis of revelation; both tasks of the method carried out in mutual interdependence. Thus, the explicitation of questions and the formulation of answers must be correlated with each other, and this correlation determines the structure of the system. Within the formal correlation of question and answer, however, Tillich sees other patterns of correlation, which give the term "correlation" at least three distinct meanings. He states:

> There is a correlation in the sense of correspondence between religious symbols and that which is symbolized by them. There is a correlation in the logical sense between concepts denoting the human and those denoting the divine. There is a correlation in the factual sense between man's ultimate concern and that about which he is ultimately concerned. The first meaning of correlation refers to the central problem of religious knowledge . . . The second meaning of correlation determines the statements about God and the world; for example the correlation of the infinite and the finite . . . The third meaning of correlation qualifies the divine-human relationship within religious experience (ST, I: 60-61).

Now in Tillich's assigning these three meanings to the method of correlation, we are already in a position to see how the problem of ultimate notions asserts itself in his system. Accepting for the moment the vagueness of the terms "correspondence," "logical" and "factual" as Tillich uses them here, the question arises as to the logical order of what are apparently three distinct tasks which the method of correlation attempts to achieve within the system. For example, can a correspondence between religious symbols and that which they symbolize be determined without first establishing with some clarity the logical relationship of the concepts denoting the human and the divine? If a correspondence cannot be determined without the logical clarification of these two types of concepts, then the correspondence meaning of correlation is dependent upon its logical meaning. If, on the other hand, such a determination can be made without reference to the logical clarification of concepts, it would seem that the relationship of symbols and concepts would become quite problematic in relation to the ideal of the system,[4] viz., the mutual interdependence and determination of its elements, and the criterion of consistency would be compromised.

A more basic problem can be seen here, however. The notions "human" and "divine," "God" and "world," "infinite" and "finite" and "divine-human relationship" stand out as the points of departure for the correlative task in all its meanings. As such, they exercise logical priority over the method of correlation in the sense that they are the assumed correlates of the process of correlation. It is in their assumed, underived status that they seem to take on the character of ultimate notions. What, then, is their relationship to each other? Are some notions ultimate and others derivative, and are there other ultimate notions which Tillich, in his brief description of the method of correlation, does not introduce here? With these questions in mind, the method of correlation takes us into a more substantive analysis of the structure of the system.

We have said that the formal "defining characteristic" of the method of correlation is the correlation of question and answer. Therefore, the structure of the system is divided between those parts which explicate the full range of questions which emerge from the structure of existence and those parts which formulate the answers to these questions on the basis of revelation.[5] Concretely, the system is divided into five major parts. We must now examine this division in some detail.

As many of Tillich's interpreters have pointed out,[6] the structure of human existence plays a central role in his system. Tillich himself has stated this clearly when he asserts that:

> Whenever man has looked at his world, he has found himself in it as a part of it. But he also has realized that he is a stranger in the world of objects, unable to penetrate it beyond a certain level of scientific analysis. And then he has become aware of the fact that he himself is the door to the deeper levels of reality, that in his own existence he has the only possible approach to existence itself. [This] . . . means that the immediate experience of one's own existing reveals something of the nature of existence generally. (ST, 1: 61).

And again:

> Man occupies a pre-eminent position in ontology, not as an outstanding object among other objects, but as that being who asks the ontological question and in whose self-awareness the ontological answer can be found. The old tradition . . . that the principles which constitute the universe must be sought in man is indirectly and involuntarily confirmed, even by the behavioristic self-restriction. "Philosophers of Life" and "existentialists" have reminded us in our time of this truth on which ontology depends (ST, 1: 168).

Tillich has insisted that while man in his total structure is pivotal for his system, as the basis from which ontological questions emerge, he denies that the answers of the Christian message are derived from the structure of human existence.[7] Question and answer are independent, but they sustain a correlative interdependence, since they arise from different sources.[8] Before the answers of the Christian message can become relevant to man, however, theological analysis must lay bare the structure of human existence in such a way that the questions of which man is vaguely aware in his "pre-ontological" state can become ontologically explicit.

For Tillich the analysis of human existence discloses, in the first place, that a distinction must be made within the structure of human existence itself between what man is essentially and what he is in his "self-estranged existence." Thus a conceptuality must be developed drawn from man's awareness both of his essential structure and his estrangement from that structure, and it must contain the questions which logically emerge from these two aspects of the structure of being. This conceptuality contains concepts grounded in man's essential character and the questions arising therein, concepts grounded in the structure of existential estrangement and the questions it provokes, and concepts which presuppose the presence of both essential and existential characteristics in man's concrete actuality and the questions which emerge out of this actuality. These concepts must be correlated with the conceptuality which is formulated in answer to these three sets of questions. The body of Tillich's systematic theology consists of concepts drawn from these three dimensions or aspects of the structure of human existence and the questions attending them and the corresponding theological concepts which constitute the structure of the Christian message (ST, 1: 67).

The conceptual system which Tillich constructs on the basis of the structure described above is centered around concepts which are appropriate to the distinctions made within the structure of being and the theological concepts (answers) formulated in relation to these distinctions.[9] The controlling concept which is grounded in the essential character of man and which functions to explicate the questions intrinsic to man's essential character, Tillich designates as "Being" and the corresponding theological concept is "God". This set of concepts constitutes the first major division of the system. The concept which denotes the situation of existential estrangement and which illuminates the questions man asks vis-a-vis this situation, Tillich identifies as "existence" and the corresponding theological concept is "Christ." With these concepts the second major division of the system is delineated. The concept which denotes the concrete actuality of man and which includes essential and existential elements is called "Life" and the corresponding theological concept is the "Spirit" (ST, 1: 66-67). This is the third major division of the system. Thus, God is the answer to the problem of being, Christ is the answer to the problem of existence, and the Spirit is the answer to the problem of life.

However, before these three main parts of the system can be developed, the epistemological foundations of the system must first be made clear. Thus, the system must begin with an analysis of reason and it must show that revelation is the answer to the questions raised within the structure of reason. "Reason and Revelation" constitute, therefore, the first part of the system. Life, insofar as it reaches its apex in man, has a dimension which is actualized only in man, viz., the dimension of history. Therefore, the last part of the system Tillich calls "History and the Kingdom of God." The system in its totality, then, consists of five parts: "Reason and revelation," "Being and God," "Existence and Christ," "Life and the Spirit," and "History and the Kingdom of God."

Now that we have an overview of the method and structure of Tillich's system, we can address ourselves to the major problems which arise in relation to the question of the ultimate notions of his thought. It is obvious that the distinction between essence and existence informs the total conceptuality of the system. Tillich, himself, acknowledges this when he asserts:

> A complete discussion of the relation of essence to existence is identical with the entire theological system. The distinction between essence and existence, which religiously speaking is the distinction between the created and the actual world, is the backbone of the whole body of theological thought. It must be elaborated in every part of the theological system (ST, 1: 204).

Do we have here, then, in the notions "essence" and "existence" two of the ultimate notions of the system? Before we can answer this question, we must consider some further problems which arise out of the conceptuality of the system.

"Being," "Existence" and "Life" also assume crucial significance for the system. In Tillich's treatment of "Reason" and "History," however, we can already see the logical subordination of these notions to more fundamental ones, and thus we can begin to discern the pattern of ultimate and derivative notions within his analysis. In regard to the treatment of reason and revelation Tillich states:

> The problem of reason and revelation is secondary to that of being and God, although it was discussed first. Like everything else, reason has being, participates in being, and is logically subordinate to being. Therefore, in the analysis of reason and the questions implied in its existential conflicts we have been forced to anticipate concepts derived from an analysis of being (ST, 1: 163).

One can see the same relationship of logical dependence in Tillich's treatment of history. While history is the most "embracing dimension" of life, yet it presupposes the prior development of the concept of life. Logically therefore the notion of history cannot be developed without the full development of those critical ideas by which the notion of life is delineated, especially the ideas of the functions of life and the concept of spirit (ST, 111: 297ff.).

Thus, the concept of reason is subordinated to the concept of being and the concept of history to the concept of life. The question naturally arises, therefore, as to the relationship of the concepts "being," "existence," and "life" to each other. It is obvious that as concepts they "hold the system together" in the sense that they each provide conceptual analysis of all facts on the basis of selected facts and that taken together they constitute a conceptual synthesis. It also seems clear that each of these concepts presupposes the others for their complete development, and one would be hard pressed to show that any one of these notions is more fundamental than the others.

Tillich sometimes talks as if some notions are more inclusive than others. For example, the concept of life as the "actuality of being" "unites the two main qualifications of being which underlie this whole system; these two main qualifications of being are the essential and the existential" (ST, III: 11-12). Clearly, then, the concept of life is more inclusive than the concept existence as Tillich uses it. However, life as the actuality of being obviously presupposes the concept of being in the same way as does the distinction between essence and existence as qualifications of being, and the concept of being cannot unite these two qualifications in the way the concept of life does, since Tillich introduces it to denote first of all the essential dimension of existence. We are forced, then, to acknowledge the irreducible circularity of these three concepts which constitute one side of the main body of the system as well as the distinction between essence and existence to which each of them on its own terms addresses itself.

In the light of this circularity, it would seem forced and self-defeating to argue that one of these notions, e.g. being or life, is more fundamental to Tillich's system than the others. Therefore, we either have to argue that all three concepts and the distinction between essence and existence they presuppose together with their correlative theological concepts or symbols constitute the ultimate notions of the system, or we must look beyond the "surface structure" of the system to its "deep structure" (Chomsky) to find them. If we take the first alternative, we would, in effect, merely be identifying the ultimate notions of the system with the system itself and thus no analytical precision would be achieved, for we could not determine the principles which lead Tillich to characterize these concepts as he does. Consequently, we must look beyond the formal concepts of the system for the ultimate notions they seek to explicate.

We shall argue, then, that there are three principles or ultimate notions which inform Tillich's system. The first ultimate notion basic to Tillich's thought is the principle of finitude. It is the structure of finitude which underlies Tillich's use of the concepts being, existence and life and to which the distinction between essence and existence is appropriate. The second ultimate notion of Tillich's system is to be discerned in his claim that there appears within the structure of finitude the awareness of that which is absolute or unconditional.[10] The unconditioned or unconditional (*Unbedingte*), which appears within the structure of finitude is the ultimate correlate of finitude in that it is the ultimate source of being and meaning and thus the radical opposite of finitude. Its contrast with finitude is precisely its unconditionedness. It is characterized both philosophically (being-itself) and theologically (God) in Tillich's thought and it is encountered within the total range of finitude: cognitively as the "depth of reason," ethically as the moral imperative, religiously as "ultimate concern" and "the Holy."[11] The third ultimate notion underlying Tillich's thought is his claim that an ultimate unity obtains between finitude and the unconditioned in spite of the presence of existential estrangement within the structure of finitude. It is this last notion which is especially important for Tillich's method, and also for his epistemology.[12]

It is now necessary to explore the content of Tillich's system in terms of these three ultimate notions. Our purpose here, however, is not to achieve an exhaustive analysis of every aspect of Tillich's system, but rather to develop the meaning and significance of the ultimate notions as they are illustrated within the total system. It is hoped that this analysis will set the stage for the more detailed analysis of Part Two.

Notes

1 Cf. R. G. Collingwood, *An Essay on Philosophical Method* (Oxford University Press, London, 1933), p. 10ff. Cf. also, D. S. Shwayder, *The Stratification of Behaviour* (The Humanities Press, N.Y., 1965) p. 11 for a more recent statement of this function of philosophy, and from a quite different posture see Martin Heidegger, *Being and Time*, tr. John Macquarrie and Edward Robinson (Harper and Row, 1962) esp. p. 188ff.

2 *A History of Christian Thought, op. cit.*, p. 473.

3 Tillich has, from his earliest writings on Schelling, maintained the principles of identity with God and man's separation from God as the foundational principles of his epistemology. These principles are stated clearly in Tillich's second dissertation on Schelling, "Mystik und Schuldbewusstsein, in Schellings Philosophischer Entwicklung." Cf.: "Mystik und Schuldbewusstsein, Gefühl der Einheit mit dem Absoluten und Bewusstsein des Gegensatzes zu Gott, Prinzip der Identität von absolutem und individuellem Geist und Erfahrung des Widerspruchs zwischen dem heiligen Herrn und dem sündigen Geschöpf: das ist eine Antinomie, deren Lösung das religiöse Denken zu allen Zeiten in der Kirche angestrebt hat und immer wieder anstreben muss. Auf der einen Seite findet der Wille zur Wahrheit erst da Befriedigung, wo die Einheit von Erkennendem und Erkanntem erreicht ist, wo das Absolute ebenso Subjekt wie Objekt der Erkenntnis ist, auf der anderen Seite deckt das Sittengesetz, wo es in seiner Tiefe erfasst wird, die Widergöttlichkeit des Wollens, die Feindschaft des Subjekts gegen Gott auf." (GW, 1, op. cit., p. 17).

4 Many of Tillich's critics have called attention to this problem. We shall return to it below. Cf. John Herman Randall, *op. cit.*, p. 160; Cf. also William P. Alston in *Religious Experience and Truth*, ed. by Sidney Hook (New York University Press, 1961), pp. 12-26.

5 The correlation of question and answer commits Tillich's theology essentially to the task of apologetics, and thus it takes seriously both the "eternal truth" of the Christian message and the temporal "situation" in which it is received. Kerygma and situation are held in a dynamic balance, both poles being determinative for Tillich's understanding of theology (ST, 1:3-8). Thus, Tom Driver oversimplifies when he says that by calling his theology "apologetic" Tillich was merely trying to say that his method is anti-Barthian. Surely the urgency of Tillich's method cannot be understood if he is seen merely to be

interested in addressing the Church. Indeed, he does wish to do that ("theology is the function of the church"), but his address must be seen vis-a-vis the massive breakdown of the meaning of Christian symbols for men both inside and outside the church. Cf. Tom Driver, USQR, *op. cit.*, p. 32.

6 Cf. Alexander J. Mckelway, *The Systematic Theology of Paul Tillich* (John Knox Press, Richmond, 1964), p. 45ff and Bernard Martin, *Paul Tillich's Doctrine of Man* (James Nisbet, London, 1966). David Hopper has argued that Tillich's emphasis on man as "microcosm" led him away from a "corporate-historical existentialism" influenced by Marx and thus away from the kairos doctrine and preoccupation with the "macrocosm" (social-political realm) to an existentialism with more individualistic applications. If Hopper is correct, human existence as such, apart from its social and historical context, would seem to be more decisive for Tillich's later thought. However, Tillich's relationship to Kierkegaard and Heidegger remains to be discussed. Cf. David Hopper, *Tillich, A Theological Portrait* (J. B. Lippincott, Philadelphia and N.Y., 1968), pp. 65-100.

7 Cf. Tillich's analysis of his theological method in comparison with Barth. "Karl Barth starts from above, from the trinity, from the revelation which is given, and then proceeds to man . . . Whereas, . . . I start with man, not deriving the divine answer from man, but starting with the question which is present in man and to which the divine revelation comes as answer." *Perspectives on Protestant Theology, op. cit.*, p. 242.

8 Cf. Bernard M. Loomer, "Tillich's Theology of Correlation," *Journal of Religion*, Vol. XXXVI, no. 3 (July, 1956), pp. 150-156. Correlation is possible because man and God have the structure of being in common. But God's answer cannot be derived from man's question, since God is not bound to the structure and man is. Hence, Tillich's rejection of supernaturalism and naturalism as non-correlative.

9 We are using the term "concept" here in a very general way to include both those notions which denote the structure of existence and those notions which denote the divine. Since, for Tillich, the analysis of existence is a philosophical task, the notions derived from this analysis are more properly concepts, while the theological notions which are correlated with the analysis of existence are symbols (ST, 1: 63-64). The word "concept" here is meant to include both ontological concepts and theological symbols.

10 One of Tillich's most forceful statements of the awareness of the unconditioned within finitude is his *My Search for Absolutes* (Simon and Schuster, N.Y., 1967). Tillich's formulations here are somewhat confusing in that he claims to find absolutes within the structure of finitude (e.g. the logical and semantic structure of the mind and its unification of sense experience; the categories and polarities; the unconditional character of the moral imperative), which point beyond themselves to the "Absolute-itself" (being-itself).

While the former absolutes seem very close to Kant's a priori conditions for experience, the Absolute-itself is the ultimate notion we are seeking. Tillich's terminology is also confusing, for he denies using the terms "unconditional" or "absolute" for God except in his early writings. Paul Tillich, "Reply to Interpretation and Criticism," *The Theology of Paul Tillich, op. cit.*, p. 340.

11   In the schema of ST, III, under the functions of life: culture (the self-creativity of life) morality (the self-integration of life) and religion (the self-transcendence of life). The unconditioned construed as Spirit overcomes the ambiguities of life in all its functions. One can see again the correlative character of the unconditioned to finitude on the basis of the former's perfection.

12   In the determination of the ultimate notions set forth here, I am indebted to Bernard M. Loomer "Tillich's Theology of Correlation" *op. cit.*, and Edgar A. Towne, *Ontological and Theological Dimensions of God in the Thought of Paul Tillich and Charles Hartshorne* (Unpublished Ph.D. dissertation, University of Chicago, 1967). Loomer's emphasis that God is correlative to man's need on the basis of the former's perfection classically conceived is accepted here. I am in agreement with Towne that the unity of unconditioned and conditioned being is one of Tillich's ultimate notions; however, I have taken the principle of finitude to include the two other ultimate notions Towne has delineated, viz., the phenomenological context of all cognition and the limitation of all literal statements to phenomena. In my view, it is the structure of finitude which determines both Tillich's epistemology and his understanding of language.

Chapter Three

The Foundational Notions
of Tillich's Thought:
The Principle of Finitude

The notion of finitude informs nearly all of Tillich's writings, but he has given it systematic consideration in Part Two of the *Systematic Theology*. Although it is not stated explicitly by Tillich, it seems clear on the basis of his discussion there that finitude is the generic feature of the "structure of being" or of what Tillich also calls the "ontological structure." For Tillich the structure of being is not to be identified with being-itself, although in one passage it does seem to be identified with "reality as a whole" (ST, I: 20). "Reality as a whole" or "being as a whole", however does not mean for Tillich "the whole of reality" or the "whole of being," since thought obviously cannot grasp the "whole" of being or reality.[1] Thought rather seeks the structure which makes reality a whole. Thought seeks the structure of being (ST, I: 18). As we have said, Tillich does not state explicitly that the "structure of being" is finite or that it is to be identified with the "ontological structure." However, in order to see if this is the case and to achieve as much clarity as possible concerning his use of these terms, we must now discuss them in some detail.

J. H. Randall has argued that Tillich in using "being as such" and "reality as a whole" as equivalent terms has confused the conceptualities of two distinct traditions and that these terms cannot be used as equivalents.[2] "Being as such," Randall argues, is derived from the Aristotelian tradition and means "the generic features of any subject matter." "Reality as a whole," on the other hand, originates in the Platonic-Neo-Platonic tradition and is employed in German Idealism to mean "a unified and unifying structure of the universe," which can be and in fact has been identified with God. The former, while exemplified in religion, is the legitimate concern of ontology or metaphysics, for Randall, while the latter is much more the object of religious "aspiration," and cannot as such be a proper ontological concern. The term "structure of being," Randall asserts, cannot be identified with both these conceptions, since they have quite different meanings.

Tillich's response to Randall's criticism is illuminating. In the first place, he passes over Randall's point that "being as such" and "reality as a whole" have different meanings. Rather, Tillich acknowledges that "'being as a whole' ['being as such'] is an ambiguous phrase, used only as the opposite of 'the whole of being.' It actually means for me no more than 'being-itself.'"[3] Secondly, there seems to be no evidence in Tillich's writings to show that he does not identify "reality as a whole," "being as a whole," and "being-itself."

There is, however, much evidence in his writings that he does make this identification; hence the validity of Randall's interpretation. Thus, when Tillich defines philosophy as "that cognitive approach to reality, in which reality as such is the object" (ST, I: 18), it is also fair to say on the basis of his statement above that "being as such" is the object of philosophy, and consequently, that "being-itself" is the "object" of philosophy. But Tillich goes on to say in the passage just quoted that "reality as such" or "reality as a whole" is the "structure which makes reality a whole." In asking the question of reality as a whole, then, philosophy asks the question of that which makes reality a whole or being a whole, and this is the question of being-itself.[4] If "being as a whole" is the same as "being-itself" for Tillich, and if "being as a whole" means the "structure of being," then it would seem, as Randall has concluded,[5] that the structure of being is identified with being-itself and therefore with the ground and power of being. Consequently, the structure of being could not have finitude as one of its generic features, since being-itself is beyond both finitude and infinity (ST, I: 237), and it could not be identified with what Tillich calls "the basic ontological structure," which is, as we shall see, a finite structure.

Tillich clearly denies, however, that the structure of being is identical with being as such, reality as such or being-itself. Rather the structure of being is grounded or rooted in being-itself, and being-itself (or God) *is* the structure of being only in the sense that it (he) "has the power of determining the structure of everything that has being (ST, I: 239)." Thus, when philosophy asks the question of the structure of being, it acknowledges that being or reality is structured, and the question of reality as a whole, being as a whole, or being-itself is the question of that which makes the structure of reality or the structure of being possible, but philosophy can ask that question only on the basis of the *givenness* itself of the structure of being. When seen in this context it is obvious that the structure of being cannot be identified with reality as a whole, being as a whole or being-itself, although Tillich's language does not always make this clear.[6]

If the structure of being, then, cannot be identified with being-itself, the question arises as to whether it can be considered a finite structure, that is, is finitude the basis of carrying out Tillich's suggestion that the structure of being should be more sharply distinguished from being-itself? Again, the answer to this question must take into account the ambiguity we have already seen surrounding Tillich's use of the term "being" and the technical concepts derived from it. The answer must be *interpretative*, attempting to bring clarity and consistency of view out of the ambiguity haunting Tillich's thought. However, the interpretation must be justified by what Tillich says, and it also must recognize that ultimate clarity and consistency may not be possible. Then, the question becomes to what extent the ambiguity or inconsistency of Tillich's thought vitiates his quest for conceptual integrity.

Perhaps the most plausible argument for the view that the structure of being is finite in Tillich can be based upon his statements regarding the relationship of philosophical thought, that is, the "categories, structural laws, and universal concepts of philosophy"

(ST, I: 20) to the structure of being. It seems clear from every passage in which Tillich discusses this question that the categories and concepts of philosophy have a direct application to the structure of being, that is, borrowing the terminology of H. N. Wieman,[7] the structure of being is "specifiable" and is, in fact, "specified" by the categories and concepts of philosophy. Moreover, it would seem that it is specified nonsymbolically or in the proper sense. In Tillich's description of the relationship of the categories and concepts to the structure of being, their literal specification of that structure seems presupposed. The following passages are offered as evidence in support of this view of the relationship of philosophical thought to the structure of being in Tillich:

(1) Philosophy asks the question of reality as a whole; it asks the question of the structure of being. And it answers in terms of categories, structural laws, and universal concepts. It must answer in ontological terms" (ST, I: 20).

(2) Theology, when dealing with our ultimate concern, presupposes in every sentence the structure of being, its categories, laws, and concepts . . . The Structure of being and *the categories and concepts describing this structure* [emphasis mine] are an implicit or explicit concern of every philosopher and of every theologian" (ST, I: 21).

(3) Of course, the philosopher, as a philosopher, neither criticizes nor augments the knowledge provided by the sciences. This knowledge forms the basis of his description of the *categories, structural laws and concepts which constitute the structure of being*" [emphasis mine] (ST, I: 22).

These passages assert clearly that the categories and concepts of philosophy describe the structure of being, but they do not state explicitly that they describe this structure literally or nonsymbolically. If they do not describe the structure of being literally, however, the reason can only be that the structure of being transcends the realm in which these categories and concepts function properly or literally, that is, the realm of finitude.[8] It seems to be a plausible conclusion, however, that the categories do describe the structure of being literally or nonsymbolically.

In the first place, it is difficult to see how Tillich can maintain that the categories and concepts *constitute* the structure of being unless they describe that structure in their proper or literal sense. Unless Tillich is using the word quite loosely, it would seem that he is committed to saying that the structure of being is in principle defined and delimited by the categories and concepts which describe it so that, in contrast to being-itself, its meaning or content is fully determined by these categories and concepts. In fact, Tillich can even refer to the categories and concepts themselves as "structures of being,"[9] and we must conclude from this that at least regarding the issue of literal specification, the term "constitutes" is to be taken seriously.[10] The categories and concepts, then, determine the structure of being in the sense that they describe literally or nonsymbolically the "texture" of that structure as one.[11]

This argument can be strengthened by calling attention to two further considerations. First, Tillich in describing the function of the categories states that they are directly, i.e. properly, related to reality. He asserts:

> Categories are the forms in which the mind grasps and shapes reality. To speak of something reasonably is to speak of it by means of the categorical forms, through "ways of speaking" which are also the forms of being. The categories are to be distinguished from logical forms which determine discourse but which are only indirectly related to reality itself. The logical forms are formal in that they abstract from the content to which the discourse refers. The categories, on the other hand, are forms which determine content (ST, I: 192).

We shall not venture to say just what Tillich has in mind here by "logical forms," perhaps mathematical entities or the symbolic language of logic, but it seems clear that he is arguing by contrasting the categories with these forms that the former do, in fact, describe reality or the structure of being directly and we conclude literally. However, secondly, the argument that the categories and concepts do describe the structure of being literally seems confirmed by Tillich's explicit claim that the structure of being provides the material for the symbolic description of being-itself or God and thus that the categories and concepts (the ontological elements) symbolize being-itself in its different dimensions (ST, I: 243). It is clear, however, that before the categories and concepts can have a symbolic meaning, they must have a literal or proper meaning,[12] and thus, if they constitute and specify directly the structure of being, and if after the structure of being has been properly specified, it provides the material for the symbolization of being-itself, it follows that the categories and concepts sustain their literal or proper meaning in relation to the structure of being.

Even though it seems plausible, then, that the categories and concepts specify the structure of being literally or nonsymbolically, the question remains as to the finitude of that structure. We shall argue here that the structure of being is finite on the basis of Tillich's clear assertion that the categories and concepts which describe literally the structure of being are themselves expressions of finitude, that is, the categories and concepts of ontology function properly or nonsymbolically within the realm of finitude. The total ontological schema, which Tillich divides into four levels of ontological concepts, implies finitude as its proper content (ST, I: 189-90; 192, 198; 202). The conclusion seems clearly justified, therefore, that because the ontological schema describes the structure of being, and because it implies or expresses finitude in each level of its conceptuality, then the structure of being must itself be finite. Thus, that which the ontological schema describes or specifies generically is the finitude of the structure of being, while it determines at the same time the "fabric" of the structure of being according to the four levels of ontological concepts.

Conceived this way, a very tentative answer to the question of the identification of the "structure of being" and the "ontological structure" may now be offered. It seems clear that Tillich intends by the "structure of being" the whole of finite reality or the inclusive structure within which all finite things stand, and it could well be equated with the word "universe."[13] The "ontological structure," which is also a finite structure, on the other hand, is the structure of self and world. It is the presupposition of the ontological question and the subject-object structure of reality. As such it is "the basic articulation of being. The self having a world to which it belongs — this highly dialectical structure — logically and experientially precedes all other structures" (ST, I: 164). We will extend Tillich's words here to assert that the ontological structure is the basic articulation of the *structure* of being and thus the former is to be identified with the latter in the sense that the ontological structure represents the basic determination of the structure of being. Thus, every entity which stands within the finite structure of being will obviously fall within the dipolar ontological structure and it would seem somewhere along the continuum from fully developed selfhood to fully developed worldhood.[14]

It is the introduction of the ontological structure of being which constitutes the major reference point of Tillich's ontological analysis, however, and this sends him at the outset toward a phenomenological ontology rather than developing whatever cosmological possibilities might attend his notion of the "structure of being."[15] It is to Tillich's analysis of the basic ontological structure, then, that we now turn our attention, for it is in relation to this analysis that the notion of finitude is fully developed.

We have seen that the structure of being and its most basic determination, the dipolar ontological structure, is defined generically by its finitude. However, the meaning of the notion of finitude itself, as Tillich understands it, has yet to be made clear. In attempting to carry out this task, we shall follow the course of Tillich's own analysis by examining the ontological schema as he has developed it, after which we shall attempt to show the meaning of finitude for Tillich as it comes into view in relationship to the ontological schema. We shall then attempt to state the critical issues which emerge around the concept of finitude as one of the foundational notions of Tillich's thought.

As we have seen, Tillich distinguishes four levels of ontological concepts, (ST, I: 164) all of which are *a priori* in the sense that they make experience possible and therefore define with increasing specificity the structure of being or the ontological structure. Therefore, they are known as the result of an analysis of experience. Taken together, they constitute what we have called the ontological schema and their task is the description[16] of the structure of being or the ontological structure. As human conceptions they correspond more or less adequately to the structural elements which constitute the structure of being.

The first level of ontological concepts is the basic ontological structure itself. This structure reflects the pre-eminent place of man within the order of being, for man is alone conscious of his participation in the structure of being. Tillich refers with approval to Heidegger's method in *Sein und Zeit* in which "*Dasein*" is "the place where the structure of being is manifest" (ST, I: 168). Thus, the ontological schema is peculiarly related to man in that it is man's being which is "uncovered" in the ontological analysis. While Tillich does not employ Heidegger's distinction between "Existenzialien" (the explicata which are uniquely relevant to Dasein) and "Kategorien" (the explicata relevant to all other entities),[17] the Heideggerian character of the ontological schema is clearly evident. Thus: "the basic structure of being and all its elements and the conditions of existence lose their meaning and their truth if they are seen as objects among objects" (ST, I: 169).

The basic ontological structure, then, is the polar structure of self and world and it points to the complex, dialectical relationship obtaining between these two poles. The self has a world to which it belongs. The fundamental datum which informs the ontological structure is not the mere existence of selves or the world, but rather the datum of *self-relatedness* which the structure implies. The self is constituted by its world and the world without the self is dead. A genuine polarity obtains, therefore, and if one pole is lost, the other is lost (ST, I: 171). It is this original, mutually reciprocal, underived polar structure with which ontology must begin. The question of that which precedes this original structure cannot be answered by ontology. It is the question to which revelation alone is the answer. (ST, I: 174).

The term "self" is used by Tillich to refer properly to the human self; however, it is more inclusive than the term "ego," because it contains in its meaning both the subconscious and the unconscious elements from which ego consciousness arises. Therefore, it is intended to include subconsciousness, the unconscious (Tillich does not make clear the distinction between the two) and ego consciousness within the total frame of self-consciousness. Because the term "self" has this more inclusive meaning than the term "ego," Tillich believes that "selfhood or self-centeredness must be attributed in some measure to all living beings and, in terms of analogy, to all individual Gestalten even in the inorganic realm" (ST, I: 169). However, man alone is a fully developed and completely centered self. He has self-consciousness in the most complete sense of the term.[18]

Man like every other being *has* an environment to which he belongs, but because he is an ego-self, man transcends every environment. Man has a world. In man, then, world and environment are to be distinguished. Environment is that within a limited space with which a being has an active interrelationship. Thus, the environment of each being is peculiarly his own. Man stamps his own subjectivity upon his immediate environment, and his subjectivity is determined by his environment. World, on the other hand, "is the structural whole which includes and transcends all environments" (ST, I: 170) and man also belongs to the world of this larger whole. Man, then, is not bound to any environment, but constantly drives beyond each limited environment toward the inclusive world.[19]

The term "world" in Tillich does not mean "the sum total of all beings." Rather it introduces the notion of structure within manifoldness, for no matter how pluralistic our interpretation of the world is, its structure abides and underlies every process. However, even though Tillich attempts to steer a middle course between the subjective excess of a philosopher like Fichte or the objective realism of Hobbes, he does concede that the structure or the order of the world is fundamentally the work of "perspective," that is, the perspective of the self which looks out past its immediate environment and structures the world according to its perspective. Thus, no matter how "discontinuous it may be in itself, the whole opposite man is *one* at least in this respect, that it is related to us perspectively" (ST, I: 170). While Tillich's language here betrays a somewhat Kantian orientation, it would seem that the notion of perspective is introduced not so much to stress the distinction between phenomena and the thing-in-itself, but rather to stress the correlative character of the self-world structure. It is useless to talk about the structure of the world apart from the self to which it appears as a structured whole. Hence, Tillich is not concerned to offer proofs for the independent existence of the world. But, on the other hand, the whole opposite the self is never merely the result of the projections of the self. It is the structure over against the self by which the self is able to encounter itself. Self and world constitute the basic ontological structure and neither pole can be abstracted from the other. Any attempt to break their polar unity will result in complete misunderstanding.[20]

The relatedness which the self-world structure requires and the ontological integrity of both poles in the correlation is easily obscured, however. Tillich formulates the issue this way:

> Whenever the self-world correlation is cut, no reunion is possible. On the other hand, if the basic structure of self-world relatedness is affirmed, it is possible to show how this structure might disappear from *cognitive* view because of the subject-object structure of reason, which is rooted in the self-world correlation and which grows out of it (ST, I: 171).

To be a self is to be separated from everything else, and thus to stand opposite the world (the Umwelt and the Mitwelt) on the basis of one's own structure of centeredness. Thus, it is inevitable that the whole overagainst the self appears as object to the self as subject. The self-world structure, then, is the basis of the subject-object structure of reason; however, it is the subject-object structure of reason which is responsible for the disappearance from cognitive view of the self-world correlation. We must attempt to see what this means for Tillich.

The structure of being, Tillich maintains, is determined by *logos*, that is, it is a rational structure. The structure of reason which is manifest within the structure of being is, therefore, subject to the same fundamental determination as is the latter, viz., the self-world structure. Ontological reason, which Tillich distinguishes from technical reason,[21] is defined as "the structure of the mind which enables it to grasp and shape reality" (ST, I: 75). The *logos* structure of the grasping-and-shaping mind, Tillich calls "subjective reason" and the *logos* structure of the grasped-and-shaped reality is called "objective reason." It is ontological reason, the logos of being, which makes the self a structure of centeredness and the world a structured whole. The self-world structure, then, defines the subject-object structure of reason. The question remains, however, as to how the self-world correlation is driven from cognitive view by the subject-object structure of reason.

Tillich's answer to this question is clear but indirect. We shall state it briefly here; however, insofar as it is relevant to the problem of the relationship of philosophy and theology we shall discuss it in more detail in Part Two. The self-world structure disappears from *cognitive* view, because the subject-object structure of reason reduces everything which falls within its purview to an object, be it God, man, or a stone. This objectification of its subject matter is inevitable for reason, since "in the logical sense everything about which a predication is made is, by this very fact, an object" (ST, I: 172). Within the logical sphere the inevitable objectification of the subject matter of reason is legitimate and necessary, since reason cannot approach its subject matter without objectifying it.[22] The problem, however, is that logical objectification has ontological presuppositions and implications in that the subjectivity of that which belongs to the subject pole of the structure is distorted ontologically by the force of the objective pole within reason. If God is brought within the subject-object structure, he ceases to be God. If the self is reduced to an object, its essential nature is lost. Objectification, then, is the source of the disappearance from cognitive view of the self-world structure.

Although Tillich does not state explicitly how this happens, it would seem that the polar self-world structure disappears within the subject-object structure of reason in that the polar unity of the structure is broken by the domination of the objective pole of reason, and thus selfhood or subjectivity is lost or nearly lost.[23] Consequently, the irreducible unity of the polar structure does not inform the deliberations of reason, but rather reason defines everything objectively, thus distorting the total structure. There is, then, in the disappearance of the self-world structure a curious, almost inexplicable state-of-affairs, which Tillich himself does not seem to notice. Man, the bearer of subjectivity and subjective reason, consistently conceives of himself and the divine in objective terms. How is this to be explained? For Tillich, it is inevitable because reason must employ objective, abstract, universal notions in order to comprehend its data.   Both philosophy and theology must abstract from the concrete situation in order to develop adequate conceptualities, but theology, perhaps more than philosophy, is aware of the dangers of objective thinking. "Theology always must remember that in speaking of God . . . It must include in its speaking of God the acknowledgment that it cannot make God an object" (ST, I: 173).[24]

The subject-object structure of reason is the fundamental expression of the finitude of reason, and consequently of the finitude of the ontological structure.   The solution of the subject-object problem of reason, especially as it involves the problem of objectification and thus the cognitive distortion of the self-world structure, as Tillich understands it, must await further discussion in Part Two. But it is important to point out here that the solution to this problem finds expression in Tillich's solution to the problem of finitude as such. Before we can attempt an analysis of that solution, however, we must continue the explication of the ontological structure so that the complete meaning of finitude can come clearly into view.

The second level of ontological concepts are what Tillich calls the "ontological elements," which consist of three "outstanding" pairs: individualization-participation, dynamics-form, and freedom-destiny. They function properly to explicate the "fabric" of the ontological structure, the self-world correlation and thus they apply directly to the human self and its world; however, they can be applied analogically to the subhuman realm and, therefore, they can be extended analogically to explicate the total structure of being (ST, I: 185). It is true that in Volume One of *Systematic Theology* Tillich is interested primarily in the explication of human being and the human world; however, the implications which the ontological elements hold for subhuman phenomena are developed in Part Four of the system.[25]

The concept of individualization is grounded in the classical philosophical intuition that the idea of difference, as Plato observed, is "spread over all things" (ST, I: 174). Every being is a "structure of centeredness," and as such it is constituted as an "individual," i.e., a unique existent, whose structural centeredness cannot be divided or replaced by any other center. Thus, "selfhood and individualization are different conceptually, but actually they are inseparable." Man is completely self-centered and therefore he is completely individualized. In all nonhuman entities, the individual is an exemplar of the universal characteristics of the species. However, with man it is the individual, rather than the species or the collective, which is of supreme ontological significance. Man, the individual, cannot be subsumed into a larger whole such that his individuality is of secondary importance in relation to the whole. The larger whole (e.g. the social order) exists to enhance the individuality of man, not to negate it. To be a self is to be individualized and to be individualized is to be "unique, unexchangeable [and] inviolable" (ST, I: 175). Difference, differentiation, selfhood all point to individualization as one of the constitutive elements of the structure of being.

Individualization stands in polar relation with participation. As a polar element, participation denotes the fundamental self-world relationship; that is, it points to the fact that the centered self is not merely the passive product of the world, at least on the level of the human self, but rather it is an active *participant* in the world through the rational structure of mind and reality. The degree of participation is correlative with the degree of individualization. The less complete the individualization of the self, the more its participation is limited to its environment. Again, man is complete individualization and he, therefore, transcends every immediate environment to participate in the world. While limited to a small section of reality (environment), nevertheless man participates in the universe (world) through the universal structures of language and concepts which make man himself universal. Man is *micro-*

cosmos, and his possession of language demonstrates his micro-cosmic character. The entire universe, then, is open to his participation (ST, I: 176).

The completely individualized, centered self is a "person" and the most complete form of the person's participation is "communion." Man as micro-cosmos participates in all forms of life, but he participates most fully only in "personal" life, that is, man has communion only with persons. "Communion," Tillich defines, as "participation in another completely centered and completely individual self. In this sense ... participation is essential for the individual, not accidental" (ST, I: 176). It is in the context of communion that the individual self encounters the resistance to himself in the form of other centered individuals by which the individual discovers himself as an individual. Without the resistance of the other, the individual self would attempt to make itself absolute. The self encounters in resistance, however, an unconditional demand placed upon itself to take the other into account. The person is born in his encounter with other persons. Thus, "persons can grow only in the communion of personal encounter" (ST, I: 177).

It is participation, in polarity with individuation, "which underlies the category of relation as a basic ontological element. Without individualization nothing would exist to be related. Without participation the category of relation would have no basis in reality" (ST, I: 177). It is important to note that Tillich calls "relation" an ontological category (Cf. ST, I: 271) but it is not treated in his discussion of the categories, even though, as we shall try to show, the category of relation would make some of his claims about the categories more intelligible than they are. Indeed, the absence of an exhaustive discussion by Tillich of the category of relation, especially as it applies to God's being, constitutes one of the chief limitations of his thought.[26]

The second pair of polar elements, dynamics and form, reveals Tillich's closest link with Aristotle and the hylomorphic tradition of medieval philosophy,[27] although both Aristotle and the medieval tradition undergo significant transformations at Tillich's hand. Form is that which anything must have in order to be. Individualization and participation presuppose special and general forms, although the two are never separated in actual being. Rather "through their union every being becomes a definite being. Whatever loses its form loses its being" (ST, I: 178). We have seen that Tillich disputes the nominalist claim that universals are mere names without a reality of their own. We have also seen that he denies that universals are duplicates of reality existing in a supramundane realm of their own. Tillich's claim that special and general forms are not to be distinguished ontologically suggests both that the general forms are never exhausted by their individual exemplars (special forms) and yet that the former cannot be considered ontologically apart from the individuals (conceptually they can be separated), but neither is their ontological significance as "powers of being" to be denied.[28]

Forms, then, are principles of individuation, but as such they should not be contrasted with content. "The form which makes a thing what it is, is its content, its *essentia*, its definite power of being" (ST, I: 178). The form of a tree, to use Tillich's favorite example, is both its general form (treehood) as well as the determination of its unique, special form as an individual tree. The question is not the separation of form and content, but rather, especially on the cultural level, whether or not the form is an "authentic" expression of content, or again on the cultural level of human meaning-forms (in contrast to "natural forms"), an expression of "spiritual substance." If the form is not an authentic expression of content or spiritual substance, then the problem of "formalism"[29] results, that is, the arbitrary imposition of a form upon substance, which has not emerged "organically" out of the situation which gave rise to the substance itself. Form, as the principle of individuation, "forms something," and that which is formed Tillich calls "dynamics." The concept of dynamics, he points out, is a very complex and problematic one, and it is questionable whether Tillich succeeds in reducing its problematicity. The problematic character of the concept lies in the fact that only that which has being can be conceived and only that which has form has being.

Dynamics is that which is subject to form, but it must be conceived apart from form, that is, as the polar contrast to form. It can be conceived, therefore, neither as something which is or as something which is not. Rather, "it is the *me on*, the potentiality of being, which is nonbeing in contrast to things that have a form, and the power of being in contrast to pure nonbeing" (ST, I: 179).

Without attempting to discuss Tillich's conception of nonbeing at this point a question must be raised here regarding his use of the concept of potentiality to designate both dynamics and form. The general form (e.g. treehood), as we have noted, is potential being and as such it is a power of being. But clearly, dynamics is also the potentiality of being, which as sheer potentiality has no form (it is nonbeing in contrast to things that have form), but which, in contrast to pure nonbeing, is the power of being. It is not at all clear, then, just how form in the sense of general form is to be distinguished from dynamics if both are defined as the potentiality of being and the power of being. Perhaps it could be argued that dynamics represents "potentiality-in-general" within the structure of being, since it is not subject to any particular form, while the potentiality of the general form is potentiality within the limits of that form, "delimited potentiality" perhaps. It does not belong to the potentiality of treehood, for example, that the specific form would be an animal rather than an oak or an elm. However, one cannot place such limits upon dynamics as such. Obviously, there are technical issues here which we cannot go into, but it should be clear that Tillich's attempt to work out the distinction between potential and actual being in terms of the dynamics-form polarity calls for further analysis and clarification.

The dynamic-form polarity finds expression in immediate human experience as the structure of "vitality" and "intentionality" (ST, I: 180). Vitality is the power of a living being to maintain and enhance its life through growth. The *Elan vital* (Bergson) is the creative thrust of the living substance toward new forms. It is the expression of dynamism in all living beings, but in man vitality becomes human because it stands in polar unity with intentionality. In man, vitality is not subject to the limitations of environment to which nonhuman, living beings are bound by natural necessity and within which the vital or dynamic element in them must be expressed. Dynamics in man reaches out beyond every environment, because he is constantly creating new worlds, both technical and spiritual. However, the drive in man toward new forms or new worlds, his essential vitality, is directed or conditioned by its polar counterpart, the intentionality of man. Intentionality is rooted in the structure of subjective reason, which is man's form of being, but it is not "rationality" or "spirituality," since both these terms denote states of affairs which are not included in the meaning of intentionality.

Intentionality defines man's being as "directed toward meaningful contents" or structures of meaning, which have an objective validity over against man.[30] The intentionality of man grasps these structures by virtue of his living in universals of which language is the most notable example. Thus, "in this context 'intention' does not mean the will to act for a purpose; it means living in tension with (and toward) something objectively valid" (ST, I: 180). It is the intentional element in man which "orders" his vitality and prevents it from becoming chaotic and self-contained. Thus, man's vitality in correlation with his intentionality, drives him beyond himself at every moment toward new forms, toward new structures of meaning (ST, I: 180-181).

The dynamism of being is reflected in the tendency of every being to transcend itself and to create new forms. However, self-transcendence is possible only on the basis of the conservation of form. Each being tends to unite identity and difference, rest and movement, conservation and change within the polar structure of dynamics and form. Consequently, *becoming* is a constitutive feature of the structure of being, but Tillich insists that becoming is intelligible only in relation to that which remains unchanged in the process of becoming. Process or becoming occurs within the structure of persisting identity, and it is the identity of being, its formative character, rather than its becoming, which seems to constitute the ultimate metaphysical datum for Tillich.[31]

The polar structure of dynamics and form, which on the human level is the polarity of vitality and intentionality, finds expression in the immediate life of man as self-transcendence and self-conservation. It is only as the essential form of man (his humanity) is conserved that man is capable of transcending any given situation. Through self-transcendence on the basis of the conservation of form, man brings the new into being, but the new is wrought by man's creativity on the basis of material at hand and is always embodied, through man's intentionality, in form. Thus, man transforms himself and the forms within which he lives. The dynamics-form polarity, then, expressed within the structure of man's humanity, i.e., the self-world structure, points both to the inevitable attack upon form by the incessant flux of temporal reality including man's vitality and the presence of structural forms within this flux which may change, but which are never absent and which determine the world as a structural whole.[32]

The third ontological polarity Tillich considers is that of "freedom and destiny." This polar structure is especially significant because in it the description of the basic ontological structure and the ontological elements reaches its fulfillment and through the actualization of freedom in conjunction with destiny within the ontological structure, the analysis is directed toward that state of actual being which Tillich calls "existence." This is the case because freedom in correlation with destiny makes existence possible by transcending the necessity of being (ST, I: 182).[33] The concept of freedom is also important theologically, because revelation is unintelligible without it.

It is the freedom of man which is Tillich's chief concern in the analysis of freedom and destiny. There are analogies to human freedom and destiny in the natural realm, which Tillich designates as the polarity of "spontaneity and law,"[34] but it is man who embodies "perfectly" the polarities of freedom and destiny just as he embodies perfectly the other polarities. Thus, "man is man because he has freedom, but he has freedom only in polar interdependence with destiny," (ST, I: 182).

Tillich acknowledges that the question of freedom has usually been discussed in contrast with necessity, but necessity he argues is a category, not an element, and its contrast is possibility, not freedom.[35] If the idea of freedom is worked out over against necessity, the resultant conceptuality is that of mechanistic determinacy (necessity) and indeterministic contingency (freedom). But this conceptuality fails to grasp the structure of being as it is experienced immediately in man himself. Rather it leads to the inevitable conflict between determinism and indeterminism, both of which conceive of the human will as a thing. Determinism asserts the tautology that a thing is a thing and thus the thingified human will can have no freedom, since a thing is by definition *bedingt*, conditioned in every sense. Indeterminism, on the other hand, in protesting against the mechanistic, deterministic thesis of determinism, accepts the basic presupposition of the latter and asserts freedom of the conditioned will rather than necessity. It thus falls into a contradiction of terms and is vitiated by the deterministic tautology. Indeterminism, then, is not conceptually adequate to analyze the existential reality of freedom, but more importantly, both determinism and indeterminism are theoretically impossible, because neither of them can justify their claim to truth. "Truth presupposes a decision for the true against the false. Both determinism and indeterminism make such a decision unintelligible" (ST, I: 183).

Since determinism and indeterminism constitute pseudo or cognitively meaningless solutions to the problem of freedom,[36] what is needed is a whole new ontological analysis of the problem. Tillich attempts to carry out this new analysis by proposing that freedom be understood not as the function of "will" but of man as a totality, "that is, of that being who is not a thing but a complete self and a rational person" (ST, I: 183). Thus, every dimension of man's self participates in his freedom. Tillich's move here involves the invocation of the whole-part conceptuality in relation to man's being. Any of the parts of man's being (e.g. the cells of his body, the unconscious and consciousness) may be separated from the centered whole which is man and may be thus determined by forces outside these parts, but the determinacy of the whole cannot be derived from the determination of any of its parts. Tillich seems to be arguing here that insofar as man is a centered whole, no matter how the parts of the whole may be determined, the determinacy of the whole is qualitatively discontinuous with the determinacy of its parts, and thus while Tillich seems to hold that the whole is determined in some sense not altogether clear, yet its freedom consists precisely in its not being determined by its parts.

It seems safe to conclude, then, that man as a total, centered self is free in the sense that he is not determined definitively by any of the dimensions of his being which constitute his selfhood. Just how this is the case, however, Tillich does not bother to demonstrate,[37] and the basic assumptions of his "argument" go unexamined. For example, one of the most obvious assumptions is that the logic which governs the part-whole relationship is adequate to delineate the nature of human freedom, and consequently, freedom seems established on Tillich's terms as a matter of logical definition. But merely to define man as free when understood as a centered whole, especially when the definition of terms involves the difficulty we have already noted with respect to the whole's being unconditioned by its parts and yet as somehow genuinely related to them, seems merely to substitute the tautology of the part-whole definition for the tautology of the thingified will. This is not to suggest that the part-whole conceptuality is in principle inadequate to the human phenomenon of freedom, but rather that Tillich's terms need much more critical definition, qualification and extension than he himself provides.

This judgment must be qualified somewhat, however, because Tillich does attempt to make the part-whole conceptuality more intelligible by describing human freedom as "deliberation, decision, and responsibility" (ST, I: 184) and by the introduction of the polar contrast of freedom, viz., destiny. Deliberation involves the act of weighing, in this case the weighing of arguments and motives. The capacity to deliberate presupposes that the self is not identical with any of its motives, but is free in relation to them (the claim that the strongest motive always wins the decision is asserted *ex post facto* and is therefore empty). Man reacts as a whole to the motives he is weighing through his personal center, and this reaction is the *decision* to exclude some possibilities and to actualize others. Again, the capacity to choose among conflicting motives presupposes that man is free over against the motives or possibilities open to him. As Tillich puts it, man's "personal center has possibilities but it is not identical with any of them" (ST, I: 184). Finally, man is responsible for his decisions in the sense that he must "respond" to the question put to him about his decisions, and he can only respond or be responsible, because he is free. No one else can answer for the decisions which he himself as a unique, centered self has made. Man is free, then, to deliberate and to decide, and because these processes cannot be determined by the motives and alternatives themselves but rather by the centered totality of man's self, he is therefore responsible.

The notion of the centered totality which is the human self needs content, and this Tillich attempts to provide through the concept of destiny. "Destiny is not a strange power which determines what shall happen to me. It is myself as given, formed by nature, history, and myself" (ST, I: 185). Destiny is the total field out of which the concrete decisions of the self arise. It is, in fact, the basis of selfhood. Destiny is the history of the self which reaches back into the past, the bodily structure which makes its own demands upon the personal center, the psychic strivings and conflicts which inform every decision, the communities in which the self has participated, the environment and the world which continuously impinge upon it. There are ineluctable structures within destiny which the self cannot alter and they must be taken into account in the determination of the meaning of human freedom, but Tillich also insists that the self is not swallowed up in these structures. Rather the self can decide how it shall relate to these structures. It can accept its destiny as the conditions and limits of its freedom or it can revolt against it. But most importantly it can through its decisions contribute to the shape of its destiny.

Freedom and destiny, then, are correlative concepts. Only he who is free can have destiny, and there can be no destiny without freedom. Destiny does not merely determine the self, but it defines the ultimate context in which the self must actualize its freedom. Man is neither the passive product of his destiny nor the "Superman" who through the exercise of his will shapes his destiny absolutely in his own image. Without the notion of *destiny*, as the condition and limit of human decision, freedom becomes a fantastic possibility, unreal or unrealizable. Without the notion of *freedom*, destiny becomes the expression of the completely determined world, the block universe where novelty and change and the alternative futures which are partially shaped by human decision are mere illusion. Man is free, but his freedom is not without its ultimate limits; man decides, but his decisions are not made in a vacuum; man is responsible, but his responsibility is not without its structural conditions outside man's personal center.[38]

The three pairs of ontological elements delineate the basic self-world structure and thus constitute the basic structure of being. Individualization, dynamics and freedom express, in the monistic language of the ontological schema, "the self-relatedness of being, its power of being something for itself," while participation, form, and destiny "express the belongingness of being, its character of being a part of the universe of being" (ST, I: 165). Self-relatedness and self-togetherness, then, constitute the continuum within which any finite entity has its being. The ideal state of being of man in whom the elements are fully present and in whom the continuum is fully expressed is that self-relatedness and self-togetherness are held in balance and the ontological elements constitute a harmonious whole. However, finitude makes such harmony and balance impossible. We shall see why this is the case below.

For Tillich, both the basic ontological structure and the ontological elements imply finitude, and the notion of finitude is worked out in relation to nonbeing. It is now necessary to discuss the Tillichian concept of nonbeing in order to understand finitude as it is developed in his thought.

Nonbeing, like being, passes into conceptual form from its foundation in the existentiality of the self. Nonbeing is the content of an encounter before it becomes a concept. It is first experienced in the shock that that which is stands threatened by possible negation. It is, in fact, the shock of nonbeing which gives rise to the question of being, but as one would expect, neither notion can be considered conceptually without the other, even though thought must begin with being as its ultimate, irreducible foundation (ST, I: 163). However, man the thinker is not bound to being. Driven by the threat to himself and his world and by his capacity to transcend every given reality through the structure of his intentionality, man can conceive of nothingness. Being implies nonbeing both logically and ontologically.

Nonbeing, however, constitutes a mystery for thought and thus is conceptually problematic. Tillich believes that human thought has attempted to avoid the notion of non-being through two fundamental strategies, one logical, the other ontological (ST, I: 187). Logically the attempt has been made to assert that nonbeing is merely the content of a negative judgment. Tillich argues that to construe nonbeing in this way is to overlook the fact that every logical structure is grounded in a prior ontological structure, that is, the self-world structure, and that negative judgments merely "uncover" the fact that the world presents itself to the self in such a way that nonbeing comes into view ontologically, that is, as rooted in the very structure of being.

An anticipated event does not occur, which means that one's judgement concerning the given state of affairs was mistaken. Nonbeing appears, then, in the sense that the world which the self structured through its anticipations and expectations is nonexistent. This condition constitutes more for Tillich than the trivial observation that we are sometimes wrong in our judgments about the world. It points rather to the ontological character of nonbeing and man's participation in it. Tillich writes:

> Thus disappointed, expectation creates the distinction between being and nonbeing. But how is such an expectation possible in the first place? What is the structure of this being which is able to transcend the given situation and

to fall into error? The answer is that man, who is this being, must be separated from his being in a way which enables him to look at it as something strange and questionable. And such a separation is actual because man participates not only in being but also in nonbeing. Therefore, the very structure which makes negative judgments possible proves the ontological character of nonbeing. Unless man participates in nonbeing, no negative judgments are possible (ST, I:187).[39]

The ontological strategy to avoid the reality and conceptual problematic of nonbeing is seen in the attempt to deprive it of its dialectical character. Nonbeing must be conceived dialectically in relation to being and thus it cannot be excluded from being. Nonbeing, then, cannot be conceived as the absolute contrast to being, since everything would be excluded from being but being-itself. The self and the world would be excluded because they participate in both being and nonbeing. Therefore, any ontological analysis of the concept of nonbeing must assert at the outset the dialectical participation of nonbeing in being.

It is the dialectical understanding of nonbeing, which Tillich finds expressed in the Greek in the distinction between *ouk on* and *me on*. *Ouk on* is the "nothing" which is defined nondialectically and thus it has no relation to being. It is absolute nonbeing. *Me on*, however, is the "nothing" which is related to being. It is relative nonbeing (ST, I: 188). Tillich suggests a third fundamental type of nonbeing, which is adumbrated but not clearly delineated in the *Systematic Theology* (Cf. ST, I: 189-190). It is the nonbeing of "otherness," that is, "in Hegelian terms, the dialectical otherness which implies nonbeing in the sense of not being 'this or that.'"[40]

It must be kept in mind that both "being" and "nonbeing" are fundamentally phenomenological, existential concepts which arise out of man's immediate encounter with the world. They are not speculative abstractions, but rather correlative notions, rational-ecstatic conceptions, which arise out of what are, for Tillich, archetypal, universal human experiences.[41] However, as we have seen, Tillich is not consistent with his own method, for he wishes to extend these conceptions beyond their capacity to explicate human existence, and thus he is open to the charge made most forcefully by Paul Edwards and John Hick[42] that the term "nonbeing" is treated as a name or description (Edwards) or hypostatised (Hick).

Of the three forms of nonbeing Tillich has formulated, it is *ouk on*, or absolute nonbeing which seems most problematic in relation to his own statements. Man as existing "stands out" of both absolute and relative nonbeing (ST, II: 20). He along with all other existing things, stands out of the "emptiness of absolute nonbeing" (*ouk on*) which means that he can be found "within the corpus of reality." Man also stands out of relative nonbeing (*me on*), which is potentiality, the "not-yet-being," which can become being. But man "stands out" of neither of these forms of nonbeing absolutely and thus he "stands in" them at the same time. He came from the absolute nothingness of *ouk on* and he must return to it, and he can never actualize completely in his existence the potentiality of *me on* in which he stands. Thus, man is a mixture of being and nonbeing.

Tillich's terminology, however, is confusing. He argues that Christian thought has rejected the Platonic notion of "me-ontic matter" and has maintained that the *nihil* out of which God creates in the *creatio ex nihilo* doctrine is *ouk on*, the undialectical negation of being (ST, I: 188). Thus, in Christian thought, *ouk on* has a cosmic dimension. However, Tillich seems to deny that the *ouk on* - *me on* distinction is adequate to one's sense of cosmic nonbeing in a comment he makes in *Philosophical Interrogations*.[43] He states:

> There is a problem not touched on by the Greek distinction, namely, the possibility of the human mind to think that there might have been nothing at all. I have called this thought the "shock of nonbeing." It is a real experience, analogous to anxiety produced by the awareness of our own individual nonbeing (before birth and after death). It can also be expressed positively as the astonishment about the fact that there is something (the "unvordenkliche" fact, as Schelling calls it). Kant, in his criticism of the cosmological argument, has attributed this "shock of nonbeing" symbolically to God when he makes God reflect about the wherefrom of his own being. I do not believe that the distinction between *me on* and *ouk on* is the answer to this experience of nonbeing.

It would seem, then, that *ouk on* and *me on* refer primarily to "our own individual nonbeing" as our sense of our absolute negation (before birth and after death) and our sense of our "not being what we are." Thus, both are rooted in the existentiality of the self. But why does *ouk on* not also designate our sense that there might not have been a world? Has Tillich not come dangerously close to severing the self-world correlation? It seems that in attempting to separate the sense of individual nonbeing and the sense of cosmic nonbeing, Tillich is reluctant to affirm the unity of self and world as it is delineated negatively in the experience of absolute nonbeing. To experience the possibility of absolute individual nonbeing is to experience at the same time the possibility of the absolute nullity of the world, and in the light of Tillich's assertions about the self-world correlation, there seems to be no adequate reason why the notion of *ouk on* does not comprehend both possibilities.

Relative or dialectical nonbeing (*me on*) is more decisive for Tillich's thought, since it has to do with the nonbeing which is present within being as potentiality. One could also say that the nonbeing of "otherness", which appears, for Tillich, in "the awareness of becoming" is also an expression of dialectical nonbeing; however, it seems clear that Tillich wishes to distinguish *me on* and the nonbeing of otherness. *Me on* is the potentiality which the existent both stands in and out of. To stand out of potentiality is to be an actual existent and thus to "have" being; however, to stand in potentiality is to experience the nonbeing of not being what one essentially is. The nonbeing of otherness, on the other hand, is the problem of becoming, the negation of "sameness" (self-identity) through the establishment of "otherness" (self-alteration). One might call this the nonbeing of not being what one actually is in the sense that one is never actually the same in each concrete moment of his life process, although, as we have seen, there is a structural identity for Tillich, which abides through all change. It is dialectical nonbeing, then, which is "contained" in being and is thus constitutive of the meaning of being. Dialectical nonbeing is inescapable if one is to think about the meaning of being at all, and it is dialectical nonbeing which defines the problem of finitude, for being and dialectical nonbeing are united in the notion of finitude.

Tillich's definition of finitude is quite straightforward: "Being, limited by nonbeing, is finitude" (ST, I: 189). Dialectical nonbeing appears within the structure of being as the "not yet" and "no more" of being. Being, subject to or conditioned by nonbeing, is finite. Tillich writes:

> [Nonbeing] confronts that which is with a definite end (finis). This is true of everything except being-itself — which is not a "thing." As the power of being, being-itself cannot have a beginning and an end. Otherwise it would have arisen out of nonbeing. But nonbeing is literally nothing except in relation to being. Being precedes nonbeing in ontological validity, as the word "nonbeing" itself indicates. Being is the beginning without a beginning, the end without an end. It is its own beginning and end, the initial power of everything that is. However, everything which participates in the power of being is "mixed" with nonbeing. It is being in process of coming from and going toward nonbeing. It is finite (ST, I: 189).

There appear, on the surface, two distinct meanings of the term "being" here. First, Tillich uses "being" and "being as such" or "being-itself" as equivalent terms. Here being is prior to nonbeing, but nonbeing is contained within it, although being is *not* limited by nonbeing. Hence the paradoxical formulation: "being is the beginning [it contains nonbeing and cannot be thought without it] without a beginning, the end without an end [it is not limited by nonbeing]."[44]   On the other hand, Tillich also uses the term "being" to mean that which participates in the power of being (being-itself), but which *is* limited by nonbeing. Thus, it can be defined directly and properly as finite (ST, I: 81).

It would seem, then, that finitude constitutes the *differentia* by which two *modes* of being are distinguished, namely, being unlimited by nonbeing (being as such or being-itself) and being limited by nonbeing (finite being). Finitude is the basis of Tillich's assertion of the ontological dependence of the creature upon God and it points to the incapacity of the creature to resist nonbeing on its own terms. Thus, to assert that being is finite is to assert that the *mode* of instantiation of being in the creature is defined by finitude.

Finitude is defined in ordinary language in contrast to infinity. To be finite is to be limited (in Tillich's term limited by nonbeing), but limitation is conceivable only in relation to some notion of the unlimited. In common sense thinking, however, the unlimited has been conceived as an infinite, timeless quantity which is immeasurable by finite standards. Tillich's conception of infinity departs significantly from that common sense notion. Infinity, Tillich argues, "is defined by the dynamic and free self-transcendence of finite being" (ST, I: 190). The conception of infinity, then, does not constitute an immeasurable realm beyond finitude. Rather it directs the mind toward its own unlimited potentialities. The mind, which is grounded in the finitude of its individual bearer can, nevertheless, transcend any finite state of affairs, but it does not drive toward an infinite object or being. Thus, the mind experiences infinity as a "demand not a thing." It is the demand of infinite self-transcendence, which drives the mind to negate every finite state of affairs in the name of its own unlimited potentiality. "Infinitude is finitude transcending itself without any *a priori* limit" (ST, I: 191).

In rooting infinity in the self-transcendence of man, a twofold consequence results. First, infinity becomes the negation of finitude or finite being and thus an expression of dialectical nonbeing. However, since infinitude is finitude (finite man) transcending itself without any a priori limit, it is difficult to see how Tillich can avoid the Hegelian-Sartrean[45] thesis that it is human consciousness which is the source of the negation of finitude and therefore an expression of dialectical nonbeing. Hence, infinity or the infinite self-transcendence of human consciousness is "the infinite negation of the finite."

However, secondly, infinity, the unlimited self-transcendence of finitude, points to man's rootage in being-itself, which is beyond the finite-infinity polarity. Here, what Tillich calls "the potential presence of the infinite" is the negation of nonbeing. It is not infinity itself which is the negation of nonbeing, but infinity, as the correlate of finitude, points to that which negates the negation of finite being, viz., being-itself. Tillich asserts:

The power of infinite self-transcendence is an expression of man's belonging to that which is beyond nonbeing, namely, to being-itself. The potential presence of the infinite (as unlimited self-transcendence) is the negation of the negative element in finitude. It is the negation of nonbeing . . . Being-itself is not infinite self-transcendence. Being-itself manifests itself to finite being in the infinite drive of the finite beyond itself. But being-itself cannot be identified with infinity, that is, with the negation of finitude. It precedes the finite, and it precedes the infinite negation of the finite (ST, I: 191).

Infinity, then, as the unlimited self-transcendence of man, is the source of the negation of finitude (nonbeing) and at the same time it points to the source of the negation of nonbeing.

Finitude as the generic feature of the ontological structure, that is, being limited by nonbeing and rooted in the dynamics of self-transcendence expresses itself in awareness as anxiety. Anxiety (Angst) is not merely an emotional state. It is rather an ontological quality. It has no object as does fear. It is the disclosure to the self of its essential finitude and thus the threat of nonbeing. To be finite is to be threatened by nonbeing and to be threatened by nonbeing is to be anxious. No finite being can escape anxiety, although the way in which ontological anxiety expresses itself within the centered personality structure is dependent upon the psychodynamic and historical conditions of each person.[46] Neurotic or compulsive forms of anxiety, which stem from the condition of anxiety as the concomitant of finitude, can be handled by psychotherapy, but there is no way of removing ontological anxiety, since it is constitutive of the meaning of finitude *qua* finitude.[47]

Thus far we have seen that finitude is the mode of instantiation of being when limited by nonbeing; that finitude is defined not in contrast to an infinite, immeasurable quantity, but rather in relation to the unlimited self-transcendence of man and thus comes into view through its own negation on the ground of the negating function of human consciousness *vis-a-vis* dialectical nonbeing; that finitude as that mode of being which is essentially threatened with its own negation presents itself in human awareness as anxiety. Hence, finitude as the generic feature of the structure of being or the ontological structure presents itself also within the ontological schema which describes the "fabric" of the ontological structure. It is now necessary to examine Tillich's analysis of the manifestation of finitude within the ontological elements and the categories, and to discuss the relationship of finitude to the distinction between essential and existential being.

Although the categories are the fourth level of ontological concepts, Tillich discusses the presence of finitude within them and the ontological elements before dealing with the third level of concepts, the essence-existence distinction. We shall follow his procedure in our discussion.

We have already pointed out that the categories are both forms of thinking and of being by which the mind grasps and shapes reality on the basis of the categorical structures both mind and reality exemplify. Therefore, the categories are ontological and thus are present in everything. The mind cannot encounter reality without them; it is necessary, therefore, for systematic theology to deal with them, since they are present even in the realm of the "unconditional" from which they are excluded by definition. The theologian is not concerned to construct a system of the categories, but rather to show their relevance in the development of the question of God. Tillich's analysis, then, betrays a very clear theological interest.

Since the categories are "forms of finitude" (ST, I: 192), they sustain a double relation to being and nonbeing. They express both being and nonbeing; hence a positive and a negative element are united in them. Because the categories are exemplified within the ontological structure, the positive and negative elements they express must be considered both in relation to the self ("from the inside") and in relation to the world ("from the outside"). The importance of the categories, then, within Tillich's system is that they express not only a union of being and nonbeing but also a union of anxiety (negative element) and courage (positive element). It is in relation to this situation that Tillich's decision to discuss only the four categories of time, space, causality, and substance is seen to be less arbitrary then it would appear to be on the surface. These categories express the problematic of finitude more dramatically than the others and thus are more readily available for purposes of theological analysis (ST, I: 193).

The category of time, the central category of finitude, expresses the negativity of nonbeing and anxiety and the positivity of being and courage as they converge in the question of the present. Nonbeing is expressed in time through the impact of the transitoriness of things and the incessant flux of time itself, which "like a mighty river sweeps all our goods away." The present seems swallowed up within the temporal process balanced as it is between the past which has transpired and the future which is not yet. The nonbeing of time creates the anxiety that the present is illusion, and that nonbeing has thus conquered being, since to be is to have a genuine present. On the other hand, it is only within the unity of the present that past and future can be experienced and thus the being of time is seen within the present itself. The creativity of the temporal process, its directness and irreversibility and the emergence of the new within it all point to time's rootage in being. Ontology in describing the character of time, strives to hold the positive and negative elements in balance, but the meaning of time is given in decision and is not derived from ontological analysis.

The nonbeing and being of time are experienced in immediate awareness in the anxiety of transitoriness and the courage of a self-affirming present. Man affirms the reality of his present even though he is aware that in change and decay everything moves toward nonbeing. This awareness is most heightened in his sense of his own death. But the anxiety which is the concomitant of the subversion of man's present by nonbeing is possible only on the basis of a courage which affirms temporality. The courage to affirm the present, then, raises the question of the ontological foundation of courage. Thus man

> affirms the present through an ontological courage which is as genuine as his anxiety about the time process . . . It is hardest for him to affirm the present because he is able to imagine a future which is not yet his own and to remember a past which is no longer his own. He must defend his present against the vision of an infinite past and of an infinite future; he is excluded from both. Man cannot escape the question of the ultimate foundation of his ontological courage (ST, I: 194).

Man's temporal present implies space, since time creates the present by its union with space.[48] The category of space, as a category of finitude, embodies the same positive and negative elements as does time. To be finite requires space. Not to have a space is not to be, and thus the drive for space is an ontological necessity. Insofar as one has space, one encounters the positivity of being within finitude. However, nonbeing reveals itself in the very spatiality of being in the realization that the spatial context of being is never given absolutely, that man neither possesses his space absolutely nor that he can rely on his space to sustain him indefinitely. The nonbeing of space is seen in the fact that man has no ultimate claim on space and that his destiny is that he will lose every space in which he posits himself. The being of space is seen in the fact that man can only experience the threat to his space on the basis of the space he occupies. The category of space includes, then, the anxiety of not-having-a-place, which is the expression of the ultimate insecurity of finitude and the courage by which man affirms the present and with it his own space. Hence:

> Everything affirms the space which it has within the universe. As long as it lives, it successfully resists the anxiety of not-having-a-place. It courageously faces the occasions when not-having-a-place becomes an actual threat. It accepts its ontological insecurity and reaches a security in this acceptance. Yet it cannot escape the question how such courage is possible. How can a being which cannot be without space accept both preliminary and final spacelessness (ST, I: 195)?

Causality also reflects the ambiguity of expressing within its categorical character the positive and the negative, being and nonbeing, anxiety and courage. Causality reflects the power of being by pointing to the efficacy of that which precedes a thing or event as its cause. It also points to the reality of that which is caused, for to be caused is to come into being and thus to possess the power of being to resist nonbeing. At the same time, causality points to the situation that that which is caused does not come into being by its own power of being. Effects, by definition, have no aseity. Only God has aseity; only he is self-caused. To be finite is to be caused, to be "thrown" into being (Heidegger), and thus to emerge within the causal nexus is to be involved in the infinite chain of causal sequence within which there is, for Tillich, no absolute terminus. The abyss of nonbeing is powerfully manifest within causality itself.

The anxiety which causality evokes in man is that "of not being in, of, and by one's self"; it is the anxiety of contingency. To be contingent is to have no necessity in one's being. The contingency of throwness also points to the possibility of extinction. Man is, but he might not be. Causality discloses the radical contingency which lies at the heart of man's being. The courage which is appropriate to the anxiety which the nonbeing of causality evokes is precisely the acceptance of one's contingency. The courageous man:

> rests in himself. Courage ignores the causal dependence of everything finite. Without this courage no life would be possible, but the question how this courage is possible remains. How can a being who is dependent on the causal nexus and its contingencies accept this dependence and, at the same time, attribute to himself a necessity and a self-reliance which contradict this dependence (ST, I: 197)?

Tillich's explication of the category of substance is worked out consciously overagainst the philosophers of function or process. These philosophers cannot avoid the question of substance, he insists, for they must speak of that which *has* functions or that which *is* in process. To speak of that which persists through change is to speak of substance, for "substance points to something underlying the flux of appearances, something which is relatively static and self-contained" (*Ibid.*). To think within the category of substance, however, also requires the notion of accidents. The accidents derive their ontological power from the substance in which they cohere, but the substance is nothing without the accidents through which it is expressed. In both the substance and accidents we see the unity of being and nonbeing, anxiety and courage.

The nonbeing implied in the category of substance is experienced through the impact of change. That which changes has no *ultimate* substantiality, for Tillich; it is held in relative nonbeing, which it is powerless to avoid. Every finite being participates in the nonbeing of change and thus in the anxiety that its substance will be lost. It is this anxiety which drove the Greeks to ask about that which does not change. Moreover, the quest for the unchangeable cannot be dismissed by the correct metaphysical assertion that the static has no priority over the dynamic, for that quest is rooted in anxiety and will not be silenced by correct metaphysics. This anxiety is present in individual and group change, and it is most radically present in the threat of death, the anticipation of the final loss of both substance and accidents. The anxiety about the loss of one's substance strikes at the very center of man's being, for it involves the loss of one's identity and the power of self-maintenance in being. We should not fail to see then the existential agony which motivates the question of the unchanging substance.[49]

The anxiety over the loss of substance is countered, of course, by man's courage. It is the courage which:

> accepts the threat of losing individual substance and the substance of being generally. Man attributes substantiality to something which proves ultimately to be accidental — a creative work, a love relation, a concrete situation, himself. This is not a self-elevation of the finite, but rather it is the courage of affirming the finite, of taking one's anxiety upon himself. The question is how such a courage is possible. How can a finite being, aware of the inescapable loss of his substance, accept this loss (ST, I: 198)?

The categories as forms of finitude express the convergence of being and nonbeing in everything finite. They show the "subjective form" in which nonbeing threatens finitude relatively, namely, in anxiety and they point to the absolute nothingness to which that which is finite must inevitably return in the extinction of death. The categories also point to the courage with which man takes his finitude upon himself, while revealing, at the same time, *that the courage found within finitude is not possible on the basis of finitude.* The question of the possibility of this courage is the question of God.

The nonbeing which is disclosed within the finitude of the ontological elements creates, at least on the analytical level, a different form of anxiety than that which is seen in the categories. The nonbeing which limits being in the form of finitude drives the polar elements away from each other and thus through the tension which results, the anxiety of finitude disrupts the polar harmony of a balanced whole.[50] The anxiety which this ontological tension evokes is not the same as that which is seen in relation to the categories, namely, "the anxiety of nonbeing simply and directly." It is rather:

> the anxiety of not being what we essentially are. It is anxiety about disintegrating and falling into nonbeing through existential disruption. It is anxiety about the breaking of the ontological tensions and the consequent destruction of the ontological structure (ST, I: 199).

The ontological elements, then, clearly presuppose the further determination of finitude as the unity of essential and existential being, (in spite of their disruption) where being is understood as instantiated under the condition of finitude.

The ontological tension which is rooted in the finitude of the ontological structure and threatens its disruption can be seen in each of the three pairs of polar elements. We shall discuss briefly this tension as it appears in each of the three polarities.

The polarities of individualization and participation move away from and against each other under the impact of the nonbeing of finitude upon them. Finite individualization, when torn from participation, produces the threat of loneliness and the consequent loss of world and communion. Finite participation, when separated from individualization under the tension of finitude, drives toward the complete absorption of the self in the collectivity of its world. This is the threat to self-relatedness through the existential surrender of the self to the embracing whole of which it is a part. The self, then, is driven by the anxiety of not being what it essentially is either to maintain its individuality, subjectivity and self-relatedness by attempting to exclude the world and the "other" from its personal center, thereby becoming increasingly isolated and lonely, or by surrendering itself to its world in its quest for participation, thus relinquishing the burden of self-relatedness and individuality through its dispersal in the collective. Under the impact of this polar tension man "oscillates anxiously between individualization and participation, aware of the fact that he ceases to be if one of the poles is lost, for the loss of either pole means the loss of both" (ST, I: 199).

The polarity of dynamics and form is subject to the same tension of finitude and thus to the threat of possible disruption, with the consequent anxiety produced by the threat. Dynamics must be actualized in form; human vitality must be embodied in cultural forms and institutions through human intentionality. Dynamics is subject to the threat of losing itself in unalterable forms and form is threatened by the chaos of dynamics seeking to preserve itself by breaking through every form. Man is anxious that his vitality will be usurped by the increasing rigidification and rationalization of form in the name of the preservation of social order. On the other hand, man's intentionality is threatened by the irrational strivings of his vitality, especially embodied in the threat of chaotic formlessness in which both vitality and intentionality would be lost. With the threat of the loss of dynamics through its embodiment in a final, unalterable form or the loss of both form and dynamics in the specter of a total chaotic formlessness, the ontological structure is thus threatened at its very center.

Freedom and destiny, the final poles Tillich attributes to the ontological structure, are threatened, through the tension of finitude, with possible disruption by the twofold threat of loss of freedom on the one hand and loss of destiny on the other. Man's freedom is threatened by the necessities in his destiny, and his destiny is threatened by the contingencies in his freedom. To preserve his freedom, man is continuously in danger of surrendering his freedom to his destiny. Man's freedom places the demand of decision upon him, but as finite freedom, man must decide overagainst a destiny the complexity and enormity of which seem to undercut any possible foundation for decision man might have in his destiny. The partiality of every decision man must make, then, drives him toward a profound anxiety about the partial acceptance of his destiny for fear that the "segment" of his destiny he accepts may not define his real destiny. Thus, he asserts his freedom arbitrarily against his destiny and consequently stands in danger of losing both his freedom and destiny (ST, I: 200).

The loss of either pole in the polarity, as we have seen, means the loss of the other. Tillich's own judgment about the contemporary situation of man is that the more arbitrary his freedom becomes, the more he is in danger of losing the meaning of his being along with his destiny. Destiny, for Tillich, is "necessity united with meaning" and not simply "meaningless fate." The threat to one's destiny is, therefore, the threat of possible meaninglessness, a threat which, for Tillich, has become actual in the widespread sense of meaninglessness in the contemporary world. The essential anxiety of man over the loss of a meaningful destiny has been transformed into existential despair over destiny as such. In the face of this situation freedom has been declared an absolute (Sartre) and has become divorced from destiny. Absolute freedom in man, however, is arbitrariness and becomes biologically and psychologically necessitated. With the loss of destiny, then, freedom is also lost (ST, I: 201).

Being and nonbeing are "mixed" in finitude in such a way that finitude carries within itself an essential threat to itself in the form of the possible loss of one's ontological structure and with it one's self. The categories express the threat to the ontological structure of not being at all, and thus raise the question of the possibility of that courage by which man takes this threat upon himself. Finitude as seen from the perspective of the categories drives man to the question of God. Finitude, however, is also subject to the threat of nonbeing which arises upon the foundation of finitude in being, namely, the threat to the essentiality of finitude, the threat that it will not be what it essentially is. It is this threat which the ontological elements articulate. While the categories raise the question of the possibility of courage, the elements raise the question of that which overcomes the existential despair which arises with the disruption of the essential structure of finitude. The ontological elements, then, point to the distinction between essence and existence and thus raise the question of the one in whom the two are united under the conditions of finitude, namely, the Christ.

The analysis of Tillich's conception of finitude cannot be completed, therefore, until we have discussed the distinction between essence and existence. It must be pointed out at once, however, that we cannot begin to treat this issue with the detail it requires, since in Tillich's own words "a complete discussion of the relation of essence to existence is identical with the entire theological system" (ST, I: 204). Our purpose here is not an exhaustive analysis of the distinction, but rather to show that the distinction is made *within* finitude and hence that finitude is logically prior to the distinction which constitutes "the backbone of the whole body of theological thought." Finitude, therefore, must be seen as one of the ultimate notions of Tillich's thought.

Tillich begins his discussion of the distinction between essence and existence by stating again that nonbeing and hence finitude is constitutive of the very meaning of the term "being." "Finitude," Tillich argues:

> in correlation with infinity, is a quality of being in the same sense as the basic structure and the polar elements. It characterizes being in its essential nature. Being is essentially related to nonbeing; the categories of finitude indicate this. And being is essentially threatened with disruption and self-destruction; the tensions of the ontological elements under the condition of finitude indicate this. But being is not essentially in a state of disruption and self-destruction. The tension between the elements does not necessarily lead to the threatened break. Since the ontological structure of being includes the polarity of freedom and destiny, nothing ontologically relevant can happen to being that is not mediated by the unity of freedom and destiny. Of course, the breaking of the ontological tensions is not a matter of accident; it is universal and is dependent on destiny. But . . . it is not a matter of structural necessity; it is mediated by freedom (ST, I: 202).

It is clear from the above passage that being as it is instantiated under the condition of finitude comprehends two fundamental states of affairs. In the first place, while related essentially to non-being, that is, nonbeing is included in the definition of being, it comprehends the state of affairs in which being "preserves" itself against the absolute threat of nonbeing as disclosed in the categories, and the harmony of the ontological elements is maintained even though under the impact of finitude their tension is real. This is being in its essential state in which it is *not in a state of disruption and self-destruction.* On the other hand, being also comprehends that state in which it is divorced from its source and ground and is thus confronted with its own deficiency in which it is destined to return to the absolute nonbeing from which it was called forth. In this state, being *is* characterized by disruption and self-destruction, since the threatened break in the polar elements has become actual; their essential tension has become actual cleavage. It is this fundamental split in the fabric of being, which Tillich sees as the basis for the distinction between essential and existential being.

The distinction between essence and existence, Tillich argues, is inevitable for every philosophy and theology. The distinction is rooted in the contrast between the ideal and the real, truth and error, good and evil. All philosophical and theological thought is driven to the question: "How can being, including within it the whole of its actuality, contain its own distortion" (ST, I: 202)? Every answer to this question must be given, however, within the framework of the essence-existence distinction.

Both essence and existence, Tillich acknowledges, are extremely ambiguous terms. They both have several distinct meanings. The notion of essence:

> can mean the nature of a thing without any valuation of it, it can mean the universals which characterize a thing, it can mean the ideas in which existing things participate, it can mean the norm by which a thing must be judged, it can mean the original goodness of everything created, and it can mean the pattern of all things in the divine mind (ST, I: 202).

Existence, on the other hand, is also subject to different meanings:

> It can mean the possibility of finding a thing within the whole of being, it can mean the actuality of what is potential in the realm of essences, it can mean the "fallen world," and it can mean a type of thinking which is aware of its existential conditions or rejects essence entirely (ST, I: 203).

The ambiguity of the various meanings of the term "essence," Tillich reduces to one basic ambiguity, namely, the ambiguity which arises between an empirical and a valuational meaning of the term. When essence is used to describe the nature of a thing or to point to a quality or a universal in which things participate, its empirical meaning is dominant. However, when essence is used to designate that from which being has "fallen" (Plato), the true and undistorted nature which is exemplified in actual being only in distortion, then its valuational meaning is invoked. This ambiguity in the term "essence," however, is grounded in the basic ambiguity of existence itself, for existence both expresses essential being and contradicts it. Consequently, essence has a purely logical character as that which makes a thing what it is (*ousia*) and it has a valuational character as that which is imperfectly embodied in the thing. Essence, then, empowers the thing to be and it stands over the imperfect, distorted actualization of the thing in judgment. The judgment of essence is precisely that existence is no longer united with essence, that in existence the potential cleavage in being has become actual.

It is clear that for Tillich the valuational meaning of essence is decisive for his theological program, and it is his concern for the valuational significance of essence which most likely explains the rather imprecise treatment of the notion at Tillich's hands. It is not at all clear, for example, how essences are to be distinguished from universals or ideas (ST, I: 254), on the one hand, or from the onto-logical element of form or the potentiality of relative nonbeing on the other. However, in spite of this ambiguity, it seems fair to say that the distinction between essence and existence is fundamentally the distinction between potential and actual being and that the major thrust of the doctrine is to show that in "standing out" of potentiality or essential being, existential being actualizes itself in such a way that its very actuality is the distortion of essence; yet existence is responsible for this distortion through the exercise of finite freedom but nevertheless set within the destiny which "from the beginning" is characterized by the tragic split between essence and existence. Thus, existence in actualizing itself is cut off or sep-arated from the power and ground of being and its own essence and is "delivered over" to its self-contradictory character, which arises out of its own actuality as exemplified in its self-destructive tendencies and within the ambiguities of actual being which is life (ST, II: 28).

It is now necessary to summarize the meaning of finitude as Tillich understands it and to show its implications as an ultimate notion for the total structure of his thought. On the surface of the system, of course, finitude drives man to the question of God, but its actual function within the system is far more complex. Finitude is decisive for understanding Tillich's full doctrine of being, for the scope of ontology, and finally the solution to the problem of finitude provides the basis for the understanding of Tillich's ultimate philosophical orientation. Consequently the notion of finitude provides a helpful insight into the relationship of philosophy and theology.

We have seen that Tillich asserts that "being is finite" (ST, I: 81), that finitude is being limited by nonbeing. We suggested that this means that the being of God is the unlimited efficacy or power to resist nonbeing. This is what seems implied in Tillich's saying that:

> "finite" means carrying within one's being the destiny not to be. It designates a limited power of being, limited between a beginning and an end, between non-being before and non-being after.[51]

Hence, to say that "being is finite" is not to define being in such a way that there are actually two meanings of the term, but rather to point to the ontological fact that the finite entities which participate in being are limited, perishing creatures. It is not literally true, then, to say that being is finite, since that very statement presupposes the ultimate disappearance of being into nonbeing and denies the priority of being over nonbeing. Rather finitude qualifies the meaning of being (without involving the fallacy of equivocation) by pointing to the mystery that the divine bestowal of being upon the beings does not posit them eternally in their being. The doctrine of finitude is Tillich's attempt to incorporate within the doctrine of being the radical contingency of human existence, which the existential analytic has uncovered. Not only does finitude drive man to the question of God, but it constitutes the human problem to be overcome. Finitude and its solution inform every part of the theological system whether it be being, existence, life or history. God as the solution of finitude underlies the whole *Systematic Theology.*[52]

We have also suggested that the distinction between essence and existence is a distinction *within* finitude. It is important to point this out because Tillich comes dangerously close to the view that existence as distinct from essence, if not evil in itself, is the locus of evil in the world.[53] We have seen that finitude as the essence of man and world is "created goodness," and the doctrine of *creatio ex nihilo* prevents the negative evaluation of finitude on the one hand and the flight from finitude as the direction of salvation on the other (ST, I: 253-254). However, unless it is stressed that essence and existence are qualifications of finitude (and thus qualifications of being instantiated under the conditions of finitude), the conclusion seems warranted that existence is, at least, an inferior mode of being in relation to essence. If the structure of finitude is good, however, then existence as the state of estrangement, disruption, and destruction is held within that goodness by virtue of its own finitude no matter how divorced from its essence it may be. Thus existence may reveal its deficiency of being in its separation from essence (it cannot be identified with essential goodness),[54] but its character as finite nonetheless grants it a certain "derived" goodness. Tillich's failure to point this out, however, constitutes another major weakness in his thought.

The distinction between essence and existence as a distinction within finitude throws further light on Tillich's conception of being. Tillich considers the notions essence and existence, on the one hand, as abstractions from the "concrete actuality of being," which is "life" (ST, II: 28; III: 12), and on the other the two main qualifications of being (ST, III: 12), such that in the latter case, Tillich can speak of essential *and* existential being. The question immediately arises as to how being is predicated of God and the creature if essence and existence are included in the meaning of being, especially in the light of Tillich's claim that God or being-itself "is beyond the contrast of essential and existential being" (ST, I: 236). Again, the cruciality of finitude as that which distinguishes God and man asserts itself. It is clear that Tillich does not wish to eliminate essence and existence from the meaning of being as it is predicated of God, but just how these terms, as qualification of the meaning of being, apply to God is not altogether clear.

In one formulation of this issue (ST, I: 236-237), it would seem that God's being "beyond the contrast of essential and existential being" means that the terms do not apply to him at all, especially in regard to the question of the divine existence. Here God is not only beyond the *contrast* of essence and existence, but *he is beyond essence and existence themselves.* In another formulation (ST, II: 22-23), however, Tillich argues that essence and existence and their unity are applied symbolically to God such that his transcending the contrast between essence and existence means that he is not subject to a conflict between the two. Here Tillich is willing to speak of the divine existentiality. Hence:

> [God's] existence, his standing out of his essence, is an expression of his essence. Essentially, he actualizes himself. He is beyond the split. But the universe is subject to the split. God alone is "perfect," a word which is exactly defined as being beyond the gap between essential and existential being. Man and his world do not have this perfection (ST, II: 23).

Perhaps the second formulation is more compatible with the analogical doctrine of being. To predicate being of God and man is to predicate, on the basis of the very meaning of being, essence and existence of both God and man. Consequently, it is not the case that there are two notions of being in Tillich, one of which includes essence and existence within its meaning and one of which does not. It is clear that being is predicated analogically because Tillich claims that essence and existence are predicated symbolically of God. The question arises, however, just how these terms function symbolically once it is seen that the terms are defined in such a way that their literal meaning is not the meaning they have within finitude but rather the meaning which is achieved by their unique, singular exemplification within the divine reality.[55] Thus, to predicate being analogically of God and man is (within Tillich's scheme) to predicate essence and existence of both God and man; however, the distinction between essence and existence within finitude is merely the further articulation of being instantiated under the conditions of finitude: essence is distinguished from existence by virtue of their being split within finitude, whereas in God there is no such split, and therefore, properly speaking, no such distinction obtains. Hence, finitude not only points to the fundamental distinction between God and man, but it also points to the ground upon which an analogical doctrine of being can be attributed to Tillich while also providing the basis for the proper distinction of terms as they are used of God and man (the ordinary and extraordinary in Hartshorne), that is, linguistic distinctions rest in the distinction between the modes of being of God and man, which finitude articulates. It should be obvious, however, that this line of interpretation makes self-contradictory Tillich's claims that God does not exist or that he is in no sense an entity and that metaphysical terms apply to God or being-itself only symbolically.

The second important point at which Tillich's conception of finitude informs his system has to do with the determination of the scope of ontology. Since we shall discuss Tillich's conception of ontology in more detail in Part Two of this essay, we shall discuss this issue quite briefly here. Ontology has as its proper task the description of the structure of being. It presupposes being in its conceptual effort, but its concepts are "less universal than being but more universal than any ontic concept, that is, more universal than any concept designating a realm of beings." (ST, I: 164). Ontology, which Tillich prefers to call the science which investigates the structure of being rather than calling it metaphysics (ST, I: 20), is in fact the science of finitude. As a descriptive science the scope of ontology is limited to the structure of finitude. The presupposition of being which ontology carries within itself is again, properly speaking, the instantiation of being under the conditions of finitude (but derived, of course, from being-itself) and therefore ontology is the science of finite being. Its entire conceptual schema delineates the nature and structure of finitude. Conceptually speaking, ontology cannot go beyond finitude, although as we shall see Tillich does not maintain this view consistently.

Two important consequences follow for Tillich's thought as a result of his limiting the scope of ontology to the description of the finite structure of being. First, we can see the roots of Tillich's rejection of natural theology in the doctrine of finitude. Ontology lays bare the sheer givenness and contingency of finitude. It originates in the shock of nonbeing and it cannot answer the question why there is something rather than nothing (ST, I: 163). Ontology itself is bound to the contingency of finitude and it can establish no cognitive route out of finitude to God. It can merely show that the question of God is implicit in finitude as such, and part of its task, for Tillich, is to make that question explicit. Hence, there is every justification for saying that Tillich's ontology is really philosophical anthropology. It should be clear, then, that Tillich's decision to replace the term "metaphysics" with the term "ontology" rests upon much more complex ground than the dualistic meanings which have come to be associated with the word "metaphysics." The metaphysical traditions (before Kant and after him) have not, generally speaking, confined metaphysical inquiry to an analysis of finitude alone, for the possibility of knowing God discursively has consistently sustained the metaphysical enterprise throughout its history. Hence, between Tillich's understanding of ontology as limited to a description of finitude and the metaphysical traditions which have claimed speculative knowledge of God or the Absolute or Infinite there is considerable incompatibility.

The second consequence is that the concepts which are employed in the ontological description of the structure of being (with the exception of the basic polarity of self and world) (ST, I: 244) provide the material for the symbolization of the divine reality, although Tillich is quick to point out that a doctrine of God cannot be derived from an ontological system (ST, I: 243). Theology, of course, speaks out of the context of revelation, but it, too, speaks within finitude and while it does not derive the doctrine of God from ontology, it derives the *conceptual* language within which the doctrine of God is cast from ontological analysis. How theology, then, can employ a conceptual language which has finitude as the context within which it functions properly to speak about that which lies beyond finitude and whose being is subject to none of the conditions of finitude, constitutes one of the major problems of Tillich's thought.

Finally, we have suggested that Tillich's solution to the problem of finitude, the problem and solution informing in one way or another the entire theological system, reveals his ultimate philosophical orientation and thus provides a fruitful context within which to explore the relationship between philosophy and theology. Again, since we shall discuss this relationship from a number of angles below, we shall attempt to discuss here the problem of finitude as Tillich understands it. We shall suggest moreover that the solution to the problem of finitude is to be discerned in the two ultimate notions which remain to be discussed.

The problem of finitude can be put very briefly. Finitude defines the very character of human reality. In its categorical character it pervades the whole realm of human knowing and doing. It colors every human project with impermanence, incompleteness, insecurity, and finally with ultimate nothingness. Finitude determines the character of the concrete content of every human life. Every finite content is real; it has being, and in its reality, human reality is constructed, that is, human reality arises out of the encounter with its world and other selves, which become, then, the finite, concrete basis for the reality of every self.

Man literally gains his sense of reality through this total finite structure. However, that which constitutes human reality, that in relation to which human reality is literally founded, the structure of finitude which is the structure of human reality is itself subject to nonbeing. Finite reality is real. It is neither illusion, nor mere appearance nor ultimate unreality, but in its very reality "finite being is a question mark" (ST, I: 209). The problem of finitude, then, is this: The whole of human reality arises out of a structure which, though real, is threatened through and through with nonbeing. The threat to the structure of finitude is the threat that man must constantly lose that which constitutes him. Thus, for Tillich, the problem of finitude is that man, who is constituted through the structure of finitude, cannot live his life on the basis of that structure. The courage of finite self-affirmation in spite of nonbeing is neither possible nor intelligible on the basis of finitude itself.

It is this situation which drives man to ask the question of God, the question implied in finitude. Consequently, God (being-itself) as that which transcends finitude and the categories, which embraces and overcomes nonbeing and thus makes courage possible is the answer to the problem of finitude in all its dimensions. It is clear, however, that in order to be the answer to the problem of finitude, God can in no sense be conditioned by finitude. What are the philosophical presuppositions which inform both Tillich's analysis of the problem of finitude and his proposed solution to that problem? Can a definite philosophical orientation be discerned in Tillich's understanding of finitude which determines both his understanding of philosophy and his understanding of the relationship of philosophy and theology? It is these questions which shall guide our investigations in Part Two of this essay. However, before turning to that task, we must now examine the two remaining ultimate notions of Tillich's thought, which we have argued rest in the claims that being-itself or God is totally unconditioned and that an ultimate unity obtains between being-itself and finitude or between unconditioned and conditioned being.

Notes

1 Tillich does argue that the philosopher looks at the "whole of reality" in order to discover the structure of reality as a whole, but the context makes clear that the philosopher is free potentially to consider the whole of reality in the sense that he does not have to look in any particular place to discover the structure of reality as a whole. Tillich does not mean, however, that the philosopher can know the whole of reality. ST, I: 23; Cf. ST, I: 19.

2 J. H. Randall, *The Theology of Paul Tillich, op. cit.*, p. 139.

3 Paul Tillich, *Ibid.*, p. 335.

4 Tillich has made it clear that being-itself is the "object" of philosophy in a passage which reveals the Platonic roots of his thought and also brings to mind the heritage of Hegel. Tillich writes: "Everything we encounter appears to us as real, as true being. But we soon notice that its reality is only transitory. It was but now it is no more. Nonbeing has swallowed it, so to speak. Or we notice that it is different from what it seemed to be, and we distinguish between its surface and its deeper, more real levels. But soon these levels also prove to be surface, and we try to penetrate into still deeper levels, toward the ultimate reality of a thing . . . In our search for the 'really real' we are driven from one level to another to a point where we cannot speak of level any more, where we must ask for that which is the ground of all levels, giving them their structure and their power of being. The search for ultimate reality beyond everything that seems to be real is the search for being-itself, for the power of being in everything that is. It is the ontological question, the root question of every philosophy." *Biblical Religion and the Search for Ultimate Reality, op. cit.*, pp. 12-13. Cf. also G. W. F. Hegel, *Phenomenology of Mind*, tr. J. B. Baillie (George Allen and Unwin, 1961), Chapters I-III.

5 *The Theology of Paul Tillich, op. cit.*, p. 160.

6 One of the most problematic passages in this regard is the following: "Thought is based on being, and it cannot leave this basis; but thought can imagine the negation of everything that is, and *it can describe the nature and structure of being which give everything that is the power of resisting nonbeing* [emphasis mine]. Mythology, cosmogony, and metaphysics have asked the question of being both implicitly and explicitly and have tried to answer it . . . [but when] this question is asked, everything disappears in the abyss of

possible nonbeing; . . . but if everything special and definite disappears in the light of the ultimate question, one must ask how an answer is possible. Does this not mean that ontology is reduced to the empty tautology that being is being? Is not the term 'structure of being' a contradiction in terms, saying that that which is beyond every structure itself has a structure (ST, I: 163-164)?" In this passage, it seems that "structure of being" has the same status as "ground of being" and "power of being," i.e., as a metaphorical description of being-itself, and its meaning seems to be that being-itself *is* the structure of being just as it is the ground and power of being. However, the view we are trying to maintain is more correctly stated by Tillich when he says "since God [or being-itself] is the ground of being, he [it] is the *ground of the structure of being*" [emphasis mine] (ST, I: 238), that is, being-itself makes possible the structure of being by its being the ground of all possibility, and it makes actual the structure of being by its being the power of being, but being-itself is not identified with the structure of being. As to Tillich's claim that being-itself has a structure, one can only wish that he would have answered his own question. It does seem clear, however, that Tillich does assert structure of being-itself (he speaks of the "structural elements of being-itself") and the structure of being-itself is the "structure which makes reality [or being] a whole," but again this is not to be confused with the structure of being. Cf. Klaus-Dieter, Norenberg, *Analogia Imaginis* (Gütersloher Verlagshaus Gerd Mohn, Gütersloh, 1966), p. 122ff.

7 Henry N. Wieman, *The Source of Human Good* (Southern Illinois University Press, Carbondale, 1946), Chapter VII. Wieman has criticized Tillich for holding that being-itself is beyond literal specification by reason. *Ibid.*, p. 33, N. 1. For a more extensive criticism of Tillich, Cf. also H. N. Wieman, *Intellectual Foundations of Faith* (Philosophical Library, N.Y., 1961), Chapter Four.

8 Cf. ST, I: 243ff, where Tillich distinguishes between the proper and symbolic meaning of the categories.

9 P. Tillich, *My Search for Absolutes, op. cit.*, p. 75ff. It should be pointed out here that Tillich denies that the categories as conceptual notions are ever complete, for as concepts they are relative human inventions, which are never formulated "once and for all," but rather are constantly undergoing criticism and transformation. But as "forms of being" they are always effective in the very struggle about their meaning (Ibid., p. 78). This means, then, that while the categories and concepts are never completely defined conceptually, nonetheless their application to the structure of being is direct and literal.

10 The categories and concepts constitute the structure of being in the sense that they are the *a priori* conditions for that structure. They are not known apart from experience, and they do not describe a static, unchanging structure. The point is that the structure of being is subject to or conditioned by

the categories and concepts, and thus they cannot apply symbolically to that structure (ST, I: 166-168).

11 P. Tillich, *Love, Power and Justice*, (Oxford University Press, New York, 1954), p. 20. Tillich here speaks of the "texture" of being-itself which ontology describes. But, of course, the "structures of being" (e.g. love, power, justice) are described properly before they can provide the symbolic or metaphorical material to symbolize being-itself. Hence, the term "texture" describes adequately the plurality of "structures" which constitute the "structure of being." However, the distinction between the structure of being as a finite structure and the structure of being-itself does not obtain in this work, which only makes Tillich's thought all the more difficult to analyze.

12 Cf. Tillich's response to W. Urban's criticism of his view of the religious symbol in *The Journal of Liberal Religion*, V. II, No. 3 (1941), p. 203: "I would admit that any symbolic knowledge presupposes some basis of nonsymbolic knowledge and that pansymbolism defeats itself."

13 The finitude of the structure of being or the "universe" has nothing to do with its being limited in space. The so-called "infinite universe" is, for Tillich, still subject to nonbeing and hence it is finite. Finitude-infinitude are not quantitative terms for Tillich as we shall presently make clear. (Cf. ST, I: 189).

14 "Metaphysical theories as well as social institutions in which selves are transformed into things contradict truth and justice, for they contradict the basic ontological structure of being, the self-world polarity in which every being participates in varying degrees of approximation to the one or the other pole. The fully developed human personality represents one pole, the mechanical tool the other" (ST, I: 173). But even the tool is not a mere thing (Ding), because it has a minimal subjectivity.

15 Cf. John E. Smith's claim that Tillich's ontological way in the philosophy of religion involves him inevitably in cosmological considerations. J. E. Smith, *Reason and God* (Yale University Press, 1961), pp. 157-72. See P. Tillich, "The Two Types of Philosophy of Religion," in *Theology of Culture*, Ed. Robert Kimball (Oxford University Press, N.Y., 1959), pp. 10-29.

16 Cf. Tillich's assertion that ontology is *descriptive* rather than *speculative*. It is the descriptive character of ontology which seems to distinguish it from metaphysics. Paul Tillich, *Love, Power, and Justice, op. cit.*, p. 23.

17 Martin Heidegger, *Being and Time, op. cit.*, p. 69ff.

18 The notion of the 'centered self' is fundamental for Tillich. The self achieves its personal center by holding the polar elements within itself in creative harmony. The threat to the self is that the harmony-in-tension of the polar ele-

ments can be disrupted and the self can lose its personal center. This is the expression of nonbeing within the life of the self. The threat of ultimate disruption is one of the possibilities rooted in the finitude of the self. Cf. *Dynamics of Faith, op. cit.*, p. 4ff.; ST, I: 198-201.

19 The distinction between world and environment has been made more rigorously by existential psychotherapeutic theory based especially on the thought of Heidegger. Rollo May has described the three modes of world commonly distinguished by this school of psychotherapy as the "Umwelt" (environment), the "Mitwelt" (the world of one's fellowman) and the "Eigenwelt" (the world of relationship to one's self). *Existence*, ed. Rollo May, Ernest Angel, Henri F. Ellenberger (Basic Books, N.Y., 1958), p. 61.

20 Tillich's analysis here seems to reveal the influence of Heidegger, although he uses none of Heidegger's technical language. "Being-in-the-world" is the fundamental state of Dasein; however, it is not the highly conscious relationship to the world which the self-world correlation is in Tillich. Rather, Dasein's being-in-the-world as a pre-ontological (pre-interpretive) state of affairs hides Dasein's own being from it and gives rise to interpretations which further obscure that being. However Heidegger also distinguishes "world" from the physical universe and environment. "World" represents the sphere of Dasein's "dealings" with things (pragmata) in which the 'world' is defined by the concernful "projects" of Dasein. Although it contains none of the brilliant phenomenological analysis of Heidegger, Tillich's notion of "perspective" would seem to approximate the former's insight that "world" is in a fundamental way the embodiment of Dasein's concerns. Cf. M. Heidegger, *Being and Time, op. cit.*, pp. 91-148.

21 Ontological reason is the structure of the mind which enables it to grasp and shape reality. It is effective not merely in cognition but throughout the whole range of human experience. "It is cognitive and aesthetic, theoretical and practical, detached and passionate, subjective and objective" (ST, I: 72). Technical reason, on the other hand, has developed out of the cognitive side of ontological reason. It has reduced reason to "reasoning," especially concerning the relationship of means to ends. The great threat, Tillich believes, since the late 19th century is that technical reason will become separated from ontological reason thus losing those universal norms it provides against which rational judgments can be made. Consequently, ends become the products of Unreason and the means of achieving these ends are developed with increasing sophistication but without regard to the question of the validity of the ends themselves. Nazi Germany is an example of the perversion of technical reason, but this phenomenon is characteristic of the total Western world in the mid-twentieth century. Cf. Herbert Marcuse, *One Dimensional Man* (Beacon Press, Boston, 1964). This book is quite problematic in its basic assumptions, but the career of technical reason has never been more powerfully described.

22 The subject-object structure is determinative for the whole finite structure of being, and it constitutes one of the essential problems of finitude "under the conditions of existence" in which the subject-object split is the defining dilemma of both *theoria* and *praxis*. Thus: "In the functions of *theoria* the gap lies between the knowing subject and the object to be known and between the expressing subject and the object to be expressed. In the functions of *praxis* the gap lies between the existing human subject and the object for which he strives — a state of essential humanity — and the gap between the existing social order and the object toward which it strives — a state of universal justice. This practical gap between subject and object has the same consequences as the theoretical gap; the subject-object scheme is not only the epistemological but also the ethical problem" (ST, III: 68).

23 This issue will be discussed in more detail in Part Two, Chapter 10.

24 The question of objective thinking in theology has occupied much discussion in recent years. A brief history of the problem and the leading positions in regard to it in Protestant and Jewish thought is James Brown, *Subject and Object in Modern Theology* (SCM Press, Ltd., London, 1955). More recently the problem of objective thinking received discussion in *New Frontiers in Theology*, Vol. 1, *The Later Heidegger and Theology*, ed. by James M. Robinson and John B. Cobb, Jr. (Harper and Row N.Y., 1963). Cf. also Schubert M. Ogden, "Theology and Objectivity" in *The Reality of God and Other Essays* (Harper and Row, N.Y., 1966), pp. 71-98. We shall return to this question in Part Two.

25 The concept of "life," David Kelsey argues (*The Fabric of Tillich's Theology, op. cit.*, p. 52ff.) is more inclusive than the concept "being" and is, therefore, an "ultimate ontological concept." Kelsey says "'Being' is used to designate a 'power inherent in everything' by which each thing 'resists all that threatens to destroy it.'" "Life," however, refers to the "actuality of being," that is, being in its concreteness, and is intended to designate the "process of actualization of potentiality that occurs in all realms of reality," and thus is not limited merely to the organic realm. Nevertheless, we cannot agree that "life" is more inclusive than "being," since the latter, is universally predicable and includes within itself the distinction between essential and existential being and their mixture just as the former does (ST, III: 11-12). It seems clear that Tillich uses the concept of "life" to designate the nonhuman and inorganic worlds. Yet, the ontological elements are exemplified in every life process, and thus their meaning is extended beyond human being and the human world (ST, III: 11-107).

26 It is the idea of relation which Charles Hartshorne has developed in great detail and which informs his critique of Tillich's doctrine of God found in *The Theology of Paul Tillich, op. cit.*, pp. 164-195. Hartshorne has discussed the problem of relation explicitly in *The Divine Relativity* (Yale University Press, 1948); the problem is also dealt with in many of his other writings.

27 Tillich has described his relationship to Aristotle thus: "And from both of them [Aristotle and Kant], I have received philosophical discipline, and from each of them one fundamental philosophical insight; from Aristotle, for my theological thinking, the distinction between the two ways of being, namely, *potential being* and *actual being*, and this permeates all my thinking. *Potential being* is the *power of being* which has not used its power but which might use it in every moment. It is not *non-being*. It is more than *non-being*, and *actual being* is what appears in time and space, and the other categories." P. Tillich, "Philosophical Background of My Theology," Lecture delivered May 12, 1960, St. Paul's University, Tokyo, Japan. Not for publication.

28 "Within the whole of being . . . there are structures which have no existence and things which have existence on the basis of structures. Treehood does not exist, although it has being, namely, potential being. But the tree in my back yard does exist. It stands out of the mere potentiality of treehood. But it stands out and exists only because it participates in that power of being which is treehood, that power which makes every tree a tree and nothing else" (ST, II: 21). Cf. also ST, I: 255.

29 Cf. ST, I: 89ff. Obviously "formalism" is a problem only in relation to those forms which are the result of human creativity.

30 *The Courage to Be*, (Yale University Press, New Haven, 1955), pp. 81-82: "Man lives 'in' meanings, in that which is valid logically, esthetically, ethically, religiously. His subjectivity is impregnated with objectivity. In every encounter with reality the structures of self and world are interdependently present." It should be clear that Tillich defines the term "meaning" within the ontological structure of self and world. "Meaninglessness" results when either pole is torn from the other. In *The Courage to Be* Tillich is concerned to delineate the meaninglessness which results in the loss of the self in collectivism and the loss of the world in some forms of Existentialism. Cf. *The Courage to Be*, Chapters 4 and 5.

31 This seems clear in Tillich's response to Hartshorne's proposal that "process-itself" is the ultimate metaphysical designation for God rather than "being-itself." Tillich remarks: "I am not convinced by any of the criticisms of my use of the phrase *esse ipsum* as the first (certainly not the last) assertion about God, that it can be omitted or replaced by anything else. Being as the negation of possible nonbeing is the basic cognitive position, which precedes in logical dignity every characterization of being. I am not disinclined to accept the process-character of being-itself . . . but before this can be said, being *qua* being must have been posited." *The Theology of Paul Tillich, op. cit.*, p. 339.

32 Tillich does allow that "chaos" can emerge within the self-transcendence-self-conservation movement of man's life at the point "between the forms," i.e., at the point where the old forms have been negated and the new forms have not yet emerged. This is not absolute chaos, however, because "being implies

form" and absolute chaos would be the negation of being and form, i.e., sheer nothingness. Thus, man's creativity is only possible on the basis of materials (forms) which are present to him, which he then transforms. This is the fundamental difference between human and divine creativity. ST, III: 50-51; ST, I: 256.

33   We shall discuss this most problematic claim in more detail in relation to Tillich's distinction between "essential" and "existential" being.

34   "An act which originates in the acting self is spontaneous . . . if it comes from the centered and self-related whole of a being. This refers not only to living beings but also to inorganic *Gestalten* which react to their individual structure. Spontaneity is interdependent with law. Law makes spontaneity possible, and law is law only because it determines spontaneous reactions" (ST, I: 185). Tillich clearly wishes to define law in such a way that the determinist-indeterminist controversy is avoided, and yet, that both dynamics and form, spontaneity and limiting structure are held in genuine balance.

35   We have not discussed the meaning or the validity of Tillich's distinction between "elements" and "categories" within the ontological schema. Perhaps the two types of concepts have their origin in Kant's distinction between the categories of discursive reason and the postulates of practical reason, in the latter of which the freedom of man and his immortality (destiny) are conspicuous examples. Practical reason must affirm these postulates regarding the nature of man even though theoretical reason must conceive man as necessitated and finite. It is also possible that the elements represent the Heideggerian distinction between the "existentialia" and the "categories." Tillich, however, insists that the elements are principles, which apply to every being, not merely to man alone. Thus, the drive toward the universality of concepts, which we shall argue in Part Two is the influence of "classical" philosophy on Tillich, prevents the development of a radically existential analysis of man and shapes decisively Tillich's theological program. The question of the existential character of Tillich's thought, which is the main concern of this essay, we shall answer in the negative.

36   In this regard Tillich often comes closer to the methods of analytic philosophy than some of his critics have acknowledged. The problem of determinism vs. indeterminism is a pseudo-problem for Tillich. So also is the question of the existence of God. Unlike the analytic philosophers, however, Tillich does not rule out the attempt to deal with the so-called perennial problems of philosophy, and thus he is not sympathetic to the analytic philosophers' attempts to limit the scope of philosophy exclusively to the analysis of language. For a more recent critique of the program and presuppositions of Anglo-American philosophy cf. Herbert Marcuse, *op. cit.*, Ch. 7 and Michael Novak, "Philosophy for the New Generation" in *American Philosophy and the Future*, ed. M. Novak (Charles Scribners' Sons, N.Y., 1968).

37 Among others, Van A. Harvey has remarked on Tillich's tendency to state his position rather than to argue it in detail. Cf. Van A. Harvey's review of *Systematic Theology*, Vol. III in *Theology Today*, Vol. XXI, No. 3, October, 1964, p. 380. Perhaps this is one of the ambiguities of writing a theological system one has been in the process of thinking through nearly half a century before it is presented to the public in final form. However, Tillich's tendency to speak *ipse dixit* in the *Systematic Theology* has not advanced the apologetic aim of his theology in some quarters.

38 The ontological polarity of freedom and destiny describes man's freedom in relation to the world; but it is not a doctrine of autonomous freedom as is found, for example, in humanism or existentialism. Man's freedom is possible not only through the condition of destiny but also through the ontological priority of being-itself, which is the condition for any finite entity to exist at all. We have suggested that on Tillich's terms it is impossible to reconcile the claims he has made regarding man's freedom, especially to actualize his finite possibilities by leaving the divine ground on the one hand and on the other the power of being-itself, which gives everything finite the power to be, but which is in no way conditioned by the decisions of the creatures. Clearly, Tillich wishes to resolve the problem of the compatibility of infinite and finite freedom dialectically, that is, finite freedom is grounded in being-itself and is continuously dependent upon it, but finite freedom is nonetheless real and genuine. Thus, he asserts dialectically that both God and man are free and that man's freedom is compatible with God's freedom and power. Tillich claims that his view of man as "finite freedom" saves him from a form of Spinozistic monism (*Philosophical Interrogations*, ed. Sydney and Beatrice Rome (Holt, Rinehart and Winston, N.Y., 1964), p. 384). Thus, man is independent of the divine ground in his actualized freedom, man "stands upon" himself and is "structurally independent" of God (ST, I: 261), but he remains at every moment ontologically dependent upon God even when he "leaves" the divine ground and resists, as he resists nonbeing, returning to it. The issue here, for this writer, is how man can be free when (1) on Tillich's own terms, man's power of being is the power of being of being-itself expressed in and through him, and (2) God's being is completely unconditioned and in no way determined by the creatures. If God's being is genuinely qualified by man's decisions, then it seems that we can assert real freedom for man. But if there is no genuine contingency in God, which I believe to be Tillich's position, then it seems that the dialectical solution is Tillich's attempt "to have his cake and eat it too" and does not constitute a logically adequate solution.

39 Cf. Jean-Paul Sartre, *Being and Nothingness* tr. Hazel E. Barnes (Philosophical Library, N.Y., 1956), p. 11: "Nonbeing does not come to things by a negative judgement; it is the negative judgment, on the contrary, which is conditioned and supported by nonbeing."

40 *Philosophical Interrogations, op. cit.*, p. 402.

41 Cf. *My Search for Absolutes, op. cit.*, pp. 81-82: "There are two concepts of being. One is the result of the most radical abstraction . . . [and] is an empty absolute. The other concept of being is the result of two profound experiences, one of them negative, the other positive. The negative experience is the shock of nonbeing that can be experienced in theoretical imagination . . . [or] in the practical experience of having to die . . . There is also a positive experience. It is the experience of *eros* . . . the love of being as such, a mystical relation to being-itself . . . a feeling for the holiness of being as being, whatever it may be."

42 Paul Edwards, "Professor Tillich's Confusions," *Mind*, Vol. 74, No. 294, 1965, pp. 206ff. and John Hick, *Scottish Journal of Theology*, Vol. 12, No. 3, 1959, pp. 291-292. Edwards' hostility to existentialism obscures his analysis, however. For him the language of existentialism is not only grammatically suspect, but it is also trivial, "a bombastic redescription of empirical fact." The technical terms of existentialism, however, cannot be dismissed on the grounds that (1) ordinary, nontechnical language functions more economically to talk about man and (2) that the technical terms of existentialism are therefore superfluous. Of course, the term "nothing" functions in negative existential judgments in ordinary language, but that is hardly the "language game" of the self thinking about what it means to be a self such that nonbeing or nothingness is a possibility which is open to it. There is a great difference between being told in ordinary language that I shall, like all men, die and thinking about my death from "inside" as it were, attempting to develop a vocabulary that can capture the existential significance of such a possibility thereby laying bare the structure of human existence. However, it is when Tillich uses this terminology more under the influence of the classical Greek tradition and Schelling and Hegel than the Existentialists that the linguistic issues urged against him become more relevant. It is at least questionable, for example, whether in speaking of nonbeing as that which being-itself "overcomes" in its own "life" as well as in the life of man that Tillich is speaking meaningfully, either existentially or grammatically no matter how symbolic such statements are. If the term "nonbeing" is hypostatized in Tillich's usage, then, it is because it is removed from its phenomenological, existential ground and made to function beyond the limits of that ground.

43 *Philosophical Interrogations, op. cit.*, p. 402.

44 Cf. ST, I: 236; 252; 270.

45 Cf. Herbert Marcuse, *Reason and Revolution* (Beacon Press, Boston, 1941) for a study of the role of negation in Hegel's thought. Cf. also J. P. Sartre, *Being and Nothingness, op. cit.*, p. 22ff.

46 Tillich's most extensive analysis of anxiety is found, of course, in *The Courage to Be*, where he attempts an "ontology of anxiety" in which he distinguishes between neurotic and existential (ontological) anxiety and suggests three

types of anxiety grounded in the three fundamental modes in which nonbeing threatens man (anxiety of fate and death, emptiness and meaninglessness, guilt, and condemnation). Bernard Martin, *op. cit.*, p. 111, has shown how the notion of anxiety shapes Tillich's entire interpretation of the cosmos, and raises the question whether anxiety is as pervasive as Tillich claims. Cf. also Paul W. Pruyser's critique "Anxiety: Affect of Cognitive State?" in *Constructive Aspects of Anxiety*, ed. S. Hiltner and K. Menninger (Abingdon Press, N.Y., 1963), pp. 121-141.

47 *The Courage to Be, op. cit.*, pp. 33-34: "Anxiety is finitude, experienced as one's own finitude. This is the natural anxiety of man as man, and in some way of all living beings. It is the anxiety of nonbeing, the awareness of one's finitude as finitude."

48 On the significance of time and space for the history of religion, see Tillich's essay "The Struggle Between Time and Space" in *Theology of Culture, op. cit.*, pp. 30-39. This essay reveals Tillich's deep suspicion of the absolutizing of space, the dynamics of which are elucidated in his discussion of space as a category.

49 Cf. Frederick Nietzsche, *Beyond Good and Evil*, tr. Walter Kaufman (Vintage Books, N.Y., 1966), p. 13: "Gradually it has become clear to me what every great philosophy so far has been: namely, the personal confession of its author and a kind of involuntary and unconscious memoir; also, the moral (or immoral) intentions in every philosophy constituted the real germ of life from which the whole plant has grown."

50 It should be stressed here that finitude in and of itself does not produce the disruption of the ontological structure. Finitude "is the possibility of losing one's ontological structure and with it one's self" (ST, I: 201). But there is no necessity in finitude that this should happen. Thus Tillich distinguishes between "essential" finitude and "existential" disruption. Tillich insists, however, that "essential" finitude is good in spite of its vulnerability to threat.

51 *Love, Power and Justice, op. cit.*, p. 39.

52 Cf. Clark Williamson's review of *Systematic Theology*, Vol. III in the *Journal of Religion*, Vol. 46, No. 2, 1966, p. 301: "The system explores five areas: reason, being, existence, life and history. The problem it finds in these five areas, respectively, are: A split between the ground and structure of reason, the basic anxiety arising from the separation of finite from infinite being, estrangement, ambiguity, and historical ambiguity. The answer to the five problems are all, in one way or another, God." We are asserting here, however, that finitude is the presupposition of the split in reason, estrangement, and the ambiguity of life and history by virtue of its openness, in principle, to non-being.

53   Tillich distinguishes a "larger" and a "narrower" sense of evil, the larger sense
      "includes both destruction and estrangement — man's existential predica-
      ment in all its characteristics" (ST, II: 60). In the narrower sense, evil is seen
      as the "consequences of the state of sin and estrangement," and the doctrine
      of evil is to be distinguished from the doctrine of sin. It is in the narrower
      sense that Tillich uses the word. Only after sin as the correlate of finite free-
      dom has been delineated "can one describe evil as the structure of self-
      destruction which is implicit in the nature of universal estrangement." (ST, II:
      61) The argument seems to be that estrangement, which is the "state" of sin
      (i.e. existence) is not evil in itself even though it cannot be identified with the
      essential goodness of man, but rather evil is implicit in estrangement and
      explicit in destruction. Does this mean that existence under the actual sway
      of destruction (which must include all existence more or less) is evil? The
      distinctions here seem somewhat arbitrary, for it is not clear how existence is
      to be saved from negative evaluation when it is within its own structure that
      evil arises. This is why the unity of essence and existence *within* finitude must
      be kept in mind.

54   Daniel D. Williams has suggested that compared with the richness of exis-
      tence, its concrete value, growth and maturity, essence is actually deficient.
      Cf. his review of *Systematic Theology*, Vol. II in the *Journal of Religion* Vol.
      46, No. 1, Part II, p. 216. This review originally appeared in *The Review of
      Religion*, Vol. XXII, Nos. 3, 4, 1958.

55   Cf. Charles Hartshorne, "Tillich and the Nontheological Meanings" in *Paul
      Tillich: Retrospect and Future, op. cit.*, pp. 19-30. Hartshorne believes that
      Tillich has failed to see that "ordinary" terms can have an "extraordinary" use
      which is quite literal in relation to the extraordinary entity to which they apply,
      namely, God. Consequently, Tillich's emphasis upon the symbolic character
      of *metaphysical* speech about God is misinformed. We are asserting here,
      however, that while Tillich holds that the terms essence and existence are
      symbolically predicated of God, that he is in fact following Hartshorne's pro-
      gram, and, therefore, that Tillich asserts in spite of himself the existence of
      God as a literal state of affairs, except existence is used in its extraordinary
      sense as that which is in harmony with essence in each moment of actualiza-
      tion. Cf. William Rowe, *op. cit.*, pp. 92-93.

Chapter Four

The Foundational Notions
of Tillich's Thought:
The Unconditionedness of Being-Itself

It is not possible here to trace the transition in Tillich's terminology as represented by his moving from the use of the term "the Unconditioned" (*das Unbedingte*) in his early writings[1] to the term "being-itself" in his later writings. Rather we seek to explicate the unconditionality of being-itself as it is formulated especially in the terms of the *Systematic Theology*. Tillich's assertion that being-itself is unconditioned is expressed fundamentally in three claims: being-itself is not *a* being; being-itself does not exist; and finally, being-itself is not subject to the categories. We shall maintain that in each of these claims it is the unconditionality of being-itself which is at stake. Before following out this argument, however, we must turn our attention to Tillich's decision to work out the doctrine of God in relation to the philosophical conception of being-itself; however, this can in no way be a full discussion of Tillich's doctrine of God.

Tillich has written: "when a doctrine of God is initiated by defining God as being-itself, the philosophical concept of being is introduced into systematic theology" (ST, II: 10). It is in the doctrine of God that the convergence of philosophy and theology can be seen most clearly in Tillich's thought. What are the motivations which have led Tillich to work out his concept of God within the framework of the philosophy of being? There seem to be at least two basic answers to this question, which are interrelated and inform much of Tillich's thought about God.

The first answer has to do with Tillich's awareness that the word "God" in its religious usage has become divorced from the total context of human experience and in its increased parochialization it has lost its meaning. Hence, a new terminology is needed which will point once again to that reality which underlies all human experience and which is manifest within the structures of mind and world and within the cultural enterprise in its totality. Nowhere is this evaluation of the semantic predicament of the word "God" more evident than in Tillich's 1923 discussion with Karl Barth and Friedrich Gogarten regarding the theology of crisis. Although Tillich defends his use of the term "the Unconditioned" in his essay, the same argument applies *mutatis mutandis* to his use of the term "being-itself." Tillich writes:

> It is impossible at present to speak as though the words in which Scripture and church refer to the unconditioned could directly achieve that which is their essential meaning. This is the fault of the Grand Inquisitor, of the law, of heteronomy, and of objectification. And all of us, theologians and non-theologians alike, share this same fate. For example, it is impossible for the one who is aware of this situation to speak of God as if this word could directly convey to him its essential richness. Therefore we must speak of the *unconditioned*. Not that this is a substantive expression; it is rather a key to open for oneself and for others the closed door to the holy of holies of the name "God." Then the key should be thrown away.[2]

We may question whether Tillich's allegiance to a philosophical conceptuality is as preliminary as this passage suggests and that it can be thrown away without much ado once the holy of holies has been reached; however, it should be clear that the word "God" no longer directs men to ultimate reality for Tillich and thus must be placed within a philosophical conceptuality which, while not being a substitute expression for "God," stands a better chance of pointing men, theoretically at least, toward the Ultimate.

The second answer to this question lies in what Tillich calls "the inescapable inner tension in the idea of God" (ST, I: 211), that is, in the tension between the concrete and the ultimate elements in the idea of God. Phenomenologically, Tillich argues, "God" is the name for that which concerns man ultimately.[3] It is the tension within the structure of man's ultimate concern, then, which is the locus of the tension in the idea of God, and it is the tension within man's ultimate concern (which is the tension in the human situation as such) which determines the religions of mankind in all their major aspects" (ST, I: 215). How is this tension to be understood? Tillich has described this tension succinctly in continuity with what we have called the problem of finitude in his thought. Ultimate concern moves between two poles:

> On the one hand, it is impossible to be concerned about something which cannot be encountered concretely, be it in the realm of reality or in the realm of the imagination. . . . The more concrete a thing is, the more the possible concern about it. The completely concrete being, the individual person, is the object of the most radical concern . . . the concern of love. On the other hand, ultimate concern must transcend every preliminary finite and concrete concern. It must transcend the whole realm of finitude in order to be the answer to the question implied in finitude. But in transcending the finite the religious concern loses the concreteness of a being-to-being relationship. It tends to become not only absolute but also abstract, provoking reactions from the concrete element. This is the inescapable inner tension in the idea of God (ST, I: 211).

The tension within the structure of ultimate concern is clearly manifest in the phenomenological description of "God." This description reveals, on the one hand, that in every religion:[4]

> Gods are beings who transcend the realm of ordinary experience in power and meaning, with whom men have relations which surpass ordinary relations in intensity and significance . . . Gods are "beings." They are experienced, named, and defined in concrete intuitive (anschaulich) terms through the exhaustive use of all the ontological elements and categories of finitude. Gods are substances, caused and causing, active and passive, remembering and anticipating, arising and disappearing in time and space. Even though they are called "highest beings," they are limited in power and significance. . . . The gods are open to error, compassion, anger, hostility, anxiety. They are images of human nature or subhuman powers raised to a superhuman realm (ST, I: 212).

In other words, the history of religion discloses that that which is a matter of ultimate concern for religious man has been consistently conceived on the basis of the concrete content which is

indispensable to that concern, that is, the whole structure of finitude which constitutes the concreteness of man's life. This is the
tendency toward concreteness in both man's ultimate concern and
the idea of God.

On the other hand, phenomenological description also reveals
that the concrete terms within which gods are understood are also
seriously qualified such that the gods are understood as transcending the categorical finitude which defines them. Thus:

> Their identity as finite substances is negated by all kinds of substantial trans-
> mutations and expansions, in spite of the sameness of their names. Their
> temporal limitations are overcome; they are called "immortals" in spite of the
> fact that their appearance and disappearance are presupposed. Their spatial
> definiteness is negated when they act as multi- or omnipresent, yet they have
> a special dwelling place with which they are intimately connected. Their sub-
> ordination to the chain of causes and effects is denied, for overwhelming or
> absolute power is attributed to them in spite of their dependence on other
> divine powers and on the influence finite beings have on them . . . They tran-
> scend their own finitude in power of being and in the embodiment of mean-
> ing (ST, I: 212-213).

In asserting that the gods are not categorically subject to finitude,
the tendency toward ultimacy in the idea of God can be clearly
seen, but at the same time the conflict between concreteness and
ultimacy becomes apparent.

The idea of God, then as a *religious idea*, is required, by definition, to perform a double conceptual task. In the first place, it
must preserve within itself the concreteness which is indispensable
to ultimate concern. However, secondly, it must strive, on the basis
of the finite, concrete elements from which it is constructed, to
point men to that which transcends everything finite and concrete
and which stands beyond every finite concern as that which is the
true content of man's ultimate concern, manifest within the finite.[5]
We come, at this point, to the most dialectical aspect of the idea of
God as Tillich understands it, and in its very dialecticality, there is
revealed one of Tillich's fundamental presuppositions regarding
the conceptual limitations of the religious idea of God.

In Tillich's essay "The Religious Symbol,"[6] the dialectical character in the idea of God is clearly stated:

But the word "God" involves a double meaning: it connotes the unconditioned transcendent, the ultimate, and also an object somehow endowed with
qualities and actions. The first is not figurative or symbolic, but is rather in
the strictest sense what it is said to be. The second, however, is really symbolic, figurative. *It is the second that is the object envisaged by the religious
consciousness* (emphasis mine) . . . But the religious consciousness is also
aware of the fact that when the word "God" is heard, this idea is figurative,
that it does not signify an object, that is, it must be transcendent. The word
"God" produces a contradiction in the consciousness, it involves something
figurative that is present in the consciousness and something not figurative
that we really have in mind and that is represented by this idea. In the word
"God" is contained at the same time that which actually functions as a representation and also the idea that it is only a representation. It has the peculiarity of transcending its own conceptual content. . . . God as an object is a
representation of the reality ultimately referred to in the religious act, but in
the word "God" this objectivity is negated and at the same time its representative character is asserted.

The idea of God is dialectical in that it stands, as a religious idea or
symbol, under the Yes and No of unconditioned reality which it
both represents and fails to represent.

As William Alston[7] has pointed out, Tillich has departed significantly from traditional conceptions of God. In Alston's terminology the living, personal being of traditional theism, which is the
"symbolizandum" of religious symbols, has become itself a symbol
in Tillich's view. It is the traditional referent of religious symbols
and symbolic language (which Tillich refers to as an "object somehow endowed with qualities and actions") which now constitutes
the symbolic, figurative element in the idea of God and thus is
understood as a symbol for ultimate reality, the unconditioned
transcendent or being-itself. Hence, "God" is a symbol of man's
ultimate concern and *ipso facto* of that about which man is ultimately concerned, the Ultimate, or as Tillich puts it: "God is the
symbol for God."[8]

If we identify the God of traditional theism (a living, personal
being who enters into a definite relationship with man) with the
concrete element in the idea of God, then, it becomes clear that for
Tillich the religious consciousness imposes a significant limitation
upon the idea of God. Or to put the issue differently: the religious

idea of God cannot, on its own terms, i.e. as constructed out of finite elements, express the ultimate element in the idea of God, since it is bound to the need for concreteness of the religious consciousness. Even when the religious consciousness, through the impact of criticism, becomes aware that what it took to be God, (i.e. "the Supreme Being," who is the referent of religious language and piety) is itself a symbol of God, it is still bound to that symbol in order to express itself.[9] It seems presupposed, therefore, that while "God" as a religious symbol points to the ultimate element in the idea of God, *it cannot express this ultimacy within itself.* How then is ultimacy to be expressed in the idea of God? It is in Tillich's attempt to answer this question that he employs the philosophical concept of being-itself.

The concept of being-itself, Tillich believes, is capable of designating the ultimate element in the idea of God. It is being-itself, then, which becomes the referent of religious symbolism, the symbolizandum of the concrete element in the idea of God. Hence:

> We cannot simply say that God is a symbol. We must say two things about him: we must say that there is a non-symbolic element in our image of God — namely, that he is ultimate reality, being-itself, ground of being, power of being; and the other, that he is the highest being in which everything that we have does exist in the most perfect way. If we say this we have in our mind the image of a highest being, a being with the characteristics of highest perfection. That means we have a symbol for that which is not symbolic in the idea of God — namely, "Being-itself."[10]

If the idea of God includes both symbolic and conceptual elements and if the symbolic element points to the ultimate but cannot express it directly in its own terms, it seems clear that an adequate idea of God must include a philosophical component. We conclude, then, that the second important reason why the doctrine of God is articulated within the philosophy of being is that the ultimate element in the idea of God can only be expressed on the basis of the philosophical doctrine of being-itself.[11] The question arises, however, as to the way in which the symbolic and the conceptual elements are related to each other in the idea of God.

The most obvious answer seems to be that the symbolic represents or designates the ultimate, which is to say that "God" as symbol (and the cluster of what Tillich calls "primary symbols" which designate divine actions and qualities)[12] represents or designates God as ultimate reality, i.e. God as being-itself. However, the non-symbolic identification of God (as the referent for the symbol "God") with being-itself is presupposed in this understanding of the relationship of the symbolic and the ultimate (nonsymbolic) in the idea of God.[13] Following William Rowe's interpretation,[14] then, we take Tillich's statement that "the being of God is being-itself" (ST, I: 235) as a univocal identity statement (the only non-symbolic statement we can make about God) in which God and being-itself are held to be identical with the consequence "that the ontological status of God and the ontological status of being-itself are not two different questions, but one and the same question."[15]

It seems clear, however, that, for Tillich, while "God" and "being-itself" are ontologically identical, at the conceptual-linguistic level a clear distinction must be made between them. A difficulty arises, however, in attempting to state Tillich's understanding of this distinction. We might attempt to argue that the distinction is grounded in the fact that "God" is irreducibly symbolic while "being-itself" remains throughout a philosophical concept. This would seem implied in Tillich's 1940 response to Urban's criticism of his view of the religious symbol. Tillich asserts that:

> the nonsymbolic element in all religious knowledge is the experience of the unconditioned as the boundary, ground, and abyss of everything conditioned. This experience is the boundary-experience of human reason and therefore expressible in negative-rational terms. But the unconditioned is not God. God is the affirmative concept pointing beyond the boundary of the negative-rational terms and therefore itself a positive-symbolic term.[16]

Apart from the difficulty of Tillich's denying that the unconditioned is God, it would seem that a clear distinction obtains between negative-rational terms (concepts in the strict sense: Tillich calls God a concept in this passage) and positive-symbolic terms (symbols). However, in discussing the same issue later

Tillich remarks that ultimate concern is the point at which nonsymbolic statements are to be made about God. Nevertheless

> the moment . . . we describe the character of this point or . . . try to formulate that for which we ask, a combination of symbolic with nonsymbolic elements occurs. If we say that God is the infinite, or the unconditional, or being-itself, we speak rationally and ecstatically at the same time. These terms precisely designate the boundary line at which both the symbolic and the non-symbolic coincide. Up to this point every statement is nonsymbolic (in the sense of religious symbol). Beyond this point every statement is symbolic (in the sense of the religious symbol). The point itself is both nonsymbolic and symbolic (ST, II: 9-10).

If we take the symbolic and the nonsymbolic to involve the distinction between symbol and concept, this passage implies that apart from the context of ultimate concern nonsymbolic speech about God involves the rational determination of the symbol "God" by the concept "being-itself" and the ecstatic determination of the concept "being-itself" by the symbol "God." Thus, rather than a basic distinction obtaining between symbol and concept, it now seems that the coincidence of symbol and concept is achieved in their synthesis such that the symbol has conceptual possibilities and the concept symbolic possibilities.[17]

In what must be one of Tillich's last remarks on this question, however, this does not seem to be the position he takes. In a very suggestive essay, Robert Scharlemann[18] proposes that the statement "God is being-itself" expresses the correlation between the symbolic and the literal, and the context in which the expression is uttered determines the logical character of the assertion, i.e. a religious context makes the assertion symbolic, but if it is an ontological utterance, it is literal. As a theological assertion it is a literal statement of the correlation of symbol (God) and concept (being-itself). Scharlemann goes on to suggest that this statement may be as much ontological as theological "since it is no closer to the religious than the philosophical," and further that the life context of its author determines whether it is theological or ontological. Hence, the religious symbol "God" can also be a concept and the concept "being-itself" can also be a religious symbol. Scharlemann then argues that "God is being-itself" (a theological statement) can be converted into "being-itself is God" (an onto-logical statement).[19]

Tillich's response to Scharlemann's proposal is negative. He states:

> I hesitate to accept this formula, the consequence of which would make the logical character of these terms dependent on the context in which they appear. The more exact formulation, I think, should be that there is an element in the term "God," namely, the fact that he is being-itself, which can become a concept if analytically separated. In the first case it is the answer to the question "What does it mean that God 'is'?" which drives to the concept of being-itself. In the second case it is the element of mystery in the experience of being (in the sense of the negation of nonbeing) that enables it to become a symbol.[20]

In rejecting the contextualist meaning of these terms "God" and "being-itself", Tillich is also rejecting their convertibility. The consequence seems to be, then, that at least one literal statement can be made about God, but no literal statement can be made about being-itself ("Every assertion about being-itself is either metaphorical or symbolic"). Moreover, if we examine Tillich's "more exact formulation," it seems to say no more than that the ultimate element in the idea of God can become a concept, i.e., being-itself can become a concept and an "element" in being-itself, its power of overcoming nonbeing, which is precisely what Tillich means ontologically by "God,"[21] can become a symbol. But this is to say, on Tillich's own terms, that God can become a symbol. The conclusion seems justified, then, that Tillich does not construe "God" as a concept, but that his identifying God with being-itself is the attempt to explicate the ultimate element in the idea of God, which the symbol "God" cannot do because of its concreteness. Hence, the ultimacy, or unconditionedness of God is to be explicated on the basis of the explication of being-itself, but this in no way reduces God to a philosophical concept.[22] To say that God is being-itself is the first thing that we must say about God, but certainly not the last.[23]

We have argued that God and being-itself are ontologically identical, but that a distinction obtains between them which Tillich seems consistently to understand as between symbol and concept, where the latter connotes especially a theoretical construct arrived at through detached reflection. This is not to suggest, however, that Tillich denies that concepts of God are possible. What he does seem to maintain is that every concept of God, when it becomes an expression of ultimate concern becomes, therefore, a symbol springing from either the concrete or the ultimate element in the idea of God. Thus, "God" remains a symbol by virtue of its rootage in ultimate concern whether it is conceptualized in religious or philosophical contexts. It seems, however, that insofar as "being-itself" is a matter of ultimate concern, it has ceased to be a purely philosophical concept and has taken on symbolic character. However, the purely philosophical claims Tillich makes about being-itself are also claims made about God.

If the philosophical concept of being-itself, then, is invoked in order to explicate the ultimate element in the idea of God, it follows that ultimacy in God must be interpreted in continuity with the ontological character of being-itself. We have suggested, therefore, that the ultimate element in the idea of God is to be explicated on the basis of the unconditionality of being-itself, that is, it is because being-itself is unconditioned that it can explicate the ultimate element in the idea of God. God is ultimate reality because he is unconditioned reality, that is, being-itself.

We have chosen to explicate the unconditionedness of God as being-itself in the light of the three claims Tillich insists are constitutive of the meaning of being-itself, namely, that being-itself is not a being, that being-itself does not exist, and that being-itself is beyond the ontological scheme, especially the categories. We shall now examine these claims in more detail.[24]

Tillich has consistently maintained that being-itself is not a being, and his claim includes not only the judgment that God as being-itself is not a being in the sense in which traditional theism has construed him, but it also includes the assertion that being-itself cannot be considered an entity in any sense. For Tillich a being is by definition subject to the structure of being, which means, as we have seen, the structure of finitude. To be subject to the structure of being is to be conditioned by finitude and its structures. As James Luther Adams has remarked: "By definition there can be no unconditioned being."[25] Hence Tillich writes:

> The being of God is being-itself. The being of God cannot be understood as the existence of a being alongside others or above others. If God is a being, he is subject to the categories of finitude, especially to space and substance. Even if he is called the "highest being" in the sense of the "most perfect" and the "most powerful" being, this situation is not changed. When applied to God, superlatives become diminutives. They place him on the level of other beings while elevating him above all of them . . . Whenever infinite or unconditioned power and meaning are attributed to the highest being, it has ceased to be a being and has become being-itself (ST, I: 235).

The assertion that being-itself is not a being does not involve the straight-forward denial that there is individuating structure or form in being-itself. As we have seen Tillich seems to hold that being-itself has form "as the meaningful structure of being-itself" (ST, I: 247). The issue rather turns on the meaning Tillich attributes to the notion of *a* being, which takes us immediately to the question of existence. Being-itself cannot be a being because it would be subject to the categories of finitude, and thus it would no longer be unconditioned. It follows, then, that the defining characteristic of *a* being is its conditionedness, i.e., its dependence upon being-itself for its being and its finite character which devolves from this state of dependence. Thus far we can say that if Tillich means by *a* being any entity which is conditioned in its being, (and not simply one that has form) and if God as being-itself is unconditioned, then it is clear why he insists that God is not a being.

However, in asserting that God does not exist as a corollary to the claim that God as being-itself is not a being, it seems that for Tillich existence is also incompatible with unconditionedness. In discussing the classical arguments for the existence of God, Tillich asserts that

> Both the concept of existence and the method of arguing to a conclusion are inadequate for the idea of God. However it is defined, the "existence of God" contradicts the idea of a creative ground of essence and existence. The ground of being cannot be found within the totality of beings, nor can the ground of essence and existence participate in the tensions and disruptions

characteristic of the transition from essence to existence. The scholastics
were right when they asserted that in God there is no difference between
essence and existence. But they perverted their insight when in spite of this
assertion they spoke of the existence of God and tried to argue in favor of it. .
. . God does not exist. He is being-itself beyond essence and existence.
Therefore, to argue that God exists is to deny him (ST, I: 205).

Tillich makes two points here in regard to his claim that God
does not exist. First, God does not exist because he is not *a* being,
that is, he is not one being to be found within the "totality of
beings." It would seem then that existence is that mode of being
which is unique to finite beings. Secondly, God does not exist
because he is not involved in the disruptions attendant upon the
transition from essence to existence, where existence includes not
only the conditionedness of essential finitude, but also the disruptions and self-destructive tendencies of that mode of being which is
separated from its essence. Thus, existence entails both the conditionedness of being a being and the state of being separated from
one's essence. Since God as being-itself is neither conditioned (he
is not a being) nor subject to the split between essence and existence, he cannot exist.

As William Rowe has argued,[26] Tillich's discussion of the existence of God must be understood within the technical meaning of
existence in his thought. This meaning includes both being subject
to the structure of finitude and being subject to the essence-existence split. Thus, whatever exists is *a* being and only that is a being
whose existence is separated from its essence. In order to be consistent with his own concepts, then, Tillich cannot consider other
meanings of existence such that the divine existence can be spoken
of without entailing either that God is conditioned in the sense of
being subject to the structure of finitude or implicated in the separation of existence from essence. Rowe has stated the issue con-
cisely:

My suggestion is that Tillich's claims may rest on a three-way equivalence of
'x exists,' 'is a being,' and 'x has an essence distinct from its act of existing.'
Assuming this to be so, it is clear that since in God there is no distinction
between essence and existence, God cannot be said to *exist* or to be *a* being.
On this view the *core* of Tillich's objection to talking about the *existence* of

God is that such talk involves making God into *a* being and, thereby, implying a distinction between essence and existence in God.[27]

The denial, then, that God as being-itself is *a* being and the claim that existence is incompatible with the being of God rests upon Tillich's concern to preserve what he calls the "divinity of the divine" (ST, I: 244-45), that is, God is not *a* being and God does not exist, because as being-itself God must be absolutely unconditioned. But the question immediately arises whether Tillich, by restricting the meaning of existence to that mode of being which is conditioned within the structure of finitude and separated from essence, can consistently speak of God at all, that is, does not the assertion that *God* is presuppose not only that God exists, but that he exists necessarily? This question takes us beyond the scope of our analysis, however, and we can only raise it in passing.[28] The important consideration here is to see the unconditionedness of God as being-itself which is at stake in Tillich's refusal to think of God as *a* being or to predicate existence of him.

The unconditionedness of being-itself as it is defined negatively in the claims that being-itself is not *a* being and does not exist is conceptualized ultimately overagainst the notion of finitude. Being-itself is in no way dependent upon anything else for its being and it is neither limited by nonbeing nor is its existence distinct from its essence. It is not surprising, then, that Tillich continues to articulate the unconditionedness of being-itself in relation to finitude by asserting that the ontological schema by which the structure of finitude is described does not apply literally to being-itself, that is, being-itself is not conditioned by any state of affairs which obtains within the structure of finitude and which is described literally by ontological concepts.

We have already seen that God as being-itself is beyond essence and existence (ST, I: 236). His existence is identical with his essence with the result that his essential potentialities are completely actualized in his existence. There is, then, no "mixture" of being and not-yet-being in him. Consequently, God is beyond the distinction between potentiality and actuality. Thus, the ontological concepts essence and existence and the distinction between potentiality and actuality they presuppose do not describe God's being. God as being-itself is unconditioned with respect to these generic features of finitude.

The ontological elements and categories do not describe literally the nature of being-itself, for being-itself is unconditioned being. Rather they provide the "material for the symbols which point to the divine life" (ST, I: 243). The categories symbolize the divine-human relationship and the ontological elements symbolize the divine life itself.[29] In asserting that the ontological elements and categories symbolize God as being-itself, Tillich is claiming that something *meaningful* is being said about God or being-itself through their symbolic use. At the same time, however, Tillich must also show that the ontological concepts do not apply to God or being-itself in their literal meaning as they do to finite beings. Hence, God cannot be conditioned in any way by the symbolic application of the ontological concepts to his being.

The unconditionedness of God as being-itself is seen clearly in the way in which the ontological elements are interpreted in their symbolization of the divine life. In finite beings the polarity of the elements entails tension and separation. However, with respect to God:

> The polar character of the ontological elements is rooted in the divine life, but the divine life is not subject to this polarity. Within the divine life, every ontological element includes its polar element completely, without tension and without the threat of dissolution, for God is being-itself. . . . God is called a person, but he is a person not in finite separation but in an absolute and unconditional participation in everything. God is called dynamic, but he is dynamic not in tension with form but in an absolute and unconditional unity with form, so that his self-transcendence is never in tension with his self-preservation, so that he always remains God. God is called "free," but he is free not in arbitrariness but in an absolute and unconditional identity with his destiny, so that he himself is his destiny, so that the essential structures of being are not strange to his freedom but are the actuality of his freedom. In this way, although the symbols used for the divine life are taken from the concrete situation of man's relationship to God, they imply God's ultimacy, the ultimacy in which the polarities of being disappear in the ground of being, in being-itself (ST, I: 243-244).

Tillich rejects the classical theological doctrine of *actus purus* in his doctrine of God. His objection to that doctrine rests upon the claim that in the doctrine of *actus purus* the dynamic element in God is usurped by form. Hence, "pure actuality, that actuality free from any element of potentiality, is a fixed result; it is not alive. . . . The God who is *actus purus* is not the living God" (ST, I: 246). It is the case that the finite and the nonbeing and anxiety which finitude entails are included in being-itself, and God as "the principle of participation" is said to "participate in the negativities of creaturely life." Nevertheless:

> God as being-itself transcends nonbeing absolutely. On the other hand, God as creative life includes the finite and, with it, nonbeing, although nonbeing is eternally conquered and the finite is eternally reunited within the infinity of the divine life. Therefore, it is meaningful to speak of a participation of the divine life in the negativities of creaturely life (ST, I: 270).

How Tillich can say, on the one hand, that God as being-itself is beyond potentiality and actuality, essence and existence, and the tension and disruption which occur in the dissolution of the polarities of the ontological elements as exemplified in finite beings (that is, beyond nonbeing) and on the other that the divine life is the eternal process of actualization of potentiality, that potentiality is real for God, that there is genuine self-transcendence (becoming) in God, that he participates in the negativities of existence, and that nonbeing is eternally conquered in him, without falling into serious self-contradictions is difficult to ascertain. He denies that these claims are to be construed either as metaphysical-constructive (ST, I: 247) or as paradox (ST, II: 90-91). Rather they are dialectical-symbolic statements, which arise out of the correlation of ultimate concern. Theologically speaking, we must say that the ontological elements cohere in God without tension or separation. His unconditionedness must be asserted consistently. But religiously speaking we must assert that God is not static identity, that he participates in the careers of his creatures and yet, without in any way compromising his unconditioned being, for "only that which is unconditional can be the expression of unconditional concern. A conditioned God is no God" (ST, 248).

The question arises, however, whether dialectical-symbolic speech about God as being-itself is not also subject to the most general rules of meaningful discourse. Tillich asserts that it is (hence the ideal of "semantic rationality" (ST, I: 54)). Without arguing from a strictly positivistic or verificationist view of language, the semantic issue to be pressed here is whether terms which presuppose some contrast in the entities in which they are exemplified are any longer meaningful when these contrasts do not obtain. What Tillich is asserting, it seems to me, in claiming the unconditional unity or identity of the ontological elements in God is that there are no distinctions or contrasts within the being of God. Hence, there seems to be no way of avoiding the conclusion that in spite of Tillich's criticisms of the *actus purus* doctrine it is the idea of the divine simplicity which informs his conception of the unconditionedness of God as being-itself. Consequently, the ontological elements become unintelligible in their symbolic application to the divine being.

The same state of affairs obtains in Tillich's discussion of the categories. Since man symbolizes the relation of God to the creature by means of the categories, Tillich introduces his discussion of this group of ontological concepts within his discussion of the doctrine of creation. However, one can only be disappointed at the brevity of the discussion in which *time* alone is given consideration.[30] Nevertheless, Tillich's discussion of time will serve to illustrate our analysis.

Tillich recognizes that if finitude is to be posited within the divine life, then the categories as forms of finitude are also present in God. Thus:

> the divine life includes temporality, but it is not subject to it. The divine eternity includes time and transcends it. The time of the divine life is determined not by the negative element of creaturely time but by the present, not by the "no longer" and the "not yet" of our time. Our time, the time which is determined by nonbeing, is the time of existence. It presupposes the separation of existence from essence and the existential disruption of the moments of time which are essentially united within the divine life (ST, I: 257).

It is clear that the distinctions within time, that is, past, present, and future, which characterize existential or creaturely time, disappear within the divine life, just as the polarities of the ontological elements disappear in God as being-itself. It would seem, then, that in saying that the divine life is not determined by the "no longer" and "not yet" of existential time, Tillich is asserting again that the temporal distinctions which give time its finite, literal meaning do not obtain within the divine life,[31] even though Tillich insists that the divine life includes temporality. But by asserting that God as being-itself is beyond every distinction or contrast which obtains within finite being, especially the essence-existence contrast, Tillich has undercut any possible way of giving meaning to the categories in their application to the divine life. If God's being is in no way conditioned by time, or as Tillich puts it if God's being includes time but is not subject to it, and if being unconditioned by time means, as it seems to, that God is beyond the temporal distinctions which are constitutive for the meaning of time, then, again, the category of time is unintelligible in relation to God as being-itself, since the simplicity of the divine being admits no contrasts within the divine life by which the term can be given meaning. This same state of affairs obviously extends to the other categories in their application to the divine life.

The attempt to counter the argument put forward here with Tillich's claim that the ontological concepts apply symbolically to the divine life will not, it seems to me, withstand critical analysis. In the first place, as we have suggested, it is extremely difficult to know how to construe the ontological statements about God's being made on the basis of the ontological concepts as symbolic statements. When Tillich argues that the polarities disappear in the divine being such that no proper distinction can be made in God between essence and existence, dynamics and form, etc., or that all temporal distinctions disappear in the divine present, clearly he is not using these terms in their literal finite meaning, but the question is whether Tillich has not given them a unique meaning in relation to God which describes his being quite literally. If the ontological statements are not to be taken literally, then why,

as William Alston has asked,[32] does Tillich seek to translate theological symbols into ontological statements?

Secondly, even if it can be demonstrated that the ontological
statements are genuinely symbolic or analogical statements, thus
saving Tillich from the charge of equivocation, that is, by showing
that the ontological concepts are being predicated of God on the
basis of their literal meaning while at the same time their literal
meaning is denied,[33] we still have to raise the question of their
symbolic meaning, because for Tillich to speak symbolically of God
is to speak *meaningfully*. We have argued, however, that the divine
simplicity defined as God as being-itself, by disavowing either distinction or conditionedness in God, renders the ontological concepts unintelligible in spite of Tillich's efforts to introduce a
dynamic, self-transcending dimension into the divine being. If the
polarities by which the elements are distinguished disappear in
being-itself, then the meaning of the terms disappear as well, just as
the meaning of time disappears when the temporal distinctions of
past, present, and future disappear.

The unconditionedness of God as being-itself, then, is informed
in its detail by the presupposition that the mode of God's being is
in radical contrast to the mode of finite beings. God's being is in
no way conditioned by finitude. Thus in contrast to Whitehead,[34]
Tillich construes the unconditionedness of being-itself as not a
being; being-itself is beyond essence and existence, potentiality and
actuality, the polarities of the ontological elements and thus their
existential disruption, and the threat of nonbeing exemplified in
the forms of finitude, the ontological categories. Hence, God is
beyond the categories themselves. As we have seen, Tillich
attempts to show that finitude and the nonbeing and anxiety it
entails is somehow posited in God, but it is clear that the finite in
no way limits, conditions or contributes to God's unconditioned
perfection.[35]

The unconditionedness of God as being-itself, then, as an ultimate notion in Tillich's thought, stands in immediate correlation
with the doctrine of finitude, for it is only by participation in the
unconditionedness of God's being that man can take upon himself

the nonbeing, anxiety, and existential disruption which is grounded in finitude. In relation to the conflicts and disruptions within the ontological elements, on the finite level, God as being-itself is the unity of being which prevents the complete destruction of the structure of being through the total dissolution of the ontological polarities (ST, I: 262). With respect to the problem of nonbeing and anxiety which is exemplified in the categories as forms of finitude, the unconditionedness of God is affirmed first in relation to causality and substance in the claim that God is the creative ground of being, who is in no way subject to the infinite regression of the causal sequence nor the contingency of origination it implies (God is *a se*); nor is he subject to the threat of the loss of his substantial identity. In relation to time, space and the subject-object structure of being the unconditionedness of God is affirmed fundamentally through the theological symbol of omnipotence. "The symbol of omnipotence," Tillich declares:

> gives the first and basic answer to the question implied in finitude. . . . Faith in the almighty God is the answer to the quest for a courage which is sufficient to conquer the anxiety of finitude. Ultimate courage is based upon participation in the ultimate power of being. When the invocation "Almighty God" is seriously pronounced, a victory over the threat of nonbeing is experienced, and an ultimate, courageous affirmation of existence is expressed. Neither finitude nor anxiety disappears, but they are taken into infinity and courage (ST, I: 273).

With respect to time, omnipotence is eternity; with respect to space it is omnipresence; and with respect to the subject-object structure it is omniscience (ST, I: 274). The unconditionedness of God defined as his eternal being (which is neither timelessness nor endless time) is the basis of the courage which overcomes the negativities of existential time (ST, I: 276). The spatial structure is rooted in God, and he participates in it without being subject to it. God's omnipresence does not mean that he is endlessly extended in space nor that he is limited to a definite space. Neither does it mean that God is spaceless. Rather it means that God is eternally present in every time and place, that his creativity as the divine ground of the spatial structure is effective in every moment and every spatial context. Thus:

> God's omnipresence overcomes the anxiety of not having a space for one's self. It provides the courage to accept the insecurities and anxieties of spatial existence. In the certainty of the omnipresent God we are always at home and not at home, rooted and uprooted, resting and wandering, being placed and displaced, known by one place and not known by any place (ST, I: 278).

As one of the features of the structure of finitude, the subject-object structure, like every other feature of finitude, is grounded in the divine life, which means that God both participates in this structure (or to put it more precisely God participates in himself through his participation in this structure) and transcends it. The divine omniscience is the theological symbol "indicating that God is not present in an all-permeating manner but that he is present spiritually" (ST, I: 279), which is to say that there is nothing strange to or hidden from the centered unity of the divine life.

The correlation of the symbol of omniscience means on the one hand that the ultimacy or unconditionedness of God as being-itself is affirmed in the claim that: "Nothing falls outside the *logos* structure of being. The dynamic element cannot break the unity of the form; the abysmal quality cannot swallow the rational quality of the divine life" (ST, I: 279). On the other hand, the existential correlate of the symbol of omniscience lies in the claim that:

> The hidden the dark, the unconscious, is present in God's spiritual life. There is no escape from it. And . . . the anxiety of the dark and hidden is overcome in the faith of the divine omniscience. . . . We know because we participate in the divine knowledge. Truth is not absolutely removed from the outreach of our finite minds, since the divine life in which we are rooted embodies all truth. In the light of the symbol of divine omniscience we experience the broken character of every finite meaning, but not as a cause for ultimate meaninglessness. The doubt about truth and meaning which is the heritage of finitude is incorporated in faith through the symbol of the divine omniscience (ST, I: 279).

It should be clear from the above that the two ultimate notions of finitude and the unconditionedness of God as being-itself stand in immediate correlation. The principle of finitude literally requires the unconditionedness of being-itself, and God as being-itself could not be the answer to the question of finitude unless he were unconditioned. Hence, to say that God as being-itself is not *a* being is to assert that being-itself is in no way subject to the structure of being, most especially to the subject-object structure. To say that God as being-itself does not exist, is to assert that God is not subject to the tragic split between essence and existence and the conflicts, disruptions, and self-destructive drives of existential being as is the structure of finitude. Finally, to say that the ontological concepts do not apply to God as being-itself in their literal, proper meaning is to place God beyond the ontological schema in the sense that the distinctions and contrasts, and thus the conditionedness which the ontological concepts presuppose in the finite entities in which they are literally exemplified are simply not applicable to the being of God as being-itself. This makes the concepts unintelligible in relation to the simplicity and ineffability[36] of being-itself. Hence, being-itself is beyond the ontological concepts and the mode of conditioned being they presuppose.

We have argued, then, that the problem of finitude requires as its solution the unconditionedness of God as being-itself. God as the ground and power of being is required to hold the finite order together. The divine simplicity and unity provides the basis by which man can live within the tensions, conflicts and disruptions of the existential order in which the ontological elements move against each other. The divine eternity overcomes the nonbeing, anxiety, despair and meaninglessness of existential time. The divine omnipresence overcomes the doubt, brokenness and fragmentariness of finite meaning and truth. Thus, the divine unconditionedness is the source and basis of the courage of man's existential self-affirmation.

However, if the unconditionedness of God as being-itself is his transcendence of finitude in every respect, even though predicating being of God also means predicating finitude and nonbeing of God, and if man's state as actualized freedom is to be separated from the power of being and his own essential being, then the question arises as to the relationship between unconditioned and conditioned being.   It is Tillich's claim that an ultimate unity obtains between being-itself and finite being which constitutes the third and final ultimate notion of his system. We must now attempt to explicate briefly this final ultimate notion, following which we shall draw Part One of this essay to a close.

Notes

1 For a critical analysis of the meaning of the term "the Unconditioned" as Tillich developed it in his early writings, see J. L. Adams, *Paul Tillich's Philosophy of Culture, Science, and Religion, op. cit.*, p. 41ff; p. 261ff. Adams points out that "the Unconditioned" contains a variety of meanings, which include: "the unconditioned transcendent, the unconditionally real, the unconditionally powerful, the unconditionally personal, the unconditionally perfect, the inaccessible holy, the eternal, the unconditional demand, and the unconditional meaning" (*Ibid.*, p. 41). However, as a concept the Unconditioned can be understood as a limiting or regulative concept and as a constitutive concept. As a *limiting* concept, the Unconditioned is a "qualification of everything in the temporo-spatial, the conditioned order" (*Ibid.*, p. 44). As such the Unconditioned is neither an order next to the conditioned order, nor does it exist. Rather it is an inescapable concept in thinking about the existential order. In its limiting function, Adams suggests that Tillich refers to it as the "negative unconditioned" in his later lectures. As a *constitutive* concept, "it connotes the participation of everything ontic in an ontological structure of being" (*Ibid.*, p. 45). As such, it is the "unconditioned of being." "The unconditioned transcendent is that which gives being to existence, as the transcendent power of being" (*Ibid.*, p. 49). This is the "positive unconditioned." The third meaning of the Unconditioned is "the unconditioned of value." Here the Unconditioned is the universal norm by which every cultural creation and human nature itself is evaluated. As universal norm, the Unconditioned appears as unconditioned demand. One cannot, in his dealings with the world, escape the demand of logic or of mathematical propositions or the demand of the person to be treated as a person. These desiderata point to the "unconditionality of the Unconditioned" as it is manifest within existence. Thus, "in confronting the limited character of our existence, in confronting the ambiguous events of the temporal order, in confronting the normative demands of truth, goodness, and beauty, we find a qualification which we intuit in reality itself, the qualification of the conditioned by the Unconditioned" (*Ibid.*, p. 49). Synthetically defined, then, the Unconditioned "refers to the unconditioned of being, of truth [value], and meaning" (*Ibid.*, p. 261). One can see many parallels here between the Unconditioned and being-itself. Cf. Lewis Ford's suggestion that in replacing "the Unconditioned" with "being-itself" Tillich moved from a Kantian to a more classical terminology, although in not

interpreting "esse" (in *esse ipsum*) as act of being, he is closer to Augustine than Thomas. "Tillich and Thomas," *op. cit.*, p. 239.

2   This discussion first appeared as "Kritisches und positives Paradox; Ein Auseinandersetzung mit Karl Barth und Friedrich Gogarten" in *Theologische Blatter*, II, No. 11 (Nov., 1923), pp. 263-69. It appears also in GW, VII, 216-25. The entire discussion between Tillich, Barth, and Gogarten as it was published in *Theologische Blatter* has been published in English translation in *The Beginnings of Dialectical Theology*, ed. James M. Robinson (John Knox Press, Richmond, 1968), Vol. I, pp. 131-162. The quotation is taken from this English translation, and is found in Tillich's response to Karl Barth's initial response to Tillich's essay.

3   The notion of "ultimate concern" is a fundamental motif in Tillich's thought. He defines both faith and religion within its terms. In *Dynamics of Faith*, Tillich roots ultimate concern within the structure of concern of man as man (DF: 1). The term itself, as Tillich points out (*Ultimate Concern*: 11) is intentionally ambiguous. It indicates, on the one hand, the subjective "state" of one's *being* ultimately concerned and, on the other, the *object* about which one is concerned, that is, the "ultimate." Ultimate concern is to be distinguished from "preliminary" concerns by virtue of: (1) subjectively, ultimate concern exceeds all preliminary concerns in seriousness, intensity, and passion (although this does not mean that ultimate concern is more emotional than preliminary concerns) and (2) the object of ultimate concern (which when truly ultimate is not an object) exceeds all objects of preliminary concern in power, meaning and importance. Thus all preliminary concerns are subordinated to one's ultimate concern, which is concern for that which has "the power of threatening and saving our being" (ST, I: 14). However, because that which is of ultimate concern to man "becomes a god to him" (ST, I: 211), it is possible for a preliminary concern to be elevated to ultimacy (idolatry), and thus a distinction must be made between "true" and "false" ultimates. Tillich suggests two criteria for making this distinction: (1) that which is truly ultimate is present within ultimate concern beyond the subject-object scheme, and (2) the finite which falsely claims ultimacy for itself is not able to transcend the subject-object scheme; therefore, a false ultimate cannot fulfill human existence; rather it produces "existential disappointment" in man (DF: 11-12). Hence, ultimate concern is never merely "subjective," and that which is truly ultimate or unconditional is never found "within the entire catalogue of finite objects which are conditioned by each other" (ST, 1:214); however, ultimate concern needs finite concerns through which to express the Ultimate. This is the source of the tension within ultimate concern itself.

4   By defining God as that which concerns man ultimately, Tillich denies that any religion is atheistic in that sense. Thus, "If God is understood as that which concerns man ultimately, early Buddhism has a concept of God just as certainly as does Vedanta Hinduism" (ST, I: 220). Atheism as protest against

a particular doctrine of God, especially when it distorts the reality of the Ultimate, is possible, but atheism in the generic sense of "being without ultimate concern" is not possible for Tillich.

5   William L. Rowe ("The Meaning of 'God' in Tillich's Theology," *Journal of Religion*, Vol. 42, No. 4, 1962, pp. 274-286) has called attention to the potential contradiction in Tillich's formulation of the concreteness and ultimacy in ultimate concern. In the first place, Tillich asserts that everything finite is less than the Ultimate. However, he further asserts that man can only be ultimately concerned about something concrete. Finally, Tillich maintains that man is ultimately concerned about the Ultimate (even though he often raises preliminary concerns to ultimacy). The potential contradiction is that, obviously, ultimate concern cannot be directed toward something concrete and at the same time be ultimate concern for the Ultimate, since the concrete is less than the Ultimate. The potential contradiction is overcome, however, when it is seen that the concrete "is the focus of our ultimate concern . . . because we take it as manifesting the Ultimate toward which our concern is directed" (Ibid: 277).

6   This essay first appeared as "Das religiose Symbol" in *Blatter fur deutsche Philosophie*, Vol. 1, No. 4, 1928. It was republished in *Religiose Verwirklichung* (Berlin, 1930). It has been translated into English by James Luther Adams and Ernest Fraenkel in *The Journal of Liberal Religion*, 2, 1940. It has been reprinted in *Daedalus*, summer, 1958 and appears as an appendix to *Religious Experience and Truth*, ed. Hook (New York University Press, 1961). The quotation here is taken from this last reference, p. 315.

7   William P. Alston, "Tillich's Conception of a Religious Symbol," *Religious Experience and Truth, op. cit.*, p. 15f.

8   *Dynamics of Faith, op. cit.*, p. 46.

9   (*Ibid.*, pp. 44-45: "Man's ultimate concern must be expressed symbolically . . . . whatever we say about that which concerns us ultimately, whether or not we call it God, has a symbolic meaning . . . In no other way can faith express itself adequately. The language of faith is the language of symbols. . . . Faith, understood as the state of being ultimately concerned, has no language other than symbols . . . and the fundamental symbol of our ultimate concern is God."

10 *Theology of Culture, op. cit.*, p. 61.

11 David Kelsey argues (*op. cit.* p. 156ff.) that there are two fundamental ways in which "God" is explicated in Tillich's thought. In the first way, "God" is a proper name, whose referent is being-itself. Thus, when ontology points out the presence of being-itself (without describing it), it also explains the meaning of "God." The second way has nothing to do with treating "God" as a

proper name, explicated through ontological analysis, but rests rather upon showing the "proper context in which to use the term, rather than identifying or describing its referent" (*Ibid.*, p. 158). Here God is not a name, "but is used to express the occurrence of a revelatory event." Kelsey concludes that these ways involve quite different logics and are "probably (!!) mutually exclusive" (*Ibid.*, p. 165). He proposes to abandon the first way as inconsistent with Tillich's theological method in favor of the second. Thus "God" like "the Christ" is a "verbal icon," an aesthetic model which may provoke attitudes toward life, but it is not involved in questions of truth-claims. It would seem, however, that it is Tillich's effort to ground religious symbols within a philosophical conceptuality precisely because without it their ultimate reference is obscured that argues most strongly against Kelsey's thesis.

12 "The Meaning and Justification of Religious Symbols," Hook, *op. cit.*, pp. 8-9.

13 *Biblical Religion and the Search for Ultimate Reality, op. cit.*, p. 85: "To ask the ontological question is a necessary task. Against Pascal I say: The God of Abraham, Isaac, and Jacob and the God of the Philosophers *is* the same God."

14 "The Meaning of 'God' in Tillich's Theology," *op. cit.*, Rowe has traced two different answers in Tillich's writings to the question whether nonsymbolic statements about God are possible and what seems to be two different evaluations of the logical status of the statement that "God is being-itself." The first answer Rowe finds in Tillich's essay, "The Religious Symbol." There Tillich argues that all knowledge of God is symbolic and, therefore, that no positive, literal statement can be made about the unconditioned transcendent (which in that essay is identical with the ultimate element in the idea of God). We do not have objective knowledge of God through symbols, but symbols provide "true awareness of God" ("The Religious Symbol", *The Journal of Liberal Religion*, vol. 2, 1940, p. 28). Therefore, every reply to William Urban's charge of "pansymbolism" (see Urban's critique of Tillich's essay in the same journal) nowhere suggests that any literal statement can be made about God. Tillich asserts rather "that the nonsymbolic element in all religious knowledge is the experience of the unconditioned as the boundary, ground, and abyss of everything conditioned" (*Ibid.*, p. 203). The second answer occurs in Vol. I of ST where it is maintained that "God is being-itself" is a nonsymbolic statement. Here Tillich designates Urban's criticism as the basis for this claim. Thus, Tillich seems to have moved from saying that no nonsymbolic statements are possible about God to asserting that there is one statement about God that is nonsymbolic, i.e. that God is being-itself.

The second shift "seems to occur" in 1957 in Vol. II of ST. Here Tillich maintains once again that "everything religion has to say about God . . . has symbolic character . . . " (ST, II: 9), and the only nonsymbolic assertion about God now "is the assertion that everything we say about God is symbolic. Such a statement is an assertion about God which itself is not symbolic" (ST,

II: 9). It would seem, then, that "'God is being-itself' is not the straight-for-ward, nonsymbolic statement he took it to be in the first volume." Rowe translates "Every statement about God is symbolic" into "Everything we say about God is symbolic," and thus "God is being-itself" is no longer a literal statement about God. Now, Rowe suggests, this position seems very close to the original position of "The Religious Symbol," but with the exception that Tillich wishes to construe "Every statement about God is a symbolic state-ment" as itself a nonsymbolic statement. Rowe thinks this is a mistake because (1) the statement is not about God, but about statements about God and (2) it does not attach any positive predicate to God and cannot, there-fore, be a literal statement (Rowe fails to mention that the statement is self-contradictory, because in its very form it denies itself, i.e. if one nonsymbolic statement about God is possible, it is not the case that "*every* statement about God is symbolic"). It would seem, then, that the position of Vol. II is just another way of saying that no literal statement can be made about God, Tillich's original position in the 1940 essay.

Rowe accepts the formulation of Vol. I (as do we) as normative, however, because Tillich does not deny it in Vol. II, but rather makes a point of saying that in restating some aspects of the doctrine of God in Vol. II the substance of his earlier thought has not changed (ST, II: 5). It should also be said in support of this decision (as Robert Scharlemann has pointed out in "Tillich's Method of Correlation: Two Proposed Revisions," *Journal of Religion*, Vol. 46, I, I, 1966, Note nine) that ST, III: 294 uses the same formulation as ST, I: 238.

15 *Ibid.*, p. 280.

16 *The Journal of Liberal Religion, op. cit.*, p. 203.

17 Cf. Lewis S. Ford, "The Three Strands of Tillich's Theory of Religious Sym-bols," *Journal of Religion*, Vol. 46, I, I, 1966, pp. 104-130. Ford argues that the symbol has both religious and metaphysical functions in Tillich's thought.

18 "Tillich's Method of Correlation: Two Proposed Revisions," *op. cit.*, p. 95ff.

19 William S. Christian, *Meaning and Truth in Religion* (Princeton University Press, Princeton, N.J., 1964), p. 39, No. 4 has also suggested that Tillich might be understood as using the term "God" as a predicate expression rather than as a logical subject. Thus, in the statement "being-itself is God" "being-itself" is the logical subject and "God" is the predicate expression.

20 Paul Tillich, "Rejoinder," *Journal of Religion*, Vol. 46, I, I, 1966, p. 185.

21 Paul Tillich, "The Meaning and Justification of Religious Symbols," Hook, *op. cit.*, p. 7. Here Tillich refers to "being-itself," "power of being," "ultimate

concern," as "metaphorical names" for that to which ontological analysis leads as the referent of religious symbolism.

22 Tillich seems to regard concepts such as "cosmic person" (Brightman) or "creative process" (Wieman) as philosophical possibilities, not religious necessities. As such, they are tentative, theoretical constructs, not existential symbols of ultimate concern. They may claim religious significance. Then they must be analyzed theologically as symbols. Tillich clearly wishes to claim religious significance for "being-itself," but in doing so "being-itself" has ceased to be a tentative philosophical concept (ST, I: 44; ST, I: 220; 235).

23 David Kelsey has stressed the trinitarian structure of Tillich's doctrine of God and the significance of the concepts "Life" and "spirit" in that doctrine. David Kelsey, *op. cit.*, p. 165ff. Cf. Paul Tillich, "Rejoinder," *Journal of Religion, op. cit.*, p. 186; Cf. also LeRoy T. Howe, "Tillich on the Trinity," *The Christian Scholar*, Vol. XLIX, No. 3, Fall, 1966, pp. 206-213 for an evaluation of the role of trinitarian thinking in Tillich's theology.

24 Although our analysis is concerned with the unconditionedness of being-itself, it is clear from the above that we are explicating at the same time the unconditionedness of God.

25 J. L. Adams, *op. cit.*, p. 46.

26 *Religious Symbols and God, op. cit.*, p. 76.

27 *Ibid.*, p. 80. Rowe has criticized Tillich for failing to consider that "existence" when predicated of God in classical theology has a unique meaning which does not entail "being subject to the conditions of finitude." Tillich, however, is not consistent on this issue, for he does seem occasionally to use existence this way. Cf. ST, II: 23; *Theology of Paul Tillich, op. cit.*, p. 339. Cf. also John Hick, *Philosophy of Religion* (Prentice-Hall, Englewood Cliffs, N.Y., 1963), pp. 6-7.

28 The least we can say here is that Tillich has given no sufficient reasons for showing that the term "existence" must be limited to the meaning he has delineated. A number of critics have argued that his refusal to think of God as an entity is self-defeating, while William Rowe has made a convincing case that although Tillich asserts that God does not exist, he is in fact committed to the view that God exists necessarily. Cf. Lewis Ford, Tillich and Thomas," *op. cit.*, pp. 243-44; John Y. Fenton, "Being-itself and Religious Symbolism," *The Journal of Religion*, Vol. XLV, No. 2, April, 1965, pp. 73-86; William R. Rowe, *Religious Symbols and God, op. cit.*, Chapter Three.

29 Tillich denies that there is symbolic material in the basic self-world structure. God cannot be thought of even symbolically as a self and neither can he be identified with the world (ST, I: 244).

30 We have already noted Tillich's discussion of the two categories of causality and substance to express the relation of being-itself to finite beings. Here the categories are no longer being used as categories but as symbols (ST, I: 237-38). Cf. also Tillich's discussion of space in relation to the question of the immanence and transcendence of God. God as being-itself is the ground of the spatial structure of the world, but as unconditioned being he is not subject to that structure. However, the world is transcendent to God just as God is transcendent to the world (ST, I: 263). Again, it is difficult to reconcile the genuine transcendence of the world with Tillich's claims regarding God as related in which it is asserted that "God as being-itself is the ground of every relation; in his life all relations are present beyond the distinctions between potentiality and actuality. But they are not the relations of God with something else. They are the inner relations of the divine life . . . But the question is whether there are external relations between God and the creature. The doctrine of creation affirms that God is the creative ground of everything in every moment. In this sense there is no creaturely independence from which an external relation between God and the creature could be derived" (ST, I: 271). Tillich does not specify *whether there is any other sense* in which his assertion of the transcendence of the world could be defended. Again, the unconditionedness of being-itself vitiates a genuine doctrine of God as related and also reveals Tillich's very close affinity with Spinoza.

31 Daniel D. Williams has identified Tillich's view of time with the *totum simul* doctrine of St. Augustine. Cf. D. D. Williams, "Tillich's Doctrine of God," *op. cit.* For an extended critique of the Augustinian concept of time in the divine life, cf. also Daniel D. Williams, *The Spirit and the Forms of Love* (Harper and Row, N.Y., 1968), Chapter V.

32 William P. Alston, "Tillich's Conception of a Religions Symbol," *op. cit.*, pp. 24-25.

33 ST, I: 239: " . . . any concrete assertion about God must be symbolic, for . . . (it) is one which uses a segment of finite experience . . . to say something about him. It transcends the content of this segment, although it also includes it. . . . The segment of finite reality . . . of a concrete assertion about God is affirmed and negated at the same time. It becomes a symbol, for a symbolic expression is one whose proper meaning is negated by that to which it points, and yet it also is affirmed by it, and this affirmation gives the symbolic expression an adequate basis for pointing beyond itself." The point being argued here is that the "proper" meaning of the ontological concepts cannot be determined on the basis of their meaning for finite entities, for Tillich has created new "proper" meanings for them in their relation to God, which does not involve negating their finite meanings but replacing them. Thus, they are not predicated of God in their finite meanings at all.

34 Alfred N. Whitehead, *Process and Reality* (The MacMillan Co., N.Y., 1929), p. 521.

25 This judgment is made in the face of the many passages in Tillich in which he seems very close to the absolute-relative, unconditioned-conditioned panentheism of Whitehead and Hartshorne. The following are representative:

(1) ST, I: 246: " . . . these concepts (the concepts of thinkers from Bohme through Hartshorne which attempt to distinguish two elements in God) . . . point symbolically to a quality of the divine life which is analogous to what appears as dynamics in the ontological structure. The divine creativity, God's participation in history, his outgoing character, are based on this dynamic element. . . . It also can be expressed as the negative element in the ground of being which is overcome but is effective as a threat and a potential disruption."

(2) ST, I: 250-251: "Human intuition of the divine always has distinguished between the abyss of the divine (the element of power) and the fullness of its content (the element of meaning), between the divine depth and the divine logos. . . . Through the Spirit (the third principle in God) the divine fullness is posited in the divine life as something definite (the content of the finite process in each of its moments?), and at the same time it is reunited in the divine ground. The finite is posited as finite within the process of the divine life, but it is reunited with the infinite within the same process. . . . The divine life is infinite mystery, but it is not infinite emptiness. It is the ground of all abundance, and it is abundant itself."

(3) ST, I: 274-275: "Since time is created in the ground of the divine life, God is essentially related to it. Insofar as everything divine transcends the split between potentiality and actuality, the same must be said of time as an element of the divine life. Special moments of time are not separated from each other; . . . Eternity is the transcendent unity of the dissected moments of existential time. It is not adequate to identify simultaneity with eternity. Simultaneity would erase the different modes of time; but time without modes is timelessness. . . . If we call God a living God, we affirm that he includes temporality and with this a relation to the modes of time. . . . The eternal includes past and future without absorbing their special character as modes of time."

(4) ST, I: 242: "Most of the so-called anthropomorphisms of the biblical picture of God are expressions of his character as living. His actions, his passions, his remembrances and anticipations, his suffering and joy, his personal relations and his plans — all these make him a living God and distinguish him from the pure absolute from being-itself".

(5) In spite of Tillich's rejection of patripassianism (ST, I: 270; ST, III: 404), he wants to assert God's taking the suffering of the world upon himself by participating in existential estrangement (ST, II: 175).

(6) ST, III: 422: " . . . the world process means something for God. . . . The eternal act of creation is driven by a love which finds fulfillment only through the other who has the freedom to reject and to accept love. God, so to speak, drives toward the actualization and essentialization of everything that has being. For the eternal dimension of what happens in the universe is the divine life itself. It is the content of the divine blessedness."

It must be kept in mind, however, that Tillich regards all these passages as symbolic descriptions of God and nowhere does he rethink God's unconditionedness in the light of these claims. There is, at best, a profound ambivalence in Tillich between the divinity of God (i.e. his unconditionedness), and his being related. As Clark Williamson has pointed out ("Review of ST, Vol, III," *Journal of Religion, op. cit.*, p. 303), Tillich can claim on the one hand that the world contributes something to God (ST, III: 422), and on the other hand, he can claim that "there is nothing which the created world can offer God. He is the only one who gives" (ST, I: 264); and again "insofar as devotional language speaks of the longing of God for his creature and insofar as mystical language speaks of the need that God has for man, the *libido* element is introduced into the notion of the divine love, but as poetic-religious symbolism, for God is not in need of anything" (ST, I: 281). We are asserting, however, that inasmuch as "God is being-itself" is a literal statement, Tillich is ultimately committed to the absolute unconditionedness of God as the most basic conceptual determination of the doctrine of God and that the doctrine of God's unconditionedness vitiates every claim he makes to suggest that God is in some element or aspect of his being conditioned by the world and the creatures. Hence, the doctrine of symbolic predication merely obscures this basic antinomy in Tillich's conception of God.

36 Cf. William Rowe, *Religious Symbols and God, op. cit.*, pp. 40-41 for the assertion that being-itself is ineffable in Tillich. `

Chapter Five

The Foundational Notions
of Tillich's Thought:
The Unity of Unconditioned
and Conditioned Being

The third fundamental notion in Tillich's thought is certainly as pervasive as the other two and bears the same critical significance for his system. In the attempt to get the notion clearly before us, we shall explicate it in its three most basic expressions; that is, in its ontological, its cognitive, and its theological terms. Naturally these three levels of discourse presuppose each other within the system, and they are separated only for purposes of analysis.

The ontological assertion of the unity of unconditioned and conditioned being can be discussed briefly since it has been presupposed in much of our discussion to this point. We have already seen that Tillich maintains that being-itself infinitely transcends finite being and thus that there is "an absolute break" between the infinite and the finite, the unconditioned and the conditioned (ST, I: 237). This means that being-itself is in no way subject to the structure of finitude. Consequently, the original unity between unconditioned and conditioned being cannot be construed as an original identity. Finitude is in principle (apart from the question of existential estrangement) to be distinguished from being-itself.

The unity of being-itself and finite being is maintained, however, in Tillich's claim that everything finite participates in being-itself. For Tillich the principle of participation involves in all of its meanings partial identity and partial nonidentity and he construes the identity of participation as an identity in the power of being.[1] The basic ontological fact is finite being is identical with being-itself by virtue of the former's participation in the power of being of being-itself. Its nonidentity, however, is also clearly maintained in Tillich. Actualized freedom in finitude is only possible on the basis of the original unity in the power of being of being-itself and finite being; nevertheless, actualized freedom drives the creature away from its uncontested unity with the ground of being, and thus the original unity of unconditioned and conditioned being is qualified by the self-differentiation (partial non-identity) of the conditioned from the unconditioned. It is not, however, completely broken, even in the state of estrangement.

For our purposes the most important consideration resulting from Tillich's notion of participation as the ontological assertion of the unity of being-itself and finite being is that it is the participation of the finite in being-itself which provides the basis for the *analogia entis* and thus for the concrete element in the idea of God (ST, I: 239). This is not to suggest, however, that the claim that God is being-itself is not also rooted in the participation of the finite in being-itself. The *analogia entis* governs the predication of symbolic material to God, which is taken from the finite realm, and which presupposes the analogy between the finite and the infinite (ST, I: 131). The analogy, of course, produces no natural knowledge of God; it is rather the only way by which anything can be *said* about God (ST, I: 240).

It is difficult to determine from Tillich's writings just how we are to understand the analogy between being-itself and finite being. Tillich, responding to W. M. Urban's critique of his essay "The Religions Symbol" asserts:

> Positive-symbolic terms presuppose . . . that the immediate reality which is used in the symbol has something to do with the transcendent reality which is

symbolized in it. Therefore I can accept the classical doctrine of "analogia entis."[2]

Tillich moves from the somewhat vague formulation that the finite reality "has something to do with" transcendent reality to the assertion that the notion of participation is used precisely "to express what was rightly intended in the medieval doctrine of *analogia entis*, namely, to show a positive point of identity."[3] This would suggest, then, that the clue to understanding the analogy between being-itself and finite being is to be found in Tillich's notion of participation, and that it involves the assertion of the ontological unity or identity of unconditioned and conditioned being.

It would seem that the basic unity or identity of being-itself and finite being for Tillich, is the identity of power and that the participation of everything finite in being-itself is finitude's participation in the power of being-itself. The conclusion seems warranted, then, that the analogy between unconditioned and conditioned being is established ontologically on the basis of power. Consequently, finite reality stands in relation to the transcendent in its most basic determination in terms of the power of transcendent reality in which it participates.[4]

It is out of this basic ontological unity between unconditioned and conditioned being that Tillich can say that any segment of finite reality can potentially symbolize God as being-itself. On the other hand, due to the non-identity of the finite with being-itself, the segment of finite reality which becomes a symbol retains its concreteness. Thus, while the ultimate element in the idea of God is delineated philosophically through the literal claim that God is being-itself, the concrete element is given symbolically through the use by the religious imagination of the finite material which informs its revelatory correlation. The important point to notice here is that the religious imagination and the finite material it uses in its symbolization of the divine is rooted in the participation of the finite in being-itself. The ultimate validity of the religious symbol, which the concrete element in the idea of God presupposes, is given in the ontological unity of unconditioned and conditioned being.

A further statement of the unity of being-itself and finite being on the ontological level of analysis can be seen most clearly in Tillich's doctrine of love. The logic of estrangement presupposes an original unity of the estranged. Love drives toward the reunion of the separated. Tillich writes:

> In man's experience of love the nature of life becomes manifest. Love is the drive towards the unity of the separated. Reunion presupposes separation of that which belongs essentially together. It would, however, be wrong to give to separation the same ontological ultimacy as to reunion. For separation presupposes an original unity. Unity embraces itself and separation, just as being comprises itself and nonbeing. It is impossible to unite that which is essentially separated. Without an ultimate belongingness, no union of one thing with another can be conceived. The absolutely strange cannot enter into a communion. But the estranged is striving for reunion. . . . Therefore love cannot be described as the union of the strange, but as the reunion of the estranged.[5]

The ontological analysis of love discloses that the drive toward the reunion of that which was originally united but which has undergone separation is the defining characteristic of love. Love on the finite level seeks to achieve the reunion of life separated from life and self from self. Thus, Tillich argues that an original unity obtains within the structure of finite being as well. However, the unity of unconditioned and conditioned being is also asserted in Tillich's concept of love. "Love as the drive toward the reunion of the separated," Tillich asserts, "can be used most emphatically of man's love for God. It unites all kinds of love and yet is something else beyond them all" (ST, III: 138).[6]

The ontological unity of being-itself and finite being is seen, then, in Tillich's notions of participation, power and love. Finite being participates in the power of being-itself and thus its identity with being-itself is established. Love, however, presupposes that the finite is separated from that with which it is at the same time united in the power of being. Consequently, love is the quest for reunion by that which is separated from its source and ground and from its fellow creatures. Hence, love includes a "mystical element" in its quest for God, that is, love inherits the original unity of unconditioned and conditioned being, but it is actualized "under the conditions of existence" through the impact of the Spiritual Presence (ST, III: 120-138). Clearly, then, the ontological unity of being-itself and finite being informs Tillich's theological analysis. We shall turn to the theological expression of the unity of being-itself and finite being below. However, we must now examine its cognitive expression.

In attempting to assess the significance of German Idealism for his own thought, Tillich has written:

> ... I am indebted to Kant's critique of knowledge, which showed me that the question of the possibility of empirical knowledge cannot be answered merely by pointing to the realm of objects. Every analysis of experience and every systematic interpretation of reality must begin at the point where subject and object meet. It is in this sense that I understand the idealist principle of identity. It is not an example of metaphysical speculation, but a principle for analyzing the basic character of all knowledge. ... By taking this principle as my point of departure, I have been able to avoid all forms of metaphysical and naturalistic positivism. Thus I am epistemologically an idealist, if idealism means the assertion of the identity of thought and being as the principle of truth.[7]

Of course, in asserting the identity of thought and being as the principle of truth, Tillich is open to all the objections which have been leveled against such a view. However, Tillich's own use of the principle of identity hardly warrants the conclusion that human reason is divine (Hamilton) or that human thought as it is expressed in the system is somehow identical with truth and thus leaps over its own finitude (Kierkegaard's critique of Hegel). Clearly, Tillich has something far more modest in mind.

The principle of identity for Tillich is immediately related to the problem of subject and object on the cognitive level as the above passage makes clear.[8] Tillich's concern is to show that every act of knowledge in which subject and object are distinguished is grounded in a structure that not only presupposes their original unity but which also presupposes the unity of the cognitive structure with that which stands beyond the subject-object split. For Tillich cognition is fundamentally an asking which arises on the basis of an original unity of the one who asks and that which is asked about, but the separation of which is the motivation for the question. Cognition, like love, is the quest for the reunion of the separated.[9]

The unity of unconditioned and conditioned being is asserted cognitively in Tillich's claim that cognition is founded by that which appears immediately within cognition but which transcends the distinction between subject and object. This is the "mystical a priori," which Tillich describes as "an immediate experience of something ultimate in value and being of which one can become intuitively aware" (ST, I: 9). The mystical a priori is

> an awareness of something that transcends the cleavage between subject and object. And if in the course of a "scientific" procedure this a priori is discovered, its discovery is possible only because it was present from the very beginning (*Ibid.*).

The mystical a priori is not to be identified with mysticism as such (ST, I: 141-42). It is a priori in the sense that it makes cognition possible, and it is mystical in the sense that it discloses the identity of subject and object in that of which cognition is intuitively aware.

Tillich has formulated the mystical a priori in relation to the philosophy of religion as "the ontological principle."[10] The ontological approach to God in the philosophy of religion is the way of overcoming estrangement. In this way "man discovers himself when he discovers God; he discovers something that is identical with himself although it transcends him infinitely."[11] Tillich identifies the ontological way with Augustine. Its basic discovery is that "God is the presupposition of the question of God," that is, "God can never be reached if he is the *object* of a question and not its *basis.*" Tillich finds the ontological way continued in the Franciscan school of 13th century scholasticism, which in the figures of Alexander of Hales, Bonaventura, and Matthew of Aquasparta asserts the immediacy of the knowledge of God. For these men God is the principle of truth and the identity of subject and object. In the Franciscan tradition:

these ultimate principles and knowledge of them are independent of the changes and relativities of the individual mind; they are unchangeable, eternal light, appearing in the logical and mathematical axioms as well as in the first categories of thought. These principles are not created functions *of* our mind, but the presence of truth itself and therefore of God, *in* our mind.[12]

It is in the Augustinian-Franciscan tradition that "the problem of the two Absolutes" (the religious and philosophical Absolutes) is solved by the affirmation that *Deus est esse.* The philosophical Absolute is constituted by those *principia per se nota*, the transcendentalia *esse, verum, bonum*, which the mind implies and which have "immediate evidence when they are noticed." Thus the Absolute as the principle of Being "is a necessary thought because it is the presupposition of all thought." It has immediate certainty and thus "the certainty of God is identical with the certainty of Being-itself."[13]

The ontological principle which emerges from this tradition, and which is normative for Tillich's thought, he formulates as follows:

Man is immediately aware of something unconditional which is the prius of the separation and interaction of subject and object, theoretically as well as practically.[14]

To say that man is immediately aware of the unconditional or that Being-itself has immediate certainty is to say that there appears within the structure of mind that which founds mind and thus makes cognition possible. As the foundation of cognition, the unconditional cannot be demonstrated, since it is the presupposition of every cognitive act. Hence, the mode of cognition which is appropriate to the unconditional can only be immediate awareness. The unity of being-itself and finite being is asserted in the cognitive sphere in the claim that the separation and interaction of subject and object presuppose the immediate awareness in the mind of the unconditional as the point of identity of subject and object without which neither separation nor interaction could be thought. Finite being is united with being-itself in the cognitive sphere in the sense that finite cognition is founded by being-itself as the unconditional and thus its foundation "shines through" in every cognitive moment, even in the estrangement of the mind from its own foundation.[15]

The cognitive unity of being-itself and finite being is expressed in Tillich's notion of the "depth of reason." "The depth of reason," Tillich explains:

> is the expression of something that is not reason but which precedes reason and is manifest through it. Reason in both its objective and subjective structures points to something which appears in these structures but which transcends them in power and meaning. This is not another field of reason which could progressively be discovered and expressed, but it is that which is expressed through every rational expression (ST, I: 79).

Reason in all its expressions presupposes the unconditional as its own depth. "Truth-itself," "beauty-itself," "justice-itself," and "love-itself" constitute the unconditional under the aspects of the cognitive, aesthetic, legal, and communal realms of reason. Every true judgment points to truth-itself; every positive act of aesthetic intuition points to beauty-itself; every authentic legal form to justice-itself and every expression of community to love-itself.

The unity of unconditioned and conditioned being within the rational sphere is clearly the basis of Tillich's theology of culture, even though the presence of myth and cult suggest that reason in existence (as distinct from essential reason) is "opaque" towards its own depth and has lost its immediate unity with its depth. Nevertheless, every cultural creation as an expression of existential reason bears the unconditional within itself although ambiguously. Culture can only be approached theologically because the unity of unconditioned and conditioned being remains intact in spite of the estrangement of existential reason.

The significance of the unity of unconditioned and conditioned being as an ultimate notion for Tillich's understanding of theology can be seen in the method of correlation and in his understanding of the solution to the split between essence and existence. The unity of unconditioned and conditioned being is the presupposition of the human question about God. Man can only ask about that with which he is in some sense already united, but because he does ask about God he is also subject to the separation of the finite from being-itself and thus to the split between essence and existence. However, essence and existence are in principle open to reunification because the unity of unconditioned and conditioned being is continuous although qualified by estrangement.[16]

Tillich insists that the cognitive unity of unconditioned and conditioned being does not provide the basis for a natural theology. Although man is aware of the *prius* of subject and object, that awareness, as we have seen, cannot fall within the context of knowledge, since being-itself cannot become an object. Natural theology, Tillich maintains, reduces God as being-itself to an object which falls within the context of knowledge. Literal knowledge is possible only of objects whose structures can be delimited by the knowing mind. Apart from the literal claim that God is being-itself, there can be only symbolic knowledge of the divine reality based on the analogy between being-itself and finite being (ST, I: 238-241). Since God is the ground of the structure of being, analogical knowledge of him is possible ontologically and actualized in the religious symbol within a revelatory correlation.

The unity of unconditioned and conditioned being does allow man, however, to ask about that to which he belongs. The method of correlation presupposes that the ontological and cognitive continuity between being-itself and finite being persists in spite of man's estrangement. Theological method, joined with philosophical analysis, consists in making explicit that of which man is already in some sense aware both in its positive and negative dimensions. Negatively, through the analysis of finitude, the ontological principle discloses the participation of finite being in being-itself and thus the power by which the threatened character of finitude is overcome.[17] Tillich is very clear, however, that the ontological principle and the theological method which it informs stand under the abyss of the divine as well as being rooted in the divine ground. The method of correlation must be thoroughly dialectical.

Tillich's consistent criticism of Barth has been that his theology is supernaturalistic rather than dialectical. In a long essay written in 1935, Tillich levels this criticism at Barth and his followers. The essay is important not only for its critique of Barth, but also because it states the unity of God and man as the presupposition of the method of correlation. Dialectical thinking, Tillich asserts:

> denies . . . that what is a purely divine possibility may be interpreted as a human possibility. But dialectical thinking maintains that the *question* about the divine possibility is a human possibility. And, further, it maintains that no question could be asked about the divine possibility unless a divine answer, even if preliminary and scarcely intelligible, were not always already available. For in order to be able to ask about God, man must already have experienced God as the goal of a possible question. Thus the human possibility of the question is no longer purely a human possibility, since it already contains answers. And without such preliminary half-intelligible answers and preliminary questions based thereon, even the ultimate answer could not be perceived.

> Barth is right in combating the identity in nature of God and man and in rejecting all attempts to find a point in man where he may be able to find and lay hold of God. He is correct in his resistance to all mysticism, which would permit union with God in the depths of man's own human nature. Apart from the Augustinian *transcende te ipsum* there is no access to God. But this precept does contain within itself the demand to proceed through self beyond self. . . . We can find God *in* us only when we rise *above* ourselves. This transcendentalizing act does not signify that we possess the transcendental. The point is that we are in quest of it. But . . . this quest is possible only because the transcendental has already dragged us out beyond ourselves as we have received answers which drive us to the quest.[18]

There is in Tillich's notion of the unity of unconditioned and conditioned being as it is expressed in the method of correlation a basic tension, perhaps even a contradiction. On the one hand, the mind has immediate awareness of being-itself in every act of discernment and cognition in which it is involved. This awareness is not conditioned by the subject-object structure of knowledge and is, therefore, beyond doubt. Since it is unmediated by any inferential or discursive process, the presence of being-itself within the mind is the priori foundation of cognition and is, therefore, actual in every moment of cognition even though the individual mind may not be aware conceptually of its presence. It is not clear, then, how Tillich can argue as he does above that there is no point in man where he can find God. If being-itself is immediately present to the mind apart from its cognitive efforts, it follows that the mind has *immediate access to the divine reality* on the basis of its own structure. How Tillich limits this immediate awareness merely to the capacity to ask the question of God or to the initiation of the quest for God is not clear.

On the other hand, the method of correlation attempts to answer the question of God, which is at the same time the question of man's finitude, on the basis of the divine answer, that is, on the basis of revelation. It is here that man passes out of the indubitable certainty of being-itself and takes upon himself the risk of faith, which is bound up with "the uncertainty about everything conditioned and concrete." While the immediate awareness of the Unconditioned is a matter of self-evidence, "the unconditional element can become a matter of ultimate concern only if it appears in a concrete embodiment;[19] however, the concrete embodiment of the unconditional has no self-evident validity or immediate certainty. Its very concreteness subjects it to the structure of being and thus to ambiguity and uncertainty. The affirmation of the unconditional *vis-a-vis* the concrete is the risk of faith.[20]

The method of correlation, then, correlates the question of God, which arises not only out of the threat of finitude but also out of the immediate certainty of the Unconditioned within the finite mind, with the revelatory answer which is given in concrete symbols and which is thus subject to uncertainty and demands risk. It is clear, however, that both question and answer correlates in the method of correlation presuppose the unity of unconditioned and conditioned being. Without the immediate certainty of being-itself as it is given continuously within the growth of the human mind, there could be neither the question of God nor the reception of the divine answer, and without the participation of everything finite in being-itself, nothing finite could represent or symbolize man's ultimate concern. Thus, the method of correlation in both its negative and positive expressions presupposes the unity of unconditioned and conditioned being such that Tillich's claims that there is no natural knowledge of God or that the natural structure of the mind discloses no point of identity with God are rendered extremely problematic if not completely implausible.[21]

Perhaps the most significant expression of the unity of being-itself and finite being on the theological level is found in the solution to the problem of the split between essence and existence within finitude. The unity of unconditioned and conditioned being is the basis by which the split between essence and existence is overcome *in principle* and their reunion is made possible. It is the unity of unconditioned and conditioned being which informs both Tillich's Christology and Eschatology. Jesus as the Christ, the New Being overcomes the split between essence and existence under the conditions of existence, and the transcendent unity of unambiguous life as expressed in the three symbols Spirit of God, Kingdom of God, and Eternal Life is the continuation of the conquest of the essence-existence split within the processes of life, within the historical process, and finally "beyond" history.

We have argued that the most basic expression of the unity of unconditioned and conditioned being on the ontological level is the participation of the finite in the power of being-itself. If this unity of power were broken, nothing finite could exist. It could not even emerge from nonbeing (ST, I: 237; ST II: 8). It is the ontological unity of unconditioned and conditioned being as power, which is the basis *in principle* for Tillich's Christological claim. Reminding us that the term "being" when predicated of God means the power to resist non-being, Tillich goes on to argue that analogously:

> the term "New Being," when applied to Jesus as the Christ, points to the power in him which conquers existential estrangement or negatively expressed to the power of resisting the forces of estrangement. To experience the New Being in Jesus as the Christ means to experience the power in him which has conquered existential estrangement in himself and in everyone who participates in him (ST, II: 125).

Since being-itself is the power of being in everything finite, it is clear that predicating the "New Being" of Jesus in these terms cannot constitute the exclusive christological claim, for being itself is the power not only in Jesus but in every other finite creature by which it resists nonbeing and thus resists the forces of estrangement. However, the claim that in Jesus as the Christ the estrangement from being-itself and the split between essence and existence is overcome in a way which is not characteristic of any other finite creature presupposes the ontological unity of everything finite with being-itself as grounded in the power of being-itself.

Indeed, the power of being to resist the forces of estrangement is actualized fully and completely in the historical existence of Jesus such that "essential God-manhood" appeared under the conditions of existence in a unique personal life. This life is discontinuous with every other human life in that in it the essential unity of God and man is not broken by estrangement. Thus, the existence of Jesus is the undistorted expression of his essence and, therefore, existential estrangement is overcome within finitude by one who was himself thoroughly finite (ST, II: 93-94; 124-135). It is overcome completely within the existential self-affirmation of Jesus himself and thus must first constitute a datum which is delimited by the boundaries of his own consciousness. In spite of Tillich's denial that the salvation of man depends upon the contingent decision of Jesus not to break his unity with God by succumbing to temptation (ST, II: 129), the personal life of Jesus in its totality is made to bear the *re-established* unity of God and man. This means not only that Jesus experienced the divine reality in his own personal life in a way qualitatively distinguished from every other human experience of the divine, but also that the *full* meaning of that experience is inaccessible to us since it is enclosed within the subjectivity of Jesus (ST, II: 124-125).

Tillich insists, then, that in a personal life in space and time, that is, under the conditions of finitude the essential unity of God and man, which is vitiated by estrangement, was re-established. Although faith cannot guarantee any of the details of this personal life, the life itself remains absolutely indispensable to the Christian claim. Hence:

> If theology ignores the fact to which the name of Jesus of Nazareth points, it ignores the basic Christian assertion that essential God-Manhood has appeared within existence and subjected itself to the conditions of existence without being conquered by them. If there were no personal life in which existential estrangement had been overcome, the New Being would have remained a quest and an expectation and would not be a reality in time and space. Only if the existence is conquered in *one* point — a personal life, rep-

resenting existence as a whole — is it conquered in principle, which means "in beginning and in power" (ST, II: 98).

The New Being, which has appeared within the personal life of Jesus has not only conquered the potential estrangement from God of that life, but it has also overcome existential estrangement *in principle*, that is, for every human life. The power of the New Being, then, transcends the life of Jesus in which it first broke into human life and history with full actuality. Wherever healing and salvation have occurred prior to the event of Jesus as the Christ or within the subsequent histories which either are or are not informed by his presence, there the power of the New Being is manifest. The New Being as it appears in Jesus as the Christ is the final and complete expression of the divine healing activity, which is co-extensive with the history of creation. This means that

> only if salvation is understood as healing and saving power through the New Being in all history is the problem put on another level. In some degree all men participate in the healing power of the New Being. Otherwise they would have no being. The self-destructive consequences of estrangement would have destroyed them. But no men are totally healed, not even those who have encountered the healing power as it appears in Jesus as the Christ. . . . If he is accepted as the Savior, what does salvation through him mean? The answer cannot be that there is no saving power apart from him but that he is the ultimate criterion of every healing and saving process. We said before that even those who have encountered him are only fragmentarily healed. But now we say that in him the healing quality is complete and unlimited. . . . Therefore, however there is saving power in mankind, it must be judged by the saving power in Jesus as the Christ (ST, II: 167-168).

The unity of unconditioned and conditioned being asserts itself at two important points in Tillich's Christology. First, it seems clear that Jesus could not have become the Christ, that is, he could not have *re-established* the unity of God and man unless that unity were already an ontological state of affairs, qualified, however, by finite freedom and existential estrangement. Tillich has to argue, although unsuccessfully it seems, that Jesus made actual through contest and decision that essential unity with God which in its potential state has always obtained as the power of being and which is now understood as saving or healing power. Tillich makes this point quite clearly when he states:

> We replace the inadequate concept "divine nature" by the concepts "eternal-God-man unity" or "Eternal God-Manhood." Such concepts replace a static essence by a dynamic relation. . . . In both of these terms the word "eternal" is added to the relational description. "Eternal" points to the general presupposition of the unique event Jesus as the Christ. This event could not have taken place if there had not been an eternal unity of God and man within the divine life. This unity in a state of pure essentiality or potentiality can become actualized through finite freedom and, in the unique event Jesus as the Christ, became actualized against existential disruption (ST, II: 148).

The appearance of essential God-Manhood under the conditions of existence is not, however, a mere necessary extension of the original dialectical unity of the finite and infinite, or conditioned and unconditioned being. The incarnation is a *paradoxical* event, not a dialectical necessity.[22] However, the question arises how Tillich can assert that the New Being in the life of Jesus is actual (and thus more complex than mere essential being) while at the same time arguing that actualized being is precisely existence which is estranged from essence. Either the actuality of Jesus is not subject to the ontological structure which drives every existent toward the transition from essence into existential estrangement and hence his actuality is unintelligible, or there can be a genuine actualization of finite being without any of the marks of estrangement which are said to characterize actual, existential being. In either case, the consistency of Tillich's system is seriously impaired.[23]

The second point in which the unity of unconditioned and conditioned being informs Tillich's Christology is seen in the fact that the unity Jesus sustains with God is construed after the model of this essential, dialectical or uncontested unity. Nowhere does this seem more clear than in Tillich's discussion of Jesus as the medium of final revelation. The essential, original unity of God and man, of unconditioned and conditioned being is maintained as long as none of the possibilities open to the finite, conditioned being are actualized, that is, as long as the unity between man and God is undiffer-

entiated by the actualization of finite possibilities within the creature. It is, however, in the movement of the creature toward finite
possibilities (the actualization of one's sexuality is one of Tillich's
examples) and their actualization that this essential, original unity
is severed, because the creature comes to value the finite *alongside*
God or in defiance of God and not in unity with God (ST, II: 129).

Jesus as the Christ, however, maintains his unity with God precisely by refusing to actualize any finite possibility open to him outside of his unity with God. He neither exploits his unity with God
for his own personal advantage, nor does he become concupiscent
toward any finite possibility. In Tillich's words:

> Jesus of Nazareth is the medium of the final revelation because he sacrifices
> himself completely to Jesus as the Christ. He not only sacrifices his life . . .
> but he also sacrifices everything in him and of him which could bring people
> to him as an "overwhelming personality" instead of bringing them to that in
> him which is greater than he and they . . . If some element is cut off from the
> universal validity of the message of Jesus as the Christ, if he is put into the
> sphere of personal achievement only, or into the sphere of history only, he is
> less than the final revelation and is neither the Christ nor the New Being.
> But Christian theology affirms that he is all this because he stands the double
> test of finality: uninterrupted unity with the ground of his being and the con-
> tinuous sacrifice of himself as Jesus to himself as the Christ (ST, I: 136-137).

Clearly, Tillich does not wish to claim that Jesus actualized no
finite possibilities within his life. He does claim, however, that the
finite does not, in fact, give Jesus the *concrete content* of his life,
because Jesus continuously sacrifices this concrete content to the
Christ. Thus, the question of God does not emerge in the consciousness of Jesus by his experiencing the anxiety and despair
which estranged man undergoes in relation to his finite possibilities
and their failure to grant him the "ontological security" he seeks.
Apart from the serious question of the consistency of Tillich's view
which was raised above, the claim here is that finitude does not
break the unity of the Christ with God. Thus, what is re-established is precisely that God-Man unity which obtained before the
Fall. We have here a very clear example of the way in which the
ultimate notion of the unity of unconditioned and conditioned

being, especially as it is stated philosophically, informs Tillich's system in a radical way.[24]

Tillich acknowledges that even with the appearance of the New Being in Jesus as the Christ, the split between essence and existence and thus existential estrangement is never fully overcome within time and history. Therefore, the question of salvation drives theological thought beyond Christology to the eschatological symbols. It is not our purpose to discuss Tillich's Eschatology in detail but rather to show how the notion of the unity of unconditioned and conditioned being also informs his understanding of that doctrine.

As one might expect, the eschatological symbols are also addressed to the split between essence and existence within the structure of life and the conquest of that split. Since Tillich introduces the eschatological symbols proper (Kingdom of God and Eternal Life) within the context of his analysis of life and history, they are preceded by his analysis of God as Spiritual Presence and the symbol "Spirit of God." It seems clear that God as Spiritual Presence is the extension of the notion of the divine creativity in relation to the dynamics of life and history. Thus, God as Spiritual Presence is the working out of God's directing creativity, which is the impact of the divine Spirit on the human spirit driving the latter beyond itself toward its ultimate fulfillment. The Spiritual Presence is active in every moment driving life beyond itself, but it includes the future dimension of God's directing creativity as expressed in the symbols "Kingdom of God" and "Eternal Life" (ST, I: 264; ST, III: 107-110).

Life as the "actuality of being" (ST, III: 11) is ambiguous. Its ambiguity is rooted in the fact

> in all life processes an essential and an existential element, created goodness and estrangement, are merged in such a way that neither one nor the other is exclusively effective. Life always includes essential and existential elements (ST, III: 107).

Put more definitively, every life process is the incomplete or imperfect realization of essential possibilities, and its existential actuality is always ambiguous in relation to these essential possibilities. It is out of the gap between essential and existential elements in every life process, but most particularly in man, that the quest for unambiguous life is initiated. Tillich writes:

> only in man as the bearer of the spirit do the ambiguities of life and the quest for unambiguous life become conscious. He experiences the ambiguity of life under all dimensions since he participates in all of them, and he experiences them immediately within himself as the ambiguity of the functions of the spirit; of morality, culture, and religion. The quest for unambiguous life arises out of these experiences: this quest is for a life which has reached that toward which it transcends itself (*Ibid.*).

Unambiguous life can never be reached out of the resources of the life processes themselves, and thus man as spirit can never reach unambiguous life out of the power of his own spirit. Man as self-transcendent spirit can seek unambiguous life out of the power of his own spirit, just as he can raise the question of God on the basis of his own finitude. Unambiguous life, however, is a creation of the divine Spirit, of Spiritual Presence (ST, III: 112). It is this creation of the Spiritual Presence which Tillich calls "The transcendent union [unity] of unambiguous life" (ST, III: 129). Ambiguous life is life lived under the power of estrangement. Unambiguous life is life lifted out of its estrangement from essential being and therefore from God and the Other and driven toward unity with its essential structure.

Tillich describes the transcendent union of unambiguous life in the following words:

> The creation of ambiguous life brings about the reunion of [essential and existential elements of being] in life processes in which actual being is the true expression of potential being, an expression, however, which is not immediate, as in "dreaming innocence," but which is realized only after estrangement, contest, and decision. In the reunion of essential and existential being, ambiguous life is raised above itself to a transcendence that it could not achieve by its own power. . . . It is the direct answer to the process of self-transcendence — which in itself remains a question (ST, III: 129).

It should be clear from this passage that just as the New Being in Jesus as the Christ is the re-establishment of the essential unity of

God and man in a personal life which actualized its finite possibilities within its unity with God, so the transcendent unity of unambiguous life is the re-establishment of essential God-man unity within the life process of historical mankind. As the unity of unconditioned and conditioned being is the model for the christological conquest of estrangement, so it is also the model for the divine Spirit's conquest of the ambiguities of life within mankind as a whole. Speaking symbolically, then, Jesus as the Christ is the manifestation of the divine intentionality for the whole creation, that is, the conquest of the estrangement, conflicts, and ambiguities which haunt the human enterprise and vitiate man's ultimate fulfillment.

This is not to suggest, however, that there is a simple continuity between the complete and final actualization of New Being in Jesus as the Christ and the creation of the transcendent unity of unambiguous life within the history of human contest and decision. The unity of the Christ with God was continuous, although he took upon himself the estrangement and ambiguity of actual life. In historical mankind, however, the transcendent unity of unambiguous life or the New Being (Tillich seems to use these terms interchangeably) is realized in time and space only fragmentarily and as anticipation (ST, III: 140).[25] Again, the transcendent unity of unambiguous life as a creation of the Spiritual Presence within life and history drives to the question of ultimate fulfillment beyond history.

The transcendent unity of unambiguous life, however, is the answer not only to the question of the self-transcendence of life within the spatio-temporal context.[26] The divine Spirit through its impact upon the human spirit within space and time overcomes the ambiguities of life as they are expressed within the three basic functions of life, self-integration (centeredness), self-creation (growth), and self-transcendence (sublimity), and it overcomes the ambiguities of the three functions of the human spirit which are rooted in these three life functions, namely, morality (self-integration), culture (self-creation), and religion (self-transcendence). Since each of these functions is actualized within space and time and thus under the conditions of the essence-existence split, the transcendent unity of unambiguous life which overcomes their ambiguities can only be fragmentary. In each case, however, the work of the divine Spirit is to restore the essential unity of unconditioned and conditioned being and thus the essential unity of the life functions themselves.[27]

The symbol "Kingdom of God" is the symbol of unambiguous life as it is encountered within history. Since history is a dimension of life, Tillich defines its ambiguities in relation to the three basic functions of life, and thus speaks of the ambiguities of historical self-integration (empire and centralization), of historical self-creativity (revolution and reaction) and of historical self-transcendence (the "third stage" as given and expected). Historical life is also a mixture of essential and existential elements, which Tillich seems to distinguish as between the "aim" of history and its concrete actualizations. In its essence:

> History in terms of the self-integration of life, drives toward a centeredness of all history-bearing groups and their individual members in an unambiguous harmony of power and justice. History, in terms of the self-creativity of life drives toward the creation of a new, unambiguous state of things. And history, in terms of the self-transcendence of life, drives toward the universal, unambiguous fulfillment of the potentiality of being (ST, III: 332).

However, under the conditions of existence, "history, while running ahead toward its ultimate aim, continuously actualizes limited aims, and in so doing it both achieves and defeats its ultimate aim" (ST, III: 339).

The drive toward historical self-integration creates empires which strive to be all-inclusive but which inevitably produce counter tendencies which work against extensive centralization and corrupt the intensive centeredness of the empire itself (ST, III: 342).   Historical self-creativity strives to create the new, but encounters the ambiguity of the resistance of the old and the conflicts between them (ST, III: 343-344). And historical self-transcendence is caught in the ambiguity of absolutizing the present moment as the ultimate aim of history or of sustaining the utopian fantasy that the ultimate aim of history is "just around the corner"

(ST, III: 345). In addition, the individual is caught up in the ambiguities of history in such a way that just as nonbeing threatens his existential self-affirmation, so the "terror of history" (Eliade) threatens his historical self-affirmation. Out of the ambiguities of history, then, arises the quest for the Kingdom of God.

Without attempting to discuss the symbol Kingdom of God in detail, we shall attempt to illustrate our thesis that the unity of unconditioned and conditioned being is the ultimate notion which informs the theological solution to the split between essence and existence by examining the role of the Kingdom of God in overcoming the ambiguities which are produced by that split within the historical process.

Tillich acknowledges that the symbol Kingdom of God has a two-fold significance: it expresses the Spiritual Presence within the dynamics of history and thus possesses an inner-historical meaning, and it answers the question of the ambiguities of history therefore assuming transhistorical significance. In its latter function it is identical with Eternal Life (ST, III: 357). In its inner-historical meaning it is the expression of the Spiritual Presence's fragmentary conquest of historical ambiguity under the conditions of historical existence. In its transhistorical meaning the Kingdom of God is the expression of the non-fragmentary conquest of the ambiguities of life in all its dimensions "beyond history." The Kingdom of God is thus the "end" of history (ST, III: 394).

It seems clear that the Kingdom of God within history conquers the ambiguities of history after the model of the unity of unconditioned and conditioned being, that is, in restoring the unity of essence and existence fragmentarily by overcoming the subject-object split. The ambiguity of historical self-integration (the drive for a universal centeredness of historical groups) Tillich reduces to the ambiguity of power and the disintegrating consequences of that ambiguity. The Kingdom of God overcomes these consequences fragmentarily by creating within the politically centered, history-bearing groups the sense of the "responsible" use of power by working against the "objectification" of those who fall under their centered control (ST, III: 385). Thus, wherever the unity of subject and object and power and justice is re-established within the external and internal drives towards universal centeredness of political groups, there is a fragmentary victory of the Kingdom of God; there essence and existence are fragmentarily united, and there the re-established unity of God and man is seen with power and meaning.   One can see this same motif expressed in the Spiritual Presence's conquest of the ambiguities of historical self-creativity and historical self-transcendence. In all three cases the quest for the unity of essence and existence, subject and object arises out of historical man's awareness of the original unity of unconditioned and conditioned being and the theological symbols correlated with that quest arise out of the impact of the Spiritual Presence as it restores that unity fragmentarily in time and space.

The decisiveness of the ultimate notion of the unity of unconditioned and conditioned being can be seen most clearly in Tillich's explication of the transhistorical side of the Kingdom of God as expressed in the symbol Eternal Life. First, Eternal Life is the symbol for the final, non-fragmentary, ultimate perfection of all finite life and thus in it the existential conflicts found within the polarities of being and the ambiguities of the three life functions they inform find their final solution. In interpreting this symbol, then:

> with regard to the three polarities of being and the corresponding three functions of life we must ask for the meaning of self-integration, self-creativity and self-transcendence in the Eternal Life. Since Eternal Life is identical with the Kingdom of God in its fulfillment, it is the non-fragmentary, total, and complete conquest of the ambiguities of life – and this under all dimensions of life, or, to use another metaphor, in all degrees of being (ST, III: 401).

Self-integration in relation to Eternal Life means that the polarity of individualization and participation are in perfect balance. Finite life remains finite, but it is now united with the divine centeredness. There is no conflict between the two poles, and thus there is no separation between the finite and the divine. Self-creativity also means that the polarity of dynamics and form are in perfect balance, for they are united in the divine creativity, and self-transcendence unites freedom and destiny in perfect balance within the unity of the divine freedom and destiny. It follows that within Eternal Life the three functions of the human spirit, morality, culture, and religion are abolished as separate functions as they were in the essential unity of God and man in "dreaming innocence." Thus, life passes through the transition from eternity to time, the transition from essence to existence, and in Eternal Life, the transition from the temporal to the eternal. In Eternal Life, the split between essence and existence has been overcome through "essentialization," which is the separation of the negative from the positive in "eternal memory." Only that part of actualized life which expresses its essence enters Eternal Life (ST, III: 400-401).

There are, of course, many critical questions concerning Tillich's Eschatology which lie beyond the scope of our analysis. We have sought to illustrate the function of the ultimate notion of the unity of unconditioned and conditioned being within Tillich's system. In the symbols Spiritual Presence, Kingdom of God and Eternal Life we have suggested that the issue here (as throughout Tillich's system) is the conquest of the split between essence and existence and that conquest is articulated both as question and answer in relation to the original unity of unconditioned and conditioned being, or the unity of God and man. The conclusion we have reached is that in both Tillich's Christology and Eschatology, this unity is re-established through the actualization of finite possibilities while at the same time the finite is lifted into unity with God. The emphases have been different for the two groups of symbols, but the underlying notion is the same; in the former this finite actualization-within-unity-with-the-divine occurs within time and space (although in the Christ in a perfect way) and within the latter group both within history (fragmentarily) and beyond history (non-fragmentarily).

The model for the re-establishment of the unity of God and man is, of course, the original unity which obtained before the impact of estrangement and the power of which not only enables man to raise the question of the unity to which he belongs and from which he is estranged but also creates the continuity between the divine and estranged man which enables the latter to receive the divine answer as it is given in the Christian symbols. It should be clear, then, that this third ultimate notion is also of crucial significance for Tillich's system.

Before drawing the first part of this essay to a close, we must attempt to state the significance of the preceding analysis for what follows in Part Two, namely, the critical investigation of Tillich's understanding of the relationship of philosophy and theology. We have argued that the ultimate notions in Tillich's thought are finitude, the unconditionedness of being-itself and the unity of being-itself and finite being and we have attempted to show how these notions are illustrated within the Tillichian system. The question now arises as to the way in which these notions relate to Tillich's understanding of philosophy and theology and their relationship.

The interpretation which needs to be made at this point in a general way is that each of these ultimate notions represent basic philosophical and theological assumptions, which not only inform Tillich's understanding of the *relationship* between philosophy and theology, but which should also provide significant clues as to his understanding of the *nature* of these disciplines as well. However, it also needs to be stressed that it is Tillich's understanding of philosophy and theology which also informs these basic assumptions of his system. Thus, we are asserting that the ultimate notions and the understanding of philosophy and theology are interdependent.

We have suggested that Tillich's understanding of finitude and its solution in the unconditionedness of being-itself arises out of the philosophical tradition in which he stands. We shall also attempt to show that both the understanding of finitude and its solution are philosophical in nature and that a fundamental conflict arises in his thought between his philosophical orientation and his claim that theology is *existential* thinking. The thesis, then, which we shall attempt to demonstrate is that Tillich's philosophical orientation is determinative for his understanding of theology and that, therefore, the claim that theology is existential thinking cannot be sustained. In order to show this, however, we must examine in some detail Tillich's understanding of existentialism. This will constitute a major part of our analysis.

Finally, we shall attempt to examine the ultimate unity Tillich asserts between philosophy and theology as grounded in the third ultimate notion, the unity of unconditioned and conditioned being. Again, we shall find the claim that theology is existential thinking incompatible with this unity. It is with these aims in mind that we now turn to Part Two of this essay.

Notes

1 *The Courage To Be, op. cit.*, p. 89.

2 *The Journal of Liberal Religion, op. cit.*, p. 203.

3 Paul Tillich, "Rejoinder," *The Journal of Religion, op. cit.*, p. 188.

4 It is the ontological unity-in-power which underlies Tillich's attempts to give content to the *Analogia entis*, for example in the notion of life (ST, I: 156).

5 *Love, Power, and Justice, op. cit.*, p. 24.

6 Tillich's doctrine of love stands in contrast to the sharp distinction between *agape* and *eros* which has been made, for example, by Anders Nygren in *Agape and Eros*, tr. Philip S. Watson (The Westminister Press, Philadelphia, 1953). Love, for Tillich, is one (*Love, Power and Justice, op. cit.*, p. 27), but there are distinctions in the qualities of love. These qualities, *epithymia* (desire) or *libido, eros, philia*, and *agape* are all expressions of the nature of love as the drive toward reunion of the separated. As such they are mutually interdependent, although *agape* is the "depth of love or love in relation to the ground of life," (*Ibid.*, p. 33), and thus it transforms all the qualities of love toward the ground of love. *Eros*, however, is an indispensable component in *agape*. "Without the *eros* toward truth, theology would not exist, and without the *eros* towards the beautiful no ritual expression would exist. Even more serious is the rejection of the *eros* quality of love with respect to God. The consequence of this rejection is that love towards God becomes an impossible concept . . . " (*Ibid.*, p. 31). It should be pointed out, however, that *eros* is sublimated in a radical way in Tillich, no doubt owing to the place of *agape* in his thought. Cf. *Ibid.*, p. 30.

7 Paul Tillich, *On the Boundary, op. cit.*, p. 82.

8 Cf. Tillich's historical sketch of the two expressions of the principle of identity in western thought (the Socratic and the Augustinian) in "Mystik und Schuldbewusstsein in Schellings Philosophischer Entwicklung," *Gesammelte Werke*, Vol. I, *op. cit.*, pp. 18-34. The principle of identity in its socratic form is the "Identitat des Allgemeinen mit dem Besonderen" and in its augustinian form the "Identitat von Subjekt und Objekt." It is the latter which informs Tillich's thought.

9   Cf. Paul Tillich, "Participation and Knowledge: Problems of an Ontology of
    Cognition," *Sociologica. Aufsätze Max Horkheimer zum sechzigste Geburtstag
    gewidmen.*, Vol. I, Eds. Theodor W. Adorno and Walter Dicks (Europaische
    Verlagsanstalt, Frankfurt a. M., 1955), pp. 201-209. Cf. also *My Search for
    Absolutes, op. cit.*, pp. 66-77. Here Tillich finds three fundamental cognitive
    modes in which the separation of subject and object is overcome and the
    absolute in knowledge is disclosed. (1) The material unity of subject and
    object in sense perception; (2) the validity of the logical and semantic struc-
    ture of the mind; and (3) the absolute certainty of the self as self. One should
    note, however, Tillich's assertion (ST, I: 174) that the relation of subject and
    object is not that of identity but one of polarity. Again, it is the assertion of
    unity rather than identity which seems to be the basic term in Tillich's ontol-
    ogy and epistemology.

10 "The Two Types of Philosophy of Religion," *Theology of Culture, op. cit.*, p.
    22.

11 *Ibid.*, p. 10.

12 *Ibid.*, p. 13.

13 *Ibid.*, pp. 15-16.

14 *Ibid.*, p. 22.

15 Perhaps the most significant critique of Tillich's view of cognition has been
    made by John Y. Fenton, "Being-itself and Religious Symbolism," *The Jour-
    nal of Religion*, Vol. XIV, No. 2, April, 1965, pp. 73-84. Fenton construes
    the ontological principle in the larger context of the claim that God is being-
    itself and thus the absolutely certain ground of thought. The ontological
    principle, then, asserts that being-itself is both the foundation of thought and
    the goal of thought. Here Fenton sees the ontological principle in relation to
    Kant's first antinomy, which requires "that actual contingent acts of
    understanding presuppose an actual absolute beginning in unconditioned
    meaning or being," which is to say, "a regressive series cannot be infinite" (p.
    77). But being-itself as the goal of thought is infinite and hence, the
    progressive series of cognition is infinite. Being-itself is both ground and
    abyss. "Cognition presupposes both that we know the real and that the real is
    unlimited" (p. 76).

    The ontological principle is a direct, nonsymbolic statement about God and a
    statement of the ultimate presupposition of thought. Fenton however ques-
    tions whether the principle has any meaning at all, since "that which is pre-
    supposed by all thought (*das Unvordenkliche*) cannot be expressed in a
    thought sequence. As soon as the principle 'God is Being-itself' is stated, the
    statement presupposes something else beyond it as the ground of the state-
    ment's meaningfulness." (p. 78). Tillich has argued (*The Interpretation of*

History, op. cit., p. 171) that statements of a basic metaphysical attitude are non-self-referring and thus beyond the context of knowledge. "For as soon as a statement of this type is made into an articulate judgment, it thereby enters into the context of knowledge and becomes subject to its own transcendental criticism" (p. 79).

If the ontological principle, then, is literally true, it is self-contradictory (it falls within the context of knowledge), and if it is symbolically true, "there is no way to discover what it means or how to use it properly" (p. 79). Fenton concludes: "Tillich's description of cognition makes cognition impossible by definition" (p. 84).

16   The original unity of God and man is so qualified by man's finite freedom to turn away from God and that Tillich is willing to assert that God in his self-manifestation (although not in his abysmal nature) is "dependent on the way man receives his manifestation. . . . The divine-human relation, and therefore God as well as man within this relation, changes with the stages of the history of revelation and with the stages of personal growth" (ST, I: 61). The question, again, is whether this language which seems to attribute relativity to the divine life is compatible with the concept of being-itself, as Tillich has developed it.

17   Cf. Fenton's argument that the ontological principle may be interpreted to state a necessary connection in thought between relative and absolute degrees of comparative qualities. "Finitude" requires the infinite as its comparative contrast. Thus, the ontological principle functions negatively "to expose the fragmentariness and ambiguity of human existence" (Fenton, *op. cit.*, pp. 77; 79). Fenton also argues that in its positive expression the ontological principle contains hidden assumptions (viz., that God is *a* being and that our cognition of being is unconditioned by the context of knowledge, i.e. finitude), which violates the dialectical unity of "yes" and "no."

18   Paul Tillich, "What is Wrong with the 'Dialectic' Theology?", *The Journal of Religion*, Vol. XV, No. 2, 1935, pp. 137; 140. This passage adumbrates Tillich's conception of God as "self transcendent" or "ecstatic" in ST, II: 5-8.

19   *Theology of Culture, op. cit.*, p. 28.

20   *Ibid.; Dynamics of Faith, op. cit.*, pp. 16-19.

21   It is the function of the ontological principle in Tillich's thought which underlies this basic problem with the method of correlation and which informs the more technical difficulties which arise with the method in regard to the interdependence of questions arising out of man's estranged existence and the answers given in the Christian symbols. The problem, for example, of determining to what extent the Christian symbols determine the questions asked or to what extent the questions determine the content of the Christian symbols

can arise, it seems, only when it is recognized that the essential unity of God and man informs both question and answer. Thus, as Fenton has suggested, (Fenton, *op. cit.*, ftnote 37), Tillich's emphasis upon the risk of faith vis-a-vis the concrete symbol can only be made intelligible (since everything finite participates in being-itself) if the ontological principle itself involves a risk into the mystery of God. Although Fenton does not draw this conclusion, it would seem to follow that the immediate certainty of being-itself must also be subject to doubt and the risk of faith. For a critical discussion of the method of correlation, cf. Robert C. Johnson, *Authority in Protestant Theology* (The Westminster Press, Philadelphia, 1959), pp. 111-143 and John B. Cobb, Jr., *Living Options in Protestant Theology* (The Westminster Press, Philadelphia, 1962), pp. 259-283. Cobb especially has argued that "we understand [Tillich's] ontological doctrines as claiming warrant in autonomous philosophical thinking outside the circle of faith. We must then recognize both that no specifically Christian act is involved in recognizing being-itself as God and that this means that Tillich's idea of God is largely determined by independent philosophical considerations" (Cobb, *op. cit.*, p. 278). Thus Cobb suggests that Tillich's claim that the philosopher does not stand within the theological circle qua philosopher means that "we must regard the work of the philosopher [including Tillich] insofar as it conditions the work of the theologian as a kind of natural theology" (*Ibid.*, p. 277).

22 Cf. Paul Tillich, "A Reinterpretation of the Doctrine of the Incarnation," *Church Quarterly Review*, Vol. CXLVII, 1949, p. 137ff.

23 Cf. Eugene H. Peters, "Tillich's Doctrine of Essence, Existence, and the Christ," *op. cit.*, p. 300: "[Tillich] maintains that 'there is no point in time and space in which created goodness was actualized and had existence. . . . Actualized creation and estranged existence are identical' [ST, II: 44]. How then can one avoid the conclusion that Jesus, like everything actual, was estranged rather than perfect? Can there be an essential existent? Granted, Tillich at times talks of essence and existence as though they were compatible. But his definitive description of the Fall as a transition from essence to existence, a transition wherein the very structure of reality is distorted, seems clearly to fly in the face of their alleged compatibility. Hence, I fail to see how it is possible within Tillich's framework to assert without contradiction that in Jesus, the New Being was actualized."

24 Cf. John B. Cobb, Jr., *op. cit.*, pp. 279-280.

25 Van A. Harvey has questioned the meaningfulness of Tillich's distinction between "ambiguous" and "fragmentary" in his review of ST, III. Cf. Van A. Harvey, *op. cit.*, pp. 379-380.

26 It is in the self-transcendence of life, however, that the influence of the notion of the unity of unconditioned and conditioned being can be seen quite clearly. Just as man asks the question of God on the basis of the original unity to

which he belongs, so life transcends itself out of that same unity." . . . Since the finite is potentially or essentially an element in the divine life, everything finite is qualified by this essential relation. And since the existential situation in which the finite is actual implies both separation from and resistance to the essential unity of the finite and the infinite, the finite is no longer actually qualified by its essential unity with the infinite. It is only in the self-transcendence of life that the "memory" of the essential unity with the infinite is preserved" (ST, III: 113-114).

27 Tillich's discussion of life and its ambiguities and their conquest, especially in the three spiritual functions of morality, culture, and religion is much too vast to be dealt with here. Suffice it to say that the unity of unconditioned and conditioned being informs profoundly Tillich's understanding of the divine Spirit's conquest of the ambiguities of these functions. The three spiritual functions are indistinguishable in their essential unity (ST, III: 95-96), which, of course, is the essential unity of unconditioned and conditioned being. Under the conditions of existence, however, they are split apart and actualized in separate spheres. The Spiritual Presence strives for their reunification through the actualization of the essential within the existential situation, albeit within the dialectic of fragmentary and ambiguous realization. The Spiritual Community is "essentiality determining existence and being resisted by existence" (ST, III: 163). As such, it overcomes the profanization and demonization of religion by overcoming the separation of religion from culture and morality, and thus conquering religion itself (ST, III: 243-245). Hence, through the assertion of the ontological principle, the churches both represent and distort the Spiritual Community, culture is driven toward theonomous forms which emerge out of the Spiritual Presence's conquest of the subject-object split in language, cognition, the aesthetic function, technology, and the personal and communal functions (education, legal forms, etc.) (ST, III: 245-265). So, too, the Spiritual Presence creates a theonomous morality in which, again, the actualization of the finite self in relation to its possibilities is achieved by being taken into the transcendent unity, which is the unity of the divine life. Thus, "In so far as the personal center is established in relation to the universal center, the encountered contents of finite reality are judged for their significance in expressing the essential being of the person before they are allowed to enter, or are barred from entering, the unity of the centered self" (ST, III: 269). In other words the actualization of finite possibilities is an expression of essential being rather than a distortion of it, and thus the unity of unconditioned and conditioned being and essence and existence is restored although fragmentarily. Hence, the model of the essential unity of being-itself and finite being is retained for the work of the Spiritual Presence. It should be clear just how significant this ultimate notion is for Tillich's thought, now seen as that which the Spiritual Presence restores. It is questionable, however, whether the notion of fragmentary restoration can save Tillich from the contradiction that it is the actualization of finite possibilities which drives the finite out of its unity with the infinite and

simultaneously out of harmony with essential being. It is my judgment that it cannot. God may be beyond the ontological conditions of being, but man surely is not. Hence, the transcendent unity of unambiguous life is ontologically unintelligible on Tillich's own terms.

PART TWO

Chapter Six

Tillich's Conception of Philosophy

The attempt to delineate Tillich's conception of philosophy is confronted with special difficulties. In the first place, few thinkers have drawn as extensively from the history of western philosophy as has Tillich. In an address delivered in Japan entitled "Philosophical Background of My Theology", Tillich traces influences from the pre-Socratics to Heidegger; however, it is not possible to find in Tillich's thought the predominating influence of any particular philosophical "school" within which his understanding of philosophy is expressed. It is true, of course, that some philosophical perspectives are incompatible with Tillich's thought, the most notable example of which would seem to be Logical Positivism. However, while certain philosophical alternatives are excluded, Tillich has no *single* historical ontology or metaphysics to recommend for theological purposes, even though, as we shall see, Tillich does stand most clearly within the tradition which began with classical Greek thought, while yet critical of that tradition.

In the second place, Tillich's career as a philosopher has been clearly defined within the limits of his theological concerns, especially in his American period.[1] Consequently, we do not find in Tillich's writings intensive and sustained reflection upon the meaning and nature of philosophy. This is not to suggest, of course, that Tillich has not given much thought to the nature of philosophy. It is to point out, however, that his thought about philosophy is nearly always determined by his religious and theological concerns, and thus it is difficult to see Tillich as an independent, "autonomous" philosopher. Tillich's claim therefore, to have stood "on the boundary" between philosophy and theology seems qualified by his theological existence.[2] The attempt, then, to isolate Tillich's conception of philosophy from his theological understanding seems arbitrary at least.

In spite of these difficulties the attempt to focus on Tillich's conception of philosophy apart from its eclectic character and the theological presuppositions which inform it would seem to have special value for our study, for it would be an attempt to take Tillich seriously as a philosopher in his own right. Keeping in mind the hazards of such a task, then, we shall now consider Tillich's conception of philosophy in some detail.

In an essay entitled "Philosophie" published in 1930,[3] Tillich argues that

> Das Wesen der Philosophie kann nur von der Philosophie selbst bestimmt werden, denn es gibt keine Instanz ausser ihr oder über ihr. Sie ist sich selbst letzte Instanz; darum ist jedes Verständnis von Philosophie Ausdruck einer philosophischen Haltung, und es ist unmöglich, allgemein über das Wesen der Philosophie zu reden.[4]

In attempting to say what the nature of philosophy is, Tillich is aware that his own philosophical attitude (*Haltung*) must be determinative for the definition of philosophy he is proposing. Thus, Tillich's proposal that as a theologian he will "suggest a definition of philosophy which is broad enough to cover most of the important philosophies which have appeared . . . in the history of philosophy" (ST, I: 18) is misleading unless it is kept in mind that the definition is an expression of Tillich's philosophical attitude and that in offering it he has entered the philosophical arena as a philosopher (ST, I: 26).[5]

The first basic feature of the nature of philosophy, for Tillich, is its radically sceptical attitude toward every human assumption. Philosophy, in attempting to define itself, will allow no human authority or convention outside itself to contribute toward that definition. Hence:

> Die Philosophie ist ihre eigene letzte Instantz. Der Anfang der Philosophie ist das Absehen von jeder möglichen Instanz ausser ihr. Er ist die Frage in der radikalen Form, die grundsätzlich nichts Vorgegebenes als vorgegeben

stehen lässt. *Die Philosophie lässt sich nichts vorgeben ausser sich selbst; sie hat keinen Anfang als das Anfangen selbst.*[6]

The philosophical attitude, then, is the attitude of the radical question. Tillich finds the roots of the philosophical attitude, the attitude of the radical question, within man himself. The possibility of the philosophical attitude is in the first place a human possibility. Man, as we have seen, is the creature who transcends himself, and thus "er nicht gebunden ist an das, was ihm begegnet, sondern in jeder Begegnung zugleich über sie hinaus sein kann."[7] By not being bound to the immediate environment, man can have a world (*Welt*), and in having a world, he can place himself opposite it and ask the question of the world in its totality. Thus, the possibility of self-transcendence which defines man as such is the ground of the possibility of philosophy. However, the mere having of this possibility within himself does not constitute the philosophical attitude. The possibility must be actualized in a definite direction before it becomes philosophy.

In not being satisfied with the immediate having of his world, self-transcendent man drives toward the question of its intelligibility, and thus he transforms that which encounters him immediately into that which is opposite (*Gegenüber*). This is the fundamental conceptual task. Tillich writes:

> Begreifen ist eine Art, in der der Mensch das ihm Begegnende hat, die Art nämlich, in der das Begegnende zum Gegenüber gemacht, als Gegenüber festgehalten und dann zerfällt wird: zerfällt in das unmittelbar Begegnende und die wahre, im Gegenüber erkennbare Gestalt. Diese Stellung des Menschen zum Begegnenden macht ihn zum Menschen; sie ist noch nicht Philosophie, sie ist der Möglichkeitsgrund der Philosophie.[8]

It is only when the encountered is grasped and broken down with the distinction between the true and the untrue clearly intended, however, that the human possibility toward that which is encountered (das Begegnende) becomes philosophy. "Philosphie ist in dem Augenblick da, wo das Gegenüber und die Zerfällung des Begegnend ausdrücklich gemeint sind."[9] Out of the human possibility of grasping the world as the opposite of man and thus the object of his fundamental interrogative drive, philosophy emerges as the self-conscious and intentional development of the interrogative attitude within the structure of pure theory, which is not antithetical to "Praxis", but which in itself does not imply any particular Praxis. Thus:

> Philosophie ist die haltung des ausdrücklichen Fragens, des Fragens, das zur Theorie führt and sich grundsätzlich in der Theorie erfüllt. *Philosophie ist diejenige Haltung, in der die spezifisch menschliche Möglichkeit des Fragens ausdrücklich wird.*[10]

It is clear that Tillich is distinguishing between a prephilosophical and a philosophical orientation toward the world, both of which are grounded in the structure of man as man. The prephilosophical attitude is the expression of the human question (which Tillich identifies in his later writings as the question of being) within the structures of myth and epic, drama and poetry. The prephilosophical thrust of the question of man as man prepares the way for the philosophical attitude and thus for philosophy itself. The prephilosophical way of asking and answering the human question is, however, without clearly defined and developed theoretical dimensions. Philosophy in developing the human question by grasping and breaking down the world as opposite within theoretical terms, takes over the heritage of the prephilosophical way and by making its questions and answers explicit establishes its continuity with that heritage, and at the same time calls it into question as a tradition of assumptions, which are not allowed to stand as assumptions.[11]

In grounding philosophy in the human act of interrogation and thus construing it as a human possibility, Tillich quite clearly sees philosophy as an enterprise intrinsic to the human spirit. Man entertains the radical question because he is man, and he, therefore, drives toward pure theory, i.e., philosophy, because he desires answers to his questions which transcend mere opinion or assumption. He desires knowledge and truth. Hence:

> Philosophy . . . is not a matter of liking or disliking. It is a matter of man as man, for man is that being who asks the question of being. Therefore, every

human being philosophizes, just as every human being moralizes and acts politically, artistically, scientifically, religiously.[12]

What does it mean, then, that man asks the radical question, the question of being, which achieves theoretical precision in philosophy? In reflecting upon the structure of man's being which makes the philosophical enterprise possible, Tillich invokes the two ultimate notions we have already discussed, namely, finitude and the unity of unconditioned and conditioned being. The question implies that we do not have that for which we ask. On the other hand, man could not ask the question of being if he did not belong to being ontologically, that is, if the power of being were not in him. However:

> Our power of being is limited. We are a mixture of being and nonbeing. This is precisely what is meant when we say that we are finite. It is man in his finitude who asks the question of being . . . But man can and must ask; he cannot avoid asking, because he belongs to the power of being from which he is separated, and he knows both that he belongs to it and that he is separated from it . . . We philosophize because we are finite and because we know that we are finite . . . We have seen that we encounter a world to which we belong and which, in our encounter with it, shows the same mixture of being and nonbeing as does our human predicament. . . . It is our finitude in interdependence with the finitude of our world which drives us to search for ultimate reality . . . Because we stand between being and nonbeing and long for a form of being that prevails against nonbeing in ourselves and in our world, we philosophize.[13]

Philosophy, then, in its most fundamental characterization, is the theoretical development of the question which is intrinsic to man's finitude and the search for that which, within cognitive terms, answers this question. We shall examine the theoretical character of philosophy below; however, it is necessary here to investigate the implications of man's finitude for the character of philosophy. Tillich seldom speaks directly of the meaning of finitude for the philosophical enterprise, but we shall maintain that is is finitude which informs Tillich's claims that philosophy has both historical and existential elements and further that it is finitude which accounts for the tensions between the historical-existential character of philosophy and its theoretical character.

In working out the character of philosophy as a human possibility, Tillich acknowledges that no general definition of philosophy has been given. Even though Tillich offers such a general definition in the *Systematic Theology*, in the 1930 essay now under consideration, he argues that any such general definition is impossible since:

> der konkrete Character der Philosophie hängt davon ab, wie die Haltung der reinen Theorie im Zusammenhang möglicher menschlicher Haltungen überhaupt steht. Das kann sehr verschieden sein. Das "Wesen" der Philosophie ist selbst historisch, nicht nur die philosophischen Lehren.[14]

Philosophy is historical in the sense that it stands in fate or destiny (*Shicksal*). It will be recalled that fate or destiny is in polar correlation with freedom, and only that which is free can be subject to fate. Hence, the freedom of philosophy is precisely its standing in fate. "Not only the philosopher as a man but also the philosopher as philosopher has a fate, and this means that philosophy itself has a fate."[15]

In Tillich's notion of the historical character of philosophy, its standing in fate, the complexity of his view of the philosophical enterprise begins to emerge. Philosophy has not only a *prehistory*, which has shaped decisively the character of philosophy as it developed in distinction from that prehistory, but philosophy itself also has a *history*, and for Tillich that history is a movement away from and a partial return to the *classical* meaning of philosophy as it was achieved in Greek thought. Thus:

> Die Philosophie steht im Schicksal, und darum ist möglich, dass sich ihr Wesen einmal *klassisch* erfullt, so dass alle ihre weiteren Verwirklichungen nur in abgeleiteter Weise den Namen Philosophie für sich beanspruchen können. Und diese Möglichkeit ist Wirklichkeit: der ursprüunglich grieschische Sinn von Philosophie ist nie wieder erreicht worden und kann nie wieder erreicht werden; denn er ruht auf dem Hintergrund der griechischen Existenz in ihrer Ganzheit.[16]

The question which arises here, however, is whether Tillich considers classical Greek philosophy the *model* to which all further philosophical activity should attempt to be as faithful as possible. It would seem that if all further development in philosophy can only claim the name "philosophy" in a derived sense, then the Greek model does exercise some normative significance for Tillich.

One way of interpreting Tillich's understanding of the fate of philosophy, then, is to see the development of philosophy after its classical origin in Greece as the history of apostasy or the fall of philosophy from its essence. There are features in Tillich's account of the "career" of philosophy which suggest this interpretation.[17] However, it would be completely incorrect to see Tillich as a classicist in his understanding of the fate of philosophy, for the tragedy of Greek philosophy is precisely its attempt to live above fate. Hence, philosophy in its classical expression cannot be the unambiguous model for subsequent philosophy because it lacks in its own theoretical foundations any serious understanding of fate. Rather classical philosophy seeks to escape fate and thus human existence itself.

"Greek philosophy", Tillich states,

> is an attempt to rise above fate. . . . Philosophy gives knowledge, a knowledge by means of which man is united with the Eternal One, beyond fate. This attitude of Greek philosophy . . . is not intelligible except as the consequence of a dire need. It is the need to overcome the bondage to fate and tragedy. . . . In such a struggle a number of different attitudes were held by the philosophers. . . . In all this diversity of attitude, however, one thing remains the same: the struggle of the philosopher against a fate-entangled, demonically controlled existence. For this reason the highest ideal for human life is found in the realm of thought, in the rising above existence. . . . Never before or afterward has the struggle of philosophy against the fear of fate achieved so rapid and decisive a victory, and never again has victorious philosophy, in turn been defeated so severely by fate.[18]

Even though Tillich refers to fate as "universal necessity" which is mixed with freedom in finite existence, it is clear that fate means for him, fundamentally, historical conditionedness. To have a fate is to be subject to the relativity of historical context, to stand within the dynamics of historical change, and thus to be denied "absolute truth". Greek philosophy, then, in seeking to overcome fate sought to overcome its historical conditionedness. Its claim to absolute knowledge beyond the exigencies of time and context, that is, beyond fate, could not be sustained, since the attitude and conceptualities of Greek philosophy were rooted within the total context of Greek existence and every Greek philosopher was radically conditioned by this context. The universal truth Greek philosophy claimed for itself beyond the common sense assumptions and opinions of the unexamined life and the mythic and poetic structures of the prephilosophical heritage as the answer to its radical question, was, in fact, radically conditioned by fate. The tragedy of the Greek philosophical experience was that in failing to see the way its own foundation was conditioned by fate, it could not endure the dissolution of its great synthesis through the impact of historical change. What seemed universal was highly particular; what seemed absolute was relative; what seemed unchangeable was altered by change. Philosophy as it was classically fulfilled carried within it the seeds of its own dissolution, namely, its blindness to its susceptibility to fate.

It is not necessary to trace Tillich's account of the fate of philosophy from the disintegration of the classical Greek synthesis to the development of modern philosophy. Two aspects of his analysis, however, should be mentioned. First, Tillich sees the emergence of Christianity as a decisive event for the fate of philosophy. In Christianity *time* conquers *space*, and the irreversible, unrepeatable directedness of time conquers the cyclical view of time in Greek thought. Consequently:

> A "gracious" destiny that brings salvation in time and history subdues a demonic fate which denies the new in history. Thus the Greek view of life and the world is overcome; and with it the presupposition of Greek philosophy as well as Greek tragedy. Never again can philosophy be what it was originally. The philosophy that wished to overcome fate is itself seized by fate and becomes something different.[19]

The religious orientation of Greek culture prevented the employment of the categories and methods of Greek philosophy, which have, for Tillich, universal significance, in "world transformation". However, Christianity altered the religious foundation of philosophy, and with the rise of Christian humanism, the Greek philosophical concepts were employed "for the technical control and the revolutionary transformation of reality".[20]   For Tillich the rise of Christian humanism shaped the destiny of philosophy in a decisive way, for now philosophy is required to develop its theoretical structure against the demand for the control and technical manipulation of the world.   For Tillich, the history of modern philosophy is a response to the demand which has grown out of the Christian humanistic understanding of the world.   "In Christian humanism the fate of Christianity and the fate of philosophy are bound together."[21]

The second point in Tillich's analysis which should be stressed is his claim that modern philosophy fails to understand its relationship to destiny in much the same way as did Greek philosophy. During the Renaissance and Enlightenment,

> philosophy . . . believed not only that it had ceased to be the "hand maid" of theology but also that it had become completely autonomous, determined only by the laws of reason and free from any religious element. But this was an illusion. During the whole course of modern culture . . . philosophy itself maintained the belief in providence. . . . It did not make the development dependent on divine actions but on the political and educational activities of man. Like philosophy itself, these activities follow the demands of reason. And reason, according to rationalistic belief, has no fate. Its principles are unchangeable . . . But it never had and never can have a fate, a unity of freedom and necessity.[22]

However, the modern mind discovered what the Greek mind could not, namely, the historical character of thought, and thus the pretensions of modern philosophy to be beyond history, fate, and tragedy were "refuted by its own history". Philosophy itself came to affirm its own historical conditionedness.

Although Tillich does not state explicitly the presuppositions of his understanding of the history of philosophy, there seems to be within it the assertion of a dialectical thrust which moves between philosophy's attempts to regain its foundation in the classical vision by denying its fateful character on the one hand, and on the other the impact upon philosophy of that understanding of historical temporality introduced by Christianity, which has not only given rise to the world transformation impulse but also to historical reason itself, and which thus drives philosophy to redefine itself overagainst the classical vision. Without oversimplifying, it seems quite possible to see Tillich's own understanding of philosophy within this same dialectic.

It is now necessary to explore Tillich's understanding of the historical character of thought and its meaning for philosophy in more detail. Tillich's analysis centers in two basic concepts, *Kairos* and *Logos*. Both of these notions are of fundamental significance for Tillich's thought and cannot receive exhaustive treatment here; however, insofar as they inform Tillich's views on history, historical knowledge and the character of thought, they must be examined.

As we have seen above, Tillich divides the history of philosophy since the Renaissance into two "lines". The predominant line has been shaped by methodological preoccupations, which means, for Tillich, that its thinking is grounded "in the timeless Logos" and "the eternal form of being is the goal of knowledge". The second line, however, worked out by thinkers like Böhme, Schelling, Schopenhauer and Nietzsche, is not directed toward the *Logos*, the eternal form of being, but seeks rather to grasp conceptually the dynamic, "form-creating process", and it is thus rooted in time. It is not rooted in time as mere duration, however, but in time as "qualitatively fulfilled", the temporal moment fraught with meaning and significance, the *Kairos*.[23]

The methodical line, then, seeks the forms which are beyond time and change and thus beyond fate. Its presupposition is that the perceiving subject can occupy "the absolute standpoint" and thus become absolute itself. Therefore;

> for the philosophy of method with all of its assumptions, the emptying of the subject is an unavoidable demand. The subject must be without content in order to receive the eternal forms ... Idealism and naive realism both believe in an absolute, contentless position of the subject.[24]

The absolute subject is the vehicle of "pure theory". Its emptying is its ascetism toward the *Kairos*; however, its filling is its *Eros* toward the timeless *Logos*. The ascetism of the absolute subject toward the *Kairos* should not be construed as its standing outside time in the sense that it seeks to grasp the *Logos* theoretically and without reference to the fate, the ultimate meaning, the qualitatively fulfilled time of the epoch in which it stands. The demand of the absolute subject occupying the absolute standpoint is the demand for a theoretical structure which is valid for all epochs quite apart from the *Kairoi* which define them.

Tillich is clearly opposed to the "akairos" character of the philosophy of method. The impact of the second line in philosophy, for Tillich, is precisely its denial that the absolute standpoint in knowledge can be reached. The perceiving subject, for the second line, stands inescapably in history and the attempt to empty himself of the concrete content of the historical moment is a denial of the full context of knowledge. Protestantism has carried forward the fate of philosophy by contributing to the dynamic of the second line. It, too, has insisted upon the historical character of knowledge, which means that a constitutive element in knowledge is decision. In Protestantism,

> the subject has no possibility of an absolute position. It cannot go out of the sphere of decision. Every part of its nature is affected by . . . contradictions. Fate and freedom reach into the act of knowledge and make it an historical deed: the Kairos determines the Logos.[25]

Tillich acknowledges that there is an element of universal validity in all knowledge; however, this is a "presupposition of the historical character of knowledge", the presupposition, namely, that the Ego (the centered self) which must make decisions "cannot itself be subjected to decisions". The universal element in knowledge is the structure of personality itself, which is not subject to fate. Hence, "whether one is personality, whether one has fate, is not a possible subject of decision, since it is the necessary presupposition of decisions."[26] The element of universal validity in knowledge, then, is the universal, *a priori* validity of the structure of personality itself.

Insofar as the knowing subject is constituted formally by logical necessity, "it rests with the security of the Logos." However, it is the position of the second line in philosophy and of Protestantism as well that the concrete content of the subject is achieved only in history, which means that genuine knowledge is acquired by decision within the cleavages and contradictions of historical existence and in the face of the demand which the *Kairos* places upon the knowing subject. "History exists where there is decision", but Tillich's analysis of decision prevents the conclusion that that about which man decides is the mere horizontal succession of historical events or that history is the mere creation of human decision without reference to anything beyond man himself.

In attempting to work out a Protestant conception of knowledge in relation to the second line in philosophy,[27] Tillich argues that the decision in which human knowledge participates, according to the religious consciousness, can refer only to the Unconditioned. The decision toward the Unconditioned, however, cannot be one decision among others; rather it is the hidden, transcendental decision, which is at the same time concrete (and therefore equivocal with respect to the Unconditioned) and yet the presupposition of every penultimate decision. It is the decision toward the Unconditioned which constitutes the meaning of history. Philosophically and religiously the transcendental decision means that:

> truth is realized in a decision regarding the Unconditioned: stated in religious terms, that all knowledge of the truth in a certain stratum is knowledge of God. There is hardly a philosophy for which this statement would not be valid.[28]

The question immediately arises, of course, how the transcendental decision can be both concrete and at the same time have to do with the Unconditioned, since as we have seen the Unconditioned cannot be identified with anything concrete. Tillich has attempted to deal with this question in a basic way in his conception of the religious symbol, some of the problems of which we have already considered. However, in his attempts both to develop a Protestant conception of knowledge and an understanding of the nature of philosophy based on that conception, Tillich introduces the notion of *Kairos* to explicate the decision toward the Unconditioned. It will be well, then, to develop the meaning of *Kairos* more carefully.

As we have seen, the *Kairos* as a temporal moment is to be distinguished from time as mere duration. Tillich employs the Greek word *Chronos* (formal or measured time) to distinguish temporal duration from the time which is *Kairos*. *Kairos* means literally "the right time". When one

> is conscious of an ongoing creative life [time] is laden with tensions, with possibilities and impossibilities, it is qualitative and full of significance. Not every thing is possible at every time, not everything is true at every time, nor is everything demanded at every moment.[29]

For Tillich the consciousness of history has little to do with the mere chronicle of events which presupposes *Chronos* time. Rather consciousness of history is consciousness of *Kairos*, those temporal moments in which the meaning of an historical epoch is fulfilled and with its fulfillment a turning point in the historical process is reached and new epochs are initiated.

If the *Kairos* is fulfilled time, the moment which expresses the ultimate meaning and significance of an epoch, the question arises as to the criteria by which the *Kairos* is to be determined, and this is the question of the formal character of the notion of *Kairos* itself apart from its concrete contents, which obviously change with changing epochs. Tillich developed two such criteria, which allow for the discernment of the kairotic moment and at the same time the formal character of the notion.

The first criterion involves the relationship of time and eternity. The *Kairos* is that temporal occasion in which the manifestation of the eternal itself within a special historical moment is accepted or to put it in another Tillichian formulation, the *Kairos* is that temporal moment "when the conditioned surrenders itself to become a vehicle for the unconditioned". In describing the relationship of unconditioned and conditioned being within the context of time and history (and thus decision) in contrast to the ontological relationship, which is itself timeless, Tillich asserts:

> The relation of the conditioned to the unconditional, in individual as well as in social life, is either an openness of the conditioned to the dynamic presence of the unconditional or a seclusion of the conditioned within itself. The finite

> life is either turned toward the infinite or turned away from it toward itself. Where there is an acceptance of the eternal manifesting itself in a special moment of history, in a kairos, there is openness to the unconditional. Such openness can be expressed in religious as well as in secular symbols as the expectation of the transcendent Kingdom of God, or the thousand years of the reign of Christ, or the third epoch of world history, or the final stage of justice and peace. However different the historical consciousness involved in the use of the one or the other of these symbols may be, the consciousness of the kairos, of the outstanding moment in history, can express itself in each of them.[30]

Kairos is, then, in the words of Adams, "the concept relating the Unconditioned to the present."[31] As such it includes both relative and absolute elements. In working out these elements within the meaning of *Kairos*, Tillich also develops a second criterion by which the *Kairos* may be determined. This is his notion of "Theonomy". Theonomy is another basic concept in Tillich's thought, which cannot be explored in detail. For Tillich, there are three fundamental attitudes or orientations toward the Unconditioned, which are disclosed within the historical process. Tillich designates these three orientations as "autonomy", "heteronomy", and "theonomy".[32] In Tillich's analysis of reason, especially with reference to the "depth of reason", these notions are brought clearly into view. Reason, which actualizes itself without regard to its own depth, is autonomous (ST, I: 83). Tillich denies that autonomy means the individual's freedom to be his own law. Rather:

> autonomy means the obedience of the individual to the law of reason, which he finds in himself as a rational being. The *nomos* ("law") of *autos* ("self") is not the law of one's personality structure. It is the law of subjective-objective reason; it is the law implied in the *logos* structure of mind and reality. Autonomous reason's . . . independence is the opposite of willfulness; it is obedience to its own essential structure, the law of reason which is the law of nature within mind and reality (ST, I: 84).

The autonomous spiritual attitude (*Geisteshaltung*), then, in contrast to theonomy, "sich auf das Bedingte richtet und auf das Unbedingte nur, um das Bedingte zu fundieren".[33] The law toward which autonomy strives is the *essential* law of the conditioned sphere, which while not asserting itself in opposition to the Unconditioned, does not constitute itself on the basis of the relationship of everything conditioned to the Unconditioned. Autonomy is the turning toward the conditioned sphere, both theoretically and practically, for its own sake and not for the sake of the Unconditioned, which theonomy sees in and through the conditioned realm.[34]

Autonomy, in the name of the essential nature of reason, strives constantly against "heteronomy". "Heteronomy", for Tillich,

> imposes a strange (*heteros*) law (*nomos*) on one or all of the functions of reason. It issues commands from "outside" on how reason should grasp and shape reality. But this "outside" is not merely outside. It represents . . . an element in reason itself, namely, the depth of reason. This makes the fight between autonomy and heteronomy dangerous and tragic . . . The basis of a genuine heteronomy is the claim to speak in the name of the ground of being and therefore in an unconditioned and ultimate way . . . Heteronomy in this sense is usually a reaction against an autonomy which has lost its depth and has become empty and powerless (ST, I: 84-85).

Heteronomy does not share the presupposition of autonomy that man can live according to the essential law of reason. Rather for the heteronomous vision it is precisely because man does not live according to universal reason that he must be subject to a law which is not identical with his rational structure and which is superior to him in authority and validity. Hence, "a heteronomous culture . . . subjects the forms and laws of thinking and acting to authoritative criteria of an ecclesiastical religion or of a political quasi-religion, even at the price of destroying the structures of rationality".[35]

It is important to note, as Tillich has asserted, that heteronomy is rooted in an element of reason itself in that it represents the depth of reason against the attempts of reason to actualize itself without reference to its depth. However, heteronomy seeks to represent the depth of reason through symbols and doctrines which, as a result of the radical autonomous critique, have lost their power to grasp reason in its essential structure; hence, heteronomy's arbitrary assertion of authority over autonomy. It is the destiny of autonomy, then, to live out of the power of those periods when the depth of reason is manifest nonheteronomously, but also over against these manifestations in its drive for self-realization. The tragedy of autonomy is that as it cuts itself off from its own depth, it becomes increasingly empty and sterile, thus opening itself to the incursions of an arbitrary and destructive heteronomy, which seeks to represent the Unconditioned unconditionally against the autonomous thrust.[36]

This situation points to the disruption of the unity of unconditioned and conditioned being under the conditions of existence. But as we have seen that unity is nonetheless effective within space and time, and both autonomy and heteronomy are rooted in it. Tillich's term for the fragmentary manifestation of the unity of unconditioned and conditioned being in time and space is "theonomy". A theonomous period in history is a period in which the conditioned forms in which the human spirit is embodied become completely transparent to the Unconditioned. Theonomy does not mean that God imposes law arbitrarily upon man's autonomous creativity. Rather:

> theonomy asserts that the superior law is, at the same time, the innermost law of man himself, rooted in the divine ground which is man's own ground; the law of life transcends man, although it is, at the same time, his own . . . A theonomous culture expresses in its creations an ultimate concern and a transcending meaning not as something strange but as its own spiritual ground. "Religion is the substance of culture and culture the form of religion." This was the most precise statement of theonomy.[37]

Theonomy is reason united with its own depth within space and time and therefore within culture and history. Its cultural expression is, as we have seen, the radical openness of every cultural form to the Unconditioned and the theonomous attitude of culture is "one in which the consciousness of the presence of the unconditional permeates and guides all cultural functions and forms. The divine, for such a state of mind, is not a problem but a presupposition. Its 'givenness' is more certain than that of anything else."[38] However, theonomy appears within history and thus it stands in dialectical relationship to autonomy and heteronomy. Tillich describes this relationship as the permanent struggle of theonomy against both independent autonomies and heteronomies within history. In this struggle,

> theonomy is prior to both; they are elements within it. But theonomy, at the same time, is posterior to both; they tend to be reunited in the theonomy from which they come. Theonomy both precedes and follows the contrasting elements it contains. The process in which this happens can be described in the following way: The original theonomous union is left behind by the rise of autonomous trends which necessarily lead to a reaction of the heteronomous element. Without the liberation of autonomy from the bondage to an "archaic", mythologically founded theonomy, the culture could not develop its potentialities. Only after their liberation from the uniting myth and the theonomous state of consciousness can philosophy and the sciences, poetry and the arts, appear. But if they achieve independence, they lose their transcendent foundation which gave them depth, unity, and ultimate meaning; and therefore, the reaction of heteronomy starts . . . The permanent struggle between autonomous independence and heteronomous reaction leads to the quest for a new theonomy . . . This quest is answered by the impact of the Spiritual Presence on culture. Wherever this impact is effective, theonomy is created . . . (ST, III: 251-252).[39]

Theonomy appears in history, which means that its concrete manifestations are relative to the historical contexts in which they occur. While theonomy is bound to the structure of quantitative time (*Chronos*), it is clear that its appearance is a radical qualification of that structure of time. Theonomy is *fulfilled* time; it is the time when an ultimate meaning and significance breaks into the temporal process and every conditioned, temporal form bears witness to its impact. Thus, the *Kairos* is to be determined, on this second criterion, by the discernment of a theonomous situation within a given cultural and historical epoch.

As we have seen theonomous periods do not possess historical permanence. The horizontal thrust of the historical process and the autonomous drive of cultural creativity constantly break the immediacy of every given theonomous period. The theonomy which informs every dimension of man's spiritual life in one period of history becomes the problematic against which autonomy revolts in a further historical period, and the progressive emptiness and formalism of the autonomous period cut off from the theonomy from which it emerged creates heteronomous reactions and also gives rise to the quest for a new theonomy. The *Kairos* as the time in which theonomy appears is, therefore, completely relative to the universal historical process as is the theonomous manifestation itself. However, *Kairos* also contains an absolute element within itself, for as the time of a theonomous manifestation, it is the expression of the absolutely valid, absolutely true meaning of an historical epoch.

In the concepts of *Kairos* and theonomy and their dialectical relations, Tillich maintains,

> the answer is given to the basic question of the philosophy of history: How can the absolute categories which characterize a genuine kairos be united with the relativity of the universal process of history? The answer is: History comes from and moves toward periods of theonomy, i.e., periods in which the conditioned is open to the unconditional without claiming to be unconditioned itself. Theonomy unites the absolute and the relative element in the interpretation of history, the demand that everything relative become the vehicle of the absolute and the insight that nothing relative can ever become absolute itself.[40]

There is a basic question, however, whether Tillich allows the tension between the absolute and the relative to stand in his notion of *Kairos*. It is clear that that which is absolute in the *Kairos* of an historical epoch is the eternal, the Unconditioned, which transcends every historical epoch and is therefore valid for every epoch. What is relative in the *Kairos*, of course, is the conceptuality (the categories and symbols) in which a given epoch grasps the Unconditioned in the theonomous moment. However, Tillich introduces distinctions within the *sense* of the term *Kairos*, which seem to undercut the relative element within it. He writes:

> Kairos in its *unique* and universal sense is, for Christian faith, the appearing of Jesus as the Christ. Kairos in its *general* and special sense for the philosopher of history is every turning point in history in which the eternal judges and transforms the temporal. Kairos in its *special* sense, as decisive for our present situation, is the coming of a new theonomy on the soil of a secularized and emptied autonomous culture.[41]

Tillich continues:

In each kairos the "Kingdom of God is at hand", for it is a world-historical, unrepeatable, unique decision for and against the unconditional. Every kairos is, therefore, implicitly the universal kairos and an actualization of the unique kairos, the appearance of the Christ.[42]

The distinctions between a *unique* and *universal* Kairos on the one hand and a *general* Kairos with special manifestations in different historical epochs presuppose, it seems, two different logics, the compatibility of which is highly questionable. To claim a unique *Kairos* in Jesus as the Christ is to claim by definition that this *Kairos* is incomparable with every other historical event.[43] Thus it is to claim that the unconditional truth is radically bound to the historical event in which the unique *Kairos* has appeared, and through its uniqueness this *Kairos* also becomes universal. The logic which informs this claim is clearly the logic of historicism, which presupposes not only that one's conceptuality is conditioned by the historical context in which it emerges, but also that the unconditional truth itself is radically historical. On the other hand to claim that there is a general *Kairos* which appears periodically in different historical circumstances in special manifestations is to invoke what might be called the logic of the eternal principle, viz., that what appears in history is above history and that each historical epoch in which a *Kairos* appears is merely an exemplification of the eternal principle of *Kairos*.

The first logic presupposes a relativity which the second does not. Clearly, in arguing against the exclusively *Logos* philosophy and in asserting the historical character of thinking, Tillich is placing himself within an historicist perspective; however in claiming that every *Kairos* is implicitly the universal *Kairos* and an actualization of the unique *Kairos*, has not Tillich qualified the historicist logic to the point that the unique *Kairos* is lost and thus capitulates to the *Kairos* as eternal principle?[44] Consequently, the relativity of the unique Kairos seems also to be lost.

We shall not attempt to resolve this issue here. Rather we are trying to show just what Tillich's claim that all thinking must be historical involves. Thus far, we have seen that historical thinking and knowledge are rooted in decision toward the Unconditioned, and that the decision toward the Unconditioned can never be timeless, but rather is made in relation to that temporal moment in which the Unconditioned breaks into the temporal moment in which the thinker stands. This temporal moment is the *Kairos* of an age, and its presence is discerned where the finitude and relativity of every conditioned form is acknowledged in relation to the eternal, the absolute and thus where a genuinely theonomous culture is created. Hence, the decision toward the Unconditioned is relative to the historical epoch and its peculiar fate. The *Kairos*, then, appears on the basis of the constellation of events, concepts, and symbols which constitute an historical epoch and the decision toward the Unconditioned must be made in relation to this concrete, historical content. The absolute subject and the absolute standpoint are impossible.

This does not mean, however that the decision toward the Unconditioned is to be equated with subjectivity. There is a place for methodical strictness in Tillich's theory of knowledge, but it is not asceticism toward the *Kairos*.

Thus:

> Only in the severest methodical concentration can that objectivity be reached which can become the fate of time. Here lies the whole gravity of the task of knowledge, the necessary asceticism which is not an asceticism toward the Kairos but toward subjectivity. For subjectivity is always "akairos" . . . Insofar as interest means subjectivity, its exclusion is a prerequisite of truth.[45]

The decision toward the Unconditioned is rooted in history and therefore it is always ambiguous.[46] However, it is not mere arbitrariness. It is a decision which has undergone the radical critique of autonomous thought and which has subjected itself to the demand and judgment of the *Kairos*. For Tillich, this means that the decision toward the Unconditioned is the transcendental unity of freedom and fate.

Thus to deny that the absolute standpoint is possible, to acknowledge that all thinking stands in history and is conditioned by the historical context, and to assert that "the possibility of recognizing truth is dependent on decision and fate and cannot be separated from the Kairos"[47] is not thereby to define truth in such a way that its impossibility follows from the historical character of knowledge. It is, however, to call into question the model of truth as the timeless knowledge of the eternal *Logos*. It is, further, to call for a dynamic conception of truth, which is rooted in the dynamic character of reality. Tillich attempts to work out this dynamic epistemology in relation to the reconstruction of the notion of the "idea".

Tillich argues that in the work of Hegel and Marx reality and truth are seen to stand in a dynamic relationship, since they are both dynamic in themselves. Both Hegel and Marx, for Tillich, achieved this dynamic view of reality by taking the historical process seriously; Hegel by subjecting history to ideality (history is the unfolding of Absolute Spirit) and Marx by asserting that ideality emerges from history, i.e., ideas are the products of concrete historical situations. Without accepting either Hegelianism or Marxism as final articulations of dynamic reality, Tillich does carry forward their insights that the historical process is dynamic and that historic reality is constitutive for the character of reality as such.[48]

The analysis of knowledge provides the point of departure for approaching the analysis of the nature of reality. "The third stratum in knowledge besides pure form and pure material, the qualitatively changeable, actually historical stratum is to be interpreted", Tillich sees following Marx,[49] "not only from the point of view of knowledge, but from reality as well."[50] The analysis of knowledge has centered in the question of decision and its ambiguity and thus the category of freedom has received predominant attention. However, freedom stands in correlation with fate, and the attempt to explicate the place of fate in knowledge leads to the question of the nature of reality.

Reality is not dynamic merely because it is subject to change, especially in its historical dimension. Rather its dynamic character lies essentially in the fact that reality has

an aspect which is subject to neither an empirical nor a rational necessity. It is fate and is therefore recognized only in the freedom of decision. But where such free — not arbitrary [i.e., accidental or subjective: cf. *Ibid.*, p. 157] —

decision occurs, there this aspect of reality, fate, is effective. This third element of knowledge thus corresponds to a third element of being. The transcendental stratum of knowledge corresponds to the transcendental stratum of being.[51]

The "transcendental stratum of being" can only mean in this context that which belongs to being, but which is, at the same time, the presupposition of all finite reality, that which is manifest in finite reality, and yet that which is in no way exhausted in finite reality, in this case, of course, historic reality, i.e., the Unconditioned. The dynamic character of reality, then, historically considered, is its fatefulness, which is nothing other than the impact of the Unconditioned upon it, driving each historic epoch toward its ultimate fulfillment, its *Kairos*, discerned in free (and thus fateful) decision *vis-a-vis* the peculiar meaning-constellations of each age.

To posit the dynamic character of reality, however, is to invite the question

how far knowledge that is the true interpretation of reality is possible, when reality itself is dynamic; while truth is usually considered the static element in every change. How is it possible to grasp the nature of that which is changing, if the nature itself is not withdrawn from the change? If reality has fateful character in the depth of its essence, how then is the perception of essence possible? This question brings us to the problem of the idea.[52]

The Platonic notion of the idea has consistently informed the philosophy of method, because it has identified the idea with the timeless, immutable, unchanging elements in reality. Thus, the idea in this tradition is static, resting in itself, and the changing, contingent, temporal order has reality only insofar as it participates in the idea. However, in the thought of Böhme and to some degree of Schelling another notion of the idea was formulated, which has informed the second line in philosophy and which Tillich clearly wishes to incorporate in his own theory of knowledge.

The idea of Böhme is itself dynamic and yet it contains a static, eternal element. Tillich's analysis is as follows:

While the Platonic idea offers eternal rest, the idea of Böhme is a unity of rest and unrest, a movable, in itself questionable, being, pregnant with infinite tensions. The idea has inner infinity, not indeed for a supposed observer but for itself, and every one who regards it is drawn into the inner infinity of the idea. There is indeed a rest, an eternal, static element in it; otherwise it would not be idea, and the unrest would have no resistance, no immutable point through which it could become evident as unrest, but this static element is not to be severed from the dynamic. Therefore, whoever regards the idea can never come to rest in it. Since, however, no absolute subject of perception is possible without rest, all interpretation of the idea can be only ambiguous. . . . This means, however, that there can be no comprehension of the essential nature of things except in decision, because the nature of things itself stands in fate and ambiguity.[53]

For Tillich a philosophical understanding of history, a metaphysics of history is impossible without the notion of the dynamic idea and its inner infinity. Also, by construing the idea dynamically the cleavage between nature and history is overcome, since it is now possible to grasp the dynamic, fateful (and thus free) character of nature itself.[54]

It is not necessary here to discuss Tillich's notion of the idea in detail, since we have already considered his concept of essence in Part One. The important point to note, however, is that the idea is dynamic because its eternal, resting character is an abstraction from its concrete, historical actualizations. Thus, to know the eternal character of the idea is to know only an aspect of it, for the nature of the idea is given fully only in its historical actualizations, in fate. The inner infinity of the idea, then, means both that the idea constantly pours itself out in existence in varied concrete constellations, which can be known only contingently and, at the same time, the idea can never be known exhaustively in either its eternal aspect or in its contingent actualizations. However, Tillich is emphatic in insisting that the idea can only be known, even in its eternal aspect, in history, in fate.

It is not only the knower, then, who stands in fate. It is also the case that

essence and fate are not strange to each other . . . Fate belongs to essential being. The idea . . . does not contrast with existence as eternal completion, in which existence imperfectly participates, but drives on toward existence, toward the pouring out of its inner infinity in the historic fate. Recognizing reality is recognizing reality as it stands in the historical fate, not beyond it. Therefore the knowledge of ideas is never complete . . . The knowledge of ideas participates in the inner infinity of ideas . . . The participation of the things in the idea corresponds just as seriously to the participation of the idea in the things. The Logos becomes flesh; it enters into time and reveals its inner infinity.[55]

That the idea stands in fate, then, is a fundamental claim of the theory of knowledge based upon the doctrine of *Kairos*, and, thus, of a Protestant theory of knowledge. However, in asserting that the idea stands in fate, that the absolute standpoint is impossible, and that consequently the truth is reached in decision in relation to the *Kairos*, a fundamental problem arises. It is clear that the *Kairos* doctrine affirms the relativity of truth. But the question arises as to the relativity of the claim that truth is relative, i.e., is not the claim that truth is relative itself relative, and, therefore, is not the foundational judgment of a Protestant theory of knowledge highly ambiguous? If it is said to be so, then the formal principle of a Protestant epistemology, the knowledge of knowledge, cannot have universal significance. If it is said to be beyond relativity and ambiguity, however, an exception to the principle is admitted and "for one bit of reality the equivocal character of being is broken. The point of view of the Unconditioned would be reached at one point."[56]

Tillich's solution to this dilemma is problematic as we have noted above. He acknowledges that if the judgment concerning the relativity of truth emerged from the context of knowledge, its character as a universally valid epistemological principle would be vitiated by the ambiguity of that context. Therefore, the principle must arise from a sphere other than the context of knowledge. It must be understood not as an ambiguous proposition, but rather as the absolutely unequivocal judgment of the relationship of the Unconditioned and conditioned and therefore the transcendental foundation of the relativity of truth and of every concrete, ambiguous judgment. "The content of this judgment is just this", then,

that our subjective thinking never can reach the unconditioned truth, that it must always remain in the realm of ambiguity. This judgment is plainly the absolute judgment which is independent of all its forms of expression, even of the one by which it is expressed here. It is the judgment which constitutes truth as truth. . . . It itself is the premise of all judging, questioning, answering. One therefore really has no right to call it a judgment in a particular sense; it is rather the metaphysical meaning implied in judging.[57]

The absolute judgment is the content of the absolute standpoint, and since neither can be reached by the knowing subject within the context of knowledge, the absolute position can have only a negative function in relation to the concrete, relative status of knowledge within history. It is the guardian viewpoint, which sees human history and human knowledge *sub specie aeternitatis*, and, therefore, it "is the guard which protects the Unconditioned, averting the encroachment of a conditioned point of view on the sphere of the Unconditioned." Thus, Tillich unites the claim that all knowledge and truth are relative, conditioned, and, therefore, ambiguous with the claim that the absolute standpoint is beyond epistemological realization and therefore functions as a boundary concept for knowledge in the view which he calls "beliefful relativism".[58] Beliefful relativism is the negation of a purely relativistic view of truth, while at the same time placing truth completely within the realm of decision, ambiguity and fate, i.e., in history.[59]

It is the purely limiting, critical function of the absolute standpoint which makes it compatible with the doctrine of *Kairos*. The *Kairos* of an age is that historical moment when the ultimate significance of the age breaks in upon it, and its ultimate significance is precisely its conditionedness before the Unconditioned as well as its capacity to represent the Unconditioned in all its conditioned forms. We can say, then, that the *Kairos* is the temporalization of the absolute standpoint. If an historical epoch responds positively to the *Kairos*, it acknowledges the radical conditionedness of its every form and creation; however, it does so always ambiguously and thus it can never claim the absolute standpoint for itself. If it responds negatively, on the other hand, it has failed to acknowledge the truth of its time. Hence:

the truth of a time is its attitude toward the Unconditioned, by which it is supported and directed. Knowledge born in the situation of the Kairos then is not knowledge growing out of the accidental arbitrary events of a period but out of the period's basic significance. . . . True knowledge is not absolute

knowledge. . . . True knowledge is knowledge born of the Kairos, that is, of
the fate of the time, of the point at which time is disturbed by eternity. . . .
The dynamic thought of truth overcomes the alternative "absolute-relative".
The Kairos is absolute insofar as it places one at this moment before the
absolute decision for or against the truth, and it is relative, insofar as it knows
that this decision is possible only as a concrete decision, as the fate of the
time. Thus the Kairos serves to reveal rather than conceal the Logos.[60]

It should be clear, now that we have examined in detail the claim
that thinking, truth, and knowledge are all historical in character,
that Tillich seems to break radically with the methodical mainline
in philosophy. In stressing the dynamic-temporal nature of reality
and the idea, the decisional character of knowledge, the historical
relativity of truth and the concreteness of the knowing subject in
relation to the manifestation of the eternal *Logos* in the *Kairos*, he
has affirmed a radically historicist epistemology. However, in
working toward an epistemology which takes history seriously,
Tillich does not eliminate the *Logos* doctrine in his thought. The
question of the relationship of *Kairos* and *Logos* naturally arises
here.

The *Logos* is the changeless rational structure of mind and reality, the eternal truth. It is present in both finite and infinite being
(ST, I: 72-79, 156), but while it is eternal in character, it is not,
therefore, static. It is, rather, dynamic in the sense, as we have
seen, that the *Logos* manifests itself within the historical process.
Its manifestation occurs in the *Kairos* of an age. Thus, the basic
relationship of *Logos* and *Kairos* is one of disclosure or revelation,
that is, the *Kairos* reveals or discloses the *Logos*. Knowledge, then,
is knowledge of the eternal *Logos*, but this knowledge is achieved
in time, the qualitative time of the *Kairos*. Consequently, Tillich's
analysis of Nietzsche is also the normative epistemological statement of the doctrine of the *Logos-Kairos* relationship. He asserts:

As it does not lessen the proportions of Socrates to emphasize his struggle
against the spirit of his age, the spirit of sophistic disintegration, so Nietzsche's stature is not diminished by a strong emphasis on the spirit he was
fighting against in his day. The more deeply a man is rooted in the Kairos
(the creative moment of time) the better is he able to reach the Logos
(universal truth).[61]

While the *Kairos* reveals the *Logos*, it is also the case that the *Kairos* is distinguishable from *Chronos* (quantitative time) only by virtue of its special relationship to the eternal *Logos*, that is, only by disclosing the *Logos* within itself. Again, the pregnant moment, the moment of ultimate significance can make no claims on its own behalf. Rather it is the *Kairos* precisely because it points to the *Logos* through the concrete content of the age in which it appears. Since the eternal *Logos* is rooted in the Unconditioned, and to know the *Logos* is at the same time to know the Unconditioned, it would seem that the ultimate cognitive value of the *Kairos* has little to do with its own uniqueness, but rather has to do with its utter abandonment to the eternal *Logos*, the Unconditioned which is the invariant "import"[62] breaking through the concrete content of every *Kairos* in every historical epoch regardless of the time or the historical circumstances in which it occurs.[63] Thus, in spite of Tillich's claim that the *Logos* can only be known by the most profound involvement in the *Kairos* in history, the historicist element in his thought seems ultimately to be subordinated to the eternal *Logos* and its ahistorical character, since what the *Kairos* yields is not, in the final analysis, a radically contingent, radically conditioned, fully historical content which can be the relative truth for the historical being who encounters it, but rather the universal truth, which reduces all significant historical moments to the same consequence, viz., to be exemplars of the Unconditioned.

Regardless of the validity of this judgment, however, it is nonetheless the case that one of the significant elements in Tillich's conception of philosophy is that it, too, is historical thinking, that it stands in fate. Just as essence and fate or idea and fate are not strange to each other, so truth and fate are not strange; therefore:

fate does not concern only the outer court of philosophy, leaving untouched the sacred precincts themselves. Fate obtrudes even into the sacred inclosure of philosophy, into the truth itself. . . . But this eternal truth, this logos above fate, is not at man's disposal . . . [it] is not itself an idea with whose help a philosophy free from fate can be created.[64]

Perhaps more than any other intellectual discipline, philosophy is concerned with the *Logos*, as its origin in the Greek experience suggests, and for Tillich philosophy can never abandon its attempt to delineate the structure of the *Logos* on the basis of universal concepts and categories. However, in seeking to serve the universal truth (*Logos*), philosophy must also acknowledge its fateful, its historical, its conditioned character. Tillich formulates the task of philosophy thus:

> If philosophy maintains its relation to the eternal logos, if philosophy is not afraid of the demonic thrust of fate, then it can quite readily accept the place of fate within thinking. It can acknowledge that it has from the beginning been subject to fate, that it has always wished to escape it, though it has never succeeded in doing so. The union of kairos and logos is the philosophical task set for us in philosophy and in all fields that are accessible to the philosophical attitude. The logos is to be taken up into the kairos, universal values into the fullness of time, truth into the fate of existence. The separation of idea and existence has to be brought to an end. . . . And it is essential to philosophy to stand in existence, to create out of time and fate. . . . Since existence itself stands in fate, it is proper that philosophy should also stand in fate. . . . The truth that stands in fate is accessible to him who stands within fate, who is himself an element of fate, for thought is a part of existence.[65]

Philosophy, then, is subject to the formal conditions which Tillich identifies with the Protestant theory of knowledge, that is, the dialectical relationship of *Logos* and *Kairos* in which universal validity is given to the deliverances of philosophy by the *Logos* and in which its existential relevance is established by the *Kairos*. Even philosophy's understanding of itself is grounded in both elements of this total epistemological structure. Hence:

> There is no point at which either logos or kairos alone is to be found. . . . Even our knowledge of the fateful character of philosophy must at the same time stand in logos and kairos. If it stood only in the kairos, it would be without validity and the assertion would be valid only for the one making it; if it stood only in the logos, it would be without fate and would therefore have no part in existence, for existence is involved in fate.[66]

The historical character of philosophy must be fully acknowledged, for Tillich. Since philosophy stands in fate, its radical question is always posed *vis-a-vis* a definite constellation of historical circumstances, its conceptuality is always conditioned by the ethos in which it arises (even though the categories, for example, have a definite transhistorical character, they are subject to reformulation in each new age),[67] and its claims to truth are rooted in radical decision toward the *Kairos*. But the question which was raised above regarding the *determinative* character of the historicist element for Tillich's thought needs also to be raised for his conception of philosophy. Before examining this question, however, we must explore briefly the implications of his claim that philosophy must create out of existence, which means that not only is there an historical element within the philosophical enterprise, but there is also an existential element.

Just as philosophy must accept the historical fate in which it stands in its orientation toward the *Logos*, so the philosopher must come to terms with the way in which his own existence enters into the formation of the theoretical structure he directs toward the *Logos*. For Tillich, however, the existential element in philosophy is defined in extremely broad terms. In a statement which reflects his mature position, Tillich asserts:

> The philosopher is driven . . . to the question of being-itself, by something else [besides his theoretical interest], the existential element. The "something else" can be called with Plato the *eros* for the idea, or with the Stoics the desire for wisdom, or with Augustine the longing for the truth-itself, or with Spinoza the intellectual love of the substance, or with Hegel the passion for the absolute, or with Hume the liberation from prejudice, or with Nietzsche the will to participate in the creative and destructive life-processes. It is always a driving force in the depths of his being that makes the philosopher a philosopher.[68]

Tillich also defines the existential element in philosophy in relation to the notion "ultimate concern". The philosopher cannot escape the impact of his own existence upon his philosophical endeavors, and it is within the impact of his existence that his ultimate concern is to be seen. Tillich seems to want to maintain, in fact, that to exist and to have an ultimate concern are identical. Note, for example, this characteristic formulation:

> The philosopher . . . "exists", and he cannot jump over the concreteness of his existence and his implicit theology. He is conditioned by his psychological,

sociological, and historical situation. And, like every human being, he exists in the power of an ultimate concern, whether or not he is fully conscious of it, whether or not he admits it to himself and to others. There is no reason why even the most scientific philosopher should not admit it, for without an ultimate concern his philosophy would be lacking in passion, seriousness, and creativity (ST, I: 24-25).

Since we shall discuss Tillich's conception of existence and Existentialism below, it is necessary here only to point out that for him the philosophical enterprise is rooted deeply within human existence and thus the truth for which it strives is ultimately truth which is relevant to human existence. However, there is a significant conflict in Tillich's conception of philosophy between the existential element in it, that which gives it its fundamental significance, its ultimate concern, and its theoretical task, which is its very reason for being. In order to state this conflict as clearly as possible, it is now necessary to examine Tillich's understanding of the theoretical task of philosophy, which will allow us, at the same time, to grasp Tillich's conception of philosophy in its totality.

We have already seen that for Tillich the driving force of philosophy is the radical question, which in its most systematic expression is the attitude of pure theory. The radical question in its negative expression is directed toward every presupposition, that is, it is the radical dismantling of every assumption from which thought might proceed; it is the "question of the question itself".[69] Philosophy, however, is not limited merely to its interrogative function or, to follow one of Tillich's later formulations, the philosophical question is the question of being, and in asking that question, philosophy seeks to know that about which it asks (ST, I: 20). This means that philosophy is critical by definition in the sense that

> it separates the multifarious materials of experience from those structures which make experience possible. There is no difference in this respect between constructive idealism and empirical realism. The question regarding the character of the general structures that make experience possible is always the same. It is *the* philosophical question (ST, I: 18-19).

The critical task of philosophy, for Tillich, is less ambitious than those philosophies which seek a complete system of reality including both the deliverances of the sciences and what Tillich calls the "structures of prescientific experience" (ST, I: 19). In every case where such systems have been attempted their historically conditioned character becomes evident, but more importantly the finitude of the human mind and its inability to grasp the whole of reality is revealed. No system stands "once and for all" and thus no system can become normative for thought, since thought constantly drives beyond its every formulation. What critical philosophy seeks, then, is not the system in this sense, but rather the general principles which have emerged from, but which are transcendent to, the history of philosophy. With the collapse of each system,

> only the general principles were left, always discussed, questioned, changed, but never destroyed, shining through the centuries, reinterpreted by every generation, inexhaustible, never antiquated or obsolete. These principles are the material of philosophy (ST, I: 19).

In seeking the general principles by which experience is possible, however, philosophy seeks to delineate the structure of reality. Its critical task, therefore, is ontological in character, that is, philosophy cannot be limited to epistemology and ethics (Neo-Kantianism) nor to "logical calculus" (logical positivism). Philosophy cannot avoid the question of being, and therefore it cannot avoid the task of speaking conceptually about the structure of being. Thus, Tillich insists that philosophy must fulfill the task which it originally set for itself under the term "metaphysics", even though he prefers the word "ontology" rather than "metaphysics" to describe that task (ST, I: 20).

It is the ontological task of philosophy, then, which informs Tillich's formal definition of philosophy. Philosophy, he proposes, is "that cognitive approach to reality in which reality as such is the object" (ST, I: 18).[70] Since we have discussed in detail in Part One the meaning of the structure of reality which philosophy seeks to grasp conceptually and the concepts and categories which constitute Tillich's developed ontology, we are concerned here to explore Tillich's understanding of the way in which philosophy achieves its cognitive grasp of reality as such.

The first thing that must be said about the way philosophy achieves its cognitive task is that it seeks "universal categories in which being is expressed." Thus, in seeking to grasp reality as such, philosophy seeks the most abstract, objective, universal generalizations of which the human mind is capable as answers to "the most general questions about the nature of reality and human existence"[71] which the mind can formulate. Philosophy, then, is not limited to the analysis of a specific sphere of reality, but rather seeks reality as a whole. Consequently, philosophy cannot be satisfied with partial notions, fragmentary and incomplete, which lack the power of universality. In seeking universal categories, then, philosophy seeks that vision of reality which is *in principle*, open to all men without exception regardless of social or historical context.

The quest for universality and objectivity also determines, for Tillich, the *stance* of the philosopher, and thus, secondly, philosophy achieves its cognitive grasp of reality as such through the "attitude" of the philosopher. The philosopher's stance toward reality as such, his cognitive attitude, is one of "detached objectivity". In order to discover the universal categories of being, the philosopher

> tries to exclude the personal, social, and historical conditions which might distort an objective vision of reality. His passion is the passion for a truth which is open to general approach, subject to general criticism, changeable in accordance with every new insight, open and communicable. . . . He assumes . . . that there is an identity, or at least an analogy, between objective and subjective reason, between the logos of reality as a whole and the logos working in him. Therefore, this logos is common; every reasonable being participates in it, uses it in asking questions and criticizing the answers received. There is no particular place to discover the structure of being; there is no particular place to stand to discover the categories of experience. The place to look is all places; the place to stand is no place at all; it is pure reason (ST, I: 22-23).

The theoretical stance of detached objectivity means that the more detached and objective the philosopher can become the more adequate will be his grasp of reality as such. However, as we have already seen, objective detachment is the ideal toward which the philosopher strives but never completely reaches, because he is also a human being and thus he can never escape fully his own particularity, his personal, social, and historical milieu. Nevertheless, the important consideration here is that objective detachment is the demand which is placed upon the philosopher, it is the *sine qua non* of philosophical activity.[72]

It is difficult to determine the meaning and consistency of Tillich's statement above that the universal categories of experience are to be sought in the "no place" of pure reason, especially when considered in the light of Tillich's earlier concerns regarding the historical, fateful character of philosophy, the contingency of the philosopher's point of view, and the relativity of a Protestant theory of knowledge. At this point we can conclude that Tillich's assertion of the potential universality of the philosopher's conceptual description of the structure of being stands in tension with his simultaneous claim that philosophy, too, is subject to the limits of finitude. The question is whether he holds the theoretical and existential poles of the philosophical enterprise in dynamic balance or whether one actually dominates the other. We shall return to this question below.

We are now in a position to summarize the defining characteristics of philosophy as Tillich has explicated them. We have shown, first, that Tillich has developed a critique of the western philosophical tradition on the grounds that from its inception in Greek thought onward it has consistently failed to see its rootage in fate and thus in its cognitive quest for the universal structure of being it has not incorporated the historically conditioned and existentially relative dimensions within its theoretical structure. For Tillich, philosophy must acknowledge its historical, existential foundation. It acknowledges the former in the realization that its conceptual framework inevitably reveals the historical context in which the philosopher stands and that consequently the "absolute standpoint" which the methodological mainline in philosophy sought is impossible. It acknowledges the latter by recognizing that the philosopher's own existence, his ultimate concern, determines the character and content of his philosophy.[73] Therefore, detached objectivity, while an ideal and demand of the philosopher can never be completely achieved.

Clearly, then, Tillich's normative vision of philosophy includes existential and historicist elements within it. However, while Tillich insists that philosophy must come to terms with these elements, they are subordinate to its theoretical task, which, as his formal definition of philosophy indicates, constitutes the very essence of philosophy. Thus the second defining characteristic of philosophy, the cognitive-speculative[74] quest for the structure of reality through the development of those universally generalizable notions within which the whole of experience can be made intelligible, has as its goal the transcending of those very conditions which Tillich has explicated by the notions of the historicity and existentiality of the philosophical enterprise. It is significant, then, that philosophical truth is essentially for Tillich objective and universal truth. The philosophical task consists in developing a universal conceptuality in which that truth can be articulated on the one hand and in escaping those historical and existential conditions which both thwart the drive toward universality and yet are inescapably present in every cognitive act on the other. In brief, philosophy must attempt to escape the inescapable.

It seems clear that Tillich has accepted the classical view of philosophy insofar as he insists that philosophical truth is objective and universal and can be achieved only in the attitude of detachment. He is, however, more aware than his philosophical predecessors (e.g., Plato and Hegel) that the finitude of the philosopher must ultimately qualify "pure" philosophical truth, but the evidence is less than persuasive that Tillich has allowed the historical and existential elements in his thought basically to qualify his *conception* of philosophy or of philosophical truth.

It is the classical vision of philosophy, therefore, which Tillich attempts to bring into relationship with theology, and as we shall see, it is the classical features of Tillich's conception of philosophy which allow him to distinguish philosophy from theology. Before we examine Tillich's understanding of the relationship of philosophy and theology, however, it is necessary now to explore his conception of theology.

Notes

1 P. Tillich, "Autobiographical Reflections", *The Theology of Paul Tillich, op. cit.*, p. 10: "These studies seemed more to foreshadow a philosopher than a theologian . . . Nevertheless I was and am a theologian, because the existential question of our ultimate concern and the existential answer of the Christian message are and always have been predominant in my spiritual life."

2 *On the Boundary, op. cit.*, pp. 46-58. Dr. David Winston of the Graduate Theological Union has suggested, in a personal conversation, that the philosophical import of Tillich's thought has not been explored by the philosophical community because of his identification with religion, and, therefore, with religious authority, which, if true, is certainly an unfortunate aspect of Tillich's destiny as a thinker.

3 First published as "Philosophie: Begriff und Wesen" in *Die Religion in Geschichte und Gegenwart* (J. C. B. Mohr, Tubingen, 2 Aufl., 1930) and reprinted as "Philosophie" in *Gesammelte Werke*, Band IV.

4 GW, IV, p. 15. Cf. ST, I: 18.

5 It is possible, of course, to define the nature of philosophy in reference to the history of philosophy as a descriptive task without expressing a philosophical attitude. However, Tillich is arguing that any *normative* definition of philosophy must be an expression of philosophical activity. It is in this sense that there is no court of appeal outside philosophy itself by which philosophy can be defined. Since Tillich offers a normative definition of philosophy, he is clearly speaking as a philosopher himself, and the definition he offers he maintains is exemplified throughout the history of philosophy within the various philosophical schools. Cf. *Biblical Religion and the Search for Ultimate Reality, op. cit.*, pp. 14-18.

6 GW, IV, *Loc. Cit.*

7 *Ibid.*, p. 16.

8 *Ibid.*

9 *Ibid.*

10 *Ibid.*

11 *Biblical Religion, op. cit.*, p. 9: "Man is by nature a philosopher, because he inescapably asks the question of being. He does it in myth and epic, in drama and poetry, in the structure and the vocabulary of any language. It is the special task of philosophy to make this question conscious and to elaborate the answers methodologically.   The prephilosophical ways of putting and answering the question of being prepares the philosophical way.   When philosophy comes into its own, it is not without a long prehistory. Without Homer's poetry, the Dionysian festivals, and the Solonic laws, and above all, without the genius of the Greek language, no Western philosophy as we have it now would have developed." Cf. Bruno Snell, *The Discovery of the Mind*, tr. T. G. Rosenmeyer (Harper & Row, N.Y., 1960), Chapter Nine for a brilliant study in the transition from prephilosophical to philosophical thinking in Greece.

12 *Biblical Religion, op. cit.*, pp. 8-9.

13 *Ibid.*, pp. 11-14. Cf. Tillich's suggestion in "Philosophie und Religion," *GW*, V, pp. 101-109 (first published as "Philosophie und Religion, grundsätzlich" in *Die Religion in Geschichte und Gegenwart, op. cit.*, Band IV) that philosophy as the attitude of the radical question, is a "Nicht-Haben", while religion as "reines Ergriffensein von dem Unbedingten" is "also ein Haben, wenn auch in der Form des "Gehabt-werdens". Thus it would seem that "Philosophie und Religion verhalten sich also wie Nicht-Haben und Haben, wie Fragen und Inder-Antwort-Stehen" (*Ibid.*, p. 101). However this does not mean that philosophy does not share in the original unity of unconditioned and conditioned being, and thus its question is also the result of the original awareness in man of that to which he belongs but from which he is separated. It is this dialectical having and not having which points to the identity of philosophy and religion (*Ibid.*, p. 103ff.). Philosophy's not having is its constant negation of the given and assumed, and its standing in a state of perplexity about being. Philosophy is *aporia*, without a way. Cf., *Biblical Religion, op. cit.*, p. 6; pp. 60-62.

14 GW, IV, *op. cit.*, p. 17.

15 *Protestant Era, op. cit.*, p. 4.

16 GW, IV, *Loc. Cit.*

17 Cf., e.g., Tillich's suggestion that with the dissipation of the classical vision of Greek philosophy in late antiquity, philosophy succumbed to its own despair and thus to scepticism. With the rise of Christianity philosophy surrendered to revelation. Thus, "it was its destiny to become merely a bond-slave. . . . [But] philosophy was not merely the innocent victim of abuse at the hands of religion. The fact that befell philosophy arose out of the inner logic of its own historical development. That philosophy should become handmaid of theology was in a genuine sense its proper fate" (*The Protestant Era, op. cit.*, p. 85).

18 *Ibid.*, pp. 5-7.

19 *Ibid.*, p. 8.

20 *Ibid.*, p. 9; Cf. GW, IV, *op. cit.*, pp. 17-19.

21 *Protestant Era, op. cit.*, p. 9. Tillich describes the career of modern philosophy thus: "Modern philosophy overcomes the existential skepticism of the last period of Greek philosophy by a methodological skepticism as the basis of mathematical science and its technical application. And there is no better or more continuous test for the truth of this type of scientific approach to nature than the fact that the technical creations which are based on it *do* work and work more effectively every day. Ethical theories for the individual and legal theories for the state, fitting this world-transforming activism of modern culture are added to the dominant philosophy of science. Disturbing interferences from the transcendent are eliminated. To this end an empiricist or rationalistic metaphysics pushes the divine out to the fringe of the world – or subordinates it to technical and moral purposes." Modern philosophy represents the methodical mainline of philosophical development worked out by Descartes and Kant, which Tillich contrasts with a second line whose concern is with the irrational, the unconscious and the demonic. The symbol of this second line is the name of Jacob Böhme. Cf. *Interpretation of History, op. cit.*, pp. 123-129.

22 *The Protestant Era, op. cit.*, p. 10.

23 *Interpretation of History, loc. cit.* Tillich's analysis is not completely consistent. He argues in his essay, "Philosophy and Fate" that Hume and Kant helped awaken philosophy to its fate, which suggests that the philosophy of method thought historically after their work. However, in "Kairos and Logos", he places both Hume and Kant within the methodical mainline, which does not think historically at all.

24 *Ibid.*, p. 130.

25 *Ibid.*, p. 135.

26 *Ibid.*, pp. 141-142.

27 *Ibid.*, p. 135: "There is a classical-humanistic conception of knowledge. It is rational and static. And there is a medieval-Catholic conception of knowledge. It is super-rational and static. But there is no Protestant conception of knowledge. It has to be irrational and "dynamic." The constitutive elements Tillich discerns in knowledge are three: first, the element of universal validity, the formal element, which is grounded in the structure of personality as such. Secondly, a material element, which is the world standing opposite the knowing subject. "Here, of course, no evidence but probability is demanded." However, any epistemology lying between Rationalism and Empiricism will

miss the third element of knowledge, viz., the decisional element proper. This element is the "meaningful interpretation of reality", the original views, the basic decisions about reality in which all knowledge is rooted. It is the third element which is explicitly religious (Protestant). *Ibid.*, pp. 141-145: "The decision which is spoken of here is not a moral one. It is moral just as little as it is intellectual. It lies in the deeper stratum upon which both of these rest and which we designate but indistinctly when we term it religious, for it is also not a question of decision in the sense of a specifically religious attitude. What is meant is the attitude toward the Unconditioned, an attitude which is freedom and fate at the same time, and out of which action as well as knowledge flows."

28 *Ibid.*, p. 141. This claim clearly presupposes the unity of unconditioned and conditioned being. To know anything finite is to know it fundamentally in its participation in being-itself, and thus to know anything is to know being-itself or God.

29 *The Protestant Era, op. cit.*, p. 33.

30 *Ibid.*, p. 43.

31 J. L. Adams, *Tillich's Philosophy, op. cit.*, p. 55.

32 Tillich has developed these notions in "Das System der Wissenschaften", "Religionsphilosophie" in GW, I, in *The Protestant Era* and in *Systematic Theology*, volumes one and three. For an attempt to provide the historical background for these concepts, cf. James L. Adams, "What Kind of Religion Has a Place in Higher Education", *Journal of Bible and Religion*, vol. XIII (1945), pp. 184-192.

33 GW, I, *op. cit.*, p. 271.

34 *The Protestant Era, op. cit.*, p. 45: "The difference ... between autonomy and theonomy is that in an autonomous culture the cultural forms appear only in their finite relationship, while in a theonomous culture they appear in their relation to the unconditional."

35 *Ibid.*, p. 57.

36 *Ibid.*, p. 46; ST, III: 249-252.

37 *The Protestant Era, op. cit.*, pp. 56-57.

38 *Ibid.*, p. 43.

39 Unlike heteronomy, however, theonomy does not destroy autonomy. The first quality of a theonomous culture is that "it communicates the experience of holiness, of something ultimate in being and meaning, in all its creations."

However, the second quality of theonomy is "the affirmation of the autonomous forms of the creative process. Theonomy would be destroyed the moment in which a valid logical conclusion was rejected in the name of the ultimate to which theonomy points and the same is true of all other activities of cultural creativity" (ST, III: 251). Autonomy is "the dynamic principle of history. Theonomy, on the other hand, is the substance and meaning of history" (*Prot. Era, op. cit.*, p. 45). Autonomy is fulfilled in theonomy, since the latter is the answer to the question implied in the former (*Ibid.*, p. 46). Cf. Tillich's attempt to read Western spiritual history in relation to the autonomy-heteronomy-theonomy dialectic: ST, I: 85-86.

40 *Prot. Era., op. cit.*, p. 47.

41 *Ibid.*, pp. 46-47.

42 *Ibid.*, p. 47.

43 Bruno Snell has illustrated the logic of uniqueness nicely by pointing to Alcibiades' sketch of Socrates in *The Symposium* in which he claims that the contradictions in Socrates' personality make it impossible for him to be compared with anyone else. "Socrates, in the opinion of Alcibiades, is incomparable and therefore incomprehensible, and that means: unique and individual." B. Snell, *The Discovery of the Mind, op. cit.*, p. 210.

44 It is these considerations which lead Gordon Kaufman ("Can a Man Serve Two Masters", *Theology Today*, Vol. 15, pp. 59-77) to conclude that the historicist element in Tillich's thought is subsumed by his predominantly ahistorical ontology. Kaufman denies that a genuine uniqueness can be claimed for the Christ on Tillich's terms, and he points out that "all of Tillich's notions which start out as historical concepts seem to go over too easily into eternally valid ideas" (*Ibid.*, p. 74 n. 47). Kaufman points out that Tillich claims that the Protestant principle is eternal, beyond the changes of history, that the Church is defined almost completely without reference to the historical reality and that neither of the two types of philosophy of religion under which all religious philosophy is subsumed makes history a central category (*loc. cit.*). A comparable judgment is made by other critics in relation to Tillich's christology. Cf. James Livingston, "Tillich's Christology and Historical Research", *Paul Tillich: Retrospect and Future, op. cit.*, pp. 42-50, and D. Moody Smith Jr., "The Historical Jesus in Paul Tillich's Christology", *Journal of Religion, op. cit.*, pp. 131-147. These latter critics both argue that history is not taken seriously by Tillich, when he argues that the risk of faith is not rooted in the radical contingency of historical knowledge.

45 *Interpretation of History, op. cit.*, pp. 147-148. Tillich makes clear in a footnote what he means by subjectivity. He states: "This warning [that subjectivity is "akairos"] is extremely important at the present moment, when servile philosophers in dictatorial countries abuse the philosophy of Kairos by identi-

fying truth and power, or truth and political leadership, or truth and blood.
·They distort the idea of decision in knowledge by confusing decision and
subjective arbitrariness" (*Ibid.*, p. 147, n. 1). No doubt Tillich is referring
here among others to Emanuel Hirsch, a German theologian, who attempted
to use the *Kairos* doctrine to support Hitler's rise to power in Germany (for
an account of Tillich's relationship to Hirsch, see David Hopper, *Tillich: A
Theological Portrait, op. cit.*, Chapter Three). It is clear, however, that what
Tillich means by subjectivity is sheer individual willfulness or preference without regard to "objective" criteria. How Tillich can use the term "subjectivity"
in this sense after Kierkegaard's pioneering work is of course a major question.

46 *Interpretation of History, op. cit.*, p. 137.

47 *Ibid.*, p. 150.

48 *Ibid.*, pp. 152-156.

49 Tillich has described his relationship to Marx thus: "My relation to Karl Marx
. . . has always been dialectical, combining a Yes and a No. The Yes was
based on the prophetic, humanistic and realistic elements in Marx's passionate style and profound thought, the No on the calculating, materialistic, and
resentful elements in Marx's analysis . . . If one considers the transformation
of the social situation in many countries, the growth of a definite self-consciousness in the industrial masses, the awakening of the social conscience of
the Christian churches, the universal application of the economic-social
method of analysis to the history of thought (note Tillich's positive evaluation
of the concept of "ideology" in Marx, *Interp. of Hist., op. cit.*, p. 154) — all this
under the influence of Marx — then the No must be balanced by a Yes . . .
As long as our thought remains autonomous, our relation to the great
historical figures must be a Yes and a No". "Autobiographical Reflections",
Theology of P. Tillich, op. cit., p. 13.

50 *Interp. of Hist., op. cit.*, p. 156.

51 *Ibid.*, p. 158.

52 *Ibid.*, pp. 158-159.

53 *Ibid.*, pp. 161-162. It seems safe to conclude that Tillich stands within the
Platonic tradition insofar as the idea has ontological reality for him. Ideas are
not merely mental constructs or linguistic conventions by which the flux of
experience is ordered. Rather ideas are dynamic principles, essences, which
have the power to become embodied in existence (cf. *Prot. Era, op. cit.*, p.
13). Tillich departs from Plato by asserting that the idea cannot be grasped
apart from its actualization in historical existence, and, then, never completely
but only ambiguously. This early essay, however, stands in contrast to

Tillich's later, more Platonic thought in which existence in actualizing itself falls away from essence.

54 In 1924, in his review of Ernst Troeltsch's *Historismus Und Seine Probleme* (first published in Theologische Literaturzeitung, XLIX (1924) and reprinted in *The Journal for the Scientific Study of Religion*, Vol. I, No. I (Oct. 1961), pp. 109-114), Tillich acknowledges that there cannot be a final dualism between historical and naturalistic approaches to reality (*Ibid.*, p. 110). However, he does not seem consistent in his views regarding nature. Cf., e.g., *Prot. Era, op. cit.*, p. 48: "There is, in the doctrine of kairos, not only the horizontal dialectic of the historical process but also the vertical dialectic operating between the unconditional and the conditioned. And, finally, there is no logical, physical, or economic necessity in the historical process, according to the doctrine of kairos. It moves through that unity of freedom and fate which distinguishes history from nature."

55 *Interp. of Hist., op. cit.*, p. 164.

56 *Ibid.*, p. 170.

57 *Interpretation of History, op. cit.*, pp. 170-171.

58 *Ibid.*, p. 171. Tillich has also characterized his epistemology in his earlier writings as "belieful realism" or "self-transcendent realism". Cf., "Gläubiger Realismus, I and II", GW, IV, *op. cit.*, pp. 77-106 ("Gläubiger Realismus II" was published as "Realism and Faith" in *The Protestant Era, op. cit.*, pp. 66-82). The notion is also developed in P. Tillich, *The Religious Situation*, tr. H. R. Niebuhr (Meridian Books, N.Y., 1962).

59 Tillich states that belieful or self-transcendent realism is the religious depth of historical realism. He distinguishes the latter from mystical and technological realism. *The Protestant Era, op. cit.*, p. 77.

60 *Interpretation of History, op. cit.*, pp. 174-175.

61 P. Tillich, "Nietzsche and the Bourgeois Spirit", *Journal of the History of Ideas*, vol. 6, 1945, p. 309.

62 We shall discuss Tillich's distinctions between substance or import, content, and form below.

63 Cf. *Interp. of Hist., op. cit.*, p. 173 for confirmation of this judgment: "A moment of time, an event, deserves the name of Kairos, fullness of time in the precise sense, if it can be regarded in its relation to the Unconditioned, and if to speak of it is . . . to speak of the Unconditioned."

64 *The Protestant Era, op. cit.*, pp. 13-14.

65　*Ibid.*, pp. 14-15.

66　*Ibid.*, p. 15.

67　James L. Adams has pointed out that Tillich's philosophy of meaning is clearly conditioned by its Judeo-Christian background and more particularly by Protestant, and especially Lutheran elements. Adams questions whether that philosophy would look the same if it had arisen on Buddhist soil, even though in one early formulation Tillich claims that philosophy is the theory of the principles of meaning (*die Sinnprinzipienlehre*: GW, I: 230ff.) and thus it discerns the universal principles of meaning which are embodied in any concrete sphere of meaning. Adams' question extends, of course, to Tillich's understanding of the history of Western philosophy. In spite of the transhistorical character of its concepts within Western history, when confronted with Eastern thought-forms, the conditioned character of Western philosophy comes clearly into relief. It is this consideration which qualifies Tillich's claim that Western philosophical concepts (e.g., the concept of being) have an *a priori*, universal character. Cf. James L. Adams, "Introduction" to P. Tillich, *What is Religion?*, tr. J. L. Adams (Harper and Row, N.Y., 1969), p. 23. This volume is a translation of three early essays by Tillich all of which are published in the *Gesammelte Werke*. They are: "Religionsphilosophie" originally published in *Lehrbuch der Philosophie*, Herausgegeben von Max Dessoir, Verlag Ullstein, Berlin, Bd 2, 1925); "Die Uberwindung des Religionsbegriffs in der religionsphilosophie" (first published in *Kant-Studien*, 1922); and "Über die Idee einer Theologie der Kultur" (first published as *Religionsphilosophie der Kultur. Zwei Entwürfe von Gustav Radbruch und Paul Tillich* (Reuther und Richard, Berlin, 1919) and published as "Uber die Idee einer Theologie der Kultur" in *Kant-Studien*, 1922).

68　P. Tillich, *Biblical Religion and the Search for Ultimate Reality, op. cit.*, p. 19.

69　GW, IV, *op. cit.*, p. 19: "Das Verhältnis [of philosophy and science] kann also so bestimmt werden dass das wissenschaftliche Fragen auf konkrete, vergegebene Gegenstandsarten geht, das philosophische Fragen auf das Fragen selbst, seinen Character und seinen Gegenstand. Das philosophische Fragen ist radikal es geht auf die Wurzeln; dahin namlich, wo das Fragen überhaupt entsteht, während Wissenschaft das Fragen und seine Gegenstände schon voraussetzt."

70　Note the slightly variant definition of philosophy given in *Biblical Religion, op. cit.*, p. 5. "Philosophy is that cognitive endeavor in which the question of being is asked," and the very early definition of philosophy as "the science of the functions of meaning and their categories" found in *What is Religion?, op. cit.*, p. 41.

71　*Dynamics of Faith, op. cit.*, p. 90: "Philosophy tries to find the universal categories in which being is experienced." Cf. *Biblical Religion, op. cit.*, p. 8:

"philosophy tries to show the presence of being and its structures in the different realms of being, in nature and in man, in history and in value, in knowledge and in religion. But in each case it is not the subject matter as such with which philosophy deals but the constitutive principles of being, that which is always present if a thing participates in the power to be and to resist nonbeing."

72 In Tillich's analysis of the relationship of the truth of philosophy and the truth of faith in *The Dynamics of Faith*, the demand of detached objectivity as the cognitive condition of the theoretical enterprise is clearly stated. Philosophy in its ontological task, Tillich argues, seeks the specification of ultimate reality in *concepts* (the basic tools of theory) in contrast to religion's quest for ultimate reality through symbols. Tillich argues that one can seek ultimate reality conceptually, i.e., theoretically, only in the position of detached objectivity. He writes: "Why does philosophy use concepts and why does faith use symbols if both try to express the same ultimate? The answer . . . is that the relation to the ultimate is not the same in each case. The philosophical relation is in principle a detached description of the basic structure in which the ultimate manifests itself. The relation of faith is in principle an involved expression of concern about the meaning of the ultimate for the faithful" (*Dynamics of Faith, op. cit.*, p. 91).

73 *Ibid.*, pp. 91-92.

74 See Tillich's defense of the speculative task of philosophy in *Biblical Religion, op. cit.*, pp. 6-8. John Cobb has argued that Tillich uses phenomenology as a descriptive discipline and ontology has a more speculative function. Of course, both phenomenology and ontology belong to philosophy as such. Cf. J. Cobb, *Living Options in Protestant Theology, op. cit.*, pp. 262ff.

Chapter Seven

Tillich's Conception of Theology: The Early Writings

Tillich's conception of theology has passed through a significant development as can be seen by comparing his earlier and later writings. There is, however, within this development a clearly consistent notion of the nature, structure and task of theology, even though one can find alternative ways in which Tillich formulates this notion within his theological career. No doubt these alternative formulations are to be explained by the differing intellectual and cultural contexts in which Tillich thought as well as the internal shifts which can be observed within his thought itself. We shall look at some of the early formulations of the character of theology in order to attempt to discern the formative components involved in the theological enterprise as Tillich understands it. Then we shall concentrate upon the mature conception as it is expressed in the *Systematic Theology* and other later writings.

We have stated previously that one of Tillich's guiding concerns is to save theology from the charge that it deals fundamentally with an esoteric and eccentric sphere of human life, a sphere which is the concern of a small minority of men, and thus whatever knowledge it may be said to have is irrelevant to the larger culture. When theology is seen this way, it is at best merely one form of knowledge besides others and the concern of a few. In this case since the object of theology is not identical with the universal structure of reality with which every cultural act is concerned, it can relate to man's cultural life only by heteronomously subjecting the autonomous forms of culture to the limited and therefore vitiating authority of its object.

The conception of theology which Tillich formulated in three relatively early essays ("On the Idea of a Theology of Culture" [1919]; "Das System der Wissenschaften" [1923]; and "The Philosophy of Religion" [1925]) is characterized by the attempt to distinguish theology from other cognitive disciplines on the one hand and on the other to establish the "relevance" of theology to these disciplines by showing that the object of theology is, in fact, the *prius* of all thought and knowledge, of every cultural form and every spiritual act. This program can be seen especially in "Das System der Wissenschaften". In speaking about this study Tillich asserts:

> I attempted to win a place for theology within the totality of human knowledge. The success of this analysis presupposes that the theonomous character of knowledge itself must be acknowledged; that is to say, we must understand that thought itself is rooted in the Absolute as the ground and abyss of meaning. Theology takes as its explicit object that which is the implicit presupposition of all knowledge. Thus theology and philosophy, religion and knowledge, embrace one another. In light of the boundary position, this appears as their real relationship.[1]

In relation to the conceptuality employed in "Das System der Wissenschaften," which has been briefly discussed above, Tillich places theology within the system of the sciences as one of the cultural sciences (in contrast to the sciences of thinking and the empirical sciences), the latter being especially concerned with the notion of meaning, its functions and categories. As Tillich's statement above indicates, theology here is brought into relationship with philosophy as another of the cultural sciences. It is necessary to examine Tillich's conception of theology, then, in relation to the conception of philosophy given in "Das System der Wissenschaften" in order to grasp clearly Tillich's conception of the theological enterprise and the relationship between theology and philosophy.[2]

Philosophy, Tillich defines as "die Zinnprinzipienlehre oder die Lehre von den geistigen Funktionen und Kategorian."[3] The concept of meaning occupies a central position in Tillich's thought, and by defining philosophy as the doctrine of the principles of meaning, Tillich establishes quite early in his thought the metadisciplinary character of philosophy, which we have observed above. Philosophy is not confined exclusively to any particular sphere of meaning as are the other disciplines, but rather it seeks to explicate the general structure of meaning which is operative in every sphere of meaning. A brief analysis of Tillich's theory of meaning should make this clear.

Meaning is a function of spirit (*Geist*). Hence, philosophy can also be defined as the doctrine of the spiritual functions and categories. The system of knowledge contains three fundamental elements, thought (*Denken*), being (*Sein*), and spirit (*Geist*) to which correspond the three groups of disciplines (*Wissenschaften*), the thought disciplines (*die Denk-oder Idealwissenschaften*), the empirical disciplines (*die Seins-oder Realwissenschaften*) and the cultural disciplines (*die Geistes-oder Normwissenschaften*). The cultural disciplines attempt to achieve a synthesis of knowledge in which the ideal and real elements are united in the act of knowledge, which is at the same time an actualization of spiritual and cultural life.

The idealistic influence under which "Das System der Wissenschaften" was written[4] makes it especially difficult to grasp Tillich's conception of spirit. However, if we take the more exhaustive formulation of the notion of spirit which appears in ST, III as a guide, it becomes clear that spirit is a concept by which Tillich is able to speak about man, which incorporates both the aspects of power and meaning which characterize human experience. Spirit comes to expression in man as the power of meaning actualization.[5] J. L. Adams has defined Tillich's use of the term spirit in "Das System der Wissenschaften" as follows:

> Spirit (*Geist*) is the concept that denotes the dynamic power of creativity in man. It is not to be identified with reason or with creative intellect; it is rather in between the two. It unites elements of the universal, the rational, the existent, the creative, and the individual. It is dependent on thought and being. Spirit is the self-determination of thought in the realm of existence.[6]

It would not be incorrect, then, to say that spirit designates the capacity of man to live in structures of meaning which are not merely identical with the biological and psychological givenness of the human reality. The power of man as a spirit-bearing Gestalt (*die geisttragende Gestalt*) is precisely the power of differentiation from the mere givenness of things in the direction of meaning. This means that

> Voraussetzung der Geistverwirklichung ist also die vollkommene Loslösung eines Seienden von der unmittelbaren Gebundenheit an seine endliche Form. Voraussetzung des Geistes ist die Freiheit.[7]

The freedom of man in the dimension of spirit is actualized in the creative, spiritual act. In Adam's words:

> Every spiritual act is . . . an individual meaningful act fusing thought and being. It is an individual meaning-fulfilling act. Considered in its cultural context, the reality in which the spirit — or the spirit-bearing form — lives and creates is meaningful reality. This meaningful reality represents the creative unity of thought, being, and intuited meaning. Thus it represents the unity of intention toward the universal and the realization of creative individuality.[8]

Meaning, then, is realized in the spiritual act, which is to say that spirit lives within the structure of meaning or as Tillich has put it "spirit is always [the medium for] the actualization of meaning." Every spiritual act intends "a systematic interconnection of meaning."[9] Consequently there are three basic elements within the structure of meaning which make the awareness of meaning possible. These are:

> First, an awareness of the interconnection of meaning in which every separate meaning stands and without which it would be meaningless. Second, an awareness of the ultimate meaningfulness of the interconnection of meaning and, through that, of every particular meaning, i.e., the consciousness of an unconditioned meaning which is present in every particular meaning. Third, an awareness of the demand under which every particular meaning stands, the demand to fulfill the unconditioned meaning.[10]

The spiritual act actualizes particular meanings, but the meaningfulness of these meanings is dependent upon the total interconnection of meaning, i.e., the "world." However, the meaningfulness of the totality of meaning is not itself grounded in that totality. Tillich asserts:

> Even the totality of meaning need not be meaningful, but rather could disappear, like every particular meaning, in the abyss (*Abgrund*) of meaninglessness, if the presupposition of an unconditioned meaningfulness were not alive in every act of meaning. This unconditionality of meaning is itself, however, not a meaning, but rather is the ground of meaning.[11]

On the basis of these distinctions in the structure of meaning, Tillich develops a more complex conceptual framework by which his notion of meaning is to be understood. The particular meanings and their interconnection, Tillich calls the "forms of meaning" and the unconditioned meaning, which is the ground of all particular meanings as well as the totality of meaning, he calls the "import of meaning" (*Sinngehalt*). The import of meaning is to be further distinguished from the delimited meaning of any form or forms of meaning, the individual import or "content" (*Inhalt*) of the particular form. The notion of the import of meaning is the expression of the motif of the unconditionality of ultimate reality (being-itself) within Tillich's philosophy of meaning. As such the import of meaning stands in the dialectical relationship of Yes and No to the forms and content of meaning. Tillich writes:

> By the import of meaning we . . . do not mean the import attaching to the significance of a particular consummation of meaning, but rather to the meaningfulness that gives to every particular meaning its reality, significance, and essentiality . . . The import of meaning has for the form of meaning on the one hand the significance of the ground of meaningfulness; on the other hand it functions over against the form as the demand for an unconditioned fulfillment in meaning, a demand with which only the complete or perfect connection of all meaning could comply — the unconditioned form. However, the unconditioned form of meaning is an idea contradictory to the relation of form and import. The meaningfulness of all meaning is the ground, but it is also the abyss of every meaning, even of an unconditioned form of meaning. The idea that in an unconditioned form of meaning the ground of meaning exhausts itself would abolish the inner infinity of meaning; it would not be able to get rid of the possibility that all meaning might sink into meaninglessness. The unconditioned meaningfulness of all meaning depends

upon the awareness of the inexhaustibility of meaning in the ground of meaning.[12]

Thus far, we have seen that the structure of meaning involves for Tillich the notions of the concrete forms of meaning, their content, their universal interconnection, and the import of meaning, that to which every form, content and the universal context of meaning refer for their ultimate meaningfulness. It is from these notions that the philosophical doctrine of the principles of meaning is derived. The principles of meaning, we have seen, Tillich breaks down into the "sinngebenden Funktionen und Kategorien." These are defined as follows:

> Unter Funktionen verstehen wir diejenigen geistigen Aktrichtungen, durch die selbständige Sinngebiete abgegrenzt werden, unter Kategorien die Formen, durch die in den Sinngebieten Objekte konstituiert werden.[13]

A function of meaning, then, is a spiritual act which demarcates a pattern or sphere of meaning from the total structure of meaning and the categories are the forms of meaning which are appropriate to a particular region of meaning, or in Tillich's more phenomenological language, which constitutes the object which is appropriate to a particular region of meaning. There is, for Tillich, both a general philosophical task of delineating the principles of meaning in themselves with the concentration upon the import of meaning rather than the forms. This is theonomous philosophy. However, there is also a philosophy of the principle of meaning, the functions and categories, of each sphere of meaning. Philosophy, then, must concentrate upon the forms of meaning, and it becomes autonomous.[14] Here philosophy becomes the philosophy of each special meaning function, i.e., philosophy of art, philosophy of law, philosophy of morality, etc.

The principles of meaning are actualized within space and time in the creative acts of spirit. Their actualization constitutes the material of meaning, and since this actualization occurs within history (*Geschichte*) the task of developing the doctrine of the material of meaning (*Die Sinnmateriallehre*) falls to the cultural science Tillich designates as "Geistesgeschichte". History of culture is distinguished from history (*Historie*) in the sense that it is not fundamentally concerned with questions of time and causality and it is distinguished from "Kulturgeschichte," since it seeks to understand the material of meaning from the point of view of the principles of meaning.[15]

The structure of meaning includes not only the principles of meaning and the materials of meaning, for Tillich. Every act of meaning is actualized in relation to norms of meaning and it is the task of the discipline Tillich calls "die Sinnormenlehre oder Systematik" to delineate the norms of meaning as they emerge out of the concrete spheres of meaning. Systematics, therefore, is concerned with the question of validity as it relates to the concrete standpoint of a particular, individual sphere of meaning. Tillich writes:

> Das Sinnprinzip, erfüllt mit dem Sinnmaterial, wird zur Sinnorm. Das Sinnprinzip ist der Intentation (*sic*) nach allgemein. Es gilt fur jede Erscheinung des von ihm getragenen Sinngebeites. Die Sinnorm ist hindurchgegangen durch die Geschichte, ist geboren an einem bestimmten historischen Ort und hat darum die Konkretheit und Besonderheit der individuellen geistigen Schöpfung. Sie ist ihrer Intention nach nicht *allgemein*, wohl aber allgemeingültig . . . Sie will die konkrete Erfüllung des abstrakt-allgemeinen Sinnprinzips sein.[16]

The doctrine of the norms of meaning seeks the universally valid, but it does so, in contrast to philosophy, not in terms of the a priori, universal forms and categories, but in relation to the concrete material of a given sphere of meaning.[17] Tillich illustrates the function of systematics in relation to the sphere of meaning with the following examples. Philosophy determines the principles of meaning of a sphere of meaning by seeking to define the universal character of the meaning sphere. Moral philosophy, for example, asks "What is morality?" and normative ethics (i.e., the systematics of morality as a sphere of meaning) asks about the norms by which the moral may be determined. Philosophy of art seeks to define the essence of art and aesthetics seeks the norms by which the beautiful is to be discerned.[18]

The schema of the cultural sciences Tillich summarizes in these terms:

> Every genuine cultural science consciously or unconsciously proceeds in [a] threefold way. It proceeds from a universal function of the spirit and the forms through which objects are constituted therein. It then shows in a critical way the actualization of this essential function in the various directions of historical development. Finally, it gives its own systematic solution on the basis of the problems that are brought to the fore by the conceptualization of the essence of the thing and by the cultural history. This threefold relationship appears as the philosophy of art, the cultural history of art, and normative aesthetics; or as the philosophy of knowing (*Erkennen*), the cultural history of science, and a normative theory of science; or as the philosophy of law, the cultural history of law, and a normative history of law, etc.[19]

It is in relation to this total schema that Tillich, in his early writings, explicates the nature of theology. As a cultural science theology is concerned with meaning. It works within the structure of meaning defined above. Tillich defines theology as "theonome Systematik", which is to say that it is, like metaphysics, directed toward the unconditioned import of meaning disclosed within the forms of meaning on the one hand, but as a normative science it is rooted in the concrete sphere of meaning on the other. This gives theology both its universal and concrete character.

A theonomous systematics, theology is "theonome Sinnormenlehre." As a theonomous science of the norms of meaning, theology cannot be considered as one science among others. Rather theology is justified only when it functions as theonomous systematics. Thus:

> Die Wahreit der Theologie is abhängig von dem Mass, in dem sie sich als selbständige Wissenschaft aufhebt und in Einheit mit der autonomen Systematik normative Geisteswissenschaft überhaupt ist.[20]

Theology, then, moves between two poles. It functions within the religious sphere, but it also points to the universally valid among the other spheres of meaning.

Properly speaking, theology is the normative science of the religious function. Consequently, it stands in dialectical relationship to the philosophy of religion and the cultural history of religion.

Tillich describes the functions and the relationship of the three disciplines thus:

> Philosophy of religion is the theory of the religious function and its categories. Theology is the normative and systematic presentation of the concrete realization of the concept "religion." The cultural history of religion acts as a bridge between philosophy of religion and theology. Thus philosophy of religion and theology are two elements of a single normative cultural science of religion . . . The separation of philosophy of religion and theology is no better founded than the separation of philosophy of art and normative aesthetics . . . Every theology is dependent upon the presupposition of a concept of the essence of religion. Every philosophy of religion is dependent upon the concept of the norm of religion. And both are dependent upon comprehension of the cultural-historical material.[21]

In this formulation of the task of theology one can see a clear distinction drawn between philosophy of religion and theology as well as the assertion of their dialectical interrelationship made on the basis of the schema of the philosophy of meaning or the unified cultural science. We must now examine two issues which Tillich's analysis of the theological task raises for us. First, we must explore in more detail the conception of theology as the normative science of religion and its relationship to the philosophy of religion. Secondly, we must ask how theology can be the meaning-boundary transcending discipline Tillich claims it is, if its task is the establishment of the norm of religion, or the religious function, i.e., if its object is in some sense religion itself. The answer to this second question lies in Tillich's conception of religion.

Tillich argues that the notion of theology as theonomous systematics was adequately realized in the Middle Ages and as such it included autonomy in itself. However, with the disintegration of the medieval synthesis, theonomy became heteronomous and theology became a particular science alongside which the autonomous sciences arose. The cultural conflict between heteronomy and autonomy theology has inherited and now finds itself involved in this conflict. "Das ist verhängnisvoll für sie geworden, denn es widerspricht ihrem Wesen, eine Wissenschaft neben anderen zu sein."[22]

In the midst of this situation, Tillich sees theology as understood both heteronomously and autonomously. In its autonomous form, theology is understood as "profan-rational" in which it is made into a science of religion, of Christianity, of faith. The strength of "dieser Auffassung liegt der richtige Gedanke zu Grunde, dass Gott nicht ein Object neben anderen sein kann und dass es darum keine Wissenschaft von Gott neben anderen Wissenschaften geben könne."[23] Liberal theology protests the reduction of theology to rational metaphysics, but liberal theology also shows that theology disappears if it is confined to a purely autonomous direction. The alternative, however, is not granting to theology some other object in place of God, since the autonomous sciences deal with all other objects. Theology would then become a "praktische Arbeitsgemeinschaft für Probleme der Religion im allgemeinen und des Christentums im besonderen", but it would "damit aber als selbständige Wissenschaft aufgehört haben zu existieren."[24]

The "religiös-heteronome" view of theology is also clearly inadequate. It

der Theologie den Charakter als selbständige Wissenschaft erhalten will, ohne doch den Mut zu haben, sie zur theonomen Geisteswissenschaft schlechthin zu machen. Sie gibt den konfessionellen Symbolen, die einer theonom erfüllten Geisteslage entstammen, absolute Bedeutung und kommt dadurch auf allen Gebieten in Konflikte mit dem autonomen Prozess. Sie halt an ihrer metaphysischen Richtung fest und weiss sich als Wissenschaft von Gott, aber sie vergisst, dass die metaphysischen Symbole abhängig sind von den Begriffen und Anschauungen, die der autonome Geistesprozess hervorbringt. Sie macht dadurch Gott zu einem Objekt neben anderen und kann den übergang in rationale Metaphysik nicht aufhalten. Sie bewirkt, wo sie herrscht, die Zerspaltung des Bewusstseins in zwei Arten von Wahrheiten, die beide den Anspruch erheben, in dem gleichen Sinne richtig zu sein. Dieser Zwiespalt würde die Einheit des Geisteslebens zersprengen, wenn nicht daurend Auswege gefunden würden: Das Opfer der Autonomie als religiöse Askese im Katholizismus, die Abschiebung des Religiösen in die persönlich-praktische Sphäre in der englisch-amerikanischen Welt, die überdeckung des Widerspruchs durch die Künste der theologischen Apologetik im lutherischen Protestantismus. Weil aber all dies Mittel unzureichend sind, so triumphiert schliesslich doch immer wieder die Auflösung der Theologie in profan-rationale Wissenschaft.[25]

When theology is understood neither autonomously nor heteronomously, but rather as theonomous systematics, it does not lose its religious substance in autonomy nor does it become preoccupied with an object or meaning function next to others. Its tasks move in a different direction. As the normative science of religion, theology is not to be confused with the "seinswissenschaftliche Betrachtung der Religion und des Christentums." Theology is to be distinguished from psychology, philology and the history of religion in general or of a particular religion. Thus, historical theology involves not only philology and history, but it goes beyond them in two directions. It is "theonome Geistesgeschichte" and "normative Exegese." As the former, historical theology is not merely concerned with the history of Christianity or of religion in general but with "den gesamten Prozess ser Geistverwirklichung."[26]

Tillich's understanding of the normative exegetical task of theology adumbrates the method of correlation of his later thought. He writes:

> . . . die Theologie arbeitet aus dem konkrete Geistprozess heraus und ist gebunden an die klassischen Symbole, in denen die theonome überzeugung ihren Ausdruck gefunden hat. Daraus ergibt sich für sie die doppelte Aufgabe, den originalen Geist der religiösen Urkunden darzustellen und ihn in das gegenwärtige Bewusststein zu überfuhren.[27]

Theology's rootage in history and its being bound to the classical symbols, points to an important feature of its nature, viz., that it is *concrete-confessional*. Theology is centered in the religious function, and religion is carried by the Church "als der symboleschaffenden Gemeinschaft." Thus

> ergibt sich der konkret konfessionelle Charakter der Theologie, der auch dann nicht fehlen würde wenn die Menschheit in *einer* Konfession zusammengeschlossen ware. Auch dann würde die Theologie individuell-schöpferisch, d.h. konfessionell sein. Ebensowenig, wie die Rechtslehre ein rationales Naturrecht, darf die Theologie eine rationale Vernuftreligion suchen. Sie kann ihr normatives System nur aus den konkreten Normen der lebendigen Konfessionen entnehmen.[28]

Tillich is quick to point out that the concrete-confessional character of theology does not vitiate its character as a cultural science.
In all his early writings, Tillich insists that theology, too, is directed
toward the universal, even though it must seek the universal
through the concrete-confessional symbol.[29] This means that theology is no less "universally valid" than philosophy itself.

As theonomous systematics, then, theology is concerned with the
meaning norms of the religious function; of course, theology must
determine the norm theonomously, i.e. by its capacity to point
beyond itself to the Unconditioned. The Unconditioned is the
import of meaning, which is not itself a concrete meaning, but the
ground and abyss of all meaning. As such it is that which is universally relevant and valid for all spheres of meaning.

The conceptual-confessional direction of theology toward the
Unconditioned establishes its theonomous character and its universal relevance, but its concrete-confessional character also grounds
it in the forms of meaning in which spirit actualizes itself. Consequently, not only must theology establish its relevance to the other
theonomous disciplines of the cultural sciences but to the
autonomous disciplines as well, i.e. not only to these theoretical
and practical disciplines which are directed toward the unconditioned import of meaning (metaphysics in the theoretical and
ethics in the practical sphere, what Tillich calls the "fundierenden"
or supporting functions) but also to the theoretical and practical
disciplines directed toward the forms of meaning (the "fundierten"
or supported functions).[30]

Theology achieves its relationship to these disciplines on the
basis of the way theonomy and autonomy are expressed within
them and within the dialectical relationship of the two attitudes.
The supporting disciplines or what we have ambiguously called the
theonomous disciplines, are more open to the "theonomous intention" while the supported disciplines obviously express the
"autonomous intention." Tillich formulates the matter thus:

> Die Dialektik von Theonomie und Autonomie ist in allen Sinnfunktionen
> wirksam, aber sie äussert sich anders in den fundierenden als in den
> fundierten Funktionen. In den fundierenden Funktionen soll das Unbe-

dingte als Unbedingtes erfasst und verwirklicht werden, in den fundierten Funktionen sollen die bedingten Formen in ihrer Selbständigkeit und Gültigkeit zur Sinnerfüllung kommen. Daraus folgt, dass eine direkte theonome Intention nur in der fundierenden Sinnspare möglicht ist, eine direkte autonome Intention nur in den fundierten Sinnsphären. Im ersten Falle wird die Autonomie nur indirekt wirksam, in der Art der Symbol wahl. Im zweiten Fall wird die Theonomie nur indirekt wirksam, in der Art der Formerfassung. Einen unmittelbaren Ausdruck der Theonomie gibt es also nur in Metaphysik und Ethik.[31]

Since there is a direct theonomous intention in metaphysics, theology becomes theonomous metaphysics at that point in its structure where theonomy is most clearly manifest.[32] Theology can become theonomous metaphysics in its dogmatic function provided that heteronomy is avoided and the autonomy of the dogmatic material is preserved on the one hand, i.e. that its symbolic character is fully acknowledged and on the other hand that the Unconditioned is grasped through the dogmatic symbol.

Tillich argues that the word "Dogmatics" means that the symbols which it uses are not subjectively selected but are rather the expression of the religious community. The concrete-confessional character of theology, i.e. its dependence upon the religious community and its symbols, Tillich reiterates, does not impair the truth value of Dogmatics. This could only happen if the symbols of the community were obligatory in the sense that the dogmatic theologian had to present orthodox dogma rather than seek "die Wahrheit im Dogma."

Dogma stands between myth and metaphysics as a rational form. It can be identified with neither but is the synthesis of both. Tillich writes:

Die unmittelbarste Form der theonomomen Metaphysik ist die Mythenbildung. Sie liegt vor der Enstehung einer autonomen Wissenschaft. Die rationalste Form ist die Metaphysik. Sie benutzt die Symbole, die eine autonome Wissenschaft ihr lifert. Aber in jedem *Mythos*, solange er mehr ist als Phantastik, liegt ein autonomes Element, ein Wille zu erkennender Welterfassung, und in jeder Metaphysik, solange sie mehr ist als Lehre von der reinen Form, liegt ein theonomous Element, ein mythischer Wille, das Unbedingte zu erfassen. Mythos und Metaphysik stehen also unter der gleichen Dialektik wie Sein und Denken, wie Gehalt und Form. Die Synthese beider ist das *Dogma*, d.h. der Versuch, wissenschaftliche Begriffe als theonome Symbole

zu verwenden . . . Wo es dagegen delingt, in schöpferischer Weise die meta-
physiche Symbolik einerseits der theonomen Grundhaltung, andererseits
dem autonomen Begriffsmaterial anzupassen, da leistet die Dogmatik die
synthetische Aufgabe, zu der sie berufen ist: Sie wird zur Theonomen Metaphysik.[33]

Theonomy can only be indirectly expressed in the supported
functions. Consequently, there can be no theonomous epistemology or aesthetics, but there can be a theonomous attitude as well as
an autonomous one expressed in both these disciplines. Tillich
concludes from this situation that theology

keine theologische Asthetik und Wissenschaftslehre geben kann. Gegenüber
dem autonomen Prozess der Sinnerfüllung hat die Theologie nur die Aufgabe, Material fur die theonome Systematik auszuwahlen. Sie kann zeigen,
welche Haltungen der Wissenschaft und Kunst der Theonomie entsprechen
und welche Begriffe und Anschauungen demegmäss für die theonome Sym-
bolbildung in Betracht kommen. Aber sie kann nicht selbst Material in den
fundierten Sphären schaffen.[34]

The relevance of theology to the supported disciplines of the
theoretical sphere consists not in interfering heteronomously with
their proper tasks, but rather of pointing to the presence within
them of an ultimate, theonomous attitude of which these disciplines themselves may be unaware and at the same time showing
how the very conceptual material of these disciplines point to the
Unconditioned or theonomy. This is clearly a task of theology of
culture about which we shall speak below.[35]

The theonomous function of theology can be seen clearly in
Tillich's expansion of the discipline of liturgics beyond the heteronomous restriction to "den spezifisch kirchlichen Andachtsfor-
men." This heteronomy has occurred especially in Protestantism,
which has confined liturgics to practical theology. However, when
liturgics is seen in the context of the supporting and supported disciplines of the cultural sciences, it cannot be confined to specific
forms of devotion of the church nor is it a discipline of practical
theology. Rather, "Die Andactsformenlehre ist die Ausstrahlung
der theonomen Metaphysik in die kunstlerische und wissenschaftliche Welterfassung."[36]

In the practical sphere, theology as the doctrine of the norms of meaning must also establish its relationship to ethics as the supporting function and law and community as the supported functions. The normative relationship of theology to these disciplines follows the same pattern as that developed for the theoretical sphere, viz., the determination of a genuine theonomy within these meaning-functions and the disciplines appropriate to them, which means avoiding heteronomy on the one hand and pointing autonomy toward its fulfillment in theonomy without negating its autonomous character on the other.

In discussing ethics as the supporting function of the practical sphere, Tillich insists that the split between theological and philosophical ethics indicates the split in truth and consciousness embodied in the cultural conflict between theonomy and autonomy. This conflict "kann nur überwunden werden durch die Einigung von theonomer Intention und autonomen Ausdrucksformen in einem theonomen Ethos."[37] This means that

Theologische Ethik ist Lehre vom theonomen Ethos (Frömmigkeitslehre). Entsprechend der Spannung von Mythos und Metaphysik besteht in der Frömmigkeitslehre die Spannung von *Kultus und Ethos*. Wie der Mythos vor Entstehung einer rationaen (sic) Wissenschaft liegt, so der Kultus vor Entstehung eines rationalen Rechts — und Gemeinschaftbewusstseins. Wie die Metaphysik die rationalen Wissenschaftsformen zur theonomen Symbolik verwendet, so das Ethos die rationalen Rechts-und Gemeinschaftsformen zur Darstellung der Frömmigkeit.[38]

Clearly, Ethos is not concerned with piety as an exclusive cultic function (just as liturgy is not confined to cultic forms of devotion alone), but rather seeks a theonomous community in which the direction toward the Unconditioned is transparent in all its forms.[39] In seeking the theonomous community, a theonomous ethos raises its critique against both heteronomy and autonomy by seeking a synthesis between cultic and ethical acts. Hence:

Auf die Synthese von Kultus und Ethos ist die Lehre von der Frömmigkeit gerichtet. Die Frömmigkeit kann wie das Dogma in heteronomer Weise Recht und Gemeinschaft und Persönlichkeit zersterenden Konflikten, die der Ausdruck dafür sind, dass die Synthese von Kultus und Ethos im theonomen Ethos nicht erreicht ist. Andererseits würde die Frömmigkeit aufhören, Ethos zu sein, wenn sie auf ihre theonome Intention verzichtet und lediglich gültige Gemeinschafts-oder Personlichkeitsformen schaffen wollte. Sie findet ihre sinngemässe Erfüllung nur in der Einheit von theonomer Intention und autonomer Verwirklichungsform.[40]

The supported functions of the practical sphere are autonomous in their intention, and as in the theoretical sphere, there can be no theonomous political science nor jurisprudence. Consequently, theology executes its normative task in relation to these disciplines by standing guard against the incursions of heteronomy into the forms of law and community and implicitly struggling toward theonomous forms of personality. It thus respects the genuinely autonomous forms of law and community, while seeking to maintain a theonomous attitude within these disciplines. Rather than concentrating upon the forms of the religious community alone

Für die Theologie ergibt sich aus dem Verhältnis der Theonomie zu Gemeinschaft und Recht eine der Andachtsformenlehre entsprechende Kultgemeindelehre. Sie wählt aus Rechts-und Gemeinschaftsformen diejenigen aus, die fur die Darstellung des theonomen Ethos bedeutungsvoll sind. Sie beschränkt sich dabei nicht auf die spezifisch kirchlichen Formen, wie sie es im Protestantismus tat, mit dem Erfolg, dass sie zu einem Teil der praktischen Theologie wurde und ihre systematische Bedeutung vergass. Sie sucht vielmehr die vom theonomen Ethos getragenen Formen in allen Gemeinschaftsund Rechtsbeziehungen auf und zeigt die Ausstrahlung des theonomen Ethos in der gesamten Sphäre der sinnerfüllten Seinsbeziehungen. Sie selbst aber kann in ihnen keine Formen schaffen. Denn nur durch das Ethos kann die Theonomie auf Recht und Gemeinschaft einwirken.[41]

Just as there can be no theological metaphysics, e.g., a rational metaphysics which seeks to prove the existence of God, so there can be no theological ethics, and consequently the duplicity of two forms of truth and the divided consciousness this presupposes is overcome by theology's being understood as theonomous systematics. There can be neither a double truth nor a double morality. Thus, theology as the doctrine of the norms of meaning works both toward a theonomous metaphysics in the theoretical sphere and a theonomous ethos in the practical sphere. It also establishes its relevance to the cultural disciplines on the one hand by pointing their autonomous forms toward the Unconditioned meaning in which they are both upheld and fulfilled in their autonomy and on the other it uses the conceptual and social forms these disciplines produce to create a theonomous cultural science. The cultural relevance of theology, then, in "Das System der Wissenschaften" could not be more obvious.[42]

Having examined the cultural function of theology as it is formulated in Tillich's early period in some detail, we return now to the question of its relationship to religion. We have seen that theology is concrete-confessional, i.e., it is bound to the classical symbols of the religious community and its primary function is the determination of the norm of religion. How, then, is theology to execute its primary task and at the same time declare itself in unity with autonomous systematics, a normative cultural science in general? There are other ways of putting the issue before us. Perhaps the most effective is this: if religion is a distinct function of meaning embodied in definite cultic communities, and if theology is grounded in the religious function, how can it claim to be at the same time theology of culture if religion is only one meaning-function of culture? It is necessary now to examine Tillich's understanding of religion and philosophy of religion to answer this question.

In his early writings, Tillich has chosen to define the issue stated above in his own terms. In his presentation of the problem before us, for example, in "The Philosophy of Religion" one can see in the background the debate in continental theology in the 20s and 30s concerning the nature of religion and revelation and the relationship of religion and culture.[43] Philosophy of religion, as we have seen, is "the theory of the religious function and its categories." However, in approaching religion, philosophy of religion finds itself confronted by a meaning-reality, which resists becoming an object of philosophy. Religion claims exemption from the generalizing concept. In fact

Concepts such as "revelation" and "redemption" stand in clear opposition to the concept "religion." They express an action happening only once, transcendent in origin and transforming in its effect on reality, while "religion" subordinates a whole series of spiritual acts and cultural creations under a general concept. "Revelation" speaks of a divine, "religion" of a human, action. "Revelation" speaks of an absolute, singular, exclusive, and self-sufficient happening; "religion" refers to merely relative occurrences, always recurring and never exclusive. "Revelation" speaks of the entrance of a new reality of life and a necessary function of the spirit. "Religion" speaks of culture, "revelation" of that which lies beyond culture. For this religion feels an assault is made upon its inmost essence when it is called religion. For that reason it closes its mind to philosophy of religion and opens itself at most to theology, insofar as the latter is nothing other than a "science" of revelation.[44]

In these terms, then, the tension between theology as the normative science of religion and theology of culture takes on an added dimension, i.e. religion stands in conflict with culture and is thus not accessible to the conceptuality of theology as a cultural science, which, as we have seen, includes the disciplines of philosophy, metaphysics, epistemology, aesthetics, ethics, political science and jurisprudence. Obviously, this character of religion puts philosophy of religion and a theology informed by it at an extreme disadvantage, for it means that the former

must either dissolve away the object it wishes to grasp or declare itself null and void. If it does not recognize religion's claim to revelation, then it misses its object and does not speak of genuine religion. If, on the other hand, it acknowledges the claim to revelation, then it becomes theology.[45]

At the same time, if theology is rooted in a revelation which is utterly discontinuous with all cultural forms, then, it can have no essential relationship to philosophy or the other cultural forms, i.e., it becomes at best a positivistic science of religion.

For Tillich this state of affairs is utterly unacceptable. From the point of view of philosophy, it can neither dissolve the religious object nor accept the claim that religion is inaccessible to its critical scrutiny. The latter alternative especially would mean not only the dissolution of philosophy of religion but of philosophy in general, for

if there is one object that remains fundamentally closed to philosophy, then philosophy's claim over every object is brought into question. For then it would . . . be in no position to draw for itself the borderline between this reserved subject matter (i.e., religion) and other fields of research. In fact, it might be possible that revelation would extend its claim to all disciplines, and that philosophy would have no weapon with which to resist this claim. If it surrenders at one point, it must surrender at every point.[46]

There is, then, an antithesis between philosophy and religion, which for Tillich is destructive of the unity of consciousness and of truth if it is not resolved by way of synthesis, which is the inner overcoming of the antithesis. "The way of synthesis alone," Tillich asserts

is genuine and legitimate. It is required, even if it fails again and again. But it is not necessary that it fail. For there is a point in the doctrine of revelation and philosophy at which the two are one. To find this point and from there to construct a synthetic solution is the decisive task of the philosophy of religion.[47]

It seems clear that theology alone cannot create the synthesis. Rather a genuine synthesis can be achieved only by theology's accepting a philosophical definition of religion and thus allowing its own character to be shaped by the philosophical definition given. This means that while the two disciplines are to be distinguished, there is a philosophical dimension to theology and a theological dimension to philosophy. Everything turns, therefore, upon the definition of religion contributed by philosophy. Neither the relationship of religion to the other spheres of meaning nor of theology to the other disciplines can be discussed without such a critical and constructive definition.

The most basic confusion to be overcome in a genuine synthesis between religion and culture is the notion that religion is a function "alongside" other functions and theology a discipline among others. Tillich asserts:

The "alongsidedness" must not be permitted to stand; that is religion and theology must not remain alongside the other functions and sciences. The synthesis under discussion . . . can be attained only if the normative science of religion [i.e., theology] is in the same sense a normative cultural science in general, and only if religion is presented not as one function alongside others but as an attitude in all the other functions.[48]

If philosophy of religion can demonstrate that religion is not confined to a specific function among others, but rather is a functional dimension in every sphere of meaning, then theology by being the normative science of religion, is necessarily related to the totality of meaning-functions in which the religious dimension is always present. Thus, what Tillich later came to call philosophical theology, in contrast to kerygmatic theology, i.e. a theology which fully acknowledges a philosophical dimension within itself, is at the same time a theology of culture, since it is within culture that the religious function (or perhaps more accurately the religious meta-function) is actualized. It is now necessary to explore the philosophical concept of religion and the cultural task implied in the understanding of theology as the normative cultural science of religion.

The philosophy of religion seeks to define the essence of religion in the direction of achieving a synthesis of religion and culture. In doing so it must not distort or compromise the "absoluteness" of religion as revelation,[49] and yet it must not admit that the absoluteness of religion makes it thereby inaccessible to philosophical analysis. Thus, a philosophical conception of the essence of religion must of necessity include, at least for purposes of analysis, both a genuine conception of the religious function and a conception of culture.

Tillich attempts his critical definition of religion and culture in the context of the schema of meaning discussed above. The two functions are both defined and distinguished by the direction of consciousness. Thus:

> If consciousness is directed toward the particular forms of meaning and their unity, we have to do with *culture*; if it is directed toward the unconditioned meaning, toward the import of meaning, we have *religion*. *Religion is directedness toward the Unconditional, and culture is directedness toward the conditioned forms and their unity.*[50]

It has to be recognized, however, that the inadequacy of this definition lies in the fact that it is artificial to separate form and import. Tillich asserts:

Form and import belong together; it is meaningless to posit the one without the other. Every cultural act contains the unconditioned meaning; it is based upon the ground of meaning; insofar as it is an act of meaning it is substantially religious. This becomes evident in the fact that it is directed toward the unity of form, that it must be subordinated to the unconditioned demand for unity of meaning. But it is not religious by intention. It is not toward the Unconditional as such that it is directed; and when it turns toward the unity of meaning . . . it does not do so with a consciously religious attitude. Culture as culture is therefore substantially, but not intentionally, religious.[51]

Of course, the converse is true for the religious act, which can only grasp the unconditioned import through the unity of conditioned forms. This means that

from the point of view of its form every religious act is therefore a cultural act; it is directed toward the totality of meaning. But it is not by intention cultural; for it does not have in mind the totality of meaning, but rather the import of meaning, the unconditioned meaning. *In the cultural act, therefore, the religious is substantial; in the religious act the cultural is formal.* Culture is the sum total of all spiritual acts directed toward the fulfillment of particular forms of meaning and their unity. Religion is the sum total of all spiritual acts directed toward grasping the unconditioned import of meaning through the fulfillment of the unity of meaning.[52]

Having qualified the original definition of religion and culture as he has, Tillich's language is not yet precise. There are not, in principle, two distinct sets of acts, cultural and religious, even though Tillich's language leads to that conclusion. This can be seen when it is considered that there can be, strictly speaking, cultural acts which are not explicitly religious, but as Tillich has acknowledged, *there can be no religious act which is not at the same time a cultural act.* Thus, when Tillich insists that the religious function is not in its essence a distinct function alongside others, he means that culture is the field in which the religious act is expressed and thus the whole of culture has religious meaning. Consequently, the particular cultural constellation called "religion" is only one, and by no means the exclusive, *form* of the religious attitude or of religion.

The definition of the essence of religion as a necessary dimension in every sphere of cultural meaning leads Tillich to explicate the presence of the religious dimension within the theoretical and practical functions of meaning. Metaphysics "is necessarily and at

all times a religious attitude. It is directedness toward the Unconditional in the theoretical sphere of the functions of the spirit."[53]
But the religious attitude is also present in the supported functions
of the theoretical sphere as well as the supporting and supported
functions of the practical sphere.[54]

The relationship of religion and culture follows from the relationship of the religious function to the other functions of meaning. As has been pointed out religion is not one function among
others, and neither is it to be identified with any particular cultural
function. Hence:

> That which is the basis of all functions of meaning cannot itself be one of
> these functions. Rather, the relation is such that the meaning-functions
> come to fulfillment in meaning only in relatedness to the unconditioned
> meaning, and that therefore the religious intention is the presupposition for
> successful meaning-fulfillment in all functions. An assertion of existence
> which is not directed toward that which exists unconditionally, an apprehen-
> sion of significance not directed toward the ground of significance, a shaping
> of the personality not directed toward the unconditionally personal, a spiri-
> tual act of love not directed toward unconditioned love, cannot be recognized
> as a successful meaning-fulfillment. Only in the "Holy Spirit" does the nature
> of spirit find its realization. It comes to realization, however, not in forms
> that stand alongside the cultural ones (through which the unconditionedness
> of religion would be dissolved) but rather precisely in the cultural forms; cul-
> ture is a form of expression of religion, and religion is the substance (*Inhalt*)
> of culture.[55]

This analysis maintains the absoluteness of religion, and at the
same time allows for the development of a philosophical conception of religion.

Consequently

> It is only in a preliminary way . . . that the philosophy of religion takes as its
> starting point the functions of meaning. This procedure serves to show that
> the meaning-functions, in their being and meaning, are grounded in the reli-
> gious, that they are forms that become meaningless and without import as
> soon as they lose the intention toward the unconditioned import of meaning.
> This outcome, however, corresponds to the demand of religion itself. It is the
> solution of the basic problem in the philosophy of religion: philosophical
> analysis is driven to the point where it apprehends itself together with all of
> culture as an expression of the religious.[56]

Theonomy is "the unity of religion and culture as a unity of unconditioned meaning-import and of conditioned meaning-form."[57] This is the authentic relationship between religion and culture. However, even though Tillich has denied that religion is a function among others or belongs to a particular sphere of meaning, he nonetheless must deal with the fact that there is indeed a religious sphere within the totality of culture which has historical embodiments, symbol systems and cultic structures, the realm of institutional religion. How is this realm to be understood philosophically?

Tillich argues that the presence of institutional religion within culture reveals a split in the theonomous unity of religion and culture, a separation between the two. The separation occurs in autonomy. Autonomy is the spirit's centering itself in conditioned forms and this "gives rise to the separation of culture from religion." This separation is contributed both from the side of culture and religion when autonomy becomes the dynamic force of the spiritual life.

> In every autonomy — that is, in every secular culture — a twofold element is implied: the "nomos," the law or structural form that is supposed to be carried out radically, corresponding to the unconditioned demand for meaning, and the "autos," the self-assertion of the conditioned, which in the process of achieving form loses the unconditioned import. Autonomy therefore is always at the same time obedience to and revolt against the Unconditional. It is obedience insofar as it subjects itself to the unconditioned demand for meaning; it is revolt insofar as it denies the unconditional meaning itself.[58]

In the face of an autonomous situation, which includes the cultural critique of the religious symbols in which the Unconditioned import has been expressed, religion absolutizes these very forms and symbols and exempts them from autonomous criticism. At the same time it claims that the Unconditioned meaning is confined to particular forms and is only apprehended within a *specific religious sphere*. At this point the separation between religion and culture is complete and has resulted in the struggle between autonomous culture and heteronomous religion. Heteronomy rises against the *hybris* of autonomy, and submits itself to the unconditioned meaning; but it does not understand the divinely ordained character of autonomy, namely, the apprehension of the pure forms and their unity. It falls victim therefore to religious *hybris*, the counterpole of cultural *hybris* [i.e., autonomy].[59]

The question arises as to the dynamics which lead continuously to the disintegration of the theonomous unity of religion and culture, and the actualizations of autonomy and heteronomy as elements within theonomy. What leads the spirit to absolutize the conditioned forms? What leads to the creation of a specific religious sphere, to religion in the institutional sense? The answer for Tillich lies in the way finitude drives toward the separation of the existential and the essential. He writes:

> But now the question arises, what about religion in the narrower and customary sense of the word, be it institutional religion or the religion of personal piety? If religion is present in all functions of the spiritual life, why has mankind developed religion as a special sphere among others, in myth, cult, devotion, and ecclesiastical institutions? The answer is, because of the tragic estrangement of man's spiritual life from its own ground and depth ... In this situation, religion makes itself the ultimate and despises the secular realm. It makes its myths and doctrines, its rites and laws into ultimates and persecutes those who do not subject themselves to it. It forgets that its own existence is a result of man's tragic estrangement from his true being. It forgets its own emergency character.[60]

One of the major tasks of philosophy of religion, then, is to seek to clarify the essential relationship of religion and culture, i.e., the character of theonomy. To do so it must proceed from both poles and refuse to let itself become exclusively identified with either pole. It should strive to show that

> the religious and the secular realm are in the same predicament. Neither of them should be in separation from the other, and both should realize that their very existence as separated is an emergency, that both of them are rooted in religion in the larger sense of the word, in the experience of ultimate concern. To the degree in which this is realized the conflicts between the religious and the secular are overcome, and religion has rediscovered its true place in man's spiritual life, namely, in its depth, out of which it gives substance, ultimate meaning, judgment, and creative courage to all functions of the human spirit.[61]

The essential definition of religion has thus become clear. It is the direction of consciousness toward the unconditioned meaning expressed in cultural forms. This means that theology has a distinct cultural task about which we shall speak in more detail below. At the moment, however, it is necessary to point out that philosophy of religion also seeks a normative conception of religion, which is at least implicit in the above formulations in which Tillich insists that religion *should* be the depth dimension of every cultural form and *not* an independent sphere or a function alongside the other functions.

Again following the pattern of the cultural sciences, philosophy of religion determines the elements of meaning of the religious function, derives the essential definition therefrom and then turns to the cultural history of religion to derive the normative concept of religion.[62] The normative concept of religion which philosophy of religion can determine in a formal way is a synthesis of the basic tendencies Tillich believes are to be within the cultural history of religion, i.e. the sacramental and the theocratic.

The sacramental attitude Tillich argues is the "primitive" spiritual condition from which all other movements of the religious consciousness derive. The notion itself presupposes a level of consciousness which is characterized by a basic unity in which the critical apparatus has not yet developed. Thus the sacramental attitude is "indifferent to the distinction between the divine and the demonic."

> This stage has been characterized as the religion of nature. But this concept is misleading, for nowhere is nature worshiped as such. Nature provides the symbols, but what they signify is not nature. It is much more accurate to speak of a religion of indifference, keeping in mind, however, that in fact a pure indifference does not exist.[63]

Both on the ground of this sacramental attitude and in opposition to it, the theocratic tendency arises. The theocratic movement attacks the sacramental indifference and drives toward the differentiation of the original sacramental consciousness. The theoretical criticism precipitates "the autonomous expulsion of every sacramental import." Thus, theocracy

> in its perfected religious form . . . must be characterized as a religion of infinite demand, a religion of law. Under the criticism of the religion of law sacramental religion can firmly cling to certain definite symbols and become heteronomous. . . . If, however, its concrete symbols are dissolved, it can be pushed forward into a radical mysticism. Insofar as mysticism aspires to go beyond everything given, it is also law, even though it be law with the demand to abolish all law and all form within the conditioned order. It is possible, therefore, to sum up this whole situation created by theocratic criticism as the stage of law in religious development, in contrast to the previous stage of the immediately given sacramental attitude.[64]

The way of synthesis, however, means that the sacramental and theocratic tendencies are not mere opposites and theocracy as a perfected form of consciousness is not merely law in contrast to the original innocence of sacramental indifference. In a much more complex way

> the goal of the whole movement . . . is the union of the theocratic demand and mystical negativity with the sacramental sanctification of some one concrete thing. Now, since this unity of the present Holy and the demanded Holy cannot be deliberately brought about, but rather can be experienced only as a breakthrough, we describe it as "a religion of grace" or a "religion of paradox."[65]

The religion of paradox, then, as the synthesis of sacramental and theocratic tendencies is the normative concept of religion for the philosophy of religion. As a gestalt of grace, the religion of paradox cannot be created by philosophy of religion and understanding it as a breakthrough means that the absoluteness of religion is preserved in the very conceptuality of philosophy of religion. Religion is not merely a creation of the human spirit; rather the religion of paradox is the revelatory perfection of the religious consciousness in which its natural structure is both affirmed and negated, preserved and lifted to a higher synthesis.

The dialectical movement from the sacramental to the religion of paradox has its counterpart in the development of the conception of God. The undifferentiated consciousness of the sacramental attitude cannot achieve "authentic representations of God," since everything in its immediacy is a potential bearer of the holy. However, the theocratic drive toward form passes through a genuine polytheism, of which Greek monarchical polytheism is the highest expression, toward mystical monotheism, which arises with the dissolution of polytheism. Mystical monotheism "elevates itself beyond all particular divinities, and symbolizes the pure import in paradoxical concepts, like Nirvana, the Beyond, and the Abyss."

Pure theocracy, however,

> is exclusively monotheistic [in the sense that it no longer retains polytheism within itself as mystical monotheism does]. It negates the many divinities from the point of view of one God who is the bearer of the unconditioned form, the jealous God who tolerates no demonic cleavages. But the more God is removed from his polytheistic basis, the more abstract, transcendent and formal he becomes. The perfected religion of grace passes through the stage of exclusive monotheism. It does not remain, however, in this sphere of law, but rather takes from sacramental polytheism a symbol that brings to full expression the religious paradox: the symbol of the divine mediator. The finite, the conditioned, which in a paradoxical way is the bearer of the Unconditional and for whose sake it surrenders itself as finite, the vision of the figure of the incarnate, lowly and dying God: this constitutes the genuine religious *mysterium*.[66]

It is here that philosophy of religion and theology meet, i.e., in relation to the norm, for it is in the concrete symbol of the divine mediator that the religion of paradox is fulfilled and thus the norm concept is to be found philosophically and explicated theologically. Theocratic criticism removes every demonic tendency from the divine mediator and the unconditioned form is borne by him. It is in the concrete symbol in which the unconditioned form is manifest completely unambiguously that "the synthesis of the tendencies of the history of religions [is] achieved."

> Only there can exclusive monotheism incorporate a polytheistic element without danger of demonic splitting, and thus be transformed from the religion of law to the religion of grace. The elucidation of this symbol in concrete form is the central task of the normative theory of religion, or theology.[67]

On these grounds Tillich draws his most fundamental distinction between philosophy of religion and theology. He asserts:

> It is not the task of philosophy of religion to decide what concrete symbol the religion of paradox can adopt, or better, what concrete symbol is fundamental for the normative concept of religion. That is the task of theology, which is necessarily confessional because it involves acknowledgment of a concrete symbol. But it does not therefore need to be less universally valid than philosophy of religion. If it has grasped the paradoxical, symbolic character of the context of faith, it must also place itself and its apprehension of the Unconditional under the No of the Unconditional. It will stand all the deeper in the religion of paradox, the more it succeeds in intuiting in its own symbol the No of the Unconditional against every symbol.[68]

Without attempting to discuss in detail Tillich's fascinating early effort to construct a philosophy of religion, we have seen that the relationship of philosophy and theology in Tillich's early thought takes on added complexity in his understanding of the relationship of theology to philosophy of religion as a branch of philosophy. This is most clear in considering that philosophy not only provides theology with a theory of meaning within which it must work, thus making itself indispensable for theology, but it also contributes more specifically a definition of religion which requires theology to surrender a narrow, positivistic understanding of itself and instead become, as an essential expression of its religious nature, a normative cultural discipline. Religion as an attitude in every cultural sphere of meaning requires that theology be understood as a theology of culture.

We raised the question above how theology could be understood as a normative science of religion and at the same time establish its relevance to the entire cultural process and the totality of cultural disciplines. The first dimension of the answer to this question, as we have seen, is that religion in its essential nature is present in every cultural function as the dimension of depth. Consequently, religion transcends the religious sphere and theology as the normative science of religion finds its object both within and beyond the religious sphere where the latter is understood as a specific cultural function among others. At this juncture, however, an observation is in order.

In spite of the fact that for Tillich the existence of religion as a sphere of its own is due to the "emergency" of estrangement, it would be incorrect to conclude that the locus of theology is to be found in culture in general. Tillich's philosophy of religion makes clear that the religious function has its own elements and categories and theology is clearly rooted within it. Theology is thoroughly confessional, i.e. it is "church" theology and its task is to determine the normative concrete symbolization of the Unconditional as a matter of ultimate concern, *first* within the religious function itself. This is its primary and foremost task. However, it will be recalled that Tillich insists that theology is just as universal in its function as philosophy in spite of its confessional character. This means, I believe, that the concrete symbol in which the religion of paradox is adequately expressed is normative for the whole of culture.

This is not, however, theology's only task. It also seeks a normative analysis of culture itself and the norm it seeks to establish for culture is theonomy. Tillich states the twofold task of theology in this way:

> The following law can now be formulated: the more the form, the greater the autonomy; the more the substance or import, the greater the theonomy. . . . The relation of import to form must be taken as resembling a line, one pole of which represents pure form and the other pole pure import. Along the line itself, however, the two are always in unity. The revelation of a predominant import consists in the fact that the form becomes more inadequate, that the reality, in its overflowing abundance, shatters the form meant to contain it; and yet this overflowing and shattering is itself still form.

> The task of a theology of culture is to follow up this process in all the spheres and creations of culture and to give it expression. Not from the standpoint of form — that would be the task of the branch of cultural science concerned — but taking the import or substance as its starting point, as theology of culture and not as cultural systematization. The concrete religious experience embodied in all great cultural phenomena must be brought into relief and a mode of expression found for them. It follows from this that in addition to theology as a normative science of religion, a theological method must be found to stand beside it in the same way that a psychological and sociological method, etc., exist alongside systematic psychology. These methods are universal; they are suited to any object; and yet they have a native soil, the particular branch of knowledge in which they originated. This is equally true of

the theological method, which is a universal application of theological questioning to all cultural values.[69]

The quest for a theological method which is rooted in the concrete standpoint of the religious sphere, and yet applicable to all the spheres of cultural creation should not be construed to mean that the unity of theology is vitiated thereby. Rather it is an attempt to enlarge the scope of theology, while acknowledging that theology stands in the split between the divine and the demonic, the sacred and the secular. Hence the theology of culture will follow the pattern of systematic theology in seeking to grasp its object, namely, the import of cultural creations. Tillich writes:

> We have assigned to theology the task of finding a systematic form of expression for a concrete religious standpoint, on the basis of the universal concepts of philosophy of religion and by means of the classifications of philosophy of history. The task of theology of culture corresponds to this. It produces a general religious analysis of all cultural creations; it provides a historical-philosophical and typological classification of the great cultural creations according to the religious substance realized in them; and it produces from its own concrete religious standpoint the ideal outline of a culture penetrated by religion.[70]

In executing its task, theology of culture produces a general religious analysis of culture, a religious typology and philosophy of cultural history, and a concrete religious systematization of culture.

We shall not attempt here to follow out the concrete cultural analysis Tillich achieves in his early essay. Our concern is to understand the relationship between theology of culture and church theology. Tillich speaks directly to this issue. His view is that theology of culture is impossible without the specifically religious culture of dogma, cultus, sacred actions, community and church. This means that

> A specific religious culture must already have come into being before we can experience religious values in culture, or develop a theology of culture . . . Church, cultus, and dogma must already have come into being, and not only that, before we can conceive of the state as church, or art as cultus, or science as a theory of faith. To be able somehow to comprehend the Holy and experience it as distinct from the profane or secular, we must take it out of context and bring it into a special sphere of cognition, or worship, of love, and of

organization. The profane or secular pole of culture . . . claims our whole attention if it is not balanced by the opposite pole; a universal profanation and desecration of life would be inevitable if no sphere of holiness existed to oppose and contradict it.[71]

It is the penetration of cultural forms by substance or import, which creates both the specifically religious sphere, on the one hand, and the larger religious substance of culture on the other. The traditional problem with the church theologian has been that he fails to see that the religious sphere was created to preserve and heighten the religious quality of culture, and thus he understands

this sphere as the expression of a definite religious "concreteness," no longer derived from culture but with an independent history going back much farther than most other cultural creations. It has evolved its own forms, each with its separate history, its independence, and its continuity, in spite of all the influences exerted by autonomous forms of culture.[72]

Working out of this traditional stance, the church theologian adopts two possible attitudes toward culture. The first, Tillich identifies with the Roman Catholic attitude in which all the aspects of culture are grouped under the term "world" and then confronted by the "kingdom of God." In this attitude the religious sphere is made identical with the religious principle and thus absolutized. Heteronomy, of course, is the result. The second attitude is the Protestant one. "Here church, cultus, and ethics are freed and seen in their relativity; but the cognitive tie, the idea of absolute knowledge as a supernatural revelation, is still retained."[73] Neither of these attitudes are theologically adequate for Tillich.

Protestant theology, Tillich maintains, must find a new attitude. It should have the following shape:

On the one hand, the distinction between religious potentiality and actuality, i.e., between religious principle and religious culture, will be strictly drawn and the character of "absoluteness" assigned only to the religious principle and not to any factor of the religious culture, not even that of its historical foundation. On the other hand, the religious principle will not be defined in purely abstract terms, nor will its concrete fulfillment be entrusted to every floating fashion of cultural development. Every effort, however, will be made

to ensure the continuity of its concrete religious standpoint. Only if this attitude is adopted can there be any positive relation between theology of
culture and the theology of church.[74]

If both the church theologian and the theologian of culture
stand in this new attitude, nonetheless the church theologian will
be more conservative than the theologian of culture. He will think
and act out of the past as well as toward the future. Continuity is a
matter of deep concern, and every issue of change is cast in refor-
matory rather than revolutionary terms. However,

the theologian of culture is not bound by any such considerations; he is a free
agent in the living cultural movement, open to accept not only any other form
but also any other spirit. It is true that he lives on the basis of a definite concreteness, for *one can live* only in concreteness; but he is prepared at any
time to enlarge and change this concreteness. As a theologian of culture, he
has no interest in ecclesiastical continuity; and this of course puts him at a
disadvantage as compared with the church theologian, since he is in danger of
becoming a fashionable religious prophet of an uncertain cultural development divided against itself.[75]

There will be tension between church theology and theology of
culture, but if both forms of theology are informed by the religious
principle, viz., that culture is the locus of the religious substance
and that the specifically religious sphere is only one cultural form
in which the religious substance is to be seen, then they can only
complement each other. In principle there is no basis for conflict
between them. In a passage which anticipates the notion of the
Protestant principle in Tillich's later thought, the basis of comple-
mentation is found in concreteness, relativity, and the absoluteness
of the religious principle itself. There can be no real opposition
between theology of culture and church theology, where

the theologian of culture acknowledges the necessity of the concrete standpoint in its continuity, and the church theologian in turn acknowledges the
relativity of every concrete form compared with the exclusive absoluteness of
the religious principle itself.[76]

The religious principle, however, does not drive theology of culture to revolt against the estrangement of finite man from his own
religious ground or substance. Theology of culture is a cultural-

spiritual activity which is also rooted in the estrangement of everything finite. Consequently,

> The cultural-theological ideal itself . . . goes farther than the distinction
> between cultural theology and ecclesiastical theology. Yet it does not
> demand a culture that eliminates the distinction drawn between the profane
> or secular pole and the holy, for that is impossible in the world of reflection
> and abstraction, but it does demand one in which the entire cultural move-
> ment is filled by a homogeneous substance, a directly spiritual material, which
> turns it into the expression of an all-embracing religious spirit. In that case,
> theology is eliminated, for it is only the expression of a split between sub-
> stance and meaning in culture.[77]

Tillich's early thought then, is characterized by the drive toward
synthesis in which the dynamic unity of consciousness and culture
can be established. It is the ideal of synthesis, (which we will suggest here, without demonstrating the claim, grows out of the foundational notion of the unity of conditioned and unconditioned
being), which shapes in a radical way the character of theology. It
is clear that Tillich's early conception of theology is decisively conditioned by the system in which it stands. Without the philosophy
of meaning, for example, the notion of theology as theonomous
systematics would be unintelligible and without the philosophical
conception of religion achieved by the philosophy of religion, the
cultural task of theology would be completely ungrounded. Thus,
any critique of the cultural task of theology as Tillich has defined it
could not be successful merely by asserting a counter model of theological inquiry (e.g., a more biblical-kerygmatic model or one that
takes church tradition as normative). Rather it would have to
begin with a critique of the validity of Tillich's philosophy of religion, an activity which Tillich would insist would be itself a philosophical venture.

Thus, we can see in Tillich's early writings some very seminal
notions which inform his mature conception of philosophy, theology, and their relationship. First, the notion of philosophy as the
cognitive search for universal notions and categories is clearly
maintained. There is no object which is closed to philosophical
analysis, i.e., the concepts and categories of meaning which

philosophy seeks to clarify have universal applicability. Consequently, theology is understood within this philosophical framework, i.e., theology executes its task by employing a definite philosophical conceptuality. This makes theology philosophical in a fundamental sense.

Secondly, the distinction between philosophy and theology is grounded in the concreteness of the theological perspective. Philosophy is abstract, objective, and universal. Theology is concrete, existential and universal. Philosophy can develop a normative concept of religion, but it is only in theology's being grasped by an existential encounter with a concrete symbol that the content of that norm can be established. Philosophy, by its very nature, cannot make such an existential decision about the concrete content of the religious norm. The theologian goes beyond the formal notion of norm to a living relationship to a concrete norm. The theologian risks his existence in the normative question in a way the philosopher does not.

Thirdly, the notion of religion in Tillich's early writings drives philosophy out of a purely profane, secular, merely critical positivistic understanding of itself. Philosophy is religious in the sense that its history, as we have seen, reveals its quest for ultimate reality, for unconditioned meaning. On the other hand, the notion of religion drives theology out of a purely ecclesiastical or confessional understanding of itself. Philosophy and theology meet in the religious nature of both enterprises. It is only when philosophy asserts its autonomous drive and theology its heteronomous drive that a conflict is possible between them. However, when both philosophy and theology stand in a genuine theonomy, the conflict between them is overcome and their ultimate unity is established.

It should be clear, then, that in his earliest writings Tillich asserts the radical interdependence of philosophy and theology. Philosophy and theology in the West have exercised a mutual influence upon one another and the influence has been both negative and positive. In some periods of history, the synthesis of the two has been achieved. In other periods, especially the modern and contemporary periods, each has tried to drive the other out of its midst as can be seen most clearly in the rise of Logical Positivism on the one hand and the Barthian theology on the other. Tillich is seeking a synthesis of unity and distinction, i.e., a synthesis in which philosophy and theology are united in the common ground of their religious character, but in which neither is to be merely identified with the other. The question which we shall explore is whether the synthesis Tillich seeks is as balanced as it would seem to be. Before approaching that question, however, we must now examine Tillich's mature conception of theology.

Notes

1 *On the Boundary, op. cit.*, 55-56.

2 The conception of philosophy articulated in "Das System der Wissenschaften" is yet another variant definition of philosophy found in Tillich's writings. It was not discussed in Chapter Five because, while the conceptuality within which philosophy is defined differs from the formal definition which was considered there, the fundamental meaning of philosophy does not seem to be changed substantially between this early definition and the later one.

3 GW, I, *op. cit.*, p. 231.

4 J. L. Adams has shown the influence of Hegel and Fichte upon Tillich's vision of the system of knowledge and the sciences. However, the metalogical method rejects both a straightforward Idealism and Realism in favor of Self-transcendant or Critical Realism. Cf. J. L. Adams, *Tillich's Phil. of Culture, Science and Religion, op. cit.*, pp. 124ff. Cf. also, GW, I, *op. cit.*, pp. 120, 235-238; *What is Religion?, op. cit.*, p. 42.

5 In ST, III, spirit with a small "s", as contrasted with the divine Spirit, is a dimension or function of life which "characterizes man as man and which is actualized in morality, culture, and religion . . . Spirit can be defined as the actualization of power and meaning in unity. Within the limits of our experience this happens only in man — in man as a whole and in all the dimensions of life which are present in him (ST, III, p. 111).

6 J. L. Adams, *op. cit.*, p. 57.

7 GW, I, *op. cit.*, p. 210.

8 J. L. Adams, *op. cit.*, p. 58.

9 *What is Religion?, op. cit.*, p. 56.

10 *Ibid.*, p. 57.

11 *Ibid.*, pp. 57-58.

12 *Ibid.*, p. 58.

13 GW, I *op. cit.*, p. 232.

14 For Tillich's discussion of autonomy and theonomy in relation to the subject at hand, see GW, I *op. cit.*, pp. 227-228.

15 *Ibid.*, pp. 238-240.

16 *Ibid.*, p. 241.

17 Tillich contrasts philosophy and systematics thus: " . . . any universal philosophical concept is empty unless it is at the same time understood to be a normative concept with a concrete basis . . . this does not constitute the difference between philosophy and the science of norms, but the fact that each works in a different direction. Philosophy provides universal, a priori categorical thought forms on the widest empirical basis and in systematic relationship with other values and essential concepts. The normative sciences provide each cultural discipline with its content, with what is peculiar to it, with what is to be regarded as valid within the specific system." *What is Religion?*, *op. cit.*, p. 158.

18 *Ibid.*, p. 157. It should be kept in mind that the universal notion of philosophy and the normative notion of systematics are dialectically interrelated, just as philosophy, cultural history, and the normative sciences constitute a unified cultural science. Tillich writes: "Out of the power of a concrete, creative realization the highest universal concept gains its validity, full of content and yet comprehensive in form; and out of a highest universal concept the normative system acquires its objective scientific significance. In every useful universal concept there is a normative concept; and in every creative 'norm' concept there is a universal concept." *Ibid.*, pp. 158-159.

19 *What is Religion?*, *op. cit.*, pp. 32-33.

20 GW, I, *op. cit.*, pp. 275-276.

21 *What is Religion?*, *op. cit.*, pp. 33-34.

22 GW, I, *op. cit.*, p. 274.

23 *Ibid.*, p. 275.

24 *Ibid.*

25 *Ibid.*

26 *Ibid.*, p. 276.

27 *Ibid.* In carrying out its exegetical task, theology must avoid the errors of allegorizing the religious documents or of heteronomously subjecting the

contemporary mind to "der exact erfassten offenbarungsurkunde." While the point is not made, the fact that the autonomy of the contemporary mind must be acknowledged suggests that the questions it raises must be incorporated within theological exegesis. One can see clear parallels between this formulation of the theological enterprise and that of the *Systematic Theology*.

28 *Ibid.*, p. 277.

29 Cf. *Ibid.*, p. 277; *What is Religion?*, *op. cit.*, p. 97.

30 Tillich follows an elaborate classificatory schema in distinguishing the structure of cultural science. As we have seen, he establishes the three elements of meaning and determines philosophy, cultural history, and systematics as the key disciplines of cultural science. Also decisive for the classification of the cultural sciences is the twofold cultural attitude (*Geisteshaltung*), autonomy and theonomy. The third criterion of classification is the grouping of the various spheres of meaning. Tillich develops a general criterion by which to achieve this task by dividing all meaning-fulfilling acts into theoretical and practical acts. Thus, there are spheres of meaning which are appropriate to the theoretical act and spheres of meaning appropriate to the practical act. Following the distinction between autonomy and theonomy, the spiritual act directed toward the Unconditioned, Tillich calls a *supporting* function. The spiritual act directed toward the forms of meaning, he calls a *supported* function. The supported functions in turn can be distinguished as between those directed toward the forms of the theoretical and practical spheres and those directed toward the import of meaning which the forms express. This schema yields the following structure: "In der theoretischen Sphäre ist die formbestimmte fundierte Funktion die *Wissenschaft* ("Epistemology" — Adams, *op. cit.*, p. 160), die gehaltsbestimmte fundierte Funktion die *Kunst* ("Aesthetics" — *Ibid.*); während die fundierende Funktion für beide die *Metaphysics* ist. In der praktischen Sphäre ist die formbestimmte fundierte Funktion das Recht ("Jurisprudence" — *Ibid.*).; die gehaltsbestimmte fundierte Funktion die *Gemeinschaft* ("Political Science" — *Ibid.*), während die fundierende Funktion für beide die Sittlichkeit ist." (GW, I, *op. cit.*, p. 230).

31 *Ibid.*, p. 278.

32 A brief explanation of Tillich's conception of metaphysics is appropriate here in order to make this point clear. Tillich insists that the understanding of metaphysics as a rational science which has emerged since the Enlightenment is to be rejected if its genuine function is to be restored to present-day thought. The chief task of metaphysics is to show "dass sie Richtung des Bewusstseins auf das Unbedingte eine notwendige, die Sinnwirklichkeit konstituierende Funktion ist. Sie hat zu zeigen, dass das Prius jeder einzelnen Sinnerfassung der unbedingt Sinn selbst, das Prius jeder Sinnform die Rich-

tung auf die unbedingte Form, und das Prius jedes Sinngehaltes der unbedingte Gehalt ist. Der Begriff des Unbedingt steht also im Zentrum des Metaphysik. Die Metaphysik ist der Wille, das Unbedingte zu erfassen" (GW, I, *op. cit.*, p. 253).

As the supporting function of epistemology and aesthetics, metaphysics is to be identified with neither. It is a "selbständige Sinnfunktion"; however, its formal means of expression is the concept. This is the epistemological element in metaphysics. But the intention of metaphysics "ist nicht gerichtet auf die Begriffe als Wirklichkeitsformen, sondern als Ausdruck des Wirklichkeitsgehaltes. Darauf gründet sich das künstlerische Element, das jeder schopferischen Metaphysik innewohnt" (*Ibid.*) The Unconditioned, however, cannot be a theoretical object nor does it exist. Consequently, metaphysics can grasp the Unconditioned only "in den Formen des Bedingten. Das ist die tiefe Paradoxie, die ihr innewohnt." The concepts which metaphysics uses to grasp the Unconditioned are conditioned forms which have their proper function within the autonomous sciences. Therefore, metaphysics uses these concepts symbolically, and it is dependent upon the autonomous sciences to produce them.

Metaphysics, then, is the doctrine of the elements of meaning (*Sinnelementenlehre*). "Auf der Grundlage der Sinnelemente erhebt sich das System der metaphysichen Symbole. Es sind drei Grundfragen, die in jeder Metaphysik ihre Antwort finden müssen, erstens die Frage nach dem Verhältnis des Unbedingte zum schöpferischen Geistesprozess, drittens die Frage nach der Sinneinheit von Seinprozess und Geistesprozess" (*Ibid.*, p. 255). The first question is answered by "Seinsmetaphysik oder Ontologie." "Geschictsmetaphysik" addresses itself to the second question, while the unity of the two culminates in the "Metaphysik der absoluten Idee" (*Ibid.*, p. 256).

The important consideration in regard to this conception of metaphysics is that it is not to be identified exclusively with the historical traditions of metaphysics (e.g., Platonic, Aristotelian, Rationalistic, Kant, Whitehead, etc.). Rather these traditions are just one form of theonomous metaphysics, which in its essence appears where consciousness seeks the Unconditioned. This means that on the purely rational level there is a distinct discipline, metaphysics, with distinct functions, even though it has no concepts of its own. However, metaphysics can also occur in other contexts, e.g., in myth, autonomous scientific concepts, or in religious symbols or dogma. This is why dogmatics can be identified as theonomous metaphysics.

33 *Ibid.*, p. 279.

34 *Ibid.*, p. 280.

35 Again one can see how this early theme has been explored in Tillich's later thought, for example, in the theologian's sensitizing the philosopher, scientist

or artist to his own hidden ultimate concern (cf. Tillich's dialogue with Einstein, Picasso, Psychoanalysis, and Existentialism in *Theology of Culture*.)

36 GW, I, *op. cit.*, p. 280.

37 *Ibid.*, p. 281.

38 *Ibid.*

39 Note this remarkable passage from *What is Religion?*, *op. cit.*, p. 173: "The religious substance shatters the autonomous form of the state: that is the profoundest meaning of idealistic 'anarchism', not to make way for a new theocracy but in favor of a theonomy built up from communities themselves and their spiritual substance. . . . Such a state . . . is what must be termed 'church' in the sense of the theology of culture; the universal human community, built up out of spiritual communities and bearing with it all cultural functions and their religious substance, with the great creative philosophers for its teachers, artists for its priests, the seers of a new ethic of the person and the community for its prophets, men who will lead it to new community goals for its bishops, leaders and recreators of the economic process for its deacons and almoners."

40 GW, I, *op. cit.*, pp. 281-282.

41 *Ibid.*, p. 283.

42 J. L. Adams summarizes the structure of theology in *Das System* thus: "Systematic theology as a theonomous theory of the norms of meaning embraces theonomous metaphysics oriented to the living confessions (dogmatics), theonomous ethics or ethos (the theory of piety), the theory of the forms of devotion (liturgics), and the theory of the cultus community; add to these disciplines the theonomous theory of the principles of meaning (philosophy or philosophy of religion) and the theonomous theory of the material of meaning (historical theology and theonomous cultural history); all together these disciplines constitute the theonomous cultural science of theology." Adams, *op. cit.*, p. 173.

43 Cf. *The Beginnings of Dialectical Theology*, v. I, ed. James M. Robinson (John Knox Press, Richmond, Virginia, 1968).

44 *What is Religion?*, *op. cit.*, pp. 27-28.

45 *Ibid.*, p. 28.

46 *Ibid.*

47 *Ibid.*, p. 30.

48 *Ibid.*, p. 34.

49 The terminology of absoluteness in regard to religion must be understood in relation to Tillich's notion of the Unconditioned. He writes: "As religion, every religion is relative, for every religion objectifies the Unconditional. As revelation, however, every religion can be absolute, for revelation is the breakthrough of the Unconditional in its unconditionality. Every religion is absolute to the degree that it is revelation, i.e., insofar as the Unconditional manifests itself within it as something unconditional, in contrast to everything relative that belongs to it as religion." *Ibid.*, p. 146.

50 *Ibid.*, p. 59.

51 *Ibid.*

52 *Ibid.*, p. 60.

53 *Ibid.*, p. 35.

54 Tillich defines the religious dimension of the theoretical and practical functions thus: "In the sphere of knowledge culture is directedness toward the conditioned forms of existence and their unity. Religion in the sphere of knowledge is directedness toward the unconditionally existing (*das unbedingt Seiende*) as the ground and abyss of all particular claims and their unity." In the aesthetic sphere, "directedness toward particular significances and their interconnections in the universal work of art is the cultural-aesthetic act. Directedness toward the unconditioned import of significance and its presentation in the universal interconnection of significance is religion." In the function of law in the practical sphere " the intention of the spirit toward a particular legal form and the ideal unity of forms, viewed apart from the meaning-ground of all right which transcends every particular right, is the cultural attitude of culture. The intention of the spirit toward the unconditionally personal as the ground of every right and the implementation of this intention in a kingdom of righteousness is the religious attitude." In the function of community "the inner directedness toward the particular forms of the realization of love and their unity is the cultural attitude in the sphere of community, the inner directedness toward unconditioned love (which at the same time is the ground as well as the abyss of any particular love) and toward the universal unity of love as its symbol, is the religious attitude."

Tillich concludes from his analysis: "Thus corresponding to the universal apprehension of the religious within the very nature of meaning itself, it has become evident that religion is immanent in all the functions of meaning, theoretical as well as practical. The twofold method of derivation from both the theoretical and the practical is of decisive importance for the apprehension of the Unconditional. The merely theoretical way makes the Unconditional into an object which, like any other object, can be manipulated or dis-

238 *The Early Writings*

posed of by the personality. But as a consequence it loses the power of unconditionedness. It can retain this power only through the [correction provided by the] practical side that makes the recognition of the unconditionally personal into an unconditionally personal demand. But conversely, the merely practical way loses the Unconditional in its quality of grounding and at the same time transcending everything real; it makes the Unconditional into a mere demand without presence. Thus, it also loses the character of unconditionedness and is changed into a product of unconditioned action. Only if it views the Unconditional as that which exists unconditionally in all of being can it preserve the element of unconditionedness. The two ways must supplement each other, and only together in their unity do they provide the living apprehension of the unconditioned meaning that constitutes the ground and abyss of all meaning." *Ibid.*, pp. 65-69.

55 *Ibid.*, p. 73. Cf. Tillich's later formulation in *The Theology of Culture, op. cit.*, p. 7. Here religion is defined as an "aspect of the human spirit," i.e., religion is not a special function of man's spiritual life, but it is the dimension of depth in all of its functions, which "means that the religious aspect points to that which is ultimate, infinite, unconditional in man's spiritual life. Religion is ultimate concern."

The circularity of religion as ultimate concern is clear from the following passage. "Ultimate concern is manifest in all creative functions of the human spirit. It is manifest in the moral sphere as the unconditional seriousness of the moral demand. Therefore, if someone rejects religion in the name of the moral function of the human spirit, he rejects religion in the name of religion. Ultimate concern is manifest in the realm of knowledge as the passionate longing for ultimate reality. Therefore, if anyone rejects religion in the name of the cognitive function of the human spirit, he rejects religion in the name of religion. Ultimate concern is manifest in the aesthetic function of the human spirit as the infinite desire to express ultimate meaning. Therefore, if anyone rejects religion in the name of the aesthetic function of the human spirit, he rejects religion in the name of religion. You cannot reject religion with ultimate seriousness, because ultimate seriousness, or the state of being ultimately concerned, is itself religion. Religion is the substance, the ground, and the depth of man's spiritual life." *Ibid.*, p. 8.

In departing somewhat from his formulations in "The Philosophy of Religion," Tillich calls religion as ultimate concern an "existential" rather than a theoretical understanding of religion. He is led to state the relationship of religion and culture thus: "Religion as ultimate concern is the meaning giving substance of culture and culture is the totality of forms in which the basic concern of religion expresses itself. In abbreviation: religion is the substance of culture, culture is the form of religion . . . Every religious act, not only in organized religion, but also in the most intimate movements of the soul, is culturally formed." *Ibid.*, pp. 41-42. One can see a clear continuity between Tillich's early and later thinking on the nature of religion. For a critical and illuminating discussion of Tillich's conception of religion as ultimate concern, Cf. John Magee, *Religion and Modern Man* (Harper and Row, New York, 1969), pp. 22-38.

56 *What is Religion?, op. cit.,* pp. 73-74.

57 *Ibid.*

58 *Ibid.,* pp. 74-75.

59 *Ibid.,* p. 75.

60 *Theology of Culture, op. cit.,* p. 9.

61 *Ibid.*

62 Tillich determines the essential elements of religion as: religion and culture, faith and "unfaith", God and the world, sacred and the secular, the divine and demonic. From the cultural history of religion, Tillich determines two major tendencies, the sacramental and the theocratic. In the categories of religion, Tillich places myth and revelation within the theoretical sphere and in the practical sphere he places the cultus and the cult fellowship. Taken together these notions constitute the body of his philosophy of religion.

63 *What is Religion?, op. cit.,* p. 92.

64 *Ibid.,* pp. 92-93.

65 *Ibid.,* p. 93.

66 *Ibid.,* pp. 95-96.

67 *Ibid.,* p. 96.

68 *Ibid.,* p. 97.

69 *Ibid.,* pp. 164-165.

70 *Ibid.,* p. 165.

71 *Ibid.,* p. 165.

72 *Ibid.,* p. 176.

73 *Ibid.,* p. 177.

74 *Ibid.,* p. 177.

75 *Ibid.,* p. 178.

76 *Ibid.*

77 *Ibid.,* pp. 178-179.

Chapter Eight

Tillich's Conception of Theology: The Later Writings

James L. Adams' claim that Tillich's early writings are of a philosophical character and that it is only after his coming to the United States that Tillich turns his attention to the more explicit theological task of working out in detail the normative science of religion or the theological system seems quite warranted.[1] However, one can see a clear continuity between the early reflections upon the nature of theology and the full-bodied conception of theology of Tillich's American period.

We have seen that theology, for Tillich, is theology of culture, and that he sought a theological method in the early years which would be applicable to the totality of the cultural process. This method is seen clearly in the *Systematic Theology*. It is both apologetic and correlational. Thus, rather than seeking the religious substance in the cultural forms (as in the early Tillich), theology seeks to *answer the questions* raised by man's cultural self-understanding.

It seems clear that the mature conception of method attempts to overcome the possible conflicts between church theology and theology of culture when they are conceived, as Tillich tended to do in his early thought, as separate but related enterprises. The mature method seeks a complete theological system, which is rooted both in the eternal message of Christian faith and the cultural "situation" in which the theologian finds himself.[2] Thus, insofar as theology is rooted in the eternal message, it is kerygmatic-church theology; insofar as it must interpret the message to the situation, it is theology of culture.

It will be recalled that in Tillich's early reflections upon the nature of theology a philosophy of meaning was developed in which the notions of form, content, and substance or import were decisive and that a philosophical conception of religion as the direction of consciousness toward the unconditioned import of meaning in all the cultural functions was also extremely important. These notions have also been determinative for the mature conception of theology. This can be seen clearly in Tillich's discussion of the nature and method of systematic theology.

As was stated above, the theological system or systematic theology is "a function of the Christian church, [and] must serve the needs of the church" (ST, I: 3).[3] As a function of the church, however, a theological system must not only satisfy the needs of the church, but it must participate in a fundamental way in the very definition of those needs. For Tillich, the needs of the church, which systematic theology seeks to meet, are twofold. First, theology must seek to state the truth of the Christian message, and, secondly, it must seek to interpret the truth of the Christian message "for every new generation." Thus, "theology moves back and forth between two poles, the eternal truth of its foundation and the temporal situation in which the eternal truth must be received" (ST, I: 3). Theology, then, must attempt to take the "situation" in which the message is to be received as seriously as it takes the Christian message itself.

The notion of the "situation" has technical significance for Tillich, and seems to correspond roughly to what he means by the cultural-historical significance of a period in his early writings. "Situation", he argues,

as one pole of all theological work, does not refer to the psychological or sociological state in which individuals or groups live. It refers to the scientific and artistic, the economic, political, and ethical forms in which they express their interpretation of existence. The "situation" to which theology must speak relevantly is not the situation of the individual as individual and not the situation of the group as group ... The "situation" theology must consider is the creative interpretation of existence, an interpretation which is carried on in every period of history under all kinds of psychological and sociological conditions. The "situation" certainly is not independent of these factors. However, theology deals with the cultural expression they have found in practice as well as in theory and not with these conditioning factors as such. . . . The "situation" to which theology must respond is the totality of man's creative self-interpretation in a special period (ST, I: 3-4).

In defining the theological task this way, Tillich is aware of what might be called the risk-benefit ratio of a theological method which moves between message and situation. The risk, as Tillich saw in his reflections upon the peculiar ambiguity of the theologian of culture, is that the Christian message may be dissolved or lost in the relativities of the cultural situation. The critique of the theology of the last two hundred years executed from the perspective of kerygmatic theology is precisely that

theology lost its own ground when it entered the situation. Apologetic theology in all these forms . . . is, from the point of view of recent kerygmatic theologians, a surrender of the kerygma, of the immovable truth. If this is an accurate reading of theological history, then the only real theology is kerygmatic theology. The "situation" cannot be entered; no answer to the questions implied in it can be given, at least not in terms which are felt to be an answer. The message must be thrown at those in the situation − thrown like a stone (ST, I: 6-7).

For Tillich, this is a real risk and any theological method which tries to go beyond the kerygmatic method, must take the latter's critique seriously.

The benefits of an apologetic method, however, move in two directions, and clearly outweigh the risks for Tillich. First, the method of correlation makes quite explicit that theology does not exist in a cultural vacuum, i.e., that its very language and concepts are drawn from a cultural process upon which it is dependent, and thus, when this is understood, the repristinatory impulse of kerygmatic theology and the conceptual and cognitive self-sufficiency it presupposes is seen to be sheer illusion. The method of correlation makes clear that by virtue of its dependence upon culture for its language and concepts, not even kerygmatic theology can avoid the "situation". Any attempt to do so is utterly self-defeating. The first benefit of the method of correlation is that it prevents theology from assuming a stance of naiveté toward culture.

The second benefit is no doubt more profound. It is rooted in the concern we have already noticed in Tillich of establishing the cultural significance or "relevance" of theology. A theological method which drives the theologian to a full and courageous participation in the "situation" will not guarantee theology's relevance to culture, but it does provide, at least, the *necessary* conditions whereby theology can establish a position in which it *could* be taken seriously by culture. The method of correlation prevents theology from taking a stance toward culture the very character of which determines its cultural irrelevance and thus its inconsequentiality for contemporary man. Thus, the method of correlation seeks to grasp the power of the kerygma for contemporary man, but it prevents its orthodox fixation. Clearly, then, the method of correlation attempts to unite kerygmatic and apologetic theology within the theological system. It seeks to avoid the cultural isolation of a purely kerygmatic theology on the one hand and the dissolution of the foundation of its message within the cultural situation on the other, i.e., it prevents the naiveté of an apologetic theology, which fails to grasp the discontinuity between message and situation. Kerygmatic and apologetic theology need each other for their mutual completion.

The ideal of the method of correlation, then, as it was in Tillich's early thought, is that of synthesis. Within the theological enterprise of the last two centuries

the perennial question has been: Can the Christian message be adapted to the modern mind without losing its essential and unique character? . . . No doubt the voices of those who have emphasized the contrast, the *diastasis*, have been louder and more impressive — men usually are more powerful in their negations than in their affirmations. But the continuous toil of those who have tried to find a union, a "synthesis," has kept theology alive. Without them traditional Christianity would have become narrow and superstitious, and the general cultural movement would have proceeded without the "thorn in the flesh" which it needed, namely, an honest theology of cultural high standing. . . . Yet certainly it is necessary to ask in every special case whether or not the apologetic bias has dissolved the Christian message. And it is further necessary to seek a theological method in which message and situation are related in such a way that neither of them is obliterated. . . . The following system is an attempt to use the "method of correlation" as a way of uniting message and situation. It tries to correlate the questions implied in the situation with the answers implied in the message (ST, I: 7-8).

The theological method is informed by the nature of systematic theology and the nature of theology is informed by method. What is the nature of theology which the method presupposes? In answering this question Tillich begins by asserting two negations regarding the nature of theology which are also to be found in his early thought. He asserts that theology is neither an empirical-inductive or a metaphysical-deductive "science." Theology cannot be deductive in a scientific sense because in every allegedly "scientific" theology one can always find elements of individual experience, valuations informed by tradition and quite personal commitments, which often decide methodological and substantial issues. No purely scientific theology in the deductive sense is possible. On the other hand, in an allegedly empirical-inductive theology one can find a priori elements, which determine the foundation upon which one decides what characteristic of reality or experience is to be the empirical basis for theology. These a priori elements are obviously not derived from experience. However, the same is true of the deductive approach as developed, for example, in classical idealism. Here

the ultimate principles in idealist theology are rational expressions of an ultimate concern; like all metaphysical ultimates, they are religious ultimates at the same time. A theology derived from them is determined by the hidden theology implied in them (ST, I: 9).

Tillich traces these two methodological alternatives to the various naturalistic and idealistic forms of theology they have produced and concludes that the theological concepts of both are "rooted in a mystical a priori, an awareness of something that transcends the cleavage between subject and object." This "mystical a priori" is always present in both deductive and inductive forms of theology and thus it undercuts their allegedly scientific character. Thus, "this is the circle which no religious philosopher can escape. And it is by no means a vicious one. Every understanding of spiritual things (*Geisteswissenschaft*) is circular" (ST, I: 9).

Every philosophy of religion, then, for Tillich, stands within the circle delimited by the "mystical a priori," which means, in brief, that the ultimate foundation of every philosophy of religion is grounded in the unity of finite and unconditioned being and consequently cannot be "established" by philosophy of religion itself. It is rather presupposed. The theologian, on the other hand, stands within the circle of the "mystical a priori," but he also occupies the "theological circle," which is more narrow than the former, i.e., the theologian

> adds to the "mystical a priori" the criterion of the Christian message. While the philosopher of religion tries to remain general and abstract in his concepts, as the concept "religion" itself indicates, the theologian is consciously and by intention specific and concrete. The difference, of course, is not absolute . . . The philosopher as philosopher, however, tries to abstract from these elements and to create generally valid concepts concerning religion. The theologian, on the other hand, claims the universal validity of the Christian message in spite of its concrete and special character. He does not justify this claim by abstracting from the concreteness of the message but by stressing its unrepeatable uniqueness. He enters the theological circle with a concrete commitment. He enters it as a member of the Christian church to perform one of the essential functions of the church — its theological self-interpretation (ST, I: 10).

It follows that a "scientific" theology, in the ordinary sense of scientific, is impossible once the nature of the theological circle is understood. The philosopher of religion does not need to stand in the theological circle in order to perform his cognitive task. The theologian, however, cannot escape it, if he is to be a theologian. He cannot claim to begin his work objectively and dispassionately; he cannot claim as his point of departure, as the philosopher does, the place which is no place, i.e., pure reason itself. Rather he thinks out of an existential decision toward a concrete content, the validity of which he cannot objectively demonstrate.

Tillich insists, speaking no doubt out of his Lutheran background, that the existential decision to occupy the theological circle is not to be equated with the faith of the theologian. To be in the theological circle is to be in the situation of faith, but no one can claim for himself that he is in the situation of faith. This means that

> no one can call himself a theologian. . . . Every theologian is committed *and* alienated; he is always in faith *and* doubt; he is inside and outside the theological circle. Sometimes the one side prevails, sometimes the other; and he is never certain which side really prevails. Therefore, one criterion alone can be applied: a person can be a theologian as long as he acknowledges the content of the theological circle as his ultimate concern. Whether this is true does not depend on his intellectual or moral or emotional state; it does not depend on the intensity and certitude of faith; it does not depend on the power of regeneration or the grade of sanctification. Rather it depends on his being ultimately concerned with the Christian message even if he is sometimes inclined to attack and to reject it (ST, I: 10).

The notion of the theological circle is an expansion of Tillich's early claim that theology is concrete-confessional, and it is used quite clearly to differentiate the theologian from the philosopher, both the philosopher in general and the philosopher of religion. The most important consequence of the doctrine of the theological circle, however, is its methodological implication, viz. that "neither the introduction nor any part of the theological system is the logical basis for the other parts. Every part is dependent on every other part" (ST, I: 11).

From the doctrine of the theological circle, Tillich develops two formal criteria for every theology. These criteria point to the religious character of theology and thus establish, as Tillich has done in his "Philosophy of Religion," theology's relationship both to culture and religion, form and import. The two criteria are derived from Tillich's notion of "ultimate concern." Ultimate concern expresses the nature of the religious concern, i.e., that in relation to which all other concerns are preliminary and finite. Tillich states:

> The religious concern is ultimate; it excludes all other concerns from ultimate significance; it makes them preliminary. The ultimate concern is unconditional, independent of any conditions of character, desire, or circumstance. The unconditional concern is total: no part of ourselves or of our world is excluded from it; there is no "place" to flee from it. The total concern is

infinite: no moment of relaxation and rest is possible in the face of a religious concern which is ultimate, unconditional, total, and infinite (ST, I: 11-12).

Through the notion of ultimate concern, Tillich attempts to point to two features of religion, viz., the "existential" character of religious experience and the inaccessibility of the religious object apart from the stance of ultimate concern. The point where these two features of religion coalesce is in the insight that the attitude of detached objectivity is completely incompatible with the stance of ultimate concern. Tillich's argument here is very important in understanding the nature of theology. "That which is ultimate," he maintains

> gives itself only to the attitude of ultimate concern. It is the correlate of an unconditional concern but not a "highest thing" called "the absolute" or "the unconditioned," about which we could argue in detached objectivity. It is the object of total surrender, demanding also the surrender of our subjectivity while we look at it. It is a matter of infinite passion and interest (Kierkegaard), making us its object whenever we try to make it our object. For this reason we have avoided terms like "the ultimate," "the unconditioned," "the universal," "the infinite," and have spoken of ultimate, unconditional, total, infinite concern (ST, I: 12).

If theology, then, is the self-interpretive expression of the religious concern, i.e. if it is rooted in the religious encounter with reality and comes to expression fundamentally out of the need of the religious encounter to interpret itself to itself,[4] then it follows that "the object of theology" is formally constituted as that which "concerns us ultimately." Consequently, "only those propositions are theological which deal with their object in so far as it can become a matter of ultimate concern for us" (ST, I: 12). This is the first formal criterion of theology. It clearly establishes the "existential" character of theology, where "existential" means being in the stance of ultimate concern.

This first formal criterion, because of its formality, functions in a boundary line capacity, at least in its negative implication. It establishes a clear boundary between theology and the whole realm of preliminary concerns and it prevents theology from interfering in the realm of preliminary concerns on the one hand and it prevents those who are occupied with the realm of preliminary concerns from interfering with the theological concern on the other. "The first formal principle of theology, guarding the boundary line between ultimate concern and preliminary concern, protects theology as well as the cultural realms on the other side of the line" (ST, I: 12).

However, the negative function of the first formal principle of theology does not exhaust its meaning. While theology does not interfere in the realm of the preliminary concerns, this does not mean that it does not adopt a positive attitude toward this realm. In a move which is quite reminiscent of the early emphasis upon form and import, Tillich argues that

> there are three possible relations of the preliminary concerns to that which concerns us ultimately. The first is mutual indifference, the second is a relation in which a preliminary concern is elevated to ultimacy, and the third is one in which a preliminary concern becomes the vehicle of the ultimate concern without claiming ultimacy for itself (ST, I: 13).

The first of these relations is incompatible with the ultimate character of the religious concern. The second is "idolatrous in its very nature," i.e., "Something essentially conditioned is taken as unconditional, something essentially partial is boosted into universality, and something essentially finite is given infinite significance" (ST, I: 13). Consequently, the third relation is the only possible one for theology. Here

> the . . . relation between the ultimate concern and the preliminary concerns makes the latter bearers and vehicles of the former. That which is a finite concern is not elevated to infinite significance, nor is it put beside the infinite, but in and through it the infinite becomes real. Nothing is excluded from this function. In and through every preliminary concern the ultimate concern can actualize itself. Whenever this happens, the preliminary concern becomes a possible object of theology. But theology deals with it only insofar as it is a medium, a vehicle, pointing beyond itself (ST, I: 13).[5]

Having established the character of theology as the existential interpretation of the religious encounter, that is, that the interpretation is given in the situation of concern and cannot be theological if it is not given in the situation of concern, and, therefore, having established also the criterion by which theology relates to the pre-liminary concerns, i.e. by which it executes its cultural function, the question now arises as to the *content* of the ultimate concern. At this juncture a formal criterion can be posited within the theological structure itself, but which is not capable of specifying the actual content of that concern. Theology, in asserting the general criteria by which it executes its task, can here state the formal conditions which any concrete content must meet before it can claim to be that which *does* concern us ultimately. The second formal criterion of theology, then, is stated thus: "Our ultimate concern is that which determines our being or not-being. Only those statements are theological which deal with their object in so far as it can become a matter of being or not-being for us" (ST, I: 14).

As we have noted in Part One, "being" refers to the total structure of finite reality, i.e. the total structure of reality which is conditioned by non-being. The meaning of "being," then, is not limited merely to existence in time and space. It is this total structure which is threatened and it is this structure about which man is ultimately concerned. In this second formal criterion of theology the full structure of ultimate concern can be seen. The first criterion delimits what Tillich elsewhere calls the subjective meaning of ultimate concern, viz., that man is capable of encountering himself in ultimate terms. The second criterion delimits the objective meaning of ultimate concern, viz., that man is ultimately concerned about that which is genuinely ultimate. Tillich writes:

> The term "ultimate concern" unites the subjective and the objective side of the act of faith — the *fides qua creditur* (the faith through which one believes) and the *fides quae creditur* (the faith which is believed). The first is the classical term for the centered act of the personality, the ultimate concern. The second is the classical term for that toward which this act is directed, the ultimate itself, expressed in symbols of the divine. This distinction is very important, but not ultimately so, for the one side cannot be without the other. There is no faith without a content toward which it is directed. There is always something meant in the act of faith. And there is no way of having the content of faith except in the act of faith.[6]

The second formal criterion of theology, then, seeks to establish that only statements about that which is genuinely ultimate can be

properly theological. Thus, while theology is rooted in the structure of human existence, or more precisely in man's religious
encounter with reality, it does not follow that the "object" of theology is merely generated out of that structure. The ultimate is not
a mere projection of faith.[7] Rather it is that which objectively has
the power of determining our being or nonbeing. The attempt to
unite existential and ontological issues within the formal structure
of theology can be seen here. It is the second formal criterion
which also establishes the philosophical character of theology in
the sense that the ultimate with which theology is ultimately
concerned is formally defined in ontological terms, i.e. in relation
to the conception of being.

The second formal criterion of theology has a twofold function.
In the first place, as we have seen, it establishes the defining characteristics of the content of ultimate concern without itself specifying that content. Thus it remains "open for contents which are
able to express 'that which determines our being or nonbeing.'"
However,

> At the same time it excludes contents which do not have this power from
> entering the theological realm. Whether it is a god who is a being beside oth-
> ers (even a highest being) or an angel who inhabits a celestial realm (called
> the realm of "spirits") or a man who possesses supranatural powers (even if
> he is called a god-man) — none of these is an object of theology if it fails to
> withstand the criticism of the second formal criterion of theology, that is, if it
> is not a matter of being or nonbeing for us (ST, I: 14-15).

The first formal principle stands as a boundary between theology
and culture. The second formal principle stands as a boundary
between that which is genuinely ultimate in the religious encounter
and those contents to be found in the history of religion which are
no longer a matter of ultimate concern. It seems clear that the
notion of ultimate concern establishes the principle of relevance
for the theological enterprise.

Theology for Tillich, we have said, arises out of the religious
encounter with reality. It is also a function of the Christian church.
On the one hand, then, theology is the interpretative component in
all religious experience, i.e., every basic religious encounter with

reality in human history has, for Tillich, an implicit or explicit theological dimension. On the other hand, Tillich argues that the career of the idea of theology within the whole history of the religious experience of mankind has come to its complete fulfillment in Christian theology. This means that Christian theology has a normative power which other theologies do not have. Tillich makes this claim thus:

> Theology is the methodical interpretation of the contents of the Christian faith. This is implicit in the preceding statements about the theological circle and about theology as a function of the Christian church. The question now arises whether there is a theology outside Christianity and, if so, whether or not the idea of theology is fulfilled in Christian theology in a perfect and final way. Indeed, this is what Christian theology claims; . . . Has it any validity beyond the periphery of the circle? It is the task of apologetic theology to prove that the Christian claim also has validity from the point of view of those outside the theological circle. Apologetic theology must show that the trends which are imminent in all religions and cultures move toward the Christian answer. This refers both to doctrines and to the theological interpretation of theology (ST, I: 15).

On what basis, then, can Christian theology make this claim? In the first place Christian theology establishes its continuity with all theology. In the broadest sense of the term, theology or reasoning (*Logos*) about God or divine things (*Theos*) is as old as religion itself. Every myth has an implicit theology which is often made explicit. Mystical speculations such as those found in Vedanta Hinduism unite meditation with theological penetration. Metaphysical speculations like those in Greek thought unite rational analysis with theological vision. Other forms of theology can be found in the social structures and interpretations of community and cultus. "All this is 'theo-logy,' *logos* of *theos*, a rational interpretation of the religious substance of rites, symbols, and myths" (ST, I: 16).

It follows that

> Christian theology is no exception. It does the same thing, but it does it in a way which implies the claim that it is *the* theology. The basis of this claim is the Christian doctrine that the Logos became flesh, that the principle of the divine self-revelation has become manifest in the event "Jesus as the Christ."

If this message is true, Christian theology has received a foundation which transcends the foundation of any other theology and which itself cannot be transcended. Christian theology has received something which is absolutely concrete and absolutely universal at the same time. No myth, no mystical vision, no metaphysical principle, no sacred law, has the concreteness of a personal life. In comparison with a personal life everything else is relatively abstract. And none of these relatively abstract foundations of theology has the universality of the Logos, which itself is the principle of universality (ST, I: 16).

Nowhere has Tillich made the implications of theology as the normative science of religion more explicit. The early theme of theology's seeking the concrete norm of religion within the philosophical framework of the religion of paradox and at the same time establishing its universality by establishing the universality of its norm has culminated in the mature doctrine of the *Logos*. It is here that one can see Tillich's affinity with the classical theological tradition just as his affinity with the classical philosophical tradition could be seen in his conception of philosophy.

The doctrine of the *Logos* unites the absolutely concrete (a personal life) and the absolutely universal (being-itself). Its normative power is precisely its transcending the abstract on the one hand and the particular on the other. The limitations of both the abstract and the particular are that

something that is merely abstract has a limited universality because it is restricted to the realities from which it is abstracted. Something that is merely particular has a limited concreteness because it must exclude other particular realities in order to maintain itself as concrete. Only that which has the power of repeating everything particular is absolutely concrete. And only that which has the power of representing everything abstract is absolutely universal. This leads to a point where the absolutely concrete and the absolutely universal are identical. And this is the point at which Christian theology emerges, the point which is described as the "Logos who has become flesh." The Logos doctrine as the doctrine of the identity of the absolutely concrete with the absolutely universal is not one theological doctrine among others; it is the only possible foundation of a Christian theology which claims to be *the* theology (ST, I: 16-17).

The *Logos* doctrine, then, establishes the concrete, existential character of theology on the one hand, and thus follows consistently from the first formal principle of theology, while on the other hand it determines the absoluteness and universality of theology by asserting that the *Logos* in Jesus as the Christ has the power of determining our being or not being and therefore follows consistently from the second formal principle of theology. This can be seen in Tillich's further claim about Jesus as the Christ. He writes:

> It is necessary to accept the vision of early Christianity that if Jesus is called the Christ he must represent everything particular and must be the point of identity between the absolutely concrete and the absolutely universal. In so far as he is absolutely concrete, the relation to him can be a completely existential concern. In so far as he is absolutely universal, the relation to him includes potentially all possible relations and can, therefore, be unconditional and infinite (ST, I: 17).

An aspect of the nature of theology, then, is that it is the "existential" interpretation of the religious encounter with reality. As existential interpretation it stands in the theological circle, which means that its object can be given to it only in the stance of ultimate concern and not by deduction or inference. Its rootage in the theological circle means that it is inescapably church theology and thus it is rooted in the message of the Christian church. There is, therefore, a kerygmatic element in systematic theology, but that element *must* be balanced or united with the apologetic task, since theology not only stands in the theological circle but in the "situation" as well. Theology can be "answering theology" because it has received that which is the norm of man's cultural, religious and moral life. The term "reception" implies that the norm was given to and not produced in the state of ultimate concern which the first formal principle of theology demands. Thus, there can be *no* demonstrative route to the content of ultimate concern. It is a matter of decision, risk and courage.

Theology is concrete-confessional as we have seen. It is also ultimately concerned about that which is universally valid. It seeks that which has the power of determining our being or nonbeing, the unconditional, the infinite, the ultimately real. In seeking unconditional reality theology stands in positive correlation with philosophy and thus the concrete-confessional or existential character of theology in no way undercuts its universality. The second formal principle of theology establishes the ontological character of theology and thus for Tillich its universal relevance to the spiritual life of man. Christian theology is the fulfillment of theology because the concrete and the universal, the existential and the ontological are identical in the event which is the foundation of Christian theology. The *Logos* is the fulfillment of the religious quest and the idea of theology found within it and the cultural quest and the idea of theonomy found within it.

The second formal principle of theology points toward the fact that theology is not only the existential interpretation of the religious encounter with reality or ultimate concern, but that its complete nature also demands that it seek to interpret the ultimate concern methodically. Tillich states:

> Theology is the existential and, at the same time, methodical interpretation of an ultimate concern. The interpretation of an ultimate concern is "existential" if it is done in the situation of concern. The interpretation of an ultimate concern is methodical if it relates the concern rationally to the whole of experience.[8]

The methodical interpretation of ultimate concern raises questions about both the method and the structure of theology. These questions are: "What are the sources of systematic theology? What is the medium of their reception? What is the norm determining the use of the sources?" (ST, I: 34).

The impact of method upon the structure of systematic theology, Tillich describes in the following terms:

> The positive element in theology . . . gives the *content* of theological work; the rational element . . . gives the *form* of theological work; and the element of immediacy . . . gives the *medium* of theological work.[9]

The positive element in theological method determines the answer to the question of the *sources* of theology; the element of immediacy circumscribes *experience* as the *medium* of theology; and the rational element in determining the *form* of theology has basic implications for the correlational character of theological method.

We shall examine each of these components of theological method in more detail.

The answer to the question of the sources of systematic theology must be given in relation to what has already been said about the theological circle, which itself determines the "positive" element in theological method. This means that theology first

> must interpret the totality of symbols, institutions, and ideas in which an ultimate concern has embodied itself; theology is, first of all, *positive*. It works on the basis, in the material, and for the purpose of an actual religion. The participation in a religious reality is a presupposition of all theology. You have to be within the circle of a concrete religion in order to interpret it existentially.[10]

The most significant consequence of the positive element of theological method is that it makes "individual theology" impossible. By this Tillich means that the theologian, while he is an individual, cannot generate the content of his ultimate concern out of his own individuality. Thus:

> The individual theologian can and should find more adequate methods of interpretation. But he cannot find that which he is asked to interpret. Concretely speaking: Christian theology is the interpretation of the message that Jesus is the Christ, and of the symbols and institutions based on this message. Theology is the methodical self-interpretation of the Christian church (1) in the direction of its foundation, the "new reality" which has become manifest in Jesus as the Christ, and (2) in the direction of the life, past and present, which is determined by this reality. The original document of the new reality is the Bible; the expression of the life determined by this new reality is the Tradition.[11]

The Bible and Tradition, then, are the two fundamental sources of systematic theology. Thus, Tillich rejects the neo-orthodox claim that the Bible is the *only* source of theology. The Bible is a product of human religion and culture; consequently, "the biblical message embraces more (and less) than the biblical books. Systematic theology, therefore, has additional sources beyond the Bible." On the other hand, the Bible is the basic source of theology, "because it is the original document about the events on which the Christian church is founded," and because it contains the original witness of those who participated in the revealing events. Their participation was their response to the happenings which became revealing events through this response. The inspiration of the biblical writers is their receptive and creative response to potentially revelatory facts. The inspiration of the writers of the New Testament is their acceptance of Jesus as the Christ, and with him, of the New Being, of which they became witnesses . . . The witnesses to that of which it is a part (ST, I: 35).

The biblical material is accessible to the systematic theologian on the basis of the labor of the historical theologian. The task of the biblical theologian is not limited, however, to the historical-critical enterprise. He must also unite his own existential commitment with his technical work, which means that this stance toward the biblical material is at the same time critical and "devotional-interpretive," "taking account of the fact that it deals with matters of ultimate concern." Thus:

Being ultimately concerned about what is really ultimate liberates the theologian from all "sacred dishonesty." It makes conservative as well as revolutionary historical criticism open to him. Only such free historical work, united with the attitude of ultimate concern, can open the Bible to the systematic theologian as his basic source (ST, I: 36).

Some forms of Protestantism, however, have failed to see that "the genesis of the Bible is an event in church history — an event in a comparatively late stage of early church history" (ST, I: 36). In using the Bible as a source, therefore, the theologian makes implicit reference to church history. The task of theological method is, of course, to make the implicit conditions of theologizing explicit, which is to say, that it must draw attention to the fact that church history is also a source of systematic theology. Tillich, therefore, rejects the radical biblicism of a truncated Protestantism and at the same time, the traditionalism of the Roman Catholic Church. In moving between these two alternatives, Tillich develops what he calls the Protestant principle for relating to the church historical tradition as a source of systematic theology. The Protestant principle neither asserts an exclusive authority of the Bible nor does it allow the papacy and church councils to decide the issues with which theology struggles. Consequently the Protestant principle frees the theologian to be genuinely ecumenical. Tillich writes:

> Protestant theology protests in the name of the Protestant Principle . . . against the identification of our ultimate concern with any creation of the church, including the biblical writings in so far as their witness to what is really ultimate concern is also a conditioned expression of their own spirituality. Therefore it is able to use all the materials provided by church history. It can make use of Greek and Roman and German and modern concepts in interpreting the biblical message; it can make use of the decisions of sectarian protests against official theology; but it is not bound to any of these concepts and decisions (ST, I; 37).[12]

The ecumenicity of the Protestant principle, however, is qualified by the theologian's own denominational background. While the positive element in theological method prevents "individual theology," it cannot rule out the impact the theologian's own concreteness has upon his theological efforts. "Therefore, the denominational tradition is a decisive source for the systematic theologian, however ecumenically he may use it" (ST, I: 38).

The church historical material also becomes accessible to the systematic theologian through the historical-critical labor of the historical theologian, who at the same time balances his ultimate concern within the structure of his work. "The historical theologian," for Tillich

> must show that in all periods Christian thought has dealt with matters of ultimate concern and that therefore it is itself a matter of ultimate concern. Systematic theology needs a history of Christian thought written from a point of view which is radically critical and, at the same time, existentially concerned (ST, I: 38).

Just as Tillich refuses to confine the sources of theology to the Bible alone, thus rejecting the orthodox Protestant position, he also denies that Tradition can be normative for theology, thus rejecting the Roman Catholic position. The question arises, however, how the Tradition is to be used if it is not normative. Tillich answers this question by asserting that the Tradition is "guiding" for the theologian. He argues:

Tradition cannot be normative in Christian theology because there is always an element in Tradition which must be judged and cannot be the judge itself. But Tradition can and must be guiding for the theologian, because it is the expression of the continuous reception of the new reality in history and because, without Tradition, no theological existence is possible . . . The guiding function of the Tradition has a positive and a negative side. Positively, the Tradition shows the questions implied in the Christian message, the main possibilities of answers, and the points in which Christians have agreed and have disagreed. Negatively, the Tradition shows answers which have generally been avoided and, above all, answers which have been characterized by the church as "heretical." He who takes the Tradition seriously must take heresies seriously. . . . He will not easily — not without the consciousness that he risks his participation in the new reality — promote a view which has been characterized as heretical by the church as a whole.[13]

It is also important to note Tillich's insistence that the historical material of both Bible and Tradition cannot be used in a probabilistic way to support any of the claims of the systematic theologian. If one approaches the historical dimension of Christian faith this way, whether it be the attempt to support the doctrine of apostolic succession or the historicity of Jesus, he fails to grasp the meaning of the "historical" as systematic theology understands it, *viz.*, as the locus of the appearance of the new reality upon which the Christian faith is based. The probabilistic approach to history is fatal for the theological enterprise and the Christian faith itself.

A broader source of systematic theology than those of Bible and Tradition is the history of religion and culture. However, Tillich acknowledges that it is difficult for the systematic theologian to appropriate these sources because, unlike the biblical and church historical sources, "neither a theological history of religion nor a theological history of culture has been theoretically conceived and practically established." On the other hand it is imperative that such disciplines be developed, since, as we have seen, the theologian lives *in* culture and draws his very conceptual tools (language, values, concepts) from it. At the same time, it is important to understand that the theologian lives in a culture *shaped* by religion, and thus both culture and religion have a profound impact upon the theologian. Beyond the immediate and unavoidable encounter with culture and religion, the systematic theologian deals with them directly in many ways. He uses culture and religion intentionally as his means of expression, he points to them for confirmation of his statements, he fights against them as contradictions of the Christian message, and, above all, he formulates the existential questions implied in them, to which his theology intends to be the answer (ST, I: 38).

The theological history of religion should attempt a typological analysis of the pre-religious and religious material in history in which it shows how the motives and types of religious expression follow from the religious concern and their presence within all religions, including Christianity. It also seeks to show the demonic distortions and new tendencies which appear in the history of religion. However, a theological history of religion does not stop there. It brings its own ultimate concern to bear upon the analysis of religion, and insofar as ultimate concern is informed by theological method

> this means that in every theological statement we must take into consideration the religious substance which is transformed and purified in the prophetic and apostolic message. Only in this sense . . . the history of religion belongs to the positive element in Christian theology. The universality of the Christian claim implies that there is no religion, not even the most primitive, which has not contributed or will not contribute to the preparation and reception of the new reality in history. In this sense the theologian always must be a "pagan" and a "Jew" and a "Greek" (humanist) and bring their spiritual substance under the criterion of the theological norm.[14]

In order for the systematic theologian to be able to appropriate culture as a source of theology, a "theology of culture" is needed. It is here that it can be seen that Tillich conceives of "theology of culture" as a discipline within the total framework of the theological disciplines (like biblical and church historical theology), but at the same time its results drive systematic theology in a basic cultural and thus apologetic direction. Thus, a "theology of culture"

> is the attempt to analyze the theory behind all cultural expressions, to discover the ultimate concern in the ground of a philosophy, a political system, an artistic style, a set of ethical or social principles. This task is analytic rather than synthetic, historical rather than systematic. It is a preparation for the work of the systematic theologian. . . . The key to the theological understanding of a cultural creation is its style. Style is a term derived from the

realm of the arts, but it can be applied to all realms of culture . . . The style of a period expresses itself in its cultural forms, its choice of objects, in the attitudes of its creative personalities, in its institutions and customs. It is an art as much as a science to "read styles". . . . This, however, is what is demanded of the theological historian of culture and in performing this function he opens up a creative source for systematic theology (ST, I: 39-40).

The sources of systematic theology, Bible, Tradition, history of religion and culture correspond to the positive element in theological method. However, not only are special disciplines required by which systematic theology may appropriate these sources, but theological method must also determine the generic structure operative within systematic theology by which these sources and their critical elaboration may be received, i.e., method must determine the *medium* of their reception. This for Tillich is the element of immediacy in theological method and its interpretation centers in the notion of "experience." Experience is the medium through which the sources are received by the systematic theologian.

Tillich's analysis of the function of experience as the medium of reception of the systematic theologian is carried out against the backdrop of the history of theology with special attention given to the Reformation, Schleiermacher, the theological development following him and the Neo-orthodox reaction to it as well as a critical analysis of the experimental or empirical theology of America. He also distinguishes three ways in which the word "experience" has been used in the context of contemporary theological and philosophical discussion. His analysis raises issues which cannot be explored here.

The main burden, however, of his discussion is to find a place for experience within theology against the claims of Neo-orthodoxy to the contrary and yet to deny that experience produces the content of the Christian faith on the one hand and that "new experience" takes the theologian beyond the confines of Christian experience and thus beyond the event Jesus as the Christ to a new center of truth and revelation on the other.

Understanding experience as the medium through which the objective sources are received, Tillich argues, excludes the reliance of the theologian on a possible post-Christian experience. But it also denies the assertion that experience is a theological source. And, finally, it denies the belief in experience which, although remaining in the Christian circle, add some new material to the other sources. Christian theology is based on the unique event Jesus the Christ, and in spite of the infinite meaning of this event it remains *this* event and, as such, the criterion of every religious experience. This experience receives and does not produce. Its productive power is restricted to the transformation of what is given to it. But this is not intended (ST, I: 46).

The theologian's experience is passive in relation to its object *in the sense that it has nothing to contribute to the constitution of the object of theology.* This means, for Tillich, that the theologian's subjectivity must be taken into account methodologically but that his subjectivity is in no way constitutive of the truth or the reality of the foundation of Christian theology. Tillich makes his case this way:

> The act of reception intends to receive and only to receive. If transformation is intended, the reception becomes falsification. The systematic theologian is bound to the Christian message which he must derive from other sources than his experience under the criterion of the norm . . . This excludes any intentional subjectivity, yet it gives to the subjectivity of the theologian that influence which a medium has on what is mediated through it. The medium colors the presentation and determines the interpretation of what it receives . . . Man's religious experience could become an independent source of systematic theology only if man were united with the source of all religious experiences, the Spiritual power in him . . . This unity is implied in the modern doctrine of man. But, as the Reformers realistically stressed against the Enthusiasts, this unity is not a fact. . . . Insight into the human situation destroys every theology which makes experience an independent source instead of a dependent medium of systematic theology (ST, I: 46).

In this latter statement one can see the impact of Tillich's conception of finitude upon the method and structure of theology. It will be recalled that finitude contains within itself the dynamics which break the original unity of finite and unconditioned being. The theologian, like all men, stands in the midst of the ruptured unity of being and hence his experience is ambiguous. Consequently, experience cannot be a source of theology. However, while the unity of finite and unconditioned being is ruptured, it is not severed under the conditions of existence, i.e. its power is still effective even in the face of the power of estrangement and separation, the rent in the fabric of being which has broken, but not destroyed, the original unity of finite and unconditioned being. Methodologically the power of the original unity can be seen in Tillich's analysis of the "mystical" or "religious a priori." After insisting, as we have seen, that "not experience, but revelation received *in* experience, gives the content of every theology," thereby drawing a clear distinction between medium and content, Tillich states:

> There is, however, one point . . . in which medium and content are identical, because in this point subject and object are identical: It is the awareness of the ultimate itself, the *esse ipsum*, which transcends the difference between subject and object and lies, as the presupposition of all doubts, beyond doubt; it is the *veritas ipsa*, as Augustine has called it. It is wrong to call this point "God" (as the ontological argument does), but it is necessary to call it "that in us which makes it impossible for us to escape God." It is the presence of the element of "ultimacy" in the structure of our existence, the basis of religious experience . . . If we use [the] phrase ["religious a priori"] . . . . we must remove every content from it and reduce it to the pure potentiality of having experiences with the character of "ultimate concern." . . . While the certainty of the pure ultimacy is ultimate, conditioned by nothing, its concrete embodiment in symbols and acts is a matter of destiny and venturing faith. Whenever we speak of religious experience, it is important to distinguish these (inseparable) elements: (1) the "point of immediate awareness of the unconditional which is empty but unconditionally certain; and (2) the "breadth" of a concrete concern which is full of content but has the conditional certainty of venturing faith. Theology deals with the second element, while presupposing the first and measuring every theological statement by the standard of the ultimacy of the ultimate concern.[15]

The positive element of theological method, then, determines the *content* and the immediate element determines the *medium* of systematic theology. However, theology also has, in addition to content and medium, a *form*, and the form of theology is determined by the *rational* element in theological method. The rational character of theology can be seen especially in the fact that theological work is *constructive* rather than *historical-descriptive* and it must use reason in its constructive task. Theology is the rational "word" about God, and, therefore, in its rational side it is the methodical interpretation of ultimate concern. Any theological proposition which violates the rational structure of man and world is both internally self-defeating and an attack upon the dignity of man.[16]

There is, however, a basic question concerning the role of reason within the structure of theology, especially in relation to the "existential" or nonrational side of theology. Tillich attempts to define the role of reason in theology by distinguishing two forms of reason. The first form of reason is generic to the structure of faith itself. The cognition implied in faith "has a completely existential, self-determining, and self-surrendering character and belongs to the faith of even the intellectually most primitive believer. Whoever participates in the New Being participates also in its truth" (ST, I: 53). Tillich calls this form of reason "self-transcending" or "ecstatic" reason. It is the organ with which we receive the contents of faith. The theologian, like every other believer, participates in the Christian message with the organ of self-transcending reason.

The theologian, however, not only participates in the truth of the New Being, but also has to express its truth in a methodical way. The form of reason by which the theologian executes this task, Tillich calls "technical" or "formal" reason. Tillich insists that

> in both cases reason is not a source of theology. It does not produce its contents. Ecstatic reason is reason grasped by an ultimate concern. Reason is overpowered, invaded, shaken by the ultimate concern. Reason does not produce an object of ultimate concern by logical procedures, as a mistaken theology tried to do in "its arguments for the existence of God." The contents of faith grasp reason. Nor does the technical or formal reason of the theologian produce its content (ST, I: 53).

Reason, then, in both its ecstatic and formal structures, is the form in which the content of Christian faith is expressed. But it is precisely at this point that the problematic or "questionable" character of theology is to be seen. For example, the formulation of the theological norm (see below) is

> a matter of personal and communal religious experience and, at the same time, a matter of the methodological judgment of the theologian. It is simultaneously received by ecstatic reason and conceived through technical reason

... The ambiguity cannot be avoided so long as there is theology ... The problem would be solved if man's formal reason were in complete harmony with his ecstatic reason, if man were living in a complete theonomy, that is, in the fullness of the Kingdom of God. One of the basic Christian truths to which theology must witness is that theology itself, like every human activity, is subject to the contradictions of man's existential situation (ST, I: 54).

At the same time, that which makes theology questionable, i.e., the simultaneous interpenetration of ecstatic and formal reason also rules out, for Tillich, a "natural" theology. The positive character of theology which grasps the ecstatic or existential reason, upon the basis of which the formal reason is brought into play, by definition is self-positing and thus brought within the horizon of technical reason by the prior existential surrender of ecstatic reason to that which grasps it. Consequently, a rational or natural theology, where these terms mean that theological propositions can be produced by a detached analysis of reality without existential participation in an ultimate concern is clearly impossible. Tillich writes:

The concepts "natural revelation" and "natural theology" are often used for a knowledge of God which is inferentially derived from the structure of reality. But, whether such conclusions are valid or not, in neither case have they the character of "revelation," and they should not be called "theological," for there is no meaningful speaking of God if he is taken as an object which is not, at the same time, the ground of the speaking about him. There is no meaningful speaking of God except in an existential attitude or in the situation of revelation. ... So we can say: There is revelation through nature; but there is no natural (rational) revelation. And there *is* theology dealing with nature; but there is no natural theology. Reason elaborates but does not produce theological propositions.[17]

Having established, then, that reason is not a source for theology and therefore its deliverances cannot be the basis for a natural theology nor a philosophy of religion, which seeks to "know" God in a detached, objectively demonstrable way, Tillich goes on to suggest some "directing principles" by which the ultimately unsolvable problem of the rational character of systematic theology can at least be understood. The first principle is a semantic one. It is incumbent upon the theologian to employ the rules of semantic clarity for every basic word he uses. The principle of *semantic rationality* demands that the theologian take seriously his use of language and seek to achieve the most precise and unambiguous terminology of which he is capable.

Semantic rationality, however, is subject to a limit and establishes a consequence for systematic theology. The limit is that the theologian, in trying to obey this first principle, cannot hope to "disambiguate" his language by construing a "pan-mathematical formalism." The realm of spiritual life with which theology deals imposes its own demands upon language, i.e., "words," in this realm, "cannot be reduced to mathematical signs, nor can sentences be reduced to mathematical equations. The power of words denoting spiritual realities lies in their connotations. The removal of these connotations leaves dead bones which have no meaning in any realm" (ST, I: 54). Words like "Spirit, "New Being" and "history" emerge out of a whole context of meanings which include anthropological, psychological and philosophical elements. The principle of semantic rationality demands that in the theological use of these words "all connotations . . . should consciously be related to each other and centered around a controlling meaning." These very examples, however, illustrate "how difficult it is to apply this principle — a difficulty which is rooted in the fact that every significant theological term cuts through several levels of meaning and that all of them contribute to the theological meaning" (ST, I: 55).

The consequence for systematic theology of the semantic situation defined by the principle of semantic rationality is "that the language of theology cannot be a sacred or revealed language." Therefore, the theologian

cannot restrict himself to the biblical terminology or to the language of classical theology. He could not avoid philosophical concepts even if he used only biblical words; and even less could he avoid them if he used only the words of the Reformers. Therefore, he should use philosophical and scientific terms whenever he deems them helpful for his task of explaining the contents of the Christian faith. The two things he must watch in doing so are semantic clarity and existential purity. He must avoid conceptual ambiguity and a possible distortion of the Christian message by the intrusion of anti-Christian ideas in the cloak of a philosophical, scientific, or poetic terminology (ST, I: 55-56).

The second principle determining the rational character of theology is that of *logical rationality*. By this principle Tillich means first that the structures which are presupposed in *any* meaningful discourse and which are formulated in the principles of logic are just as inescapable for theology as for another discipline. "Theology is as dependent on formal logic as any other science. This must be maintained against both philosophical and theological protests." The issue here, for Tillich, is to show that genuinely *dialectical* thinking, which in its most complete philosophical formulation in the person of Hegel was a protest against formal logic, is not incompatible with formal logic. Tillich asserts:

Dialectics follows the movements of thought or the movement of reality through yes and no, but it describes it in logically correct terms. The same concept always is used in the same sense; and, if the meaning of the concept changes, the dialectician describes it in logically correct terms. . . . formal logic (is not) contradicted when, in the dogma of the Trinity, the divine life is described as a trinity within a unity. The doctrine of the Trinity does not affirm the logical nonsense that three is one and one is three; it describes in dialectical terms the inner movement of the divine life as an eternal separation from itself and return to itself. Theology is not expected to accept a senseless combination of words, that is, genuine logical contradictions. Dialectical thinking is not in conflict with the structure of thinking (ST, I: 56).

This means, for Tillich, that there is a clear place for paradox within the structure of systematic theology, but that the paradoxical statement does not contradict the logical structure of thought. The various *paradoxa* found within Christian thought do not indulge in logical contradictions; rather they

want to express the conviction that God's acting transcends all possible human expectations and all necessary human preparations. It transcends but does not destroy, finite reason; for God acts through the Logos which is the transcendent and transcending source of the Logos structure of thought and being. . . . Paradoxical means "against the opinion," namely, the opinion of finite reason. Paradox points to the fact that in God's acting finite reason is superseded but not annihilated; it expresses this fact in terms which are not logically contradictory but which are supposed to point beyond the realm in which finite reason is applicable . . . There is, in the last analysis, only *one* genuine paradox in the Christian message — the appearance of that which conquers existence under the conditions of existence. . . . The acceptance of this paradox is not the acceptance of the absurd, but it is the state of being grasped by the power of that which breaks into our experience with the principle of logical rationality. Paradox has its logical place (ST, I: 57).[18]

The third and final principle defining the rational character of theology Tillich specifies as that of *methodological rationality*. This principle maintains that theology as an intellectual discipline "follows a method, that is, a definite way of deriving and stating its propositions." The method peculiar to systematic theology is, "dependent on many non-rational factors . . . , but, once it has been established, it must be carried through rationally and consistently." This consideration leads Tillich to assert: "The final expression of consistency in applying methodological rationality is the theological system" (ST, I: 58). Since we have discussed the role of system in Tillich's thought in Part One, we turn now to a more detailed discussion of the actual method employed in systematic theology, which Tillich argues, embodies the principle of methodological rationality.

We have seen that for Tillich the nature of theology is defined by a non-rational (but not irrational) or "existential" side and a rational or methodological side, that it is an existential-methodical interpretation of a religious encounter with reality or an ultimate concern and that its non-rational and rational sides are strictly interdependent. We have also seen that both the non-rational and rational sides are reflected in theological method insofar as there are positive, immediate (non-rational) and rational elements within theological method itself. Thus, theological method is grounded in the *nature* of theology and the *structure* of systematic theology follows from the methodological elaboration of the nature of theology. The method of correlation presupposes the nature of theology and it is actualized within the structure of theology. Tillich has formulated this issue thus:

The cognitive relation in theology reveals the existential and transcending character of the ground of objects in time and space. Therefore, no method can be developed without a prior knowledge of the object to which it is applied. For systematic theology this means that its method is derived from a prior knowledge of the system which is to be built by the method (ST, I: 60).

It is Tillich's contention that the history of theology reveals that the method of correlation has always been used in theological reflection and discourse. It is true that this method has often been used with various degrees of consciousness. The issue here is to develop the method of correlation with explicit consciousness, "especially if the apologetic point of view is to prevail." This means quite clearly constructing a theology in which "the contents of the Christian faith [are explained] through existential questions and theological answers in mutual interdependence" (ST, I: 60).

We have already seen in Part One that the method of correlation is carried out on three levels within the structure of theology. The correspondence between symbol and symbolizandum is correlative and thus bears central significance for the problem of religious knowledge; there is a logical correlation between concepts denoting the human and the divine, which "determine statements about God and the world," and there is a factual correlation between "man's ultimate concern and that about which he is ultimately concerned. . . . The third meaning of correlation qualifies the divine-human relationship within religious experience" (ST, I: 60-61).

It is especially the third meaning of correlation which is problematic for theologians such as Karl Barth. Barth has protested this meaning of correlation on the grounds that it makes God in some sense dependent upon man. Tillich's response to this criticism brings him as close in his writings as one can find to the absolute-relative position of dipolar theism. He writes:

> . . . although God in his abysmal nature is in no way dependent on man, God in his self-manifestation to man is dependent on the way man receives his manifestation. This is true even if the doctrine of predestination, namely, that this way is foreordained by God and entirely independent of human freedom, is maintained. The divine-human relation, and therefore God as well as man within this relation, changes with the stages of the history of revelation and with the stages of every personal development. There is a mutual interdependence between "God for us" and "we for God." God's wrath and God's grace are not contrasts in the "heart" of God (Luther), in the depth of

his being; but they are contrasts in the divine-human relationship. The divine-human relation is a correlation. The "divine-human encounter" (Emil Brunner) means something real for both sides. It is an actual correlation, in the third sense of the term (ST, I: 61).[19]

Again, as we have argued above the essence of the method of correlation depends upon the three foundational notions we have analyzed, especially upon the notions of finitude and the unity of finite and unconditioned being. These notions are the ultimate presuppositions of the method of correlation, without which the method itself could not "function." Just as medium and content are identical at one point, namely, within the structure of the "mystical" or "religious a priori" (which is the expression of the unity of finite and unconditioned being) so also question and answer, or form and content (substance) are identical at the same point. Tillich asserts:

> The divine-human relationship is a correlation also in its cognitive side. Symbolically speaking, God answers man's questions, and under the impact of God's answers man asks them. Theology formulates the questions implied in human existence, and theology formulates the answers implied in human existence. This is a circle which drives man to a point where question and answer are not separated. This point, however, is not a moment in time. *It belongs to man's essential being, to the unity of his finitude with the infinity in which he was created . . . and from which he is separated.* A symptom of both the essential unity and the existential separation of finite man from his infinity is his ability to ask about the infinite to which he belongs; the fact that he must ask about it indicates that he is separated from it (ST, I: 61, Emphasis Mine).[20]

The procedure of the method of correlation is interesting for our purposes because it defines, in part, the relationship of philosophy and theology in a way which differs significantly from the early understanding of the relationship we have explored below. Rather than philosophy's providing the principles of meaning within which theology as theonomous or normative systematics works, now philosophy provides the questions to which theology gives the answers. Following its method, then,

> systematic theology proceeds in the following way: it makes an analysis of the human situation out of which the existential questions arise, and it demon-

strates that the symbols used in the Christian message are the answers to these questions. The analysis of the human situation is done in terms which today are called "existential." Such analyses are much older than existentialism; they are, indeed, as old as man's thinking about himself, and they have been expressed in various kinds of conceptualization since the beginning of philosophy (ST, I: 62).

Tillich is quite explicit in stating that the analysis of existence or of the human situation from which the questions arise, to which the Christian symbols and their theological elaboration are the answers, is a philosophical task even if it is done by a theologian. However, if this task is undertaken by a philosopher, who is not intentionally a theologian, his analysis is placed within a broader philosophical construction with no explicit reference to the theological answers. The theologian, on the other hand, who works as a philosopher insofar as the analysis of human existence is concerned, differs from the latter in that he "tries to correlate the material of his analysis with the theological concepts he derives from the Christian faith." It should not be concluded that this makes the philosophical work of the theologian heteronomous, because

As a theologian he does not tell himself what is philosophically true. As a philosopher he does not tell himself what is theologically true. But he cannot help seeing human existence and existence generally in such a way that the Christian symbols appear meaningful and understandable to him. His eyes are partially focused by his ultimate concern, which is true of every philosopher. Nevertheless, his act of seeing is autonomous, for it is determined only by the object as it is given in his experience. If he sees something he did not expect to see in the light of his theological answer, he holds fast to what he has seen and reformulates the theological answer. He is certain that nothing he sees can change the substance of his answer, because this substance is the *logos* of being, manifest in Jesus as the Christ. If this were not his presupposition, he would have to sacrifice his philosophical honesty or his theological concern (ST, I: 63-64).[21]

The method of correlation, then, defines the formal relationship between theology and philosophy and asserts that theology is dependent upon philosophy insofar as the objective and universal determination of the structure of existence is concerned, and although Tillich has not made the point explicit here, philosophy is dependent upon theology for the answers to the questions this analysis reveals. We shall explore this relationship in more detail in the next chapter. The point to be made here is that a relationship of mutual interdependence between philosophy and theology is required by the method of correlation, which as we have seen, shapes the *form* of question and answer, although the *substance* of the Christian message is unaffected by this relationship (ST, I: 64). The answers cannot be derived from the questions or the analysis of existence they presuppose (this would violate the existential-positivistic character of theology), but the form in which the answer is given is shaped by the form of the question.

The method of correlation also replaces three inadequate methods which Tillich believes have also been used in attempting to relate message and situation. In one way or another these methods violate the dialectical relationship of Yes and No which obtains between the content of the Christian faith and the cultural milieu in which it is received. In Tillich's description of these methodologies, their respective inadequacies can be seen.

> The first method can be called supranatualistic, in that it takes the Christian message to be a sum of revealed truths which have fallen into the human situation like strange bodies from a strange world. No mediation to the human situation is possible. . . . The second method to be rejected can be called "naturalistic or humanistic." It derives the Christian message from man's natural state. It develops its answer out of human existence, unaware that human existence itself is the question. . . . Questions and answers were put on the same level of human creativity. Everything was said by man, nothing to man. But revelation is "spoken" to man, not by man to himself. The third method to be rejected can be called "dualistic," inasmuch as it builds a supranatural structure on a natural substructure. This method . . . is aware of the problem which the method of correlation tries to meet. It realizes that, in spite of the infinite gap between man's spirit and God's spirit, there must be a positive relation between them. It tries to express this relation by positing a body of theological truth which man can reach through his own efforts, or in terms of a self-contradictory expression, through "natural revelation" (ST, I: 64-65).

The method of correlation is neither supranaturalistic, humanistic, nor dualistic. Taking "self-transcending realism" as its point of departure, the method of correlation resolves "natural theology into the analysis of existence and [it resolves] supranatural theology into the answers given to the questions implied in existence" (ST, I: 66).22 In the method of correlation

> the Christian message provides the answers to the questions implied in human existence. These answers are contained in the revelatory events on which Christianity is based and are taken by systematic theology *from* the sources, *through* the medium, *under* the norm (ST, I: 64).

We have departed somewhat from Tillich's own discussion by choosing to discuss the norm of systematic theology after our discussion of its nature, method, and structure. It will be recalled, however, that in his earliest formulations, Tillich stressed the normative character of theology, and thus no discussion of his conception of theology would be complete without an analysis of the norm under which theological construction is directed.

We have seen that in his "Philosophy of Religion" Tillich argues that whatever concrete norm theology decides upon, it will fall within the philosophical conception of the religion of grace or paradox. Here we have a clue from the early Tillich as to the determination of the norm of systematic theology in his mature thought. If Tillich is to argue consistently that there is only *one* genuine paradox within the Christian message, *viz.*, the appearance of that which conquers existence under the conditions of existence, then it follows that the norm of systematic theology will be grounded in that central paradox.

Tillich argues that the history of the Christian faith reveals a variety of norms which emerged out of special situations and as a result of unique demands. Consequently:

> the norm grows; it is not produced intentionally; its appearance is not the work of theological reflection but of the Spiritual life of the church, for the church is the "home" of systematic theology. Here alone do the sources and the norms of theology have actual existence. At this place alone can experience occur as the medium of systematic theology (ST, I: 48).

The articulation of the norm of systematic theology then, is a creative act of theological reflection, which occurs within the matrix of the church historical development in which the theologian stands and the cultural situation which impinges upon him. As such the articulation of any norm can only be attempted with reservations and ambiguity. "In order to be a genuine norm," Tillich writes, "it must not be a private opinion of the theologian but the expression of an encounter of the church with the Christian message."

In rejecting the completely arbitrary standpoint of the individual theologian (what Tillich would call theological subjectivism) in the articulation of the theological norm, Tillich, again, brings to bear the impact of the positive element of theological method upon theological reflection. However, it also needs to be seen that Tillich does not thereby deny relativity in theology. The norms of systematic theology seen in the history of the church are relative and not absolute, which is to say, that they will change and be replaced as new cultural situations emerge to which the Christian message must be related. Consequently, the norm which Tillich offers, he understands, is not final. It, too, will be replaced.

The relativity in theological method, therefore, leads Tillich to reject, as we have seen, the normative claims of Bible and Tradition. Clearly a genuine norm, on Tillich's terms, will have to be rooted in Bible and Tradition, but it cannot be identical with them. What is not relative in the theological norm, therefore, is the event upon which Bible and Tradition are based. But Bible and Tradition, as well as the *formulation* of the norm, are relative. The implications of Tillich's distinction between the *source* and *medium* of theology and the *norm* of theology can now be seen. The norm determines the way both sources and medium are to be used in theological construction.

Tillich characteristically develops his conception of the norm of systematic theology out of his determination of the cultural situation with which he believes the church is confronted. The philosophical analysis of the human situation, which the method of correlation demands, reveals the following results:

It is not an exaggeration to say that today man experiences his present situation in terms of disruption, conflict, self-destruction, meaninglessness, and despair in all realms of life. This experience is expressed in the arts and in literature, conceptualized in existential philosophy, actualized in political cleavages of all kinds, and analyzed in the psychology of the unconscious. It has given theology a new understanding of the demonic-tragic structures of individual and social life. The question arising out of this experience is not, as in the Reformation, the question of a merciful God and the forgiveness of sins; nor is it, as in the early Greek church, the question of finitude, of death and error; nor is it the question of culture and society. It is the question of a reality in which the self-estrangement of our existence is overcome, a reality of reconciliation and reunion, of creativity, meaning, and hope (ST, I: 49).

The assumption here is that in the historical epoch of the Reformation, the felt need of man was forgiveness of sin by a merciful God and that the material norm of Luther's theology, the justification by faith, was, although unconscious to Luther, established correlatively to that need. The same can be said of the historical period of the early Greek church where the quest to overcome the power of finitude, death, and error determined the theological norm of this period. Thus, it is the cultural aspirations and self-definitions of a period which determine the interpretation of the theological norm, and consequently, Tillich seeks to develop the *interpretation* of the theological norm which is implicit in the self-understanding of contemporary western man. He is convinced that there is a consensus on several different cultural fronts that contemporary man's situation is defined by disruption, conflict, self-destruction, meaninglessness, and despair. This, of course, is a creative philosophical decision on Tillich's part, the gravity of which can be seen in the fact that the articulation of the norm by which theological reflection is to be guided is determined by it.

What contemporary western man seeks, then, whether he knows it or not, is that which can overcome existence under the conditions of existence, that is, he seeks release from his disrupted, meaningless, despair-ridden existence. He longs to participate in that which is not characterized by the old realities, but in the new reality which offers integration, meaning, and fulfillment. This reality, the Christian faith proclaims, has appeared in historical existence. The theological norm which emerges out of the power which is present in historical existence, Tillich formulates as the "New Being." He writes:

If the Christian message is understood as the message of the "New Being," an answer is given to the question implied in our present situation and in every human situation. But this answer is not sufficient. It leads immediately to the further question, "Where is the New Being manifest?" Systematic theology answers this question by saying: "In Jesus the Christ." . . . He who is the Christ is he who brings the new eon, the new reality. And it is the man Jesus who in a paradoxical assertion is called the Christ. Without this paradox the New Being would be an ideal, not a reality, and consequently not an answer to the question implied in our human situation. The material norm of systematic theology, used in the present system and considered the most adequate to the present apologetic situation, is the "New Being in Jesus as the Christ." If this is combined with the critical principle of all theology, one can say that the material norm of systematic theology today is the New Being in Jesus as the Christ as our ultimate concern. This norm is the criterion for the use of all the sources of systematic theology (ST, I: 50).

For theological reflection to be carried out consistently under the norm of the "New Being in Jesus as the Christ," then, its every proposition must be directed, on the one hand, toward the explication of the human situation as disrupted, meaningless, and caught in the grip of despair and on the other it must give witness to the presence of that reality in personal and social-historical existence which overcomes the power of these dynamics within the structure and under the condition of existence. In a very real sense, theology is a response to power, and it is the theologian's own participation in the power of the New Being which allows him to look courageously at the human predicament without turning away from the sometimes terrifying and overwhelming marks of estrangement and fallenness to be seen there, while not succumbing to hopelessness and despair himself. The task, which the norm Tillich has defined for theologizing places upon the theologian is enormous. He must speak with utter honesty about the human condition, which means cutting through the personal and cultural illusions men use to hide themselves from the depths of their own reality. At the same time, he must speak the word of hope and salvation, which stands against every false hope and every spurious salvation.

Our analyses of Tillich's conceptions of philosophy and theology have brought us to the point where we must now attempt systematically to define his conception of their relationship. We have seen that there are both similarities and differences in the two enterprises. We shall now attempt to determine the way in which Tillich defines them and their relationship to each other.

Notes

1 Adams, *op. cit.*, p. 259.

2 Perhaps one can see in the mature period a crystallization of Tillich's identity as a theologian, even though he insists that he remained on the boundary between philosophy and theology, church and secular society, religion and culture. It would be difficult imagining Tillich's responding in his mature period as he did to Barth in the early 20's in regard to the theological task: "Thus our attention is directed beyond all these allusions to where there is *only* allusion, where the Yes and No shine in perfect brightness. This may be called philosophy of culture because the allusion to this ultimate is not expressed in the words of Scripture and of the Church. For our situation forces us, as theologians, to be *not* theologians but philosophers of culture." *The Beginnings of Dialectical Theology, op. cit.*, p. 157.

3 We are using the terms "theological system" or "systematic theology" as Tillich has defined them. "Theology is often identified with systematic theology. Although this terminology is bad, because it excludes historical and practical theology from their full part in the whole world of theology, it indicates that theology is essentially systematic. The word 'system' has a narrower and a larger meaning. In its narrower sense the word points to the ideal of a deductive method in which a whole of interdependent presuppositions is derived from highest principles. Attempts have been made to develop such a system in the history of Christian thought. But the positive element in theology utterly resists a 'system' in this sense; it includes openness and undermines a closed system. But 'system' has also a larger sense. It designates a whole of propositions which are consistent, interdependent, and developed according to a definite method. In this sense all classical theology was systematic, and no theology . . . can surrender the systematic idea. Every meaningful fragment is an implicit system, as every system is an explicit fragment."   P. Tillich, "The Problem of Theological Method," *Four Existentialist Theologians*, ed. Will Herberg (Doubleday & Co., Garden City, N.Y., 1958), p. 250. (Hereafter "Theological Method"). Cf. also the brief discussion of "system" in Part One above.

4 Cf. "Theological Method," *op. cit.*, p. 240: "The presupposition of theology is that there is a special encounter with reality — or a special way in which reality imposes itself on us — which is ordinarily called religious. And it is the

presupposition of this paper that having a religious encounter with reality means being ultimately concerned about reality."

5   One can see what amounts to the distinction between form and import more clearly in the following passage: "Pictures, poems, and music can become objects of theology, not from the point of view of their aesthetic form, but from the point of view of their power of expressing some aspects of that which concerns us ultimately, in and through their aesthetic form. Physical or historical or psychological insights can become objects of theology, not from the point of view of their cognitive form, but from the point of view of their power of revealing some aspects of that which concerns us ultimately in and through their cognitive form . . ." (ST, I: 13). The existential character of theology, i.e., its having to speak out of the situation of ultimate concern, which the first formal principle establishes, means that "no object is excluded from theology if this criterion [of ultimate concern] is applied, not even a piece of stone; and no object is in itself a matter of theology, not even God as an object of inference. This makes theology absolutely universal, on the one hand, and absolutely definite, on the other hand. Theology has to deal with everything, but only under the theological criterion, the ultimate concern." "Theological Method," *op. cit.*, p. 241.

6   *Dynamics of Faith, op. cit.*, p. 10.

7   Tillich quite self-consciously makes this point in his early "Philosophy of Religion", *What is Religion?, op. cit.*, p. 79: "In a metalogical philosophy of religion one can speak of God only insofar as he is intended in a religious act. An extrareligious speaking of God contradicts the methodological as well as the material presuppositions. God is the object intended in faith, and beyond that nothing. This, however, is not to say that the object is as it were to be made into a product of the subject, as though God were a creation of faith. Rather, faith as faith is determined by its directedness toward the Unconditional; and the reality of the Unconditioned is the foundation of every assertion regarding reality. But the act of grasping the Unconditional is an act of faith; without faith the Unconditional is not apprehensible." Cf. also ST, I: 212 and Tillich's comments on Feuerbach, Marx, and Freud in *A History of Christian Thought, op. cit.*, pp. 435-439.

8   "Theological Method", *op. cit.*, p. 241.

9   *Ibid.*, p. 247.

10 *Ibid.*, pp. 242-243.

11 *Ibid.*, pp. 243-244.

12 The notion of the "Protestant Principle" is another seminal concept to be found in Tillich's thought. Tillich argues in *The Protestant Era* that

"Protestantism is understood as a special historical embodiment of a universally significant principle. This principle, in which one side of the divine-human relationship is expressed, is effective in all periods of history; it is indicated in the great religions of mankind; it has been powerfully pronounced by the Jewish prophets; it is manifest in the picture of Jesus as the Christ; it has been rediscovered time and again in the life of the church and was established as the sole foundation of the churches of the Reformation; and it will challenge these churches whenever they leave their foundation . . . It is the critical and dynamic source of all Protestant realizations, but it is not identical with any of them. It cannot be confined by a definition. It is not exhausted by any historical religion; it is not identical with the structure of the Reformation or of early Christianity or even with a religious form at all. It transcends them as it transcends any cultural form. On the other hand, it can appear in all of them; it is a living, moving, restless power in them; . . . The Protestant principle . . . contains the divine and human protest against any absolute claim made for a relative-reality, even if this claim is made by a Protestant church. The Protestant principle is the judge of every religious and cultural reality, including the religion and culture which calls itself Protestant . . . [It] is the theological expression of the true relation between the unconditional and the conditioned or, religiously speaking, between God and man . . . It is the guardian against the attempts of the finite and conditioned to usurp the place of the unconditional in thinking and acting." *The Protestant Era, op. cit.*, pp. xi-xii; 163.

With respect to the question of tradition, Tillich supplements the Protestant principle with the notion of "Catholic substance." "The Protestant principle . . . is not restricted to the churches of the Reformation or to any other church; it [is] . . . an expression of the Spiritual Community . . . It alone is not enough; it needs the 'Catholic substance', the concrete embodiment of the Spiritual Presence; but it is the criterion of the demonization (and profanization) of such embodiment. It is the expression of the victory of the Spirit over religion" (ST, III: 245).

13 "Theological Method," *op. cit.*, pp. 245-246.

14 *Ibid.*, p. 245.

15 *Ibid.*, p. 49; Cf. also "The Two Types of Philosophy of Religion," in *Theology of Culture, op. cit.* for a more detailed analysis of the "mystical" or "religious *a priori*" in the ontological type of philosophy of religion, the validity of which Tillich asserts against the cosmological type, the latter making knowledge of God an inferential process, and thus the philosophical source for "natural" theology.

16 Cf. *Dynamics of Faith, op. cit.*, p. 74ff.

17 "Theological Method," *op. cit.*, p. 251. It should be noted here that some of Tillich's interpreters have, in fact, maintained that he is not successful in attempting to eliminate a natural theology from his own thought. Cf. John Cobb, *Living Options in Protestant Theology, op. cit.*, pp. 276-283.

18 Cf. also ST, II: 90-92.

19 On the basis of our analysis of the unconditionedness of God as being-itself in Part One, we can only conclude again that while Tillich would seem to be advocating an absolute-relative view of God here that, in fact, the claim that God's being in his self-manifestation is qualified or conditioned by man's reception of it or lack thereof cannot be consistently maintained. It is regrettable that Tillich in this passage does not attempt to show just *how* God is "dependent" upon man, rather than merely asserting this dependence. We can see no evidence in Tillich to conclude that he would assert a genuine relativism in God, which would include the claim, as C. Harteshorne has argued in *The Divine Relativity* (Yale University Press, New Haven, 1948), that insofar as God's self-manifestation is known or received by man, He is, therefore, genuinely qualified by that knowledge and changes because of it, or that insofar as He is not known or received by man, His "experience" is to that degree incomplete. Cf. also Schubert Ogden's critique of Tillich in *The Reality of God, op. cit.*, pp. 54-55. We conclude, then, on the basis of our previous analysis that Tillich cannot sustain his claim that God is genuinely qualified or dependent upon man in his self-manifestation, and, therefore, is involved, in some aspect of his being, in change.

20 Tillich has formulated the same issue in terms of form and substance. This formulation reveals both the significance of the foundational notions for theological method and also the impact of the rational element of theological method upon theological propositions, that element, too, being rooted in the unity of finite and unconditioned being. " . . . the question arises as to whether the 'elaboration' of the positive element in theology does not introduce a rational element into the substance itself. The urgency of this question is obvious when we look at the large number of philosophical concepts which have been used for theological purposes [which the principle of semantic rationality demands] throughout the whole history of Christian thought . . ."

" . . . the method of correlation establishes a mutual interdependence between questions and answers. The question implied in human existence determines the meaning and the theological interpretation of the answers as they appear in the classical religious symbols. The form of the questions, whether primitive or philosophical, is decisive for the theological form in which the answer is given. And, conversely, the substance of the question is determined by the substance of the answer. Nobody is able to ask questions concerning God, revelation, Christ, etc., who has not already received some answer. So we can say: With respect to man's ultimate concern the questions contain the substance of the answers, and the answers are shaped by the form of the questions. Here the rational element in theological method has a determining influence on theological propositions — not on their substance but on their form. But there is no way of saying a priori how much substance is hidden in the form. This can be said only in the process of theological work, and never fully. The reception of the 'new reality', is always conditioned by the 'old reality,' which is conquered and fulfilled by it. This is the reason why early Christianity formulated the doctrine of the Logos, who has appeared in a unique way in Jesus as the Christ and is, at the same time, the universal principle of revelation in religion and culture. In this way the old reality can be considered as preparation for the new one; and the philosophical form is ultimately related to the substance of the theological answer instead of being alien to it. It seems to me that without some form of a Logos doctrine (even if the term 'Logos' is not used), no theology — certainly no apologetic theology — is possible." "Theological Method," *op. cit.*, pp. 251; 253-254.

It should be noted that in this passage Tillich denies that the rational component determines substance. However, both question and answer, form and substance presuppose reason and they also presuppose their identity at the point where they arise, viz., the awareness of that which is beyond subject and object. This is the ontological foundation for the Logos doctrine as well. However, there is an historical component, which Tillich seems to ontologize, *viz.*, the concrete content of the Christian message itself. Men may ask the question of ultimate reality on the basis of the ontological unity of finite and unconditioned being, but it does not follow that the specifically Christian answers to these questions are as universal as the questions themselves, as the presence of other religious answers in human history clearly demonstrates. Thus, a serious question may be raised as to whether form and substance, question and answer are as interdependent as Tillich thinks. It is here again that one can begin to see the way in which the philosophical quest for universal truth determines the theological enterprise for Tillich, and thus negates both the "existential" and historical character of theology. This also raises the question as to whether Tillich's claim that all religious answers not given in the symbol of Jesus as the Christ are mere "preparations" for the Christian answer can rescue Tillich from the charge that he has eternalized and universalized the Christian substance at the expense of its essential historicity. Thus, it would seem that Tillich is not correct in denying that the "elaboration" has introduced a rational element into the Christian substance. The rational-philosophical concern for universal truth has clearly led Tillich to make claims for the Christian substance which it is not at all obvious it can sustain, the Logos doctrine notwithstanding.

If this analysis is correct, a twofold state of affairs arises for theological method. On the one hand, the Christian substance has, in fact, been conditioned by its rational elaboration, especially where the presuppositions of reason are determined by the philosophical quest for universal truth. On the other, the Christian substance determined by its rational elaboration, in fact, determines that very elaboration insofar as the latter involves the development of the question to which the Christian substance is the answer, i.e., the substance of the answer determines the substance of the question, a condition, we have seen, Tillich readily admits. The objection to the method of correlation, however, receives its force when it is seen that the relationship between question and answer in the Christian substance is an historical-cultural one and not ontological as Tillich seems to think the Logos doctrine implies. We shall return to this question below.

21 It should be noted here that the method of correlation answers the question "Natural theology or Philosophy of religion?" for systematic theology by taking the philosophical element of both "into the structure of the system itself." This means that "for the organization of systematic theology . . . no special discipline called 'philosophy of religion' belongs to the realm of systematic theology" (ST, I: 30).

22 Cf., "Theological Method," *op. cit.*, p. 238.

Chapter Nine

Philosophy and Theology: Tillich's Conception of Their Relationship

The analysis of the development of the conceptions of philosophy and theology in Tillich's thought clearly reveals that from his earliest reflections onward he has consistently construed the relationship of the two disciplines to be one of positive, mutual interaction. At the outset we can say that for Tillich the relationship between philosophy and theology means that neither can exist independently of the other. The ideal of a purely positivistic philosophy devoid of any religious or theological concern classically expressed in A. J. Ayer's *Language, Truth and Logic* and a kerygmatic theology untouched by philosophical concepts most clearly seen in Barth's enterprise are from Tillich's stance both philosophically and theologically naive. The former is largely a specialized development within philosophy, which is important and necessary, but in relation to the history of philosophy, it cannot claim to be the whole of philosophy itself. Historically

the most . . . significant philosophies show not only the greatest power of thought but the most passionate concern about the meaning of the ultimate whose manifestations they describe. One needs only to be reminded of the Indian and Greek philosophers, almost without exception, and the modern philosophers from Leibnitz and Spinoza to Kant and Hegel. If it seems that the positivistic line of philosophers from Locke and Hume to present-day logical positivism is an exception to this rule, one must consider that the task to which these philosophers restricted themselves were special problems of the doctrine of knowledge and, in our time especially, analyses of the linguistic tools of scientific knowledge. *This certainly is a justified and very important endeavor, but is not philosophy in the traditional sense* (emphasis mine).[1]

However problematic Tillich's claim may be that Locke and Hume restricted themselves to problems of knowledge, what is clear is that the traditional or classical conception of philosophy is both normative for the conception of philosophy as we have seen and includes within itself a religious or theological dimension which does not allow philosophy to trivalize its meaning by denying it or to escape a positive relationship to theology.

The conception of theology which asserts its independence from philosophy is, to Tillich's mind, completely unaware of the impact of philosophical concepts and ideas upon its own reflections and language. To be independent of philosophy, a theology would have to show that its language and concepts are *sui generis*. Barth's attempt to create a dogmatic theology which is "unspoiled" by philosophy is abortive, for Tillich, precisely because he fails to understand that the Word of God, which Barth claims as the exclusive source of Dogmatics embodied in Scripture and Church, is received in human thought and culture and is thus received upon a soil which has been prepared by philosophical activity. Thus, Barth is blind to the philosophical concepts and presuppositions, which are implicit in the structure of his own theology. Tillich is adamant on this point. He asserts:

> It is infuriating to see how biblical theologians, when explaining the concepts of the Old or New Testament writers, use most of the terms created by the toil of philosophers and the ingenuity of the speculative mind and then dismiss, with cheap denunciations, the work from which their language has been immensely enriched. No theologian should be taken seriously as a theologian, even if he is a great Christian and a great scholar, if his work shows that he does not take philosophy seriously.[2]

Apart from this general assertion regarding the relationship of philosophy and theology, however, the task remains to explore this positive relationship in detail. We may begin by stating that the first assumption which informs Tillich's conception of the relationship is that philosophy and theology are two distinct cultural forms of inquiry with distinct methods, delimited fields of knowledge (although philosophy's field is in principle the whole of reality), and distinct objects, which are, nonetheless, if not identical, at least comparable at a common point. Their distinctiveness gives rise to divergences in their relationship to each other while their comparability gives rise to a convergence in the same relationship.

We have noted that, for Tillich, philosophy's primary task is ontological, that is, it asks the question of being and it seeks to answer its question by describing the structure of being in objective, universal concepts and categories. What we have not made explicit regarding theology, however, even though the two formal theological criteria presuppose it, is that it too, asks the question of being. In fact, philosophy and theology "necessarily" ask the question of being. Philosophy necessarily asks the question of being because it seeks universal truth as the fulfillment of its theoretical task. "Theology," as its two formal criteria demand,

> necessarily asks the same question, for that which concerns us ultimately must belong to reality as a whole; it must belong to being. Otherwise we could not encounter it, and it could not concern us. Of course, it cannot be one being among others; then it would not concern us infinitely. It must be the ground of our being, that which determines our being or not-being, the ultimate and unconditional power of being. . . . Theology, when dealing with our ultimate concern, presupposes in every sentence the structure of being, its categories, laws, and concepts. Theology, therefore, cannot escape the question of being any more easily than can philosophy (ST, I: 20-21).

Not only does theology presuppose the structure of being and its categories, laws, and concepts, but it uses terms which have emerged from a history of philosophical activity. Hence,

> the theologian must take seriously the terms he uses. They must be known to him in the whole depth and breadth of their meaning. Therefore, the systematic theologian must be a philosopher in critical understanding even if not in creative power (ST, I: 21).

An aspect of the comparability, then, of philosophy and theology is that as cognitive disciplines they cannot escape the ontological question and the structure of being that question presupposes. Thus:

the structure of being and the categories and concepts describing this structure are an implicit or explicit concern of every philosopher and of every theologian. Neither of them can avoid the ontological question. Attempts from both sides to avoid it have proved abortive. If this is the situation, the question becomes the more urgent: What is the relation between the ontological question asked by the philosopher and the ontological question asked by the theologian (ST, I: 21-22)?

It is clear that the ontological task of philosophy, the cognitive quest for reality as a whole, prevents any attempted divisions between philosophy and theology. Tillich remarks:

> . . . philosophy asks the question concerning being-itself. This implies that philosophy primarily does not ask about the special character of the beings, the things and events, the ideas and values, the souls and bodies which share being. Philosophy asks what about this being itself. Therefore, all philosophers have developed a "first philosophy," as Aristotle calls it, namely, an interpretation of being. And from this they go on to the description of the different classes of beings and to the system of their interdependence, the world. It is easy to make a simple division between philosophy and theology, if philosophy deals only with the second realm, with the sciences, and attempts to unite their last results in a picture of the world. But philosophy, before attempting a description of the world in unity with all kinds of scientific and nonscientific experience, tries to understand being itself and the categories and structures which are common to all kinds of beings. This makes the division between philosophy and theology impossible, for, whatever the relation of God, world, and man may be, it lies in the frame of being; and any interpretation of the meaning and structure of being as being, unavoidably has consequences for the interpretation of God, man, and the world in their interrelations.[3]

If there can be no division between philosophy and theology, then theology cannot be merely kerygmatic theology. An adequate theology must acknowledge its philosophical character without, as was noted, losing its kerygmatic foundation. This means that, for Tillich, only philosophical theology can be an adequate theology. The fact that the two types of theology — philosophical and kerygmatic — have developed relatively independently of each other should not conceal their underlying unity and the need for synthesis. "This duality," says Tillich,

> is natural. It is implied in the very word "theology," the syllable "theo" pointing to the *kerygma*, in which God is revealed, and the syllable "logy"

pointing to the endeavor of human reason to receive the message. This implies further that kerygmatic and philosophical theology demand each other and are wrong in the moment they become exclusive. No kerygmatic theology ever existed which did not use philosophical terms and methods. And no philosophical theology ever existed — deserving the name "theology" — which did not try to explain the content of the message. Therefore, the theological ideal is the complete unity of both types, an ideal which is reached only by the greatest theologians and even by them only approximately.[4]

It would seem, then, that the universality of philosophy's question, i.e., the question of being has implications for theology's conceptuality precisely because of its generality and universality, and one of its most basic implications is that theology cannot seek to conceptualize its object apart from the frame of being, that it, too, must ask the question of being. We return, therefore, to Tillich's quiry as to the relation of the question asked by philosophy and theology.

Being is inescapable for philosophy *and* theology. Both philosophy and theology ask the question of being; however, they ask the question of being from different perspectives. Tillich defines these perspectives thus: "Philosophy deals with the structure of being in itself; theology deals with the meaning of being for us" (ST, I: 22). What philosophy and theology have in common, then, is being and the cognitive quest for its structure, laws and categories, and it is this which accounts for the convergence in their relationship. However, since both are perspectival stances toward being, the differences in perspective will also account for their structural contrasts, or the divergence in their relationship.

As Tillich's definition of the differences in the perspectives of philosophy and theology suggest, the first point of divergence is to be seen in their respective cognitive attitudes. The philosopher

although driven by the philosophical *eros* . . . tries to maintain a detached objectivity toward being and its structure. He tries to exclude the personal, social, and historical conditions which might distort an objective vision of reality. His passion is the passion for a truth which is open to general approach, subject to general criticism, changeable in accordance with every new insight, open and communicable. In all these respects he feels no different from the scientist, historian, psychologist, etc. He collaborates with them. . . . Of course, the philosopher as a philosopher, neither criticizes nor augments the knowledge provided by the sciences. This knowledge forms the basis of his description of the categories, structural laws, and concepts which constitute the structure of being. In this respect the philosopher is as dependent on the scientist as he is dependent on his own prescientific observation of reality — often more dependent. This relation to the sciences . . . strengthens the detached, objective attitude of the philosopher. Even in the intuitive-synthetic side of his procedure he tries to exclude influences which are not purely determined by his object (ST, I: 22).

The theologian, on the other hand, occupies a quite different cognitive stance. His fundamental attitude is not *detachment*, but *involvement*. Rather than seeking objective truth by negating his own personal interests or concerns, the theologian

looks at his object . . . with passion, fear, and love. This is not the *eros* of the philosopher or his passion for objective truth; it is the love which accepts saving, and therefore personal, truth. The basic attitude of the theologian is commitment to the content he expounds. Detachment would be a denial of the very nature of this content. The attitude of the theologian is "existential." He is involved — with the whole of his existence, with his finitude and his anxiety, with his self-contradictions and his despair, with the healing forces in him and in his social situation. Every theological statement derives its seriousness from these elements of existence. The theologian, in short, is determined by his faith. Every theology presupposes that the theologian is in the theological circle. This contradicts the open, infinite, and changeable character of philosophical truth. . . . Theology is necessarily existential, and no theology can escape the theological circle (ST, I: 22-23).

There is, secondly, a divergence in the relationship of philosophy and theology in regard to their *sources*. Philosophy, as we have seen, takes the whole of reality as its object "to discover within it the structure of reality as a whole." It presupposes that there is a common rational structure in both world and mind and that every reasonable being participates in this structure, using it both to question the nature of reality and to answer these questions. It is this common, universal structure in mind and reality which constitutes the basis of objective truth, for all reasonable men can discern the truth of being regardless of their concreteness by virtue of their participation in the rational structure of being. Philosophy, therefore, is not confined to a particular place in order to define the structure of being. Its source of knowledge is "everyplace" because the same structure appears in whatever place the philosopher looks for it. Philosophy's truth is objective and universal because it can be achieved quite apart from the concreteness and particularity of the knower and in systematic contrast to the attitude of personal interest or concern.

The source of theology, however, is much more limited. That which is a matter of ultimate concern to the theologian is not in fact manifest in every place; rather it appears in a concrete history, which at least insofar as its appearance is concerned, excludes other histories. Thus, for the theologian,

> the source of his knowledge is not the universal Logos but the Logos "who became flesh," that is, the logos manifesting itself in a particular historical event. And the medium through which he receives the manifestation of the *logos* is not common rationality but the church, its traditions and its present reality. He speaks in the church about the foundation of the church. And he speaks because he is grasped by the power of this foundation and by the community built upon it. The concrete logos which he sees is received through believing commitment and not, like the universal logos at which the philosopher looks, through rational detachment (ST, I: 23-24).

Not only is there a divergence in the relationship of philosophy and theology with regard to cognitive stance and sources of knowledge, but, thirdly, there is a divergence in their *content*. While philosophy and theology speak about the *same* object, Tillich argues, they nonetheless speak at the same time about something different. Philosophy speaks about being in relation to its cosmological implications. It experiences being as rational and explanatory, i.e., being is experienced and understood as the source and structure of reality and it is only in relation to being, then, that reality can be made intelligible. Hence the philosopher

> deals with the categories of being in relation to the material which is structured by them. He deals with causality as it appears in physics or psychology; he analyzes biological or historical time; he discusses astronomical as well as microcosmic space. He describes the epistemological subject and the relation of person and community. He presents the characteristics of life and spirit in their dependence, and independence of, each other. He defines nature and history in their mutual limits and tries to penetrate into ontology and logic of being and non-being (ST, I: 24).

The theologian, while also speaking about being, experiences it not only as rational and explanatory, but also as *saving* or, as John Macquarrie has argued, as "gracious."[5] Theological assertions, in contrast to the cosmological assertions of philosophy, are soteriological. This means that theology relates the concepts and categories of ontology to the quest for a "new being." The theologian

> discusses causality in relation to a *prima causa*, the ground of the whole series of causes and effects; he deals with time in relation to eternity, with space in relation to man's existential homelessness. He speaks of the self-estrangement of the subject, about the spiritual center of personal life, and about community as a possible embodiment of the "New Being." He relates the structures of life to the creative ground of life and the structures of spirit to the divine Spirit. He speaks of the participation of nature in the "history of salvation," about the victory of being over non-being (ST, I: 24).

The relationship of divergence between philosophy and theology is, however, only one side of the total relationship between the two. There is also a counterbalancing relationship of *convergence*, for Tillich, between philosophy and theology. This convergence is rooted in the fact that both the philosopher and the theologian exist, which means that every philosophy carries an implicit theology within it, since existence can never close itself absolutely to the impact of ultimate concern. Philosophy is basically theoretical, and as we have seen, the more it assumes the attitude of detachment toward the existential dimension of the philosopher, the more successfully it can execute its theoretical task. Theology, on the other hand, is basically existential, and it can execute its task only by becoming involved in the questions of existence. However, it would be incorrect to say that philosophy is *purely* theoretical and theology is purely existential. Rather:

> We have searched for the object or question of philosophy, and we have discovered that a theological element, an ultimate concern, gives the impulse to philosophy. We have searched for the object or question of theology, and we have discovered that a philosophical element is implied in theology — the question of the meaning and structure of being and its manifestation in the different realms of being. Philosophy and theology . . . are convergent as far as both are existential and theoretical at the same time. They are divergent

as far as philosophy is basically theoretical and theology is basically existential.[6]

The basically theoretical character of philosophy is the reason why it can speak of being and the beings as if they did not concern the philosopher at all. The basically existential character of theology allows it to become exclusively kerygmatic. However, neither of these positions has been maintained absolutely, for

> as theology always has created a philosophical theology, so philosophers always have tried to reach existential significance, to give a prophetic message, to found a sect, to start a religious-political movement, or to become mystics. But in doing so they were philosophical theologians and were considered as such by followers and foes. Most creative philosophers have been theological in this sense.[7]

Hence:

> Every creative philosopher is a hidden theologian (sometimes even a declared theologian). He is a theologian in the degree to which his existential situation and his ultimate concern shape his philosophical vision. He is a theologian in the degree to which his intuition of the universal *logos* of the structure of reality as a whole is formed by a particular *logos* which appears to him on his particular place and reveals to him the meaning of the whole. And he is a theologian in the degree to which the particular *logos* is a matter of active commitment within a special community (ST, I: 25).

Not only is it impossible to repress the existential element in philosophy altogether, but Tillich further argues, that only those philosophies which have been informed in some way by the existential dimension — only those have creative power and genuine historical significance. "Only noncreative philosophy," he asserts,

> cuts itself off entirely from its existential basis. It has in its hands the shell, not the substance, of philosophy. It is school and not life and therefore not philosophy, but the trading of old philosophical merchandise.[8]

The philosopher, however, does not *intend* to be a theologian. His intention rather is

> to serve the universal *logos*. He tries to turn away from his existential situation, including his ultimate concern, toward a place above all particular places, toward pure reality. The conflict between the intention of becoming

universal and the destiny of remaining particular characterizes every philosophical existence. It is its burden and its greatness (ST, I: 25).

The theologian, on the other hand, turns toward his concreteness, his particularity, i.e., the existential situation in which his
ultimate concern is manifest. He does this, however, not in a confessional posture, but rather to assert

> the universal validity, the *logos* structure, of what concerns him ultimately.
> And he can do this only in an attitude of detachment from his existential situ-
> ation and in obedience to the universal logos. This obligates him to be critical
> of every special expression of his ultimate concern. He cannot affirm any
> tradition and any authority except through a "No" and a "Yes." And it is
> always possible that he may not be able to go all the way from the "No" to
> the "Yes". . . . Theology, since it serves not only the concrete but also the
> universal *logos*, can become a stumbling block for the church and a demonic
> temptation for the theologian. The detachment required in honest
> theological work can destroy the necessary involvement of faith. This tension
> is the burden and the greatness of every theological work (ST, I: 25-26).

The convergence between philosophy and theology, then, seems
to include at least two claims. First, that both philosophy and theology are matters of ultimate concern insofar as the *existence* of
philosopher and theologian inform the two enterprises respectively, but methodogically theology is rooted in the concreteness of
the existential concern while philosophy must seek to transcend
the particularity of the philosopher's existence in order to grasp the
universal *Logos*. Secondly, that the assertions of philosophy and
theology have universal significance because they are both cognitive specifications of the universal *Logos* of being, philosophy is in
principle cosmological, conceptual, theoretical, while theology is in
principle soteriological, symbolic, and existential.

The divergence and convergence between theology and philosophy permits neither a conflict between them nor their synthesis. A
conflict, Tillich argues, "presupposes a common basis on which to
fight." However, no such common basis is available to the philosopher and theologian. If they fight, they do so either on a philosophical or theological basis. If the theologian needs the concep-

tuality of philosophy, he must either appropriate it from a philosopher or he must become a philosopher himself. This means that

> the theologian has no right whatsoever to argue for a philosophical opinion in the name of his ultimate concern or on the basis of the theological circle. He is obliged to argue for a philosophical decision in the name of the universal *logos* and from the place which is no place: pure reason. . . . Conflicts on the philosophical level are conflicts between two philosophers, one of whom happens to be a theologian, but they are not conflicts between theology and philosophy (ST, I: 26).

Frequently, open conflict between philosopher and theologian does not occur on the philosophical level at all, but rather the hidden theologian in the philosopher (his ultimate concern) drives him to fight with the professed theologian, especially where a theological analysis of the philosopher's ideas requires the recognition of existentially conditioned elements in them. The philosopher in seeking the position of pure reason in order to conceptualize the universal *Logos* is reluctant to acknowledge the impact his own existence has upon his ideas, since that is to qualify seriously their universality. But, Tillich argues, the theologian must struggle against this tendency in the philosopher, for the *truth value* of any philosophy depends upon the creative "amalgamation" of existential passion and rational power. "The insight into this situation," Tillich asserts:

> is, at the same time, an insight into the fact that two philosophers, one of whom happens to be a theologian, can fight with each other and that two theologians, one of whom happens to be a philosopher, can fight with each other; but there is no possible conflict between theology and philosophy because there is no common basis for such a conflict (ST, I: 27).

Just as no conflict is possible between philosophy and theology, so there can be no synthesis between them for precisely the same reason, *viz.*, that there is no common basis on which they both stand. This means, for Tillich, that there can be no "Christian philosophy" as such where that term denotes a "philosophy which does not look at the universal *logos* but at the assumed or actual demands of a Christian theology" (ST, I: 28). This is not to deny, however, the impact of Christianity upon the philosophy of the West. One might speak of a "Christian philosophy" in the sense that, as James Ross asserts, "Christian culture has become the *form* of Western thought,"[9] and, therefore, all modern philosophy is Christian insofar as Christianity constitutes the meaning structure in relation to which western philosophy has shaped its own career. However, even though Christianity is a *character indelebilis* inscribed upon the body of western philosophy the notion of a philosophy which is intentionally Christian, which submits to the authority of the Christian Church or whose conceptuality is developed in special reference to the claims of the Christian message is fallacious. "There is nothing," says Tillich,

> in heaven and earth, or beyond them, to which the philosopher must subject himself except the universal *logos* of being as it gives itself to him in experience. Therefore, the idea of a "Christian philosophy" in the narrower sense of a philosophy which is intentionally Christian must be rejected. The fact that every modern philosophy has grown on Christian soil . . . has nothing to do with the self-contradicting ideal of a "Christian philosophy." Christianity does not need a "Christian philosophy" in the narrower sense of the word. The Christian claim that the *logos* who has become concrete in Jesus as the Christ is at the same time the universal *logos* includes the claim that wherever the *logos* is at work it agrees with the Christian message. No philosophy which is obedient to the universal *logos* can contradict the concrete *logos*, the Logos "who became flesh" (ST, I: 28).

The question naturally arises here as to why the universal *Logos* in which both philosophy and theology are grounded cannot be the common basis for the two disciplines, allowing both conflict and synthesis. The answer that suggests itself is that even though the universal *Logos* of being is the matrix in relation to which both philosophy and theology achieve their validity as cultural (and therefore spiritual) disciplines, nonetheless the *Logos* of being is disclosed within these disciplines in such a way that there is a qualitative distinction in the disclosure, which both determines the essential character of theology and philosophy and just as essentially determines their differentiation. Thus, while it is the same universal *Logos* of being which is the object of both philosophy and theology, it is apprehended under quite different aspects in the two disciplines.   Philosophy grasps the rational structure of the *Logos* of being, those universal, permanent, necessary, unchanging principles which are evident throughout the whole manifold of immediate experience and can thus be discerned from the "no place" of pure reason.   Here, the *Logos* of being is seen in its cosmological aspect, satisfying the most profound needs of the mind to know and therefore determining philosophy's essential character as theoretical detachment from the concreteness, particularity, and flux of immediate experience, and as the cognitive attempt to see reality "sub specie aeternitatus."

Theology, on the other hand, encounters the "graciousness" of the universal *Logos* of being, its power not only to sustain the universal structure of being but to manifest itself salvifically within concrete, historical events.   Theology apprehends the *Logos* of being under its soteriological aspect and therefore it is defined by the freedom of being-itself to disclose itself not in universal categories which any critical mind can discern, but rather in terms of particular occasions which persuade not by their rational self-evidence but by their power to transform the existence of those (including the theologian) who participate in them.   Hence, theology's chief cognitive tool is not the concept but the symbol, not a system of categorical notions, but myth.   Its stance is not essentially that of theoretical detachment, but participation in a given structure of historical events, symbolic forms, and a community of experience which is informed by these events and forms.   In short, theology is existential thinking.   Theology needs philosophy to delineate the structure of being and to show that its concrete truth is at the same time the universal truth of being-itself.[10]

However, the distinction between philosophy and theology which informs Tillich's thought, while asserting the unity of truth and knowledge as they are rooted in the universal structure of being and, therefore, the ultimate unity of philosophy and theology themselves, yet clearly presupposes (1) that the universal *Logos* in its cosmological aspect is *in principle* accessible to the inquiring mind without regard to questions of the unique disclosure of the *Logos*, or of the determinative historical events in which the unique disclosure is received, and thus without regard to particular contexts without which the mind could not be grasped by the *Logos* and (2) that philosophy, therefore, cannot apprehend the *Logos* of being in its *totality*, i.e., philosophy does not experience the *Logos* soteriologically, while theology, having received a unique disclosure of the *Logos*, is able to grasp it not only in its cosmological aspect, drawing upon the work of philosophy, but in its soteriological aspect as well, that is, in its totality.

It seems a legitimate conclusion, then, that for Tillich, theology is in a more privileged position in regard to the *Logos* (and thus the structure of truth) than is philosophy. Since its privileged condition is the result of theology's being rooted in a particular historical context in which a definitive and final disclosure of the nature and power of the *Logos* has occurred, and since that disclosure cannot be received in the stance of theoretical detachment alone, but rather only in a state of profound existential involvement, it would seem to follow that it is its privileged character in relation to the *Logos* that ultimately distinguishes theology from philosophy.[11]

If our claim is correct that theology, for Tillich, stands in a privileged relationship to the *Logos* of being by virtue of its capacity to grasp not only its rational structure with the help of philosophy but also to appropriate the soteriological power of the *Logos*, then we are in a position to see the cruciality of his argument that philosophy is the detached search for the universal structure of being, the vehicle through which man's cognitive needs are satisfied, while theology is the existential response to the totality of the *Logos* of being in which the complete structure of man's "noetic" or spiritual needs is fulfilled. If what is at stake in this argument is nothing less than the question of man's salvation as a total person, then it is clear that theology bears within its structure a task of the greatest urgency and profundity, namely, the cognitive-symbolic delineation of that which is the ultimate answer to the driving questions of human existence and destiny.

Obviously, theology cannot reflect upon the problematic of the human predicament and participate in the power which overcomes that predicament in a state of detachment, since the very existence and identity of the theologian and theology itself are at issue in the theological enterprise. The price theology pays for its privileged position is that it must speak in "fear and trembling." Consequently, it can only be detached and critical toward the concrete expressions of its ultimate concern, but never toward the ultimate concern itself. Theology is existential thinking, for Tillich, precisely because it has received the answer to the most persistent, problematic, and agonizing questions men can ask themselves about the meaning of human existence. Therein lies the basic distinction between philosophy and theology.

We may conclude, then, that in spite of Tillich's many qualifications to the contrary in which it is suggested that philosophy moves within the existential orbit and theology must exercise critical detachment in its interpretative task, nonetheless the most fundamental distinction between philosophy and theology lies in their basic "attitudes" or stances toward their subject-matter and further that their points of convergence and divergence presuppose this basic distinction. Thus, Tillich's claim that philosophy is the detached, objective search for the universal forms and structures of being, while theology is the existential reception and interpretation of the meaning of being for us is generic to his entire enterprise. Therefore, the intelligibility of Tillich's use of philosophy within his theological program rests to a considerable extent upon his understanding both of existential thinking and theology as a form of existential thinking. In pursuing our analysis, we shall examine three issues: we shall need to examine the basic themes of existential philosophy, we shall need to explore Tillich's critique of existentialism and his conception of existential thinking in more detail; and we shall need to ask whether he has executed his theological program in a way that is consistent with his basic definition of the nature of theology.

Notes

1   *Dynamics of Faith, op. cit.*, p. 92.

2   *Biblical Religion, op. cit.*, p. 9. Cf. Daniel D. Williams' claim that there are indeed clear philosophical orientations, especially that of Kant, in both Barth's and Brunner's theologies. Daniel D. Williams, "Barth and Brunner on Philosophy," *The Journal of Religion*, vol. XXVII, no. 4 (1947).

3   *The Protestant Era, op. cit.*, pp. 85-86.

4   *Ibid.*, p. 84.

5   John Macquarrie, "How is Theology Possible?", *Union Seminary Quarterly Review*, Vol. XVIII, No. 2, Winter, 1963.

6   *The Protestant Era, op., cit.*, p. 88.

7   *Ibid.*, p. 89.

8   *Ibid.*

9   James Ross, "On the Relationship of Philosophy and Theology," *Union Seminary Quarterly Review*, Vol. XXVI, No. I, Fall 1970, p. 16.

10 Langdon Gilkey, whose work perhaps reveals the impact of Tillich's thought more than any other contemporary American theologian, has written a brief, but suggestive essay on the history of the interaction between philosophy and Christian theology and reaches a very Tillichian conclusion about their relationship. He writes: "Christian theology must contain philosophical or ontological elements (1) in order that the ontological uniqueness, universality, and decisiveness of God to each creature be adequately expressed, that is, in order that *God* be properly conceived theologically; and (2) in order that the universality and the decisiveness of the problem to which religion addresses itself and of the resolution which is offered be expressed, that is, in order that its salvation be properly conceived theologically. Thus some form of general ontology, some philosophical view of man's nature, and some form of philosophy of history must be implicit in any Christian theology that is internally consistent and externally intelligible."

"On the other hand, Christian theology must retain mythical elements for two reasons: (1) In order that the ultimacy, freedom, and transcendence of the divine over the system of things be expressed in determinate and not merely in negative terms . . . For only the ontic, the phenomenal, and the historical can express the absolute uniqueness, and the intentionality of the sacred on the one hand, and its strange and unique relatedness to the beings on the other . . . Thus even in the most sophisticated philosophical theology, myth returns to express the height of the divine transcendence and sacrality and its unique omnipresent and everlasting relatedness to the universal structures of what is."

"(2) Christian theology must contain mythical categories because its understanding of the transcendence and the sacrality of the divine is grounded in particular past events within the general stream of temporal passage and contains promises for the particularity of history in the future. God here is thus related to particular events, and at the most *concrete*, phenomenal level. . . . Philosophical conceptuality, because of the utter universality of its categories, tends to negate as relevant to truth universally not only the transcendence of the divine over the structures of natural things, but even more the concreteness, decisiveness, and uniqueness of particular events and histories in the passage of time." *Religion and the Scientific Future* (Harper and Row, N.Y., 1970) pp. 115-117.

11   It is considerations like these that seem to have led James Ross to conclude that Tillich adheres to elements of the scholastic distinction between philosophy and theology, which he defines thus: "(i) Philosophical science begins with what is self-evident to human reason; theology begins with what is revealed, augmenting it with the demonstrations of philosophy. (ii) Philosophy is properly demonstrative, and its conclusions are established, if they are strictly deduced from rational first principles; theology is only analogously demonstrative since some of its first principles have their evidence externally (by divine authority). (iii) All the premises and steps of philosophical establishment are accessible to and assessable by natural reason; not so theology." James Ross, *op., cit.*, pp. 7-8. Tillich does speak of a "saving transformation and an illuminating revelation" within philosophical activity. Tillich writes: "Ontology presupposes a conversion, an opening of the eyes, a revelatory experience. It is not a matter of detached observation, analysis, and hypothesis. Only he who is involved in ultimate reality, only he who has encountered it as a matter of existential concern, can try to speak about it meaningfully. In this sense one must say that there is faith in the philosopher . . . faith as the state of being grasped by ultimate reality." However, Tillich goes on to qualify this philosophical conversion to the point that the privileged position of theology is upheld. Thus, "Certainly philosophical conversion and philosophical faith are not identical with conversion and faith in biblical religion. The latter are related equally to all functions of man's spiritual life, to his whole personality. There is no preponderance of the cognitive function as it is in philosophical conversion and philosophical faith. But even philosophical

conversion and philosophical faith are not restricted to the cognitive function, for this function, if it is existentially moved, cannot be separated from the other functions. Philosophical conversion changes not only the thinking of the philosopher but also his being. But this being remains in the background, while in religious conversion it is in the foreground. Religious conversion, therefore, is more embracing. It includes the possibility of philosophical conversion, just as religious faith includes the possibility of ontological awareness." *Biblical Religion and the Search for Ultimate Reality, op. cit.,* pp. 65-66.

Chapter Ten

The Problem in Historical Perspective

Part One:

The Conception of Philosophy and Truth in Greek Thought

If our analysis is plausible to this point, the basic distinction in Tillich's thought between philosophy and theology rests not so much upon distinctions within the two disciplines themselves, as it does upon the revelatory and soteriological character of being-itself. Thus, while being is not opaque to thought, that is, philosophy can know the structures and categories which characterize being, yet there are decisive disclosures of being in which not only man's cognitive needs but the exigency of his total predicament is overcome *in principle* and fragmentarily *in actuality*. Philosophy is not excluded from the salvation events rooted in the disclosure of being-itself, since, as Tillich makes clear, reason itself participates in the healing power of the New Being in Jesus as the Christ (ST, I: 155); however, the philosophical enterprise is not dependent upon a self-conscious philosophical appropriation of the Christian message, since philosophy can know the essential structure of being even under the conditions of estranged existence. Christian theology, however, is impossible without the unique disclosure of being-itself, which is the very foundation of theology as well as the basis under the conditions of estranged existence for the fragmentary reconstitution of essence and existence and thus the salvation of the whole created order.

Because the theological enterprise is rooted in the ontological power which overcomes the existential predicament of man, in a way in which philosophy is not, we have suggested that theology stands in a *privileged* relationship to being. The privileged relationship of theology to being, however, does not empower it to dictate to philosophy the shape its inquiry shall take on the one hand nor does it grant theology's independence from philosophy on the other, even though theology may be said to be the *fulfillment* of philosophy just as revelation is the fulfillment of reason. Philosophy, then, is the expression of *autonomous* reason (it is the attitude of the radical question), which means that its total conceptual achievement is subject to the ground of being, which it cannot know totally on the basis of its own structure and method as question. Theology is an expression of *theonomous* reason which means that it has received the disclosure of the ground of being within its cognitive structure as answer.

In relation to the structures of philosophy and theology, Tillich has characterized the position of the two in terms of their basic stances toward their objects. Philosophy is confined to an analysis of the structure of being. The structure of being does not disclose itself, but rather is subject to cognitive specification through an active achievement of the human mind. Therefore, philosophy does not apprehend the structure of being through an act of reception (even though, of course, the structure of being is "given" — philosophy does not invent it), but through the conceptual delineation of that structure.

This means that philosophy, in order to achieve the most universal, objective, and general notions of which the human mind is capable, is intentionally detached and objective toward the concrete concerns of existence. Theology, on the other hand, arises in an act of reception and that which it receives is a matter of ultimate concern not only to the existence of the theologian but *in principle* an ultimate concern for all men. The theologian, therefore, cannot separate his existence from the import of that which he receives, since what he receives is unintelligible without the correlation of the existential concerns in relation to which the disclosure of being-itself is received. The cognitive stance of theology is not, therefore, detached toward the deliverance of existence, but rather profoundly involved in the existential question, and it seeks to show above all else, the *relevance* of being-itself and the truth which is rooted in it to the resolution of the existential question. This makes theology, as we have seen, intentionally existential thinking in contrast to the detached, objective thinking of philosophy.

We have argued above that it is Tillich's emphasis upon the philosopher's intentionality to transcend his concrete existence and its concerns to achieve the ideal of universal and objective truth which places him in the "classical" tradition in regard to the conception of the nature of philosophy. It is necessary to develop this claim in more detail. In doing so, however, we are generalizing from the history of philosophy, and therefore, our argument will not be characterized by an exhaustive historical exegesis, which such a question obviously deserves.

If our analysis is correct that for Tillich the philosophical enterprise achieved its normative or essential definition in the Greek experience, then we have an historical basis upon which to link Tillich to the *classical* conception of philosophy, for it is precisely in the struggle of the Greek mind to know reality that the notion of truth as correlated with objectivity, universality and eternity emerges, and, consequently, it is in this same struggle that philosophy is conceived of as the discipline by which human thought most nearly approximates the divine by virtue of its capacity to transcend the particularity of the philosopher's existence and to see reality from the divine point of view.

It is among the Greeks that the notion of the *philosopher* as a unique kind of human being takes shape. Among the presocratics, the philosopher is one who is distinguished from other men by virtue of his singleminded preoccupation with the order of the cosmos and his self-elevation to the level of the divine mind through the act of knowledge. The knowledge he seeks removes him from the level of the precritical self and its inchoate involvement in the world of common sense meanings, which lie only on the surface of reality. Werner Jaeger has described the early Greek philosophers thus:

The most notable feature in the character of the first philosophers − of course they did not call themselves by that Platonic name − is their intellectual devotion to knowledge, their absorption in studying Existence for its own sake. Their singlemindedness was admired and yet considered paradoxical by the later Greeks, and doubtless by their contemporaries too. Their scholarly disregard for the things which others held important − money, honour, even home and family − their apparent forgetfulness of their own interests, and their indifference to popular enthusiasms, begot many famous anecdotes. These stories were carefully collected and handed down . . . as examples and models of the *Bios Theoretikos*, which Plato declared was the true *praxis* of the philosopher. In them the philosopher is the great eccentric, an uncanny but lovable character, who deliberately isolates himself from the society of men in order to live for his studies. He is childishly naive, awkward and impractical; he lives in eternity, not in time and space. While watching some celestial phenomenon, the wise Thales falls into a well, and his Thracian maid jeers at him for wanting to look at things in heaven when he cannot see what is at his own feet. Pythagoras, asked why he lives, replies, 'To look at heaven and nature.' Anaxagoras is accused of caring nothing for his kinsfolk and his country, but points to heaven and says, 'There is my country.' These anecdotes all refer to the philosopher's inexplicable interest in the structure of the cosmos, in what was then called (in a deeper sense) meteorology − the knowledge of things in the heights. His behaviour and aspirations seem to the common people to be bizarre and over-ambitious: the Greeks used to think that a deep scholar was unhappy, because he was *Perittos*. The full sense of the word is untranslatable, but it denotes a quality bordering on hybris, for the thinker overpasses the boundary between the human and the divine mind.[1]

The very lifestyle of the early Greek thinkers, who were later to be designated "philosophers" by Plato, suggests the model of truth and the philosophical route to achieve that truth which we have identified as characteristic of the classical tradition. There can be seen the first movement toward the philosopher's detachment from his own personal and societal concreteness which is the primary condition of the *Bios Theoretikos* in the classical tradition, and thus his attempt at objectivity and the identification with the eternal, universal structures which obtain for all rational minds. The presocratic thinkers, of course, disagree as to the designation of these structures; however, they are in agreement that such structures exist and that they can be apprehended by extricating oneself from the world of appearance and penetrating to their nature.

It is in the work of Plato and Aristotle, however, that the classical conceptions of truth and the philosophical enterprise achieve their most profound formulations.

Plato's dialogues reflect his attempt to think both about the nature of philosophy on the one hand and to resolve the ambiguities of his own philosophical doctrines on the other. It is in the former task that we are primarily interested here.

According to Jaeger, the word "philosophy" originally meant "culture" (*Bildung*) among the Greeks and only came to be construed as a rational discipline or science in the circle of Socrates and Plato. The presocratics called their thinking activity *ístoríe* or wisdom (*sophíe*),[2] and we may thus conclude that the notion of a rigorous intellectual discipline by means of which the truth about reality may be obtained, exemplified in the unique lifestyle of the thinker (who himself must possess outstanding qualities of mind and spirit), and which is called "philosophy" was most fully developed by Plato and constitutes his unique contribution to the intellectual life of the West.

In *The Republic* Plato describes both the nature of philosophy and the philosopher. In books V and VI, his most developed theory of the nature of philosophy and the philosopher and the relationship of philosophy to the state is found. It is significant that Plato introduces his discussion of the nature of philosophy by distinguishing between knowledge, ignorance, and opinion in relation to being and nonbeing. Knowledge is correlated, of course, with being and ignorance with non-being.[3] Opinion, however, is correlated with a state of affairs intermediate between being (knowledge) and nonbeing (ignorance). It is the cognitive stance of those whose minds are limited to the manifold of experience. Those who live by opinion can appreciate beautiful things, for example, but they have no grasp of beauty itself, the absolute, eternal essence in relation to which every particular beautiful entity receives its ontological foundation as beautiful. Not to be able to grasp the structure of reality through the eternal essences, forms, or ideas, is to be caught in the realm between being and non-being, the realm of contingent plurality in which there is neither unity or ultimate coherence. The philosopher, on the other hand, has knowledge (or exists in relation to being) because he "is able to distinguish the idea from the objects which participate in the idea, neither putting the objects in the place of the idea nor the idea in the place of the objects."[4]

The philosopher, then, is neither caught in the grip of ignorance nor opinion, because through his vision he can "see the absolute and eternal and immutable," the ultimately real patterns, which are exemplified in the world of flux and which provide men with the absolute certainty and authority by which they may conduct their lives. However, as Plato is profoundly aware, only a very rare person, the philosopher, is able to extricate himself from the regions of nonbeing and partial being in order to know the real, and he does so only by identifying with the "absolute and eternal and immutable" to such an extent that he transcends every relative and partial viewpoint and becomes "the friend of God."[5]

As the "friend of God," the philosopher detaches himself from the world of becoming and its proximate concerns, and through the ascent of his own soul becomes identified with the universal, immutable, and eternal realm of being and thus with truth itself. Plato makes clear that the more the philosopher becomes rooted in being, the more he undergoes a basic ontological transformation in his own existence. This transformation enables the philosopher to achieve the divine point of view, to see man and the world from the vantage point of eternity, although as long as he remains mortal (finite), the philosopher will never embody the philosophical perspective perfectly.

Plato's vision of the philosophical life is clearly expressed in a passage from *The Republic*. He states:

> For he, Adeimantus, whose mind is fixed upon true being, has surely no time to look down upon the affairs of earth, or to be filled with malice and envy, contending against men; his eye is ever directed towards things fixed and immutable, which he sees neither injuring nor injured by one another, but all in order moving according to reason; these he imitates, and to these he will, as far as he can, conform himself. . . . And the philosopher holding converse with the divine order, becomes orderly and divine, as far as the nature of man allows; but like every one else, he will suffer from detraction.[6]

The demand of detachment, then, is for the philosopher to purge himself of every idiosyncratic element in himself and to extricate himself from the power of time and all temporal forms. He does this by imitating the *Paradeigma*, which the true order of being affords.[7] The philosopher's life is, thus, the triumph of rationality, where the rational is the universal, the immutable, and the eternal.[8] It is through philosophical activity, therefore, that man, in a very real sense, becomes divine for Plato.

Aristotle's discontinuity with Plato may be seen in his denial of the separation (*Chorismos*) of the eternal, immutable, and universal order of being from the concrete particulars, that is, for Aristotle, *Ousia* (being) is the *Hypokeimenon*, the ground of each particular thing, which may be *defined* apart from the particular, but which is *real* only in its embodied form in the particular.[9] There is continuity, however, between Plato and Aristotle, and thus between the two streams of philosophical development originating from them, in their conceptions of truth or knowledge and the philosophical enterprise.

Werner Marx's study *Heidegger and the Tradition*[10] identifies Aristotle's contribution to the classical tradition in terms of the four basic traits by which he characterizes the nature of being (*Ousia*), that is, its "eternalness," its necessity, its selfsameness, and its intelligibility. The philosopher will achieve wisdom or knowledge of a truly scientific nature if he understands *what* a thing is and *why* it is, in other words if he understands the *causes* of things.[11] It is through an adequate conception of being and its power, its causal efficacy, that the philosopher achieves that transcendent knowledge of the world, which liberates him from opinion and belief.

First philosophy (metaphysics), then, seeks to understand being *qua* being. However,there are many senses of the term being, and in *The Categories*, Aristotle distinguishes between a "first ousia" and a "second ousia," the genus-species distinction being instances of the latter.[12] It is the meaning of the former, the "first ousia," however, which is important for our study. The point we wish to make here about Aritstotle's characterization of being in the primary sense in terms of the four traits delineated by Marx is that they place the object of knowledge beyond the power of time, beyond contingency, beyond the power of radical novelty,[13] and beyond the power of cognitive ambiguity. In effect, *Ousia* is the most objective, universal and inclusive conception the human mind can formulate for Aristotle, and, thus, the features of the classical tradition we have identified as normative in regard to the question of truth (the truth is objective and universal) are maintained in Aristotle's thought.

The question that remains is whether Aristotle conceives the philosophical enterprise in continuity with the tradition. That he did seems clear when one explores the meaning of the intelligibility of *Ousia* and his conception of the essence of man. Aristotle is convinced that the ultimate structure of reality, *Ousia* in the first sense, is ordered, and, therefore, knowable. The intelligibility of *Ousia* then, is its eternalness, its necessity, and its complex self-identity through change, that is, *Ousia* is permeated by *Logos*. It is, therefore, "thinkable" both because it is intrinsically rational and because man is endowed with *Logos* as well. Not only is *Ousia* thinkable, but it can be specified in speech.[14] Marx has rendered Aristotle's conception of the intelligibility of *Ousia* thus:

> For Aristotle, the Being and essence of the particular being [is] in principle unconditionally and unobstructedly intelligible. This intelligibility resulted for Aristotle from the supposition of an unconditional sovereignty of the principle of complete transparence. The early Greeks had already termed this principle the *nous*. Thus Aristotle, expressly referring to this insight of Anaxagoras, declares that *"nous* governs." Aristotle conceived this sovereignty of the *nous* in the likeness of the light (*phos*). The *energeia* of the *nous poietikos* is like the effectiveness of the light, which through its shining, confers "transparency" on everything and transforms the "potential" colors into "actual" colors. . . . Owing to the *nous, ousia* is luminous, transparent, "noetic," i.e., "thinkable." Only because ousia is thinkable, because it is ready for thinking, man, through the intuitive beholding *noesis*, is able to think it. . . . The basic trait of the intelligibility of *ousia* "establishes" its thinkability by human thinking. . . . In Aristotle the basic trait of the intelligibility of *ousia* is also connected with the truth (alethia) in the sense that every obstruction of this intelligibility, whether through error or semblance, is excluded. To *noesis*, to the intuitive beholding comprehension of the "simple," of the *ousia*, the latter shows itself in its truth. "Neither semblance nor error is here possi-

ble," Aristotle expressly remarks at the end of Book IX of the *Metaphysics*. This cryptic passage must be interpreted to mean that the essence must be completely and wholly intelligible, completely undisguised, "lucid and transparent;" otherwise the *noesis* cannot grasp it unerringly through a simple "contract" (*thigein*).[15]

Because of the rational principle in man, errors in judgment can be overcome. In fact, for Aristotle, it is man's supreme task to actualize his rationality, for it is his rationality which is the divine dimension in man. In *The Nicomachean Ethics*, Aristotle asserts the following of reason:

> If happiness is activity in accordance with virtue, it is reasonable that it should be in accordance with the highest virtue; and this will be that of the best thing in us. Whether it be reason or something else that is this element which is thought to be our natural ruler and guide and to take thought of things noble and divine, whether it be itself also divine or only the most divine element in us, the activity of this in accordance with its proper virtue will be perfect happiness. That this activity is contemplative we have already said.
>
> . . . Firstly, this activity is the best (since not only is reason the best thing in us, but the objects of reason are the best of knowable objects); and, secondly, it is the most continuous, since we can contemplate truth more continuously than we can do anything. And we think happiness has pleasure mingled with it, but the activity of philosophic wisdom is admittedly the pleasantest of virtuous activities; at all events the pursuit of it is thought to offer pleasures marvelous for their purity and their enduringness, and it is to be expected that those who know will pass their time more pleasantly than those who inquire. And the self-sufficiency that is spoken of must belong most to the contemplative activity . . . [and] the philosopher, even when by himself, can contemplate truth, and the better the wiser he is; he can perhaps do so better if his has fellow-workers, but still he is the most self-sufficient . . .
>
> But such a life would be too high for man; for it is not in so far as he is man that he will live so, but in so far as something divine is present in him; and by so much as this is superior to our composite nature is its activity superior to that which is the exercise of the other kind of virtue. If reason is divine, then, in comparison with man, the life according to it is divine in comparison with human life. But we must not follow those who advise us, being men, to think of human things, and, being mortal, of mortal things, but must, so far as we can, make ourselves immortal, and strain every nerve to live in accordance with the best thing in us; for even if it be small in bulk, much more does it in power and worth surpass everything. This would seem strange, then, if he were to choose not the life of his self but that of something else.[16]

It is through the power of *Nous*, then, that man is apotheosized for Aristotle. The intelligibility of *Ousia* and man's rational capacity to delineate that intelligibility through knowledge and discourse, constitute the *Logos* of reality, and the more man contemplates this *Logos*, the more he approaches the divine. By grasping the eternal and necessary connections among things and formulating these connections in conceptual terms, man grasps the intelligible structure of the cosmos. In this sense we can say that the notion of truth is defined by its objectivity, universality, and its inverse relation to the idiosyncratic, the particular, the concrete, thereby establishing Aristotle's continuity with the classical tradition. We may quote Marx again for clarification of this issue:

> A look at the essence, scope, and aim of *epistēmē* affords additional evidence that Aristotle understood *ousia*, the object of *epistēmē* in that wider sense, as equally intelligible in principle as the objects of *epistēmē* in the narrower sense and that he therefore regarded its complete knowability through human "science" as possible. The various essential determinations of *epistēmē*, above all in the *Analytics* and the *Nicomachean Ethics*, are grounded especially on the basic traits of *ousia*: its "eternalness," necessity, and selfsameness. Guided by the *noesis*, which has already apprehended *ousia* and the first principles, *epistēmē* in the narrower sense − in contrast to practice (technical, ethical, and political action) − is directed only to the "necessary", "eternal" and "selfsame" universals (*ta katholou*), which stand in an order ruled by laws and in fundamental connections. This order, as a "logical" one, is so established that it can be wholly and completely grasped by the scientist's *legein* through the exhibiting of causes, syl-logism, demonstration (*apodeixis*) and definition (*horismos*). For this reason, knowledge itself can be characterized as "necessary"; it is valid "forever and everywhere" and in this sense is "universal."[17]

Aristotle's dependency upon the Eleatic thinkers and Plato in regard to the nature of truth and the philosophical enterprise can be further substantiated by examining his own conception of the philosophical life. We have seen above that reason is "the best thing" in man for Aristotle. He further maintains that the philosopher is he who gives himself to the contemplation of the rational structure of the cosmos. He does not assert explicitly (as does Plato) that in doing so the philosopher "imitates" the divine; however, it is clear that the philosopher patterns himself after the divine contemplative activity.   As Aristotle puts it in the *Meta-physics*:

> And thinking in itself deals with that which is best in itself, and that which is thinking in the fullest sense with that which is best in the fullest sense. And thought thinks on itself because it shares the nature of the object of thought; for it becomes an object of thought in coming into contact with and thinking its objects, so that thought and object of thought are the same. For that which is *capable* of receiving the object of thought, i.e., the essence, is thought. But it is *active* when it possesses this object. Therefore the possession rather than the receptivity is the divine element which thought seems to contain, and the act of contemplation is what is most pleasant and best. If, then, God is always in that good state in which we sometimes are, this compels our wonder; and if in a better this compels it yet more. And God is in a better state. And life also belongs to God; for the actuality of thought is life, and God is that actuality; and God's self-dependent actuality is life most good and eternal. We say therefore that God is a living being, eternal, most good, so that life and duration continuous and eternal belong to God; for this *is* God.[18]

The "state in which we sometimes are" and in which God is always is the state of thought thinking itself, which the philosopher seeks to actualize increasingly in his own life. Clearly, God is the model for such activity, and the philosopher can only achieve such dynamic rational contemplation by transcending the particulars, at least conceptually, toward the universal, eternal, and necessary. Aristotle does not stress the tension between the higher philosophical nature and sensible existence as does Plato; however, it is clear that the philosophical life involved as much for Aristotle as for his predecessors that quest for unchanging, eternal, universal, objective, and necessary truth and its formulation in the concept, holding the promise of the divinization of the thinker, the "friend of God," which so fascinated the Greek philosophical mind.

As we have seen, Tillich's own analysis of the two lines of development in philosophy since Descartes suggests that the formulation of the nature of philosophy worked out in the Greek experience has radically shaped the methodological main line of philosophy into the modern period. Tillich's own conception of philosophy, we are arguing, has also been deeply influenced by this tradition, even though he has tried to incorporate the insights of the second line of development into his own thought, especially its critique of a purely essentialist conception of philosophical method, knowledge, and truth. Clearly, Tillich has tried to maintain his synthetic stance in relation to these two lines of development in philosophy, most clearly in relation to the existentialist revolt against the essentialism of the philosophical tradition. It is now necessary to evaluate Tillich's criticism of existentialism, first by considering some key doctrines in the existentialist movement as they are expressed in the thought of Kierkegaard and Heidegger, and secondly, by developing a critical analysis of Tillich's evaluation of this philosophical movement. We shall then attempt to assess his total conception of the relationship of philosophy and theology in the light of the material which emerges from our preliminary analysis.

Part Two

The Substance of Existentialism: Kierkegaard and Heidegger

The *locus classicus* of the revolt against the philosophical tradition is found in Kierkegaard's relatively early work *Fear and Trembling*. Kierkegaard wrote *Fear and Trembling* soon after the famous dissolution of his engagement to Regina, and after a brief period of study in Berlin where he heard Schelling's lectures. There is no doubt that Kierkegaard's break with Regina influenced the issues he seeks to resolve in *Fear and Trembling*; however, the standard interpretation that Kierkegaard terminated his relationship to Regina in order to realize his "absolute relation to God," a decision which was necessary because the former diluted the latter, and that this is the meaning of *Fear and Trembling*,[1] we shall argue is quite inadequate in helping us understand what Kierkegaard is up to in this book. We shall further argue that the discoveries Kierkegaard makes in *Fear and Trembling* exercise enormous influence over the remainder of his thought as well as the existentialist movement following him.

As is well-known, Kierkegaard's entire literary effort was in one way or another, conceived and executed in radical opposition to "the System," which is, of course, Hegel.[2]   There is much Kierkegaard says against Hegel which cannot be taken seriously as philosophical analysis, because of its *ad hominem* character. However, in spite of his excessive execrations against the Hegelian juggernaut, Kierkegaard formulates a critique, not only of Hegel, but *mutatis mutandis* of the entire classical philosophical tradition, which deserves our critical attention.

It is significant that Kierkegaard states in his Preface to *Fear and Trembling* that

> the present writer is nothing of a philosopher; he is, *poetice et eleganter*, an amateur writer who neither writes the System nor promises of the System, who neither subscribes to the System nor ascribes anything to it.[3]

To be a philosopher, for Kierkegaard, means, in the first place, the commitment to an intellectual substance (the history of philosophy) and methodology, which has as its fundamental task the transcendence of the philosopher's own individuality, concreteness and ethical existence in the world. In refusing to call himself a philosopher, Kierkegaard is saying "no" to this entire enterprise and at the same time attempting nothing less than a revolution in thought, an experiment, which has as its only goal the delineation of the character of human existence and the confrontation of the existing person with himself, so that he might choose his existence rather than forfeit it in an act of self-deception, which latter act is only reinforced by the philosophical tradition itself. Obviously, such an understanding is fraught with difficulty, the discussion of which must be deferred until we have considered Kierkegaard's argument in some detail.

Fear and Trembling opens with Kierkegaard's famous consideration of the biblical story of Abraham and Isaac. For Kierkegaard, Abraham is the exemplar of faith, whom Kierkegaard tells us again and again, he, himself, cannot imitate. But how does Abraham exemplify faith, and what does Kierkegaard mean by the notion of faith, which he thinks Abraham exemplifies? Our contention is that Kierkegaard is attempting to construct a notion of faith, which, while it is developed in relation to, yet cannot be construed as continuous with, the normative Christian understanding of faith. I would further contend that in *Fear and Trembling*, at least, Kierkegaard cannot be understood as a traditional Christian at all.

In order to develop his conception of faith, Kierkegaard subjects what for him are two fallacious notions of faith to critical scrutiny. The first may be called the naive *religious* view of faith and the second we may designate as the *philosophical* (Hegelian) view of faith. Kierkegaard is radically opposed to both of these views of faith.

The naive religious view of faith seems to be expressed in at least two meanings in *Fear and Trembling*. The first meaning construes faith as that rather half-hearted, self-protective attitude, which one assumes, with not a little resentment, in the face of the uncertainties of life. In describing Abraham's making the movement of infinite resignation (a notion we shall discuss below), Kierkegaard writes:

> Upon this pinnacle stands Abraham. The last stage he loses sight of is the infinite resignation. He really goes further, and reaches faith; for all these caricatures of faith, the miserable luke-warm indolence which thinks, "There surely is no instant need, it is not worth while sorrowing before the time," the pitiful hope which says, "One cannot know what is going to happen . . . it might possibly be after all" — these caricatures of faith are part and parcel of life's wretchedness, and the infinite resignation has already consigned them to infinite contempt.[4]

The second meaning of faith of the naive religious perspective is somewhat more difficult to identify. It is the notion that faith is the expectation, which one waits faithfully to have fulfilled, that either (1) God will intervene in the course of events and vindicate one's belief that he will do so (a variation on this theme is to see natural and historical events as the will of God) or (2) that in spite of the vicissitudes of one's temporal existence, one's ultimate fulfillment lies beyond time and history in "the next world." We shall argue that we cannot understand Kierkegaard's interpretation of Abraham if we construe his faith as his expectation that God would not in fact require him to sacrifice Isaac, that he would intervene at the last moment as the *Deus ex Machina* and spare Isaac. At best, such an interpretation would deprive the story of Abraham of its most basic ingredient for Kierkegaard, namely, *dread*, and at worse it would reduce faith to a sort of game played between God and Abraham in which God puts Abraham to the test to determine the depth of his faithfulness and in which Abraham plays the game to please God because he has nothing ultimately to lose. Faith cannot mean for Kierkegaard this kind of vulgar manipulation.

We reject this interpretation of the meaning of faith in *Fear and Trembling* even though Kierkegaard's language at points lends itself to such an interpretation. For example:

> [Abraham] believed that God would not require Isaac of him, whereas he was willing nevertheless to sacrifice him if it was required. He believed by virtue of the absurd; for there could be no question of human calculation, and it was indeed the absurd that God who required it of him should the next instant recall the requirement.[5]

By insisting that faith is not a matter of human calculation, it should be clear that Kierkegaard does not mean that faith is a kind of calculated risk, which man can execute by "second-guessing" God. On the surface, however, it does seem as if Abraham's faith is his responding to God's voice that he should sacrifice Isaac (his most precious possession) and having his faith rewarded by God's changing his mind and allowing him to keep Isaac. Our claim that this meaning of faith is negated by considering Kierkegaard's total argument and that this is not what Kierkegaard means by Abraham's getting Isaac back again awaits further explication.

The second option of the naive religious understanding of faith, Kierkegaard rejects flatly:

> Let us go further. We let Isaac be really sacrificed. Abraham believed. He did not believe that some day he would be blessed in the beyond but that he would be happy here in the world. God could give him a new Isaac, could call to life him who had been sacrificed.[6]

Not only does Kierkegaard find these naive views of faith wanting, but he rejects the Hegelian view of faith as well. Faith is not a "lower immediacy," i.e., a level in man's development in which ultimate reality is grasped in aesthetic and pictorial images and which philosophy must critically dissolve to make way for the

"Notion," the rational concept, in which Absolute Knowledge is obtained. Kierkegaard insists that one cannot go "beyond faith," as Hegel's mature philosophy of religion maintains, to a philosophical conceptuality that adequately clarifies that truth of which the religious imagination has only a vague, ambiguous presentiment in its acts and symbols. "Love has its priests," Kierkegaard complains,

> and sometimes one hears a voice which knows how to defend it; but of faith one hears never a word. Who speaks in honor of this passion? Philosophy goes further. Theology sits rouged at the window and courts its favor, offering to sell her charms to philosophy. It is supposed to be difficult to understand Hegel, but to understand Abraham is a trifle. To go beyond Hegel is a miracle, but to get beyond Abraham is the easiest thing of all. . . . [Faith] is the highest thing, and . . . it is dishonest of philosophy to give something else instead of it and to make light of faith. Philosophy cannot and should not give faith, but it should understand itself and know what it has to offer and take nothing away, and least of all should fool people out of something as if it were nothing.[7]

Having rejected these notions of faith, Kierkegaard proceeds to construct his own conception. In his "Preliminary Expectoration," Kierkegaard sees Abraham as the exemplar of faith by his "making the movements of faith," which involves his simultaneously relinquishing his claim to Isaac, the supreme joy and fulfillment of his life, and receiving Isaac back again. The movement of faith is made at each moment by "virtue of the absurd," which is to say that faith is grounded in "the paradox." In order to obtain a clear understanding of Kierkegaard's conception of faith, then, it is necessary to "unpack" the meaning of these terms which constitute the Kierkegaardian idea of faith.

The essence of Kierkegaard's notion of faith is contained in the following passages, which are quoted here at length:

> For the movements of faith must constantly be made by virtue of the absurd, yet in such a way, be it observed, that one does not lose the finite but gains it every inch. For my part I can well describe the movements of faith, but I cannot make them . . . I make the movements of infinity, whereas faith does the opposite: after having made the movements of infinity, it makes those of finiteness. Hail to him who can make those movements, he performs the marvelous, and I shall never grow tired of admiring him, whether he be Abraham or a slave in Abraham's house; whether he be a professor of

philosophy or a servant-girl, I look only at the movements. . . . The *knights of the infinite resignation* are easily recognized: their gait is gliding and assured. Those on the other hand who carry the jewel of faith are likely to be delusive, because their outward appearance bears a striking resemblance to that which both the infinite resignation and faith profoundly despise . . . to Philistinism.

I candidly admit that in my practice I have not found any reliable example of the *knight of faith*, though I would not therefore deny that every second man may be such an example. . . . One can discover nothing of that aloof and superior nature [in the knight of faith] whereby one recognizes the knight of the infinite. He takes a delight in everything, and whenever one sees him taking part in a particular pleasure, he does it with the persistence which is the mark of the earthly man whose soul is absorbed in such things. . . . And yet he is no genius, for in vain I have sought in him the incommensurability of genius. . . . He lives as carefree as a ne'er-do-well, *and yet he buys up the acceptable time at the dearest price, for he does not do the least thing except by virtue of the absurd.* And yet, . . . this man has made and every instant is making the movements of infinity. With infinite resignation he has drained the cup of life's profound sadness, he knows the bliss of the infinite, he senses the pain of renouncing everything, the dearest things he possesses in the world, and yet finiteness tastes to him just as good as to one who never knew anything higher, for his continuance in the finite did not bear a trace of the cowed and fearful spirit produced by the process of training; and yet he has this full sense of security in enjoying it, as though the finite life were the surest thing of all. And yet, the whole earthly form he exhibits is a new creation by virtue of the absurd. He resigned everything infinitely, and then he grasped everything again by virtue of the absurd. He constantly makes the movements of infinity, but he does this with such correctness and assurance that he constantly gets the finite out of it. (emphasis mine).[8]

After developing the contrast between the knight of infinite resignation and the knight of faith, and rather cryptically defining the movements of faith from resignation to a regaining of the finite, Kierkegaard proceeds to explicate the movements of faith in "a definite instance which will serve to illustrate their relation to reality, *for upon this everything turns*" (emphasis mine).[9] It is here, I would suggest, that Kierkegaard's revolt against the classical philosophical tradition is most apparent, for he is about to delineate his conception of existence in relation to a concrete experience open to anyone, an experience, as we shall see, which opens the possibility of a decision for which there is utterly no rational justification, and which defines the truth for the individual who makes it, a truth which itself is unique and individual.

Imagine, says Kierkegaard, a young swain who falls in love with a princess, and "the whole content of his life consists in this love."[10] However, it is not possible for the love relationship to be actualized. The common sense attitude would advise that the swain surrender this hopeless unrequited love, but he refuses, for he is fully aware that in his feelings for the princess his whole sense of reality is posited, that his entire identity is grounded in his love for the princess, that in fact he cannot be who he is without his love, and to surrender his love would be to deny his own personal reality. This the young swain refuses to do. Rather:

> he makes sure that this really is the content of his life, and his soul is too healthy and too proud to squander the least thing upon an inebriation. He is not cowardly, he is not afraid of letting love creep into his most secret, his most hidden thoughts, to let it twine in innumerable coils about every ligament of his consciousness — if the love becomes an unhappy love, he will never be able to tear himself loose from it. He feels a blissful rapture in letting love tingle through every nerve, and yet his soul is as solemn as that of the man who has drained the poisoned goblet and feels how the juice permeates every drop of blood — for this instant *is life and death*.[11]

Having posited the meaning of his personal existence in his love for the princess, the swain is then confronted with the impossibility of his love. It is in relation to this impossibility that he "makes the movements," which must be understood as having been made "normally," i.e., as the result of a passionate (existential) participation in one's situation (and not merely as a reflection upon it). Fully lucid, then, that his love is impossible, the swain, whom Kierkegaard now designates as the knight of resignation, must first

> have power to concentrate the whole content of life and the whole significance of reality in one single wish. If a man lacks this concentration, this intensity, if his soul from the beginning is dispersed in the multifarious, he never comes to the point of making the movement, ... — in short, he is not a knight. In the next place the knight will have the power to concentrate the whole result of the operations of thought in one act of consciousness. If he lacks this intensity, if his soul from the beginning is dispersed in the multifarious, he will never get time to make the movements, he will be constantly running errands in life, never enter into eternity, for even at the instant when he is closest to it he will suddenly discover that he has forgotten something for which he must go back. He will think that to enter eternity is possible the

next instant, and that also is perfectly true, but by such considerations one never reaches the point of making the movements, but by their aid sinks deeper and deeper into the mire.[12]

The movement of resignation consists at the outset of becoming fully aware of the unifying power which devolves to the self in relation to the finite content of its life, *when one chooses to concentrate one's existence upon this content.* The knight of resignation is beyond the aesthetic sphere of existence by virtue of his singleminded, unconditioned commitment to his love, thus precluding the project of living totally in the realm of possibility.[13] In allowing his love to define his existence, the knight of resignation achieves a sense of identity and reality, which for Kierkegaard, lifts him above the level of the relatively undifferentiated, anonymous, pseudo-existence of the crowd and thus establishes his integrity as a person. It is precisely the knight of resignation's awareness of his integrity as a person, which is achieved through his love, which compels him *not* to give it up. As Kierkegaard has put it:

> The knight does not contradict himself, and it is a contradiction to forget the whole content of one's life and yet remain the same man. To become another man he feels no inclination, nor does he by any means regard this as greatness. Only the lower natures forget themselves and become something new. Thus the butterfly has entirely forgotten that it was a caterpillar, perhaps it may in turn so entirely forget it was a butterfly that it becomes a fish. The deeper natures never forget themselves and never become anything else than what they were.[14]

And yet, the love between the knight and the princess is impossible. The knight will not give it up and his love for the princess cannot be actualized either. At this point the movement of resignation is complete, which consists in keeping the love alive *without* sustaining an immediate, concrete relationship to the beloved. What is common to these strategies of resignation is the knight's relinquishing his claim to the object of his love thereby becoming reconciled to existence in pain.

One way of making the movement of resignation is to transform one's love of the princess into a love for the Eternal. Hence:

> So the knight remembers everything, but precisely this remembrance is pain, and yet by the infinite resignation he is reconciled with existence. Love for the princess became for him the expression for an eternal love, assumed a religious character, was transfigured into a love for the Eternal Being, which did to be sure deny him the fulfillment of his love, *yet reconciled him again by the eternal consciousness of its validity in the form of eternity, which no reality can take from him* (emphasis mine).[15]

Although Kierkegaard does not make the historical reference here, St. Augustine can be seen as embodying this particular form of resignation when he tells us in *The Confessions* of the death of his friend in the love of whom "I had poured out my soul upon the dust, in loving one that must die, as if he would never die." Rather than love any finite creature unconditionally again, Augustine grounds the love of the finite in the prior love of the eternal God, i.e., one loves God absolutely and the finite relatively. Augustine writes:

> Blessed whoso loveth Thee, and his friend in Thee, and his enemy for Thee. For he alone loses none dear to him, to whom all are dear in Him who cannot be lost. And who is this but our God, the God that made heaven and earth, and filleth them, because by filling them He created them? Thee none loseth, but who leaveth. And who leaveth Thee, whither goeth or whether fleeth he, but from Thee well-pleased, to Thee displeased?[16]

Thus, the knight of resignation may still love the princess, but only as his love is transmuted through his love of the eternal, whom he will never lose.

The second strategy of resignation is to reverse the impossibility of the love of the princess into a possibility by spiritualizing it. In this move the knight

> expresses it spiritually by waving his claim to it. The wish which would carry him out into reality, but was wrecked upon the impossibility, is now bent inward, but it is not therefore lost, neither is it forgotten. At one moment it is the obscure emotion of the wish within him which awakens recollections, at another moment he awakens them himself; for he is too proud to be willing that what was the whole content of his life should be the thing of a fleeting moment. He keeps his love young, and along with him it increases in years and in beauty. On the other hand, he has no need of the intervention of the finite for the further growth of his love . . . because he recollects her in an eternal sense. . . . [17]

In this strategy of resignation, the knight commits himself to the memory of his beloved and pursues his memory as Dante pursued Beatrice, as the transcendent, ideal woman, whom he was not able to love in reality; while there may be other persons in his life, none of them can compare to the transcendent memory of the beloved.

A third strategy of resignation is for the knight to become self-sufficient by maintaining his sense of reality in relation to the beloved as memory, and never allowing himself to care for anyone else. As Kierkegaard puts it:

> There was one who also believed that he had made the movement; but lo, time passed, the princess did something else, she married — a prince, let us say — then his soul lost the elasticity of resignation. Thereby he knew that he had not made the movement rightly; for he who has made the act of resignation infinitely is sufficient unto himself. The knight does not annul his resignation, he preserves his love just as young as it was in its first moment, he never lets it go from him, precisely because he makes the movements infinitely. What the princess does, cannot disturb him, it is only the lower natures which find in other people the law for their actions, which find the premises for their actions outside themselves.[18]

In the infinite resignation man finds "peace and rest" by becoming reconciled to existence through pain. While Kierkegaard has used the example of the love relationship to explicate the structure of resignation, his insight cannot be limited to that relationship; rather he is uncovering, in terms of Heidegger's distinctions, an *ontological* structure through an *ontic* one. It is that ontological structure we shall now attempt to elucidate.[19]

The issue to be resolved in Kierkegaard's example is not that of unrequited love, *but rather the problem which emerges when a person becomes aware that his whole sense of reality is posited in relation to a finite value which is itself contingent, temporal, and utterly threatened.* The swain sustains a *defining relationship*[20] to the princess, which is to say that the princess has come to have an ultimate meaning for him in the sense that she is a life necessity for him, i.e., he is who he is, his identity and personal reality are given, in relationship to the princess. Kierkegaard is arguing nothing less than that in the relationship to the beloved, the swain achieves a sense of absolute meaning, which the classical theological tradition asserts obtains only in man's relationship to God; however, the swain achieves this absolute meaning in relationship to a finite creature, who is not divine, but on the contrary, is the very contrast of the divine: limited in space and time, impermanent, and whom the swain will ultimately lose.

On the ontological level, then, the absolute meaning is not itself absolute, and thus the various strategies of resignation are ways in which the knight of resignation maintains his meaning without the risk and dread of a continuing, concrete, and immediate relationship to the princess. What the knight of resignation denies himself, then, is the ultimate fulfillment of a concrete relationship to the princess in order to protect himself from the constant dread that he will lose that in relation to which his sense of reality is posited through rejection, perhaps, or death.

The knight of resignation has achieved an authentic lucidity about himself and the world in which he lives, namely, that the absolute meaning he has achieved in his defining relationship to the finite princess is ultimately threatened, and that if he loses her, he loses his own sense of reality and identity. He, therefore, resigns himself to the fact that that which provides him with absolute meaning he will ultimately lose, which is for Kierkegaard the truth of finite existence. He becomes reconciled to existence in pain by refusing to enter into a concrete relationship to the princess and thus defends himself from the dread which is the inevitable component of the concrete meaning of his life. He thereby dilutes the full meaning of the defining relationship through the strategy of resignation. He is protected from the pain of dread, but he loses the ultimate fulfillment Kierkegaard is convinced can be given in the defining relationship. The knight of resignation cannot deny himself, but he cannot endure the terror of a total commitment to the meaning of his life either. Therein lies his tragedy for Kierkegaard.

"For the act of resignation," says Kierkegaard,

faith is not required, for what I gain by resignation is my eternal consciousness, and this is a purely philosophical movement which I dare say I am able to make if it is required, and which I can train myself to make, for whenever any finiteness would get the mastery over me, I starve myself until I can make the movement, for my eternal consciousness is my love to God, and for me this is higher than everything. For the act of resignation faith is not required, but it is needed when it is the case of acquiring the very least thing more than my eternal consciousness, for this is the paradoxical.[21]

Kierkegaard in this passage continues to develop his critique of the classical philosophical tradition. The stance of detached objectivity, we have argued, allows the philosopher to see the world *sub species aeternitatus*, that is, in his eternal consciousness, which is directed toward the eternal God of the classical philosophical vision. Resignation is a philosophical movement for Kierkegaard precisely because it opens to the philosopher the awareness of the ontological insufficiency of the finite to provide the permanent, unchanging, and therefore universal truth which the philosopher seeks, and, at the same time, allows him to live in relation to the eternal order of being in his eternal consciousness by rationalizing his movement away from the finite, the latter alone providing, for Kierkegaard, the absolute fulfillment of one's own personal truth. Classical philosophy, in leading the thinker away from the finite and the dread of an absolute commitment to it, originates in an act of cowardice, the ultimate outcome of which is to deprive the philosopher of his own subjectivity.

The infinite resignation is the last stage prior to faith. If one has not posited the meaning of his existence in the defining relationship to a finite value on the one hand and on the other achieved the lucidity that that in relation to which he has achieved his personal meaning, because it is finite, he will ultimately lose, if he has not made the movement of resignation, then he cannot possibly make the movement of faith, for resignation consists in becoming fully aware of the contingency of oneself and one's world, especially that in one's world one values most. Faith, for Kierkegaard, must not be based upon an illusion, and, therefore, it must include the lucidity of the movement of resignation within its structure or else its integrity is lost.

However, faith goes beyond resignation. Kierkegaard writes:

Now we will let the knight of faith appear in the role just described. He makes exactly the same movements as the other knight, infinitely renounces claim to the love which is the content of his life, he is reconciled in pain; but then occurs the prodigy, he makes still another movement more wonderful than all, for he says, "I believe nevertheless that I shall get her, in virtue, that is, of the absurd, in virtue of the fact that with God all things are possible." The absurd is not one of the factors which can be discriminated within the proper compass of the understanding: it is not identical with the improbable, the unexpected, the unforeseen. At the moment when the knight made the act of resignation, he was convinced, humanly speaking, of the impossibility. This was the result reached by the understanding, and he had sufficient energy to think it. On the other hand, in an infinite sense it was possible, namely, by renouncing it; but this sort of possessing is at the same time a relinquishing, and yet there is no absurdity in this for the understanding, for the understanding continued to be in the right in affirming that in the world of the finite where it holds sway this was and remained an impossibility. This is quite as clear to the knight of faith, so that the only thing that can save him is the absurd and this he grasps by faith.[22]

The knight of faith, then, makes the movement of resignation but goes on to make the movement of faith by virtue of the absurd in which, in Kierkegaard's example, he both renounces his claim to the princess and gets her back again. But what does this mean? Kierkegaard states briefly but explicitly in what the experience of faith consists. Thus:

It is about the temporal, the finite, everything turns in this case. . . . To exist in such a way that my opposition to existence is expressed as the most beautiful and assured harmony with it, is something I cannot do. And yet it must be glorious to get the princess, that is what I say every instant, and the knight of resignation who does not say it is a deceiver, he has not had only one wish, and he has not kept the wish young by his pain. Perhaps there was one who thought it fitting enough that the wish was no longer vivid, that the barb of pain was dulled, but such a man is no knight. A free-born soul who caught himself entertaining such thoughts would despise himself and begin over again, above all he would not permit his soul to be deceived by itself. And yet it must be glorious to get the princess, and yet the knight of faith is the only happy one, the heir apparent to the finite. Whereas the knight of resignation is a stranger and a foreigner. Thus to get the princess, to live with her joyfully and happily day in and day out (for it is also conceivable that the knight of resignation might get the princess, but that his soul had discerned the impossibility of their future happiness), thus to live joyfully and happily every instant by virtue of the absurd, every instant to see the sword hanging over the head of the beloved, and yet not to find response in the pain of resignation, but joy by virtue of the absurd — this is marvelous. He who does it is great, the only great man.[23]

It should be clear now that Kierkegaard's example of unrequited love is meant to focus not upon the experience of unfulfilled love, but rather upon the experience of having one's sense of reality posited in relation to a finite value. The knight of faith does not get the princess back again by some mere contingency, a stroke of good luck: he gets her back by courageously continuing to posit his personal meaning, his sense of identity and reality, in relation to the princess even as he is as fully aware as is the knight of resignation that the princess is finite. He sustains a concrete relationship to the princess whereas the knight of resignation does not, which means that he takes upon himself the dread of the relationship and thereby achieves the ultimate meaning of his existence. This is the meaning of faith for Kierkegaard; the courage of sustaining one's sense of reality and meaning in relation to the finite world, paradoxically achieving *ultimate* fulfillment in relation to the finite by virtue of the absurd.

The paradox and the absurd in *Fear and Trembling* do not mean, as they do in Kierkegaard's later thought, the "God in Time," or the "God-Man," i.e., the Christian assertion of the Incarnation. Rather they refer to the experience, which is sheer heresy in relation to the classical philosophical tradition, of achieving ultimate fulfillment and meaning (what Kierkegaard calls eternal happiness) in time, or more precisely, in relation to that which is thoroughly temporal, the finite itself. This experience is paradoxical and absurd only if it is seen against the background of both the classical philosophical and theological traditions of the West in which man's eternal felicity is grounded in the infinite, eternal, immutable order of being beyond or "above" the finite world.

The knight of faith, then, is one who achieves a definitive sense of reality, an ultimate meaning in relation to a personal, idiosyncratic, concrete and fully contingent value, and this concrete content becomes, even though Kierkegaard does not make this point explicitly in *Fear and Trembling*, the personal truth of the knight of faith. To distinguish his own view of truth even more decisively from that conception of truth found in the philosophical tradition, Kierkegaard explores a series of *problemata* derived from his analysis of Abraham. The first two problemata, namely, "is there such a thing as a teleological suspension of the ethical?" and "is there such a thing as an absolute duty toward God?" bear further consideration.

Again, we shall argue that Abraham means for Kierkegaard one who willingly and consciously allows his identity to be shaped by a passionate relationship to a finite value and who takes upon himself the dread of the relationship by both repeatedly acknowledging the threat to his identity for valuing that which itself is threatened (surrendering his claim to the finite) and yet maintaining his identity and personal fulfillment by continuously affirming his concrete relationship to that which defines his identity and meaning (getting the finite back again). We must keep this model of the knight of faith in mind as we examine the meaning of duty and the ethical in *Fear and Trembling*.

"The ethical," says Kierkegaard;

> is the universal, and as the universal it applies to everyone, which may be expressed from another point of view by saying that it applies every instant. It reposes immanently in itself, it has nothing without itself which is its *telos*, but is itself *telos* for everything outside it, and when this has been incorporated by the ethical it can go no further. Conceived immediately as physical and psychical, the particular individual is the individual who has his *telos* in the universal, and his ethical task is to express himself constantly in it, to abolish his particularity in order to become the universal. As soon as the individual would assert himself in his particularity over against the universal he sins, and only by recognizing this can he again reconcile himself with the universal. . . . If this be the highest thing that can be said of man and of his existence, then the ethical has the same character as man's eternal blessedness, which to all eternity and at every instant is his *telos*. . . .[24]

However controversial Kierkegaard's assertion here in relation to the history of ethical theory may be again he is convinced that the philosophical tradition from Socrates, Plato and Aristotle through Kant to Hegel has in common the view that moral duty cannot rest upon the individual's particular circumstances, but rather the moral imperative, as the truth itself, must be universal and objective, the only adequate ground for wise moral action. Hence, the ethical is the universal and the ethical task of the individual is to divest himself of his particularity (to edit a perfect edition of oneself as Kierkegaard put it), i.e., his inclinations, common sense notions of right and wrong, habits, motives of reward (even though doing justice for its own sake brings man's highest happiness according to Plato), concrete preferences, self-interest, partial perspectives, and translate his actions into universal moral terms, or as Kant has it "act on that maxim through which you can at the same time will it should become a universal law." Just as in knowledge the philosopher knows universal and objective truth so in action the philosopher (hence all men) should act in accord with objective and universal moral principles.

Kierkegaard's argument against the tradition is comparable to his argument concerning the meaning of faith. He will appeal to a concrete experience, open to anyone, which stands as a counterexample to the claim that all significant moral action is subsumed under universal moral rules. Abraham provides such a counterexample.

On the ethical level, the paradox of faith is that

> the particular is higher than the universal — yet in such a way, be it observed, that the movement repeats itself, and that consequently the individual, after having been in the universal, now as the particular isolates himself as higher than the universal. If this be not faith, then Abraham is lost, then faith has never existed in the world. . . . because it has always existed. For if the ethical (i.e., the moral) is the highest thing, and if nothing incommensurable remains in man in any other way but as the evil (i.e., the particular which has to be expressed in the universal), then one needs no other categories besides those which the Greeks possessed or which by consistent thinking can be derived from them.[25]

Kierkegaard is convinced, however, that there is something "incommensurable" in man's experience, illustrated in the figure of Abraham, which demands a "teleological suspension of the ethical." Abraham receives the command from God to sacrifice Isaac, which means that the command from God takes precedence over the ethical ("Thou shall not kill"), i.e., the ethical injunction against murder is momentarily set aside by a higher duty, namely, to obey the will of God. If Abraham obeys the divine command, which for him is compelling, he is outside the sphere of the ethical, and as the individual "before God" he is higher than the ethical, i.e., the universal. The ethical has been teleologically suspended, and Abraham as the knight of faith acts "by virtue of the absurd." Kierkegaard writes:

> He acts by virtue of the absurd, for it is precisely absurd that he as the partic-
> ular is higher than the universal. This paradox cannot be mediated; for as
> soon as he begins to do this he has to admit that he was in temptation
> (*Anfectung*), and if such was the case, he never gets to the point of sacrificing
> Isaac, or, if he has sacrificed Isaac, he must turn back repentantly to the uni-
> versal. By virtue of the absurd he gets Isaac again. Abraham is therefore at
> no instant a tragic hero but something quite different, either a murderer or a
> believer. The middle term which saves the tragic hero, Abraham has not.[26]

The tragic hero must commit an act, which on the surface vio-lates the universal (e.g. Agamemnon's sacrifice of Iphigenia); how-ever, his act is grounded in the universal itself. Even though his act is tragic, it must be done, for the universal both demands and justi-fies the act. Thus, Agamemnon must sacrifice Iphigenia in order to save his people. The tragic hero here is thus consoled by the uni-versal: the legitimacy of what he does is established by the univer-sal.

Not so the knight of faith, says Kierkegaard:

> It was not for the sake of saving a people, not to maintain the idea of the
> state, that Abraham did this, and not in order to reconcile angry deities. If
> there could be a question of the deity being angry, he was angry only with
> Abraham, and Abraham's whole action stands in no relation to the universal,
> is a purely private undertaking.[27]

If Abraham is not motivated by the universal demand of the ethical, the question as to why he chose to sacrifice Isaac arises. Kierkegaard answers:

> He did it for God's sake because God required this proof of his faith; for his
> own sake he did it in order that he might furnish the proof. The unity of
> these two points of view is perfectly expressed by the word which has always
> been used to characterize this situation: it is a trial, a temptation ... A temp-
> tation — but what does this mean? What ordinarily tempts a man is that

which would keep him from doing his duty, but in this case the temptation is itself the ethical . . . which would keep him from doing God's will. But what then is duty? Duty is precisely the expression for God's will.[28]

As we shall see, everything depends upon becoming clear as to Kierkegaard's conception of the "will of God"; however, before we attempt to do that it is necessary to examine the meaning of the teleological suspension of the ethical in more detail. As we have seen the knight of faith is to be distinguished from the knight of resignation and the tragic hero. In defining duty as the expression for God's will, Kierkegaard states:

Here is evident the necessity of a new category if one would understand Abraham. Such a relationship to the deity paganism did not know. The tragic hero does not enter into any private relationship with the deity, but for him the ethical is the divine, hence the paradox implied in his situation can be mediated in the universal. . . . He who denies himself and sacrifices himself for duty gives up the finite in order to grasp the infinite, and that man is secure enough. The tragic hero gives up the certain for the still more certain, and the eye of the beholder rests upon him confidently. But he who gives up the universal in order to grasp something still higher which is not the universal — what is he doing?[29]

In Kierkegaard's initial analysis of the knight of faith, he argued that the knight of faith gives up the finite and paradoxically gets the finite back again. We interpreted Kierkegaard to mean by that the knight of faith gives up the finite by moving from that "lower immediacy" of experience which takes the world for granted (where the critical question is not raised) to a state of lucidity in which he sees that the finite is in principle threatened, but rather than finding his ultimate meaning in the infinite, and eternal, i.e., the Absolute of classical philosophy, he enters into a passionate relationship to that which defines his reality (a higher immediacy), namely the finite itself, thus going beyond the classical tradition in relation to which his fulfillment through the finite is absurd.

If the knight of faith refuses to give his life meaning in relation to that which is beyond time and the whole problematic of finitude, but rather seeks to actualize the meaning he has found in the finite, it follows that he individuates himself in relation to a structure of meaning which is personal and unique to him and *cannot* be subsumed by a more universal and objective structure of meaning. Therefore, the knight of faith's most profound truth and most urgent meaning is outside the realm of the universal, or in Tillich's language, the essential. So too with the knight of faith's moral existence. Kierkegaard is arguing that the knight of faith's relationship to his defining meaning places him under a moral imperative, (namely to do what his meaning demands, since he cannot be faithful to his own identity if he does not), which cannot be reduced to a universal moral principle and thus places him outside of and in opposition to the universal.

The paradox of faith, then, at the ethical level, is that the individual is higher than the universal. On the surface, Kierkegaard's treatment of Abraham seems clear: his obedience to God takes precedence over the ethical, and it is God's command received in his private experience to which he must be faithful, even though the universal ethical principle (a father should love his son) forbids that he actualize God's command. Thus, one way of seeing the problematic Kierkegaard is uncovering, is that represented by Martin Buber. He writes:

> When God commands one to murder his son, the immorality of the immoral is suspended for the duration of this situation. What is more, that which is otherwise purely evil is for the duration of this situation purely good because it has become pleasing to God. In the place of the universal and the universally valid steps something which is founded exclusively in the personal relation between God and "the Single One." But just through this the ethical, the universal and the universally valid, is relativized. Its values and laws are banished from the absolute into the relative; for that which is a duty in the sphere of the ethical possesses no absoluteness as soon as it is confronted with the absolute duty toward God.[30]

Again, Kierkegaard's words lend themselves to this interpretation, but if we follow it there seems no way to avoid the conclusion that it is not the individual who is higher than the universal, as Kierkegaard claims, but rather God who is higher, and further that given the trans-personal character of the conception of God, Abraham's decision to sacrifice Isaac is justified if God exists, at least as a linguistic convention, and if it can be shown that acts which, within a purely ethical frame of reference, can be construed as immoral are in fact moral at a higher level as expressions of the divine *telos* or purpose. If such is the case, then all that Kierkegaard says about Abraham's aloneness and his inability to make himself intelligible to others and thereby his inability to justify his action to others simply collapses. If we are to make sense of the problematic Kierkegaard has before us, we must abandon the surface meaning of Abraham and Isaac.

It is the case, of course, that in relation to the personal command, the ethical is relativized. But now we must ask what it means to say that this command comes from God. A crucial passage will facilitate our own interpretation:

> The paradox of faith is this, that the individual is higher than the universal, that the individual . . . determines his relation to the universal by his relation to the absolute, not his relation to the absolute by his relation to the universal. The paradox can also be expressed by saying that there is an absolute duty toward God; for in this relationship of duty the individual as an individual stands related absolutely to the absolute. . . . In the story of Abraham we find such a paradox. His relation to Isaac, ethically expressed, is this, that the father should love the son. This ethical relation is reduced to a relative position in contrast with the absolute relation to God. . . . The paradox of faith has lost the intermediate term, i.e., the universal. On the one side it has the expression for the extremist egoism (doing the dreadful thing it does for one's own sake); on the other side the expression for the most absolute self-sacrificing (doing it for God's sake). Faith itself cannot be mediated into the universal, for it would thereby be destroyed. Faith is this paradox, and the individual absolutely cannot make himself intelligible to anybody. . . . Either the individual becomes a knight of faith by assuming the burden of the paradox, or he never becomes one. In these regions partnership is unthinkable. *Every more precise explication of what is to be understood by Isaac the individual can give only to himself.* And even if one were able, generally speaking, to define ever so precisely what should be intended by Isaac (which moreover would be the most ludicrous self-contradiction, i.e., that the particular individual who definitely stands outside the universal is subsumed under universal categories precisely when he has to act as the individual who stands outside the universal), the individual nevertheless will never be able to assure himself by the aid of others that this application is appropriate, but he can do so only by himself as the individual . . . for only the individual becomes a knight of faith as the particular individual, and this is the greatness of this knighthood . . . ; but this also is its terror (emphasis mine).[31]

If we take Kierkegaard's statement that everything turns on the finite in understanding the knight of faith as our interpretative clue, and attempt to work with his statement that each individual must give the meaning of Isaac to himself on the basis of that clue, we may conclude that the counter-example Kierkegaard is seeking to develop includes the notion of ethical existence based precisely upon one's personal circumstance, where one's identity is defined by the concrete content of one's life and further that that concrete content exercises an absolute demand upon the one whose identity is defined by it such that he cannot be who he is unless he is faithful to that demand.   Thus, God as the absolute refers, not to the Judeo-Christian conception of God as personal, transcendent Other, who places man under the moral imperative derived from his own being as Lord, nor to the metaphysical Absolute of Hegelian philosophy, but rather to the unique relationship the individual sustains to the finite values which define his existence, where the individual has achieved the self-knowledge by which he distinguishes himself from the general meanings of his culture, including the classical philosophical structure of meaning, and individuates himself in relation to his unique personal meanings.

Perhaps at this point we can render Kierkegaard's analysis more concrete by presenting an example, like the swain and the princess, which he failed to do, beyond the example of Abraham himself, in his discussion of the teleological suspension of the ethical. Consider the example, widespread in our culture, of the married man (or woman), who finds himself deeply in love with a woman (man) outside his marriage such that his sense of reality is posited in relation to the woman. She becomes for him a "life necessity," that is, his sense of reality is so defined by the relationship to his lover that he cannot be who he is unless he actualizes his relationship to her; the meaning he derives from the relationship is absolute for him. To become a knight of faith the man must: (1) determine with as much clarity as possible that the relationship is essential to his existence, that is, that he cannot be himself without it; and (2) passionately sustain a concrete relationship to the woman.

If he decides to actualize his relationship to the woman, that is, if he places himself in an "absolute relationship to the absolute," he is immediately outside the universally ethical, which in this case is that a husband should not commit adultery but remain faithful to his wife, whether he decides to divorce her or not (we shall leave aside the question whether the injunction against adultery is a universally valid moral principle and assume that it is). Neither can he appeal to any principle outside the relationship to justify himself (e.g. that an extramarital relationship makes him a more adequate husband to his wife, that as an autonomous person he should actualize his possibilities, that his lover needs his love to feel her own value as a person, etc.), since none of these options are *necessary* to achieve the results projected. The man is "without excuse" (Sartre). From the perspective of the ethical his act is totally selfish, and yet it was done in response to the absolute command of the relationship (God). Such a man, for Kierkegaard, is a knight of faith if he takes upon himself the dread of being faithful to that which is essential to his identity and sense of reality and he is fully aware that he has elevated himself above the ethical. He is a knight of faith no matter how tragic the consequences of his act may be for himself and those around him.

Kierkegaard's position immediately raises several important problems, which he himself attempts to anticipate. In the first place, the teleological suspension of the ethical is not a form of antinomianism. It asserts that in terms of the individual's most fundamental reality, his personal existence, he is higher than the universal and cannot be subsumed by the universal. There are some choices we must make, which can only be made alone and for which we must assume full responsibility, and these choices establish our individuality, our personal significance and identity, our sense of who we are as uniquely existing human beings, and for Kierkegaard, *contra* the tradition, achieving our individuality through the passionate and dreadful relationship to the concrete content of our lives, without which we are ultimately incomplete, is the supreme ethical task confronting us. But to say that the individual is higher than the universal, is not to say that he is above or beyond the ethical in the sense that he is free to actualize any impulse or fantasy he wishes no matter how irrational or destructive.

Just as the individual, in order to become a knight of faith, must achieve that lucidity regarding the human condition which is the pre-supposition of resignation, so he must also be in the universal, where he affirms that every finite content is relative in relation to the universal. It is on this basis, I contend, that the "several criteria" Kierkegaard thinks are available to distinguish the knight of faith from the fanatic, the megalomaniac, the psychopath, and "the philistine" (the one in Kierkegaard's writings who is caught in the "lower immediacy" of experience and thereby absolutizes the finite without having raised the philosophical question) are established. Kierkegaard writes:

> Whether the individual is in temptation (*Anfectung*) or is a knight of faith only the individual can decide. Nevertheless it is possible to construct from the paradox several criteria which he too can understand who is not within the paradox.[32]

The first criterion is:

> The true knight of faith is always absolute isolation, the false knight is sectarian. This sectarianism is an attempt to leap away from the narrow path of the paradox and become a tragic hero at a cheap price. The tragic hero expresses the universal and sacrifices himself for it. The sectarian punchinello, instead of that, has a private theatre, i.e., several good friends and comrades who represent the universal about as well as the beadles in *The Golden Snuffbox* represent justice. The knight of faith, on the contrary, is the paradox, is the individual, absolutely nothing but the individual, without connections or pretense. . . . The sectaries deafen one another by their noise and racket, hold the dread off by their shrieks, and such hallowing company of sportsmen think they are storming heaven and think they are on the same path as the knight of faith who in the solitude of the universe never hears any human voice but walks alone with his dreadful responsibility.[33]

The second criterion is based on the isolation of the knight of faith:

> The knight of faith is obliged to rely upon himself alone, he feels the pain of not being able to make himself intelligible to others, but he feels no vain

desire to guide others. The pain is the assurance that he is in the right way, this vain desire he does not know, he is too serious for that. . . . The true knight of faith is a witness, never a teacher, and therein lies his deep humanity, which is worth a good deal more than this participation in others' weal and woe which is honored by the name of sympathy, whereas in fact it is nothing but vanity.[34]

As inadequately developed as these "criteria" are, let us attempt to use them to defend Kierkegaard from the charge of antinomianism in his ethical thought. The question is: is not Kierkegaard open to the charge that by placing the individual above the universal, he has thereby undercut the grounds for distinguishing between good and evil acts and thus made it possible for evil acts to be construed after the model of the knight of faith? Could not one, for example (returning for the moment to the literal meaning of Abraham and Isaac), driven by a compulsion to murder someone (e.g., Hitler) were he reflective enough, justify this compulsion on the grounds that he wishes to be a knight of faith? And if he were willing not to justify his compulsion in terms of the universal, to take full responsibility for it, would he not then be a knight of faith?

I can see no grounds in Kierkegaard's thought for concluding that under no circumstance would the knight of faith ever find himself having to act in such a way that not only would his act be above the universal, but that from the point of view of the ethical would also be reprehensible. However, it must be stressed that Kierkegaard's emphasis upon lucidity, individuality, and freedom distinguishes the knight of faith from most of the garden-variety forms of pathological behavior with which his own acts might be identified. The knight of faith understands and accepts the universal (i.e., the moral law), although Kierkegaard conceived him to show that the universal does not subsume all forms of moral action. Secondly, the knight of faith is fully lucid in regard to the fact that the concrete content of his life in relation to which he acts is, in fact, essential to his own self-identity, and yet, Kierkegaard insists that the knight must choose his values; he becomes individuated through his choices. Thus, even though his finite values are essential or necessary to his existence, they are nonetheless chosen, i.e., they are products of freedom; the knight of faith freely chooses to invest his life with the meaning they afford, and thus he was free not to choose them. This immediately removes the knight, in principle, from all forms of conscious and unconscious compulsion. Thus, to return to our example, if the knight of faith ever found himself in a position where he would have to take someone's life to be himself (an extreme case to be sure), the act would have to be free, psychologically speaking, from all those dynamics which usually motivate such acts. Obviously a serious question can be raised as to whether any one can achieve that level of self-knowledge and detachment from the "lower immediacy" of one's self to act lucidly and freely, but there can be no doubt that is Kierkegaard's goal for the knight of faith.

Thus, the knight of faith is alone, he cannot obtain confirmation for his decisions from the universal or any human group, he cannot recommend that others follow him, neither can he advise others as to what they should do. He must decide to what in the world of the finite he shall commit himself, thereby gaining his real self (as opposed to his biological, psychological or conventional self), taking upon himself the anxiety of living fully in the finite, as well as in the paradox that it is only in relation to the finite that ultimate fulfillment is possible.[35]

We have devoted this much attention to Kierkegaard's *Fear and Trembling*, because it is crucial not only for understanding his thought, but it is also important in understanding the philosophical movement which stems from him. On the basis of the analysis in *Fear and Trembling* we must now attempt to explicate Kierkegaard's notions of *existence, objectivity, and the truth as subjectivity*.

The achievement of *Fear and Trembling* is a brilliant, if incompletely expressed, insight into the nature of human existence. As we have tried to show, it represents Kierkegaard's case, at what one might call the phenomenological level, against the classical philosophical tradition's conceptions of truth and the nature of man, especially as that tradition came to fruition in the thought of

Hegel. Kierkegaard's major objection to that tradition is that the uniquely existing individual has been lost within a structure of meaning which places ultimate significance upon the universal concept, rationality, the cognitive self and the task of becoming objective as the highest end of man. Against this structure of meaning Kierkegaard asserts a conception of lived existence in contrast to a merely logical definition, defines truth as subjectivity and insists that the task of becoming subjective is the highest end of man. We must examine these assertions in more detail.

The self, for Kierkegaard, as Huston Smith has said, is a synthesis, a synthesis of the infinite and the finite, the temporal and the eternal, freedom and necessity.[36] In saying the self is eternal and infinite, Kierkegaard is not using these terms in their quantitative sense, but rather as qualities of experience, and he argues, they function as actual human needs (what Abraham Maslow might call B [Being] needs), which must be fulfilled if man is to become a fully real self. For Kierkegaard man has a need for that which does not change (the eternal) as well as a content outside of himself which has an ultimate (infinite) significance and can evoke an infinite (i.e., unqualified, absolute) concern. And yet, the self is fully finite, confronted with a full range of possibilities (freedom), and defined by biological and historical facticity (necessity). There is, then, a fundamental dichotomy running through human existence, and thus, the unity of the self is disrupted by this dichotomy. Furthermore, Kierkegaard is convinced that the self cannot overcome this dichotomy out of its own resources. It must be grasped by something outside itself which can do justice to both terms of the dichotomy, that is, the eternal, the infinite and possibility, as well as the temporal, the finite and facticity.

The classical philosophical tradition facilitated that lucidity in man in which he becomes aware of his need for the infinite and eternal as well as the awareness (the source of despair) of human finitude and temporality. Kierkegaard is appreciative of the contribution of philosophy in awakening man to himself and placing before him the task of becoming a real self; however he is in radical disagreement with the model of authentic selfhood, which he believes is characteristic of the classical philosophical tradition. This disagreement, and his own alternative to the classical tradition, are apparent in his critique of Hegel. Kierkegaard asserts:

> The way of objective reflection makes the subject accidental, and thereby transforms existence into something indifferent, something vanishing. Away from the subject the objective way of reflection leads to the objective truth, and while the subject and his subjectivity becomes indifferent, the truth also becomes indifferent, and this indifference is precisely its objective validity; for all interest, like all decisiveness, is rooted in subjectivity. The way of objective reflection leads to abstract thought, to mathematics, to historical knowledge of different kinds; and always it leads away from the subject, whose existence or non-existence, and from the objective point of view quite rightly, becomes infinitely indifferent. Quite rightly, since as Hamlet says, existence and non-existence have only subjective significance.[37]

Thus, Hegel does not deal with the subjectivity of the individual, because he is committed to the way of objective reflection whose fundamental instrument is the Concept. But, says Kierkegaard, the basic question is whether existence can be reduced to a concept. To do so is to deal with existence at the level of abstraction, and this is to deal only with the concept of existence not with the existing individual. As Robert Solomon has written:

> According to Kierkegaard's (and Schelling's) critique, the system can speak of only what is logically common to all "existents," that is, all instantiations for x in the ill-formed formula "x exists" (Heidegger's Being and not actual beings). Thus, Kant's Transcendental Logic exposes those concepts which are necessary conditions for "consciousness in general" while Hegel's Logic traces the development of the concepts of a literally "general consciousness" which are necessary for Spiritual self-consciousness in "The Idea." In both of these philosophies, the concern is only for the Universal, the *a priori*, and the analysis of those fundamental concepts or Categories in logic. Logic, however, cannot capture the peculiarities of an individual person — his feelings, particular thoughts, emotions, dispositions — in short, all of those non-universal aspects of a person to which we refer as his personality. The kind of "understanding" Kierkegaard demands of philosophy is just this sort of understanding, of psychological differences rather than logical similarities. The business of philosophy is the recognition of oneself as unique and peculiar, and not the recognition of oneself as an instance of the concept of "humanity."[38]

It is the existing individual, then, which must become the center of the philosophical enterprise not as an instantiation of Absolute Spirit or man *qua* man, but rather as a unique reality in his own right. Thus, philosophy must move from the abstract "I-am-I," the cognitive subject to the concrete ethical existence of the individual person. Kierkegaard says:

> Existence constitutes the highest interest of the existing individual, and his interest in his existence constitutes his reality. What reality is, cannot be expressed in the language of abstraction. . . . Abstract thought considers both possibility and reality, but its concept of reality is a false reflection, since the medium within which the concept is thought is not reality, but possibility. Abstract thought can get hold of reality only by nullifying it, and this nullification of reality consists in transforming it into possibility. . . . The only reality to which an existing individual may have a relation that is more than cognitive, is his own reality, the fact that he exists; this reality constitutes his absolute interest. Abstract thought requires him to become disinterested in order to acquire knowledge; the ethical demand is that he become infinitely interested in existing.

> The only reality that exists for an existing individual is his own ethical reality. To every other reality he stands in a cognitive relation; but true knowledge [for the classical tradition] consists in translating the real into the possible. . . . The real subject is not the cognitive subject, since in knowing he moves in the sphere of the possible; the real subject is the ethically existing subject.[39]

Kierkegaard, then, is making two closely related arguments against Hegel, and the tradition. He is asserting (1) that the ideal of objectivity in knowledge, i.e., the search for universal concepts, uncontaminated by the concrete interests, situations, needs, passions and desires of the knower, is, in fact, an illusion, at least insofar as its claim that all reality, including the human subject, can be fully grasped and comprehended within these universal concepts is concerned, and (2) that the very task of becoming objective in order to achieve objective knowledge further compounds the illusion and thus deprives man of his most fundamental reality, namely, himself in his irreducible concreteness and subjectivity. Man is not in the first place a cognitive subject, but an existing individual who must give his life meaning by freely choosing the concrete content of his life utterly without rational justification or support: "The real subject is the ethically existing subject."

To assert that the real subject is the ethically existing subject is to say that man's highest task is to decide who he shall be from among contending and incompatible possibilities. Man's ethical existence is paradoxical existence, for Kierkegaard, precisely because the incompatible possibilities which are open to him cannot be "mediated," that is, resolved at the logical, rational level. Solomon has stated Kierkegaard's argument with Hegel on this issue well. He writes:

> In Hegel's *Logic*, no paradox was absolute, that is, unresolvable. A paradox or contradiction, an opposed set of ideas, could always be resolved by finding a "higher synthesis" or a further idea which embraced the central principles of the opposed theses. . . . Paradox ("contradiction," "opposition"), thus broadly conceived, exists between various conceptions — the conception of God as transcendent and of man as separated from God. Conceptions could be mediated in Logic in the movement of conceptual thought to the resolution of such oppositions. . . . In Hegel, all such paradoxes or contradictions, including those of morality and religion as well as those of traditional Logic (narrowly conceived) could be so mediated.

> It is important to note that Kierkegaard agreed with Hegel that such mediation of paradox was possible, and that Hegel had succeeded in doing so in his *Science of Logic*. However, such mediation was possible only between concepts, and Kierkegaard complains that Hegel once again has confused concepts — that is, what is universal — with existence — that is, what is particular to an individual. Logic, properly conceived as the science of concepts, was amenable to Hegel's treatment, but existence proper, namely, the existence of the individual, was not reducible to a concept, and the paradoxes which existed for an individual could not be mediated. . . . The logical paradoxes . . . can be mediated. . . . However, the paradoxes of morality and religion, and here "paradox" refers not to an opposition of concepts but an opposition of courses of action, are not part of logic and so cannot be mediated. These paradoxes are Absolute, and cannot be resolved through the reflection of logic.[40]

In asserting that the ethical dilemmas of the existing individual are impervious to logical or conceptual resolution, Kierkegaard is referring to the paradigm situation exemplified in the person of Abraham and the teleological suspension of the ethical, where he must make a choice for which no rational justification can be given.

Thus, Kierkegaard's notion of the "existing individual" begins to emerge in the arena of ethical choice where one is confronted with choices he must make in relation to alternatives which are a matter of ultimate significance, i.e., where the choice commits one to a life style which defines the meaning of one's existence.

Kierkegaard's argument is that an analysis of the situation in which a person finds himself in having to make ultimate choices about his life discloses that, contrary to Hegel and the classical tradition, if is simply not the case that rational (universal and objective) arguments can be presented as indubitable criteria for one's choice, but rather that one must decide on the basis of one's own criterion that the value one affirms is a "life necessity."

This personal, individual criterion is not compatible with the classical conception of rationality. Thus, Kierkegaard's analysis has lead him to a kind of irrationalism in his understanding of human existence, where that term means that in relation to the ultimate choices a person must make, which commit him to a definitive way of life, no universal and objective reasons can be given for the choice he makes, and where he finds himself having to decide between incompatible alternatives (e.g., Sartre's famous example of the young man who had to decide between joining the resistance and staying home with his mother), the paradox of this situation can be resolved not by logical mediation but only through his free and passionate decision.

The question arises, however, on what grounds Kierkegaard can exclude Reason from the ethical task of the individual. Again we will draw upon Solomon's analysis to answer this question:

How does one come to have an alternative set of goals or a way of life? Because these are ultimate, one cannot appeal them to some more ultimate consideration. These are what Kant referred to as *categorical* imperatives, those which cannot be defended on the basis of some further imperative. Kant attempted to justify one set of these ultimate values by an appeal to pure practical reason; by showing that these values are (transcendentally) necessary for any morality. However, one can still ask, as Hegel sometimes points out, why one ought to be moral. In a Kierkegaardian vain, even if one were to agree that these principles Kant identifies as categorical imperatives are necessary for any morality, any particular individual might ask why he should have to follow Reason's dictates. In other words, even if we grant that certain principles can be defended by appeal to Reason, one can then turn about and challenge the value of Reason itself. "Granted I ought to do 'x' because it is the moral thing, why should I be reasonable?" What can the Kantian answer to this?

Kierkegaard claims that no answer can be given, for the value of Reason can be challenged as any particular ethical principle might be challenged. How, then, does one decide whether to be reasonable, to follow the dictates of reason and be moral? There is no way, for any further suggested criterion . . . can be challenged in precisely the same way.[41]

It is in relation to the paradigm of Abraham or the knight of faith, we would argue, that Kierkegaard's claims that the real subject is the ethically existing subject and that the truth is subjectivity can best be understood. The ethical task is to become subjective, since "subjectivity is truth, subjectivity is reality."[42] It should be clear, however, that what Kierkegaard means by subjectivity is not what the classical tradition has meant by it. Kierkegaard states, in commenting upon Christianity as the religion of subjectivity, that:

Christianity proposes to endow the individual with an eternal happiness, a good which is not distributed wholesale, but only to one individual at a time. Though Christianity assumes that there inheres in the subjectivity of the individual, as being the potentiality of the appropriation of this good, the possibility for its acceptance, it does not assume that the subjectivity is immediately ready for such acceptance. . . . The development or transformation of the individual's subjectivity, its infinite concentration in itself over against the conception of an eternal happiness, that highest good of the infinite — this constitutes the developed potentiality of the primary potentiality which subjectivity as such presents . . .

It is commonly assumed that no art or skill is required in order to be subjective. To be sure, every human being is a bit of a subject, in a sense. But now to strive to become what one already is: who would take the pains to waste his time on such a task, involving the greatest imaginable degree of resignation? . . . No indeed, thinking about the highfalutin is very much more attractive and glorious.

When one overlooks this little distinction, humoristic from the Socratic standpoint and infinitely anxious from the Christian, between being something like a subject so called, and being a subject, . . . then it becomes wisdom, the admired wisdom of our own age, that it is the task of the subject increasingly to divest himself of his subjectivity in order to become more and more objective. It is easy to see what this guidance understands by being a subject of a sort. *It understands by it quite rightly the accidental, the angular, the selfish, the eccentric, and so forth, all of which every human being can have* *enough of. Nor does Christianity deny that such things should be gotten rid of;* *it has never been a friend of loutishness.* But the difference is that philosophy teaches that the way is to become objective, while Christianity teaches that the way is to become subjective (emphasis mine).[43]

Subjectivity is a potentiality in man, which Kierkegaard often equates with his essential humanity,[44] that needs to be developed. It does not refer to that spectrum of common sense notions, customs, prejudices, eccentricities, emotional perceptions, blind and fanatical commitments with which the term is usually associated. Authentic subjectivity, as we have stated, emerges when an individual is confronted with his awareness of himself as a finite human being, constituted in relation to finite values which he must choose, for the choice of which there is no rational justification, and which are radically threatened. Thus, subjectivity, for Kierkegaard, includes the notions of lucidity, freedom, passion, risk, choice, the concrete content of one's life, the irrational commitment to that content in time, and having to assume responsibility for one's commitment.

To say that truth is subjectivity is to ground truth not in the universal concept, the objectivity of which is precisely its being true for all men everywhere, but rather in the life experience of the individual person. Kierkegaard defines the subjective truth as "an objective uncertainty held fast in an appropriation-process of the most passionate inwardness."[45] It is, then, the definitive truth of the individual person, won in the arena of dread and decision, which cannot be translated into objective terms that Kierkegaard wishes to place at the center of the philosophical enterprise and that is the basis of the revolution he initiated in Western thought. One final point needs to be discussed before briefly examining the existentialist movement rooted in Kierkegaard's thought.

We quoted a passage above from *Fear and Trembling* in which Kierkegaard denies that he is a philosopher. In the *Concluding Unscientific Postscript* Kierkegaard introduces the notion of "the subjective thinker" and continuously draws a contrast between the speculative philosopher and the subjective thinker. We have seen that his conception of truth as subjectivity is set in opposition to the philosophical conception of truth as objectivity, and the ethical task of the individual in contrast to the universally ethical. Yet, we have also seen that Kierkegaard delineates the structure of human existence in terms of subjectivity, finitude, freedom, dread, the demand to choose, paradox, the absurd, and commitment, and one can clearly see the distinction Heidegger makes between authentic and inauthentic existence implicit in Kierkegaard's writings as between one who chooses his existence and one who does not; furthermore to say that truth is subjectivity is to make an objective statement about the nature of truth which is made independently of any given individual. It is obvious that, for Kierkegaard, men should value subjectivity, since it is subjectivity that makes them essentially human. It is clear, then, that even though he denies it, Kierkegaard is very much a philosopher, and the question is whether or not he can escape objectivity, and if not, is there not, as Tillich has argued, a vitiating self-contradiction in Kierkegaard's thought?

"A point rarely appreciated by defender's of Kierkegaard's notion of subjectivity," writes Solomon,

> [is] that Kierkegaard is blinded by his insistence on valuing the subjective or personal individual so as to thoroughly confuse (as he accuses Hegel of confusing) existence with the concept of existence. Kierkegaard, as much as Hegel, is concerned to show the nature of the concept of "individual existence," but he differs radically in his analysis of "existence." Accordingly much of what Kierkegaard claims, for example, the (logical) necessity of choice and commitment, is to be interpreted just as much as a conceptual claim as Hegel's discussion of "Being" in the beginning of the Logic. . . . The notion of "subjectivity" is very different from the doctrines attributed to Kierkegaard to the effect that he rediscovered or "rescued" the "subjective individual" from the "concept." If this is supposed to mean that Kierkegaard ceased to talk about the concept of individual existence, then it must be an incorrect interpretation of Kierkegaard. Whether Kierkegaard admits that he is doing conceptual analysis or not, nothing can be clearer from his writings than the claim that the very concept of "the individual" entails the notions of "passion," "choice," "commitment" and "freedom."
>
> . . . It must be understood that this claim of subjectivity cannot be extended to Kierkegaard's writings as a whole; otherwise the "objective" framework within which he proves the subjectivity of choices of ultimate values collapses.

... In fact, ... Kierkegaard's own philosophy can be best understood as a kind of conceptual analysis ("logic") no less than the philosophy of Kant and Hegel. This logical rejection of "logic", or, more properly, the rejection of certain claims of a logic in a metalogical analysis will be a point of continuous confusion in those twentieth-century philosophers most influenced by Kierkegaard.[46]

We have reached here an ambiguity in the "life" of thought, which a perceptual system grounded in rigorous subjectivity can readily appreciate, namely, the inability of an individual thinker to understand completely the full implications of his own thought project. This is especially true of a thinker as complex as Kierkegaard. He simply failed to see clearly and address himself explicitly to the logic-metalogic problem; however, it is my opinion that there are resources implicit within Kierkegaard's thought which can counter the charge of a vitiating self-contradiction within his thought.

Let us accept Solomon's helpful insight that Kierkegaard is doing philosophy, where philosophy means at least the employment of Reason to achieve a conceptual analysis of a dimension or dimensions of reality, in Kierkegaard's case, the dimension of human existence itself, and let us further agree that Kierkegaard, in order to achieve this conceptual analysis, has established "cognitive distance" (objectivity) toward his own existence and the concrete existence of all men. Thus, we are accepting here Tillich's statement that there can be no existentialist analysis without some cognitive detachment on the part of the thinker involved.

Having said this, however, it is just as necessary to urge the following considerations. The charge of a vitiating self-contradiction in Kierkegaard's thought can be overcome, I submit, if it can be seen, as I believe it can, that Kierkegaard is challenging a philosophical consensus in regard to the nature of truth and the ultimate *telos* of human existence in the name of philosophy and with the conceptual tools of philosophy by delineating a new *paradigm* of subjectivity in relation to which the *paradigm* of objectivity, which Kierkegaard believes has dominated Western philosophy since the Greeks, is simply unable adequately to understand. By challenging the omnicompetence of the traditional paradigm of objectivity, Kierkegaard thereby initiated a "conceptual crisis" (Kuhn), a revolution in philosophy itself which has yet to be fully worked out.[47] Thus Kierkegaard uses Reason to show the limits of Reason, he uses conceptual analysis to uncover the existing individual whose most definitive subjective truth is without rational justification, be it noted, *in relation to the paradigm of objectivity*, and thus uses philosophy to define the purpose of philosophy, namely, to facilitate the return of the individual to himself by urging him to choose who he shall be, which latter task, i.e., the choice, philosophy cannot do for him.

Even though Kierkegaard had little use for objective truth, he did not wish to deny that such truth is possible. A completely objective system is possible for God, but the finite knower can only achieve approximations of objective truth. What he did want to argue, however, is that objective truth is *ultimately irrelevant* to the most urgent, issues of human existence. Hence:

> All essential knowledge relates to existence, or only such knowledge as has an essential relationship to existence is essential knowledge. All knowledge which does not inwardly relate itself to existence, in the reflection of inwardness, is essentially viewed, accidental knowledge; its degree and scope is essentially indifferent. . . . Knowledge has an essential relationship to the knower, who is essentially an existing individual, and that for this reason all essential knowledge is essentially related to existence. Only ethical and ethico-religious knowledge has an essential relationship to the existence of the knower.[48]

It follows that if philosophy which is bound by the paradigm of objectivity delivers irrelevant knowledge (truth) to man, then philosophy itself, insofar as it is committed to that paradigm, is also irrelevant to man. Thus, Kierkegaard, as a philosopher, wishes to restore philosophy to a relevant position in relation to man himself. After having laid the foundation for such a revolution/restoration, however, Kierkegaard fails to carry it through in relation to philosophy, but turns rather to the project of interpreting the Christian faith through the new paradigm of subjectivity which he initially articulated in *Fear and Trembling*.[49] The existentialist movement in the 20th Century is the attempt to carry through this revolution/restoration by building on Kierkegaard's foundation.

It is Martin Heidegger who first seized upon Kierkegaard's ideas and developed them into the philosophy of existentialism. The Sartre of *Being and Nothingness* is clearly dependent upon Heidegger's views, and while there are significant differences between them, it seems fair to say that Sartre has basically carried through in his own terms the ideas that were first fully articulated by Heidegger. Certainly, it is Heidegger's *Being and Time*, which is acknowledged by the philosophical world, and Tillich himself recognizes, as a key expression of the existential philosophy. However, Heidegger, in his subsequent work has not only refused to call himself an existentialist, but has repudiated several crucial themes in *Being and Time* in his most recent move toward a more radical form of non-conceptual mysticism of Being.[50]

It is beyond the scope of our study to give our attention to the critical problems which have emerged in the interpretation of Heidegger's "post-existentialist" phase. What we shall attempt to do here is analyze the way in which the conceptual revolution in philosophy initiated by Kierkegaard has been carried through by Heidegger, after which we shall return to our evaluation of Tillich's conception of the relationship between philosophy and theology. We shall pursue our analysis of contemporary existentialism with the following assumption: Heidegger's achievement in *Being and Time* stands as an independent philosophical realization and his thought must be evaluated, not in the first place in relation to what he himself has said about it, but rather on its own terms. The early Heidegger has left his mark upon philosophy, he has given impetus to one of the most influential movements in philosophy in our time, and consequently the insights he has made available to the world need to be considered as components of the present philosophical situation regardless of the course of his own subsequent career.

We have seen that the major thrust of Kierkegaard's conceptual revolution was to call philosophy back to the existing individual in his full concreteness and thus away from the abstract cognitive subject, the transcendental ego and the various other philosophical conceptions of man which ignore or negate the whole dimension of his "practical" concerns. Heidegger takes up Kierkegaard's concern for the existing individual in *Being and Time* by placing him at the center of his inquiry, and even though he does not employ Kierkegaard's terms "objectivity" and "subjectivity," he clearly works within that distinction.[51] In fact, Heidegger goes beyond Kierkegaard by denying the theoretical-practical distinction altogether.

The continuity in Heidegger's thought is defined by his persistent concern both in his early and later writings with the problem of Being. Heidegger is convinced that the question of Being has neither been adequately formulated nor adequately answered in the history of philosophy. One of the reasons why philosophy has failed to understand Being is because it has not developed an adequate *conception* of Being. Philosophers have claimed that the concept of Being is the most universal of concepts, that it is indefinable, and that it is self-evident. However, in investigating these claims, it becomes clear to Heidegger that those are hardly the last words to be spoken on the question. Rather, Being is a "stranger" to philosophy and the whole question of Being must be reformulated.

In attempting this reformulation, the Heidegger of *Being and Time* develops one of the most sustained analyses in Western philosophy of the nature of human existence, for he is convinced that an adequate conception of Being can only be achieved by first examining the being of the one who asks the question of Being, that is the being of human existence, which Heidegger calls *Dasein*. We cannot adequately formulate the conception of Being unless we analyze Dasein's being, because

> Dasein is an entity which does not just occur among other entities. Rather it is ontically distinguished by the fact that, in its very Being, that Being is an *issue* for it. But in that case, this is a constitutive state of Dasein's Being, and this implies that Dasein, in its Being, has a relationship towards that Being — a relationship which itself is one of Being. And this means further that there is some way in which Dasein understands itself in its Being, and that to some degree it does so explicitly. It is peculiar to this entity that with and through

its Being, this Being is disclosed to it. *Understanding of Being is itself a definite characteristic of Dasein's Being.* Dasein is ontically distinctive in that it is ontological.[52]

The structure of Dasein, then, establishes its priority in formulating the conception of Being. Heidegger develops this claim further. "The kind of Being towards which Dasein can comport itself," he writes,

> in one way or another, and always does comport itself somehow, we call "existence" [Existenz] . . . Dasein always understands itself in terms of its existence — in terms of a possibility of itself: to be itself or not itself. Dasein has either chosen these possibilities itself, or got itself into them, or grown up in them already. Only the particular Dasein decides its existence, whether it does so by taking hold or neglecting. The question of existence never gets straightened out except through existing itself. The understanding of oneself which leads along *this way* we call "existential." The question of existence is one of Dasein's ontical "affairs." This does not require that the ontological structure of existence should be theoretically transparent. The question about that structure aims at the analysis . . . of what constitutes existence. The context of such structures we call "existentiality." Its analytic has the character of an understanding which is not existentiell, but rather *existential.*[53]

It will be necessary to examine the meaning of the ontic-ontological and the existentiell-existential distinctions in more detail below. Before doing this, however, we must note that what Heidegger has claimed thus far is that Dasein in its ontic condition carries within itself a pre-ontological understanding of Being and that one of its essential possibilities is that it can make that understanding explicitly ontological. This very ontologicality of Dasein establishes its priority in the exploration of the meaning of Being. Heidegger states:

> . . . Whenever an ontology takes as its theme entities whose character of Being is other than that of Dasein, it has its own foundation and motivation in Dasein's own ontical structure, in which a pre-ontological understanding of Being is comprised as a definite characteristic.

> Therefore *fundamental ontology*, from which alone all other ontologies can take their rise, must be sought in the *existential analytic of Dasein.*

Dasein accordingly takes priority over all other entities in several ways. The first priority is an *ontical* one: Dasein is an entity whose Being has the determinate character of existence. The second priority is an *ontological* one: Dasein is in itself "ontological," because existence is thus determinative for it. But with equal primordiality Dasein also possesses — as constitutive for its understanding of existence — an understanding of the Being of all entities of a character other than its own. Dasein has therefore a third priority as providing the ontico-ontological condition for the possibility of any ontologies. Thus Dasein has turned out to be, more than any other entity, the one which must first be interrogated ontologically.[54]

The priority of Dasein means, therefore, that

the results of the existential analytic, on its part, are ultimately *existentiell*, that is, *ontical*. Only if the inquiry of philosophical research is itself seized upon in an existentiell manner as a possibility of the Being of each existing Dasein, does it become at all possible to disclose the existentiality of existence and to undertake an adequately founded ontological problematic. But with this the ontical priority of the question of being has also become plain.[55]

The existential structure of Dasein, then, is the portal through which the thinker must pass in order to formulate adequately the question of Being. In doing so, however, he must begin with the ontic-existentiell condition of Dasein. This proposal, as we shall attempt to show, will make Heidegger's approach (which is dependent upon Kierkegaard) to fundamental ontology unique within the Western tradition of systematic philosophy. A more careful look at the distinctions Heidegger has now introduced is in order before showing this, however.

To say that Dasein is "ontical" is to say that each Dasein exists concretely, that is, in a specific historical, social, cultural, national, geographical and community context. There is no "Dasein-in-general"; rather each Dasein is radically particular, and Heidegger uses the term "ontic" to stress this particularity of Dasein. However, while Dasein shares the particularity of any existent entity, it contains within itself another possibility, which does not extend to other existent entities, namely, the possibility of transcending the particularity of its concrete existence to achieve an understanding of those necessary and universal conditions which are intrinsic to the existence of each particular Dasein, that is, an understanding, at the level of thought, of the Being of Dasein. Dasein is that onti-cally existing entity "whose Being is an issue for it." Dasein, there-fore, is also *ontological* in that it is driven by the very structure of its own existence to ask the question of Being. Ontology, therefore, is grounded in the ontological character of Dasein, and as Solomon has indicated, the ontic-ontological distinction in relation to Dasein is really the distinction between the pre-reflective and the reflec-tive or the pre-philosophical and the philosophical.[56] Ontology makes the pre-reflective ontic truths explicit.

The existentielle-existential distinction closely parallels the ontic-ontological distinction. Ontic truth is roughly equivalent to empirical truth for Heidegger. Ontological truth, on the other hand, is necessary truth or a priori truth. Existentielle truth, then,

is related to "ontical," and is the specific application of "ontical" to Dasein. Thus we can speak of the ontical structures of a tree, but can speak of exis-tentielle structures of only Dasein. "Existentielle" when applied to Dasein, always refers to the nonessential. A statement about the existentielle struc-ture of Dasein (for example, that human beings tend to worry about weight-gain) are (sic) always empirical statements. "Existential," on the other hand, is "ontological" applied specifically to Dasein. An "existential structure" of Dasein is an essential structure; all statements about Dasein's existential structures (or *existentialia*) are *a priori* (for example, that Dasein is "in-the-world"). Ontological (*a priori*) features of all other entities are called "categories" (after Kant).[57]

Heidegger's point of departure, then, presupposes the empirical-a priori distinction in the theory of knowledge, and insofar as there are *necessary* and *universal* truths, that is, ontological truths, for Heidegger, he clearly stands within the classical philosophical tradi-tion. However, ontological truths unrelated to human existence are of a secondary order in relation to the existential (ontological) truths of Dasein. Heidegger is, therefore, continuing the Kierkegaardian revolution, while at the same time addressing him-self to the metalogical-logical issues which were unresolved in Kierkegaard's thought. Human existence, for Heidegger, has a universal, necessary, a priori structure which is accessible to con-ceptual analysis. This structure has been oversimplified by con-ceiving of Dasein *vis-a-vis* the *categories* which apply to the natural universe, that is, Dasein is conceived after the model of physical things. However, the categories of traditional metaphysics do not adequately describe the ontological structure of Dasein, because Dasein cannot be reduced to a "thing." Heidegger therefore proposes the development of a unique set of concepts which do adequately describe the nature of Dasein. These are the *existentialia*.

"Existentialia," as Calvin Schrag has written,

> as distinct from categories, are thus seen as the ontological elements which provide the necessary condition for human existence. In this sense they can properly be understood as *a priori* and transcendental elements. Heidegger states clearly that *a priori* in no way designates an *a priori* construction of the mind. Nor are existentialia *a priori* in the sense of being known prior to man's concrete historical experience, but are *a priori* in that they are constituents presupposed in the reality of existence itself. In this sense one can also properly speak of them as transcendental. They are present in the concrete existent, providing its very condition of being, but at the same time, they lie beyond every particular instance of concrete existence. All knowledge of the structures of human being is therefore transcendental knowledge.[58]

The question immediately arises as to whether Heidegger has not really turned the existentialist revolution in a predominantly essentialist direction by positing that there are universal, necessary, ontological truths which existential phenomenology seeks. Schrag has provided an analysis by which this question can be answered negatively. He states:

> Heidegger's phenomenology is consistently geared to a fundamental ontology of existence (*Existenzialontologie*). Yet we have seen that Heidegger's task is to delineate the ontological elements present in the structure of existence — elements which are universal and transcendental. How then do these ontological elements or *existentialia* differ from the universal essences of Husserl's Wesenswissenschaft and from essentialist philosophy in general? First of all it must be said that they differ from the essences of essentialist philosophy in that they are peculiar determinants of *human* existence, applicable to this mode of being and *only* to this mode of being. But they are distinct from essences in another sense. Like essences they are universal, but they are universals which are *present in the process of actualization itself*. Whereas essences are potential, i.e., universal structures which may or may not become actual, *existentialia* share in the concrete actuality of existence and are realized in this actuality. . . .

Heidegger's phenomenological ontology must therefore be understood as a delineation of the universal structures present in the actualization of existence. This existence is indelibly historical, grounded in the modes of temporality.[59]

Dasein's existence is through and through temporal, that is, historical, and thus Heidegger is seeking to delineate conceptually those historical *a priori* structures which are (1) timeless only in the sense that they are the conditions for any particular Dasein to be and are therefore universal and necessary for Dasein; and yet (2) they are temporal in that they are simultaneously fully actual within the particular existence of each concrete Dasein. Hence:

The historical Dasein, for Heidegger, is understood *through* history rather than through nature. Historical relativism is overcome by way of a delineation of the universal conditions which underlie man's concrete, historical, lived experience. In the same way it could be said that Heidegger has provided Kierkegaard's human subjectivity with ontological feet on which to walk. Such an ontology of subjectivity was already implied in Kierkegaard's ethico-religious concepts. His primary intent had to do with an elucidation of human subjectivity in its concrete ethical and religious encounters, but in describing these concrete encounters he already pointed to the structural determinants which underlie this subjectivity. The descriptions in the voluminous writings of Kierkegaard are hardly descriptions of the private and adventitious details of his personal life. They already suggest a method and approach to an elucidation of the human situation in which the question of what it means to exist can be systematically argued. It has been the task of Heidegger's philosophy to set forth an explicit phenomenological method through which a systematic delineation of the structural determinants of existence can be achieved. He has attempted to show that human existence is not simply an unknowable and discontinuous succession of lived experiences, but that in its radical historicity it is grounded in ontological structures which provide the condition for its historical freedom.[60]

In Tillich's terms, Heidegger stands clearly within the second "line" of development in the history of philosophy in that he asserts the historicity of human existence and all its projects; therefore, philosophy itself is historical. In his distinction between "categories" and "existentialia," then, Heidegger has made a decisive move in continuing the existentialist critique of the philosophy of essence. He has, in the first place, placed the human subject at the center of the philosophical enterprise, not merely as the abstract cognitive subject, but rather as a totality whose very uniqueness in relation to all other natural entities requires a unique set of concepts if it is to be fully understood. In the second place, Heidegger has attempted to formulate a notion of the essence of Dasein which both lends itself to conceptual analysis on the one hand and on the other grounds the essence of man within the temporal (historical) actualizations of human decisionality and freedom. Man's essence for Heidegger, is both his openness to possibilities which are uniquely his own and that which he makes of himself in relation to his unique possibilities.

Heidegger, unlike Sartre (who maintains that "existence *precedes* essence"),[61] insists that "the essence of man rests in existence,"[62] i.e., that essence and *Existenz* are identical when it is seen that *Existenz* is possibility.[63] Hence, existence is not that which has fallen away from essence, as in Tillich, but rather existence is the actualization of essential possibilities, apart from the actualization of which there is no human essence. We must return to this very important contrast between Tillich and Heidegger below.

That Dasein is ontological, that is, that it contains within its ontic preoccupations the possibility of understanding its unique existential structure, and thus Being as such, leads Heidegger to distinguish, as we have seen, between Dasein's pre-philosophical and philosophical relationship to itself. Any adequate philosophical understanding of Dasein must be grounded in its pre-philosophical, ordinary, average, everyday structure or else philosophy becomes guilty, as Kierkegaard charged, of imposing upon Dasein highly abstract notions which either distort or ignore its fundamental uniqueness and concreteness. Thus, the *a priori existentialia* must arise from and be utterly faithful to Dasein's average, everyday concreteness, that is, they must illuminate or make explicit the pre-philosophical understanding of existence which is given in Dasein's everyday comportment toward itself, the world, other Daseins and Being as such.

There are two *existentialia* Heidegger specifies, which we shall examine because they will illuminate his conception of truth.

These are Dasein as "Being-in-the-world" and Dasein's Being-in-the-world as "concern" or "care." For Heidegger Dasein's average everydayness cannot be understood apart from its dwelling in a world which is inseparable from Dasein itself and in relation to which Dasein's existence as "care" comes into view or as Heidegger is more apt to say "discloses itself."

Being-in-the-world, then, is an a priori condition for Dasein's being at all. Heidegger makes two very important assertions in relation to this state of affairs. In the first place, Dasein does not reside in the world in the way in which Things which are "present-at-hand" occupy space. To be sure, Dasein occupies space as do rocks, chairs, and traffic lights, and it is clearly possible to understand Dasein's existence in the world as an object to be quantified as, for example, the demographer must do. Dasein can be conceptualized as an object present-to-hand and, for Heidegger, this has been the basic approach of philosophy in its history, culminating in the objectification of man in science. However, while Dasein can be understood this way, its essential being cannot be grasped in these terms.

Dasein as Being-in-the-world means that

> Being-in . . . is a state of Dasein's Being; it is an existentiale. So one cannot think of it as the Being-present-at-hand of some corporeal Thing (such as a human body) 'in' an entity which is present-at-hand. Nor does the term 'Being-in' mean a spatial 'in-one-anotherness' of things present-at-hand, any more than the word 'in' primordially signifies a spatial relationship of this kind. 'In' is derived from 'innan' — 'to reside', 'habitare', 'to dwell' . . . 'An' signifies 'I am accustomed,' 'I am familiar with,' 'I look after something'. . . . The entity to which Being-in in this signification belongs is one which we have characterized as that entity which in each case I myself am [bin]. The expression 'bin' is connected with 'bei,' and so 'ich bin' [I am] means in its turn 'I reside' or 'dwell alongside' the world, as that which is familiar to me in such and such a way. 'Being' [sein] as the infinitive of 'ich bin' (that is to say, when it is understood as an existentiale), signifies 'to reside alongside . . . ', 'to be familiar with . . . '. *Being-in is thus the formal existential expression for the Being of Dasein, which has Being-in-the-world as its essential state.*[64]

The first assertion, contained in this elaborate etymological study, concerning the existentiale "Being-in-the-world" is that, unlike physical objects, Dasein dwells in a world or sustains a relationship to the world in which the latter is "constituted" by an ordering of meaning in Dasein itself. Thus, what Heidegger calls the "worldhood of the world" means that the world is the world *for* Dasein, i.e., the world as an existentiale of Dasein is a structure of meaning which originates and is maintained on the basis of Dasein's own subjectivity. Heidegger writes:

> 'Being alongside' the world in the sense of being absorbed in the world . . . is an existentiale founded upon Being-in. . . . As an existentiale, 'Being-along-side' the world never means anything like the Being-present-at-hand-together of Things that occur. There is no such thing as the 'side-by-side-ness' of an entity called 'Dasein' with another entity called 'world'. . . . Whenever Dasein is, it is as a Fact; and the factuality of such a Fact is what we shall call Dasein's *facticity* . . . Dasein's facticity is such that its Being-in-the-world has always dispersed itself or even split itself up into definite ways of Being-in. The multiplicity of these is indicated by the following examples: having to do with something, producing something, attending to something and looking after it, making use of something, giving something up and letting it go, undertaking, accomplishing, evincing, interrogating, considering, discussing, determining . . . [65]

There are a number of issues in the philosophical tradition, which Heidegger is combating with his phenomenological analysis of Dasein as Being-in-the-world. Perhaps the most persistent of these issues mediated through Descartes and Husserl is the problem of an ultimate skepticism about the reality of the world when philosophy begins with the *cogito*, the ego consciousness, the subject-self, which in its transcendental certitude provides the methodological starting point for philosophy, but which cannot provide epistemological access of equal certitude to the object or totality of objects (world) which the naive subject thinks is given in its experience. Heidegger is seeking to overcome the subject-object dichotomy by denying that there is a substantial ego or consciousness, which is separate from the world, and which can "bracket" (Husserl) or doubt the "external" world while its own reality remains in tact. For Heidegger, according to Solomon:

> Dasein is not a subject but undermines the traditional distinction between 'subject' and 'object' because Dasein is introduced and defined as 'Being-in-the-world.' Dasein cannot be distinguished, even in logic, from its existence

in the world . . . There is, therefore, no 'I' which can be substantially distinguished from the world in general, and there can be no bracketing or doubt-
ing of things 'outside of' consciousness. Once we have given up the notion of
an indubitable 'primitive' ego and the resultant metaphors ('contents of consciousness,' the 'external world'), traditional epistemological problems cannot
be raised.[66]

To say the world is "constituted" in and through Dasein is not to
say that the world is *merely* Dasein's projection, that it has no reality of its own. While it is the case, for Heidegger, that the world as
a structure of meaning is created by Dasein, this structure achieves
a kind of "overagainstness" to Dasein, that is, it becomes, in Peter
Berger's language "objectivated" in the forms of society and culture which are:

experienced by man as elements of an objective world. Society confronts
man as external, subjectively opaque and coercive facticity. Indeed, society is
commonly apprehended by man as virtually equivalent to the physical universe in its objective presence — a 'second nature,' indeed. Society is experienced as given 'out there,' extraneous to subjective consciousness and not
controllable by the latter.[67]

Thus, for Heidegger,

Being-in-the-world is the only possible standpoint, the only logically possible
standpoint. . . . There can be no talk of Dasein apart from its Being-in-the-
world, and no sense to talk about the world apart from Dasein. . . . Heidegger's philosophy rejects idealism, because it rejects the self or consciousness
to which all 'reality' belongs according to idealism; it also rejects realism,
however, for it makes no sense to suppose that there might be a world apart
from Dasein. . . .

Heidegger accepts an equivalent of Husserl's notion of 'transcendental constitution' but rejects the notion of 'transcendental constitution by the
subject.' This should raise no problems if we avoid thinking of constitution as
an activity performed by an agent on some object. 'The world is constituted
by Dasein and Dasein is constituted by the world' means simply that there is
no sense to any reference beyond Dasein and no sense to separating Dasein
from the world.[68]

Dasein, then, as Being-in-the-world or as constituting the world
and being constituted by it means that Dasein endows the world
with meaning, which in turn becomes externalized and "feeds

back" upon Dasein itself, shaping the latter's sense of itself and of reality. Heidegger, in positing Being-in-the-world as an a priori existentiale structure of Dasein has rendered ontologically intelligible Kierkegaard's discovery that there can be a priori synthetic, subjective, i.e., uniquely personal, truths for man which both he creates by opening himself to them existentially and which create him by defining his sense of personal and social reality.

The second basic assertion Heidegger makes, of interest to us, in regard to the ontological structure Being-in-the-world has to do with the "primitive" or pre-ontological *mode* of Dasein's absorption or involvement in the world. Heidegger wishes to show that our theoretical attitude toward the world, especially expressed in philosophy and science, and the theoretical constructs resulting therefrom are *derived*, second-order phenomena, and they are derived from a more basic, and for Heidegger, long over-looked relationship Dasein sustains to the world. The problem here, for Heidegger, is that this more basic state of Dasein as Being-in-the-world gets concealed by the very process of philosophical and scientific knowledge in which Dasein "wrongly" explains itself, because

> Dasein itself — and this means also its Being-in-the-world — gets its ontological understanding of itself in the first instance from those entities which it itself is *not* but which it encounters 'within' its world, and from the Being which they possess.[69]

Dasein's tendency to conceal itself from itself, which we shall examine in more detail below, has been expressed in Dasein's systematic attempts to know itself and the world; however, Being-in-the-world, as a basic state of Dasein

> Both in Dasein and for it, . . . is always in some way familiar [bekannt]. Now if it is also to become known [erkannt], the *knowing* which such a task explicitly implies takes itself (as a knowing of the world [Welterkennen] as the chief exemplification of the 'soul's' relationship to the world. Knowing the world [noein] — or rather addressing oneself to the 'world' and discussing it (logos) — thus functions as the primary mode of Being-in-the-world, even though Being-in-the-world does not as such get conceived . . . And even though Being-in-the-world is something of which one has pre-phenomenological

experience and acquaintance [*erfahren* und *gekannt*], it becomes *invisible* if one interprets it in a way which is ontologically inappropriate. . . .

Thus the phenomenon of Being-in has for the most part been represented exclusively by a single exemplar — knowing the world. This has not only been the case in epistemology; for even practical behaviour has been understood as behaviour which is 'non-theoretical' and 'theoretical.'[70]

There is a mode of Dasein's Being which is prior to knowing the world in the theoretical sense and upon which knowing the world in that sense is founded. It is this mode of Being which must be explicated, for it is this mode of Being that is "essentially constitutive for Dasein's Being" and within which the worldhood of the world appears. We saw above that Dasein's facticity dispersed its Being-in-the-world into "definite ways of Being-in," some examples of which were given by Heidegger. "All these ways of Being-in have *concern* as their kind of Being," says Heidegger, where "concern will be used . . . as an ontological term for an *existentiale*, and will designate the Being of a possible way of Being-in-the-world." Heidegger tells us he has chosen this term "not because Dasein happens to be proximally and to a large extent 'practical' and economic, but because the Being of Dasein itself is to be made visible as *care*. This expression too is to be taken as an ontological structural concept."[71]

Thus far we have seen that for Heidegger Being-in-the-world as concern is to be contrasted with the theoretical attitude, the latter's involving a far more detached stance toward the world. Heidegger states:

Proximally, this Being-already-alongside is not just a fixed staring at something that is purely present-at-hand. Being-in-the-world, as concern, is *fascinated* by the world with which it is concerned. If knowing is to be possible as a way of determining the nature of the present-at-hand by observing it, then there must first be a *deficiency* in our having-to-do with the world concernfully. When concern holds back [Sichenthalten] from any kind of producing, manipulating, and the like, it puts itself into what is now the sole remaining mode of Being-in, the mode of just tarrying alongside . . . [*das Nur-noch-verweilen bei* . . .] This kind of Being towards the world is one which lets us encounter entities within-the-world purely in the way they look (*eidos*), just that; on the basis of this kind of Being, and as a mode of it, looking explicitly at what we encounter is possible. . . . Such looking-at enters the mode of dwelling autonomously alongside entities within-the-world. In this kind of '*dwelling*' as a holding-oneself-back from any manipulation or utilization, the *perception* of the present-at-hand is consummated.[72]

Heidegger is arguing here that Dasein's project of knowing the world theoretically emerges at that point when its spontaneous, "pragmatic" involvement in the world is severed or where there is a deficiency in the mode of Being of concern. A question which we shall seek to answer is how it is that Dasein moves from its concrete involvement with the world in which the objects with which it is involved are not there to be observed in the stance of detached seeing, but rather *used*, to the theoretical enterprise? We shall return to this question below.

Dasein's Being as concern, then, is the "primordial," everyday mode of Being in which Dasein encounters its world basically as a "workshop." This mode of Being-in-the-world, says Heidegger:

We shall also call our 'dealings' in the world and *with* entities within-the-world. Such dealings have already dispersed themselves into manifold ways of concern. This kind of dealing which is closest to us is . . . not a bare perceptual cognition, but rather that kind of concern which manipulates things and puts them to use; and this has its own kind of 'knowledge.'[73]

The mode of concern is not just one of the ways Dasein may choose to relate to the world. This is "the way in which everyday Dasein always *is*," and thus the entities within the world get founded in their own ontological character on the basis of Dasein's concernful state of involvement with them. Pursuing the metaphor of the world as a "workshop", it is appropriate for Heidegger to define the Being of the entities within the world with which Dasein has to do in concern as "equipment" (*das Zeug*). Dasein, then, finds itself in a world the Being of the entities of which get founded in terms of Dasein's purposes for them, and Dasein's purposes constitute a "referential totality" in relation to which every particular entity gets taken up into an equipmental network. Hence Heidegger states:

Taken strictly, there 'is' no such thing as *an* equipment. To the Being of any equipment there always belongs a totality of equipment, in which it can be this equipment that it is. Equipment is essentially 'something in-order-to ...' [*"etwas un zu* ... "]. A totality of equipment is constituted by various ways of the 'in-order-to,' such as serviceability, conduciveness, usability, manipulability.[74]

Dasein dwells in the world concernfully as one who has "things to do." This having things to do of Dasein determines the contexts in which the "equipmentality of equipment" appears. Heidegger explains:

In the 'in-order-to' as a structure there lies an *assignment* or *reference* of something to something. . . . Equipment — in accordance with its equipmentality — always is in terms of [*aus*] its belonging to other equipment: inkstand, pen, ink, paper, blotting pad, table, lamp, furniture, windows, doors, room. These 'Things' never show themselves proximally as they are for themselves, so as to add up to a sum of *realia* and fill up a room. What we encounter as closest to us . . . is the room; and we encounter it not as something 'between four walls' in a geometrical spatial sense, but as equipment for residing. Out of this the 'arrangement' emerges, and it is in this that any 'individual' item of equipment shows itself. Before it does so, a totality of equipment has already been discovered.[75]

The world as referential totality which is grounded in Dasein's most practical concerns and in relation to which objects receive their assignments as equipment as they are useful for Dasein's purposes (both human artifacts and the objects of nature) is the world in which, Heidegger says, Dasein exists as Being-in. It is a world, then, whose meaning is totally dependent upon Dasein's projects. Not only do the entities within the world of Dasein's practical concern become visible as equipment, that is once we have penetrated to the most primordial level of Dasein's everyday Being-in-the-world, but equipment also possesses the kind of Being which Heidegger calls "readiness-to-hand" [*Zuhandenheit*].

In order to illustrate the Being of equipment as readiness-to-hand, Heidegger chooses the example of hammering with a hammer. "The hammering," Heidegger points out,

does not simply have knowledge about [um] the hammer's character as equipment, but it has appropriated this equipment in a way which could not possibly be more suitable. In dealings such as this, where something is put to use, our concern subordinates itself to the 'in-order-to' which is constitutive for the equipment we are employing at the time; the less we just stare at the hammer-Thing, and the more we seize hold of it and use it, the more primordial does our relationship to it become, and the more unveiledly is it encountered as that which it is — as equipment. The hammering itself uncovers the specific 'manipulability' [*"Handlichkeit"*] of the hammer. . . . If we look at Things just 'theoretically,' we can get along without understanding readiness-to-hand. But when we deal with them by using them and manipulating them, this activity is not a blind one: it has its own kind of sight, by which our manipulation is guided and from which it acquires its specific Thingly character. Dealings with equipment subordinate themselves to the manifold assignments of the 'in-order-to'. And the sight with which they thus accommodate themselves is circumspection.[76]

Equipment, when it functions as equipment, is distinguished from the entities in the world whose Being is presence-at-hand. The being of equipment is readiness-to-hand, which is to say that Dasein becomes so absorbed in the purpose, the "in-order-to" for which the equipment functions that, even while Dasein uses it, the actual physical reality of the equipment disappears from Dasein's awareness, even as it facilitates the "in-order-to," the more its Being as ready-to-hand is established. Heidegger asserts:

The ready-to-hand is not grasped theoretically at all, nor is it itself the sort of thing that circumspection takes as proximally as a circumspective theme. The peculiarity of what is proximally ready-to-hand is that, in its readiness-to-hand, it must, as it were, withdraw [*Zuruckzuziehen*] in order to be ready-to-hand quite authentically. That with which our everyday dealings proximally dwell is not the tools themselves [*die Werkzeuge selbst*]. On the contrary, that with which we concern ourselves primarily is the work — that which is to be produced at the time; and this is accordingly ready-to-hand too. The work bears with it that referential totality within which the equipment is encountered.[77]

Dasein's essential Being-in-the-world, then, is in terms of tasks to be done in which Dasein becomes absorbed and in this essential state the world is founded as a network of purposes (meanings) and equipment. Knowing how to use this equipment is not adequately explicated by calling it "atheoretical" or merely practical. Dasein's "practical" involvement in the world has its own kind of knowledge, the knowledge of *circumspection* as opposed to the theoretical knowledge of observation, and Heidegger insists, the knowledge of circumspection, grounded in Dasein's Being as concern is in no way inferior to theoretical knowledge. In fact, theoretical knowledge is also rooted in concern. The implications of this claim we shall return to below.

The explication of Dasein's Being-in-the-world as concern, confronting not Things but tools or equipment which emerge from the background of Dasein's purposes and the phenomenological determination of the Being of equipment as ready-to-hand, to this point, have been established basically by an appeal to intuition. Heidegger now wants to show how "the world" discloses itself from this network of Dasein's practical concerns and the equipment it encounters, since "the world itself is not an entity within-the-world."[78]

Heidegger develops two important theses in *Being and Time* about the world. He argues, first, that Dasein, because of its basic absorption in the world, tends to "forget" the world, or more precisely, fails to see that it is "not-at-home" in the world which it nonetheless dwells within. Thus, while Dasein is pre-ontologically "familiar" with the world, in its everyday Being-in-the-world, the worldhood of the world seldom becomes explicit. Secondly, Dasein has also tended to obscure the structure of worldhood by conceiving it as an object of cognitive specification, especially in the attempt, for which Heidegger has complete scorn, to prove the existence of the world.[79]

Thus, rather than leaving the concept of "the world" at the purely intuitive level or trying to prove the existence of the world, Heidegger delineates an experiential Gestalt in which he argues the worldhood of the world "discloses itself."

The referential totality within which equipment receives their assignments can break down. A tool can become conspicuous by its unusability for a task Dasein wished to accomplish with it. Or a tool can be missing and thus becomes *obtrusive* by its absence. Or a tool can present itself as neither unusable or missing, but simply "in the way," as perhaps obsolete, in which case its *obstinacy* intrudes upon Dasein's awareness.[80] In each of these cases, that which was ready-to-hand becomes present-at-hand, the referential totality has been temporarily disrupted by the inaccessibility of the equipment, and Dasein's stance shifts from being unaware of the tool and absorbed in the task it facilitates to a focal awareness upon the tool itself in its inert resistance to Dasein's own concern. The equipment becomes a thing to be observed rather than used. At the same time, Dasein is placed at odds (even if only slightly irritated) with the referential equipment world in which it dwells concernfully. Suddenly this world can no longer be taken for granted. It is "overagainst" Dasein; no longer a smoothly functioning extension of Dasein itself. In this moment Dasein and world are distinguished. Hence:

> When equipment cannot be used, this implies that the constitutive assignment of the "in-order-to" to a "toward-this" has been thus circumspectively aroused, we catch sight of the "towards-this" itself, and along with it everything connected with the work — the whole 'workshop' — as that wherein concern always dwells. The context of equipment is lit up, not as something never seen before, but as a totality constantly sighted beforehand in circumspection. With this totality, however, the world announces itself.[81]

It is in this experience that Heidegger finds one of the sources for the shift in Dasein's orientation toward the world from one of spontaneous absorption in it, guided by the *knowledge of how to use equipment,* which is the way everyday Dasein essentially is, to the orientation of detached observation and the theoretical knowledge appropriate to the consideration of *Things,* i.e., *knowledge that.* The theoretical enterprise originates, for Heidegger, as Solomon has put it, as a response to disaster within Dasein's concrete equipment world,[82] or as we shall see below within Dasein itself, and thus it is also an expression of concern.

Thus far we have seen that Heidegger defines Dasein essentially as *Being-in-the-world* and *concern.* The second major theme in Heidegger's analysis which needs to be considered briefly here is his further definition of Dasein as *care* (Concern-*Besorge*; Care-*Sorge*). Concern has to do basically with Dasein's interest in "getting things done" and thus appears in relation to the referential totality of equipment and purpose. Care, on the other hand, is the expression of Dasein's concern for itself. Solomon's remarks are helpful here:

> Man's concerns are not limited to his concern to get a task completed, to use a tool to do a job; man is ultimately concerned about *himself*, and it is this ultimate concern which is care. Dasein (care) is essentially self-concern. This is not to be interpreted in the vulgar sense in which it is said that man is essentially selfish . . . but he is concerned for himself in a primarily philosophical way. He is not only concerned to obtain food, territory, sexual gratification for himself, he is concerned to gain philosophical enlightenment. The concern for himself is basically the concern to find out who he is. Care is the search for self-identity.[83]

Dasein is, it will be recalled, *ontological*, which is to say fundamentally that Dasein is capable of self-knowledge where self-knowledge means knowledge of those essential structures without which Dasein could not be at all. That Dasein is ontological, then, means that it can raise the question of Being or what is the same thing, at least in the preliminary analysis of *Being and Time*, the question of self-identity, and in raising the question of Being penetrate to an understanding of those essential structures of its existence in relation to which it receives the possibility of answering the question of self-identity either in terms of its own individuality and uniqueness (authenticity) or in terms of a *derived* identity appropriated from others uncritically and therefore without the agony or the joy of autonomous self-definition (inauthenticity).

If Dasein's existence as *care* is the ontological structure from which the question of self-identity emerges, then the possibility of self-recognition must also be an ontological structure of Dasein, that is, self-recognition must be given in Dasein's pre-ontological awareness, to be sure, however, only at a very vague and implicit level; and such self-recognition must be capable of ontological analysis or explication. Thus, Heidegger must show us where that possibility is present in Dasein's ontical preoccupations and he must also bring that possibility into explicit articulation.

We have seen that one of the experiences given in Dasein's everydayness in which Dasein is "delivered over to itself" and distinguished momentarily from its world is when the equipment world itself breaks down. The other possibility of self-recognition is given when Dasein "breaks down." This is not to say that Dasein ceases to function the way a piece of equipment does, although in some cases Dasein's breakdown can lead to a minimal kind of functionality. Rather when Dasein breaks down, it undergoes a peculiar kind of experience in which it no longer functions smoothly and non-problematically in its ordinary, everyday world.

In order to understand this experience in its full context, it is necessary to discuss briefly some other *existentiale* structures of Dasein. For Heidegger, ontological self-recognition requires that Dasein grasp itself as possibility, which we have seen, Heidegger defines as Dasein's *Existenz*. *Existenz* is not only Dasein's possibilities, but it also includes the notion of *understanding* (*Verstehen*); also, self-recognition involves Dasein's seeing itself as *facticity* (*Faktizität*) and as *falling* (*Verfallen*) or *fallenness*.

We have seen that Dasein's original or "primordial" relationship to the world is not a cognitive one but rather one of practical concern. Dasein "knows how" to dwell in this equipment world, even though it may not be able to put this knowledge into theoretical perspective. This practical knowing how is a dimension of the understanding which is equiprimordial with Dasein's *Existenz*. However, since Dasein *is* possibility (it does not just *have* possibilities), Heidegger also means by understanding, Dasein's capacity to project its possibilities forward on the basis of its own uniqueness. Thus Dasein's possibilities are specific to individual Dasein, and consequently, there are no *a priori* given possibilities that every Dasein has to actualize in order to be human. What possibility means, then, for Heidegger basically is life alternatives projected by Dasein's understanding from among which Dasein *can* choose. Solomon states:

> Possibility, for Heidegger, is any envisionable structure for Being-in-the-world. Because of the peculiar structure of Dasein as being-in-the-world, any structure of Being-in-the-world is a structure of Dasein itself. In less Heideggerian language, all understanding or conceiving of the world is at one and the same time an understanding or conceiving of oneself. One's conception of the world and one's conception of oneself are inseparable; these conceptions are (Dasein's) possibilities. . . .

Like Kant, Heidegger gives a central place in his philosophy to the concept of 'understanding' . . . Understanding is the projection of fundamental possibilities into the future, the laying of plans and designs. Understanding of the world is thus a thinking of the world in terms of one's structuring and restructuring of it; it is also a thinking of oneself and of structuring and restructuring oneself.[84]

Upon the structure of *Existenz* two basic possibilities present themselves as the *modes* in which Dasein relates to its possibilities. Heidegger remarks:

Dasein always understands itself in terms of its existence — in terms of a possibility of itself: to be itself or not itself. Dasein has either chosen these possibilities itself, or got itself into them, or grown up in them already. Only the particular Dasein decides its existence, whether it does so by taking hold or by neglecting. The question of existence never gets straightened out except through existing itself.[85]

Dasein is itself if it has chosen its possibilities lucidly and resolutely, taking full responsibility for its choices as its own. Then Dasein is said to exist *authentically (eigentlich)*. Dasein is *not* itself, however, if somehow it defines itself in such a way that its basic structure as possibility, i.e., freedom to choose, is obscured, denied or neglected. Then Dasein does not take responsibility for its decisions but rather finds some "justification" for itself outside the structure of its own *Existenz*. In this case Dasein is said to exist "inauthentically" *(Uneigentlich)*. Both these basic modes of existence arise from Dasein's irreducible "mineness." Says Heidegger:

. . . in each case [i.e. with each individual Dasein] Dasein is mine to be in one way or another. Dasein has always made some sort of decision as to the way in which it is in each case mine [*je meines*]. That entity which in its Being has this very Being as an issue, comports itself towards its Being as its own most possibility. In each case Dasein is its possibility, and it 'has' this possibility but not just as a property [*eigenschaftlich*], as something present-at-hand would. And because Dasein is in each case essentially its own possibility, it *can*, in its very Being, 'choose' itself and win itself; it can also lose itself and never win itself; or only 'seem' to do so. But only in so far as it is essentially something which can be *authentic* — that is, something of its own — can it have lost itself and not yet won itself. As modes of Being, authenticity and inauthenticity . . . are both grounded in the fact that any Dasein whatsoever is characterized by *mineness*.[86]

These two basic possibilities of Dasein are given content in relation to the two other existentiale structures involved in ontological self-recognition. Not only is Dasein possibility; it is also *facticity*. By facticity Heidegger means all those features of Dasein which have not been chosen, but rather are the concrete "givens" of Dasein's existence. Dasein does not exist as Being-in-the-world in general. Each Dasein finds itself in a specific world, in a specific time and place, with these parents, this body, born into this social class. To be sure Dasein can choose to change specific worlds, but it cannot choose not to have a world, or not to have a body, and it cannot choose not to have its own past. The existentiale structure of *facticity*, then, is the whole range of facts, which define Dasein, but which, because they are not chosen, are not features of Dasein's *Existenz*. Not choosing them means that Dasein's facticity is that of *contingency* into which it has been "thrown" without reason or purpose. Dasein is, in relation to its facticity, just "there" as "thrownness" (*Geworfenheit*).

Ontological self-recognition requires for Heidegger that Dasein recognize its facticity and the contingency it makes manifest. Ontological self-recognition is possible because this existentiale structure discloses itself to the understanding in the various moods (*Stimmung*) of Dasein. A mood or a "state-of-mind" is philosophically significant, for Heidegger, because moods reveal to Dasein at the pre-cognitive level of the understanding one of the essential ontological structures of Dasein, namely, its facticity and thrownness. A mood, then, is not for Heidegger, a mere subjective datum to be ignored or disregarded by philosophy. A mood rather is a potentially disclosive event for Dasein, which, even though Dasein seeks to evade that which is disclosed in its moods, is ontologically significant.

Moods disclose three states of affairs, for Heidegger, in which the ontological structure of facticity is laid bare. In the first place a mood discloses Dasein's thrownness into a world which is already there for Dasein's circumspective concern. Thus, secondly, moods disclose what Heidegger calls "Being-in-the-world as a whole," which Heidegger adds, "makes it possible first of all to direct

oneself towards something."[87]   Moods "tune" Dasein in to its
Being-in-the-world by again "delivering Dasein over to itself"
momentarily, thus severing Dasein's ordinary absorption in the
world, so that Dasein's Being-in-the-world becomes "lit up" for it
as a whole.   In being "aroused," as it were, from its ordinary
absorption in the world through its moods, Dasein has its own most
basic mode of Being-in-the-world brought before it, which is the
third state of affairs disclosed by mood.   Heidegger puts it thus:

> But to be affected by the unserviceable, resistant, or threatening character
> [*Bedrohlichkeit*] of that which is ready-to-hand, becomes ontologically possi-
> ble only in so far as Being-in as such has been determined existentially
> before-hand in such a manner that what it encounters within-the-world can
> "matter" to it in this way. The fact that this sort of thing can "matter" to it is
> grounded in one's state-of-mind; and as a state-of-mind it has already dis-
> closed the world — as something which is in the state-of-mind of fearing (or
> fearlessness) can discover that what is environmentally ready-to-hand is
> threatening. Dasein's openness to the world is constituted existentially by the
> attunement of a state-of-mind.[88]

Dasein's facticity is mediated to it through its moods.   When
Dasein is depressed, bored, afraid, restless, angry, lonely, or frus-
trated, its facticity is radically "colored" by these states-of-mind,
presenting itself as a burden, an emptiness, a threat, a routine, an
intractable opponent, or a deprivation.   So too with more positive
moods.   In each case the average, ordinary world of Dasein's facti-
cal contingency is given to Dasein's awareness in its moods as that
into which it is thrown without excuse, reason or purpose, and it is
precisely this disclosure from which Dasein in its ordinary everydayness evasively "turns away."[89]

To say that Dasein "proximally and for the most part" turns away
from that which is disclosed in mood points to a third existential
structure involved in the ontological self-recognition of Dasein,
which Heidegger calls "fallenness." Fallenness is the mode of Dasein's Being-in-the-world where the existentiale of Being-in
includes equiprimordially the existentiale of Being-with. Thus:

> . . . the world is always the one that I share with Others. The world of Dasein
> is a *with-world* (*Mitwelt*). Being-in is Being-with Others. Their Being-in-
> themselves-within-the-world is Dasein-with (*Mitdasein*).[90]

Heidegger takes great pains to make the point that Dasein becomes conscious of itself only in relation to others. Even Dasein's being alone can have meaning only in relation to others. Furthermore, we do not become conscious of ourselves as subjects and then by inference establish the subjectivity of others whom we encounter as objects present-at-hand. Just as Being-in-the-world is constitutive of Dasein so also is Being-with-Others. Dasein is not an isolated ego; rather Dasein is only given to itself in relation to others, and knowing itself is simultaneously to know (in the sense of to be familiar with) others: self-awareness and awareness of others are equiprimordial.

Heidegger further argues that Dasein's original everyday comportment toward others is comparable to its comportment toward tools; however, people cannot be used like tools, even though others first appear to Dasein in the same referential context of "getting things done." Thus, Dasein does not stand in relation to others in circumspection, but rather in *solicitude* (*Fürsorge*), which means that Dasein cannot relate to others as equipment ready-to-hand.[91]

Dasein's facticity, then, includes being thrown into the with-world of others, who constitute what Heidegger calls the "they" (*das-Man*). Dasein in its everydayness becomes absorbed in its environmental world of tools and its with-world of other Daseins. The more it becomes concernfully (solicitously) absorbed in its with-world the less it is itself. But if Dasein is not itself in its Being-with-Others, who is it? Dasein is, Heidegger answers, the "they". Heidegger writes:

> . . . Dasein, as everyday Being-with-one-another, stands in *subjection* [*Botmassigkeit*] to Others. It itself is not; its Being has been taken away by the Others. Dasein's everyday possibilities of Being are for the Others to dispose of as thy please. These Others, moreover, are not *definite* Others. On the contrary, any Other can represent them. What is decisive is just that inconspicuous domination by Others which has already been taken over unawares from Dasein as Being-with. One belongs to the Others one-self and enhances their power. 'The Others' whom one thus designates in order to cover up the fact of one's belonging to them essentially oneself, are those who proximally and for the most part 'are there' in everyday Being-with-one-another. The "who" is not this one, not that one, not one-self [*man selbst*],

not some people [*einige*], and not the sum of them all. The 'who' is the neuter, the 'they' [*das Man*].[92]

The existentiale of fallenness pertains specifically to Dasein's being in subjection to the "they." The "they," the public determines Dasein's identity according to the former's norms and tastes. Here is Solomon's analysis:

> Dasein as Being-with is a part of the public, has his identity in his social roles; he is a college professor, a medical student, a nobody (does nothing for society). These social roles are defined, not by the individual, but by the public itself. We have already seen that Dasein has, as one of its essential characteristics, Existenz, or possibilities. As Being-with, as one of the public, Dasein resigns his right to project these possibilities for himself . . . these possibilities, because they are 'disposed of' by the public instead of by oneself, no longer become one's own responsibility. . . . The power to determine what Dasein is belongs not to oneself, and thus the self of Dasein is not a personal self but the self of the anonymous public, the others. . . .
>
> As *das Man*, Dasein's understanding of his own possibilities is restricted to the standards of success and failure which are imposed by *das Man*, by no one in particular. This reduces all individual differences to mere differences of 'distance,' more or less satisfaction of these impersonal standards. The goal of *das Man* is thus to be average.[93]

Dasein's fallenness in *das Man* means fundamentally that it lives out of a pseudo-identity which is bestowed upon it by the "they" and is largely introjected uncritically and unconsciously by Dasein itself. Thus Dasein's possibilities are "leveled down" to the public's consensus as to what is possible, which is to say, what is possible for "everyone," and Dasein is thereby "disburdened" of the responsibility of deciding as itself what its possibilities shall be. Dasein's continuing "temptation" as Being-in-the-world and Being-with is to surrender its freedom to choose who it shall be to the tranquillizing power of the "they," which relieves Dasein of the burden of having to be itself authentically, that is, of having to achieve an identity out of its own resources and grounded in the most rigorous and lucid self-recognition of which the existential understanding is capable. The fallenness of Dasein is a pervasive existentiale condition, which is never completely eradicated from Dasein's being; however, one of the possibilities open to Dasein is that of extricating itself from the identity-conferring power of the "they" and the inauthentic mode of Being into which such power lures Dasein. Even though Heidegger does not put it in these terms such extrication is Dasein's ultimate ethical task.

We have seen that moods are potentially disclosive intrasubjective events in which the possibility is given to Dasein in terms of its own consciousness of coming to an authentic recognition of itself. We have also seen that, for Heidegger, such self-recognition is most possible within the context of a unique, one might even say, privileged experience in which Dasein temporarily "breaks down," and is, therefore, most radically brought before itself, which is to say, brought before its possibilities. This experience Heidegger analyzes as a mood or state-of-mind and yet it is a "basic state-of-mind" and constitutes a "distinctive way in which Dasein is disclosed." It is the state-of-mind of "anxiety" (*Angst*).

Heidegger's argument is that the mood of anxiety is distinctively disclosive because it illuminates both Dasein's tendency to "flee" from itself by becoming absorbed in the world of its concerns and the "they," and at the same time it illuminates that "in the face of which" Dasein flees. Heidegger distinguishes anxiety from fear by asserting that fear as a mood is Dasein's awareness of an entity-within-the-world which is "detrimental" to Dasein itself and from which Dasein "shrinks back," and thus Dasein "is not necessarily fleeing whenever one shrinks back in the face of something or turns away from it." The "fleeing" of falling, however, is not a flight from a concrete entity-within-the-world. Rather:

In falling, Dasein turns away from itself. That in the face of which it thus shrinks back must, in any case, be an entity with the character of threatening; yet this entity has the same kind of Being as the one that shrinks back: it is Dasein itself. That in the face of which it thus shrinks back cannot be taken as something 'fearsome'. . . .

Thus the turning away of falling is not a fleeing that is founded upon a fear of entities within-the-world. Fleeing that is so grounded is still less a character of this turning away, when what this turning-away does is precisely to *turn thither* towards entities within-the-world by absorbing itself in them. The turning away of falling is grounded rather in anxiety, which in turn is what first makes fear possible.[94]

Anxiety and fear are comparable in that they are both moods which register Dasein's being threatened; however, in anxiety Dasein is threatened by that which "is completely indefinite."

> Accordingly, when something threatening brings itself close, anxiety does not 'see' any definite 'here' or 'yonder' from which it comes. That in the face of which one has anxiety is characterized by the fact that what threatens is *nowhere.* . . . It is so close that it is oppressive and stifles one's breath, and yet it is nowhere. . . . The obstinacy of the "nothing and nowhere within-the-world" means as phenomenon that *the world as such is that in the face of which one has anxiety.*[95]

In the state of anxiety, then, Dasein is threatened by nothing in particular, but rather by its very Being-in-the-world as thrown possibility; in brief Dasein is threatened by Dasein itself. Anxiety is a privileged, though painful, experience for Dasein precisely because it wrests Dasein from its comfortable, tranquillizing pseudo-identity in the "they" and throws it back upon itself and its unique possibilities. Heidegger states:

> In anxiety what is environmentally ready-to-hand sinks away, and so, in general, do entities within-the-world. The 'world' can offer nothing more, and neither can the Dasein-with of Others. Anxiety thus takes away from Dasein the possibility of understanding itself, as it falls, in terms of the 'world' and the way things have been publicly interpreted. Anxiety throws Dasein back upon that which it is anxious about — its authentic potentiality-for-Being-in-the-world, which as something that understands, projects itself essentially upon possibilities. Therefore, with that which it is anxious about, anxiety discloses Dasein as *Being-possible*, and indeed as the only kind of thing which it can be of its own accord as something individualized in individualization [*vereinzeltes in der Vereinzelung*].[96]

Anxiety thus brings Dasein's unique possibilities before itself and consequently its *Existenz* as "Being-free." In the experience of anxiety the conventional worlds of meaning of the "they" in which Dasein lives comfortably "sink away," i.e., they lose their extrinsic "substantiality" and "necessity," which Dasein in its average every-dayness tends to attribute to them. In disclosing to Dasein itself its structure as Being-free, anxiety thus makes Dasein feel "uncanny" [*unheimlichkeit*] in relation to its everyday world and its pseudo-identity collapses. Dasein is no longer "at home" in the public world of the "they."

To say, then, that anxiety individualizes Dasein is to say that it requires Dasein to become aware that it can never complete the project of disowning its "mineness" by fleeing into the inauthentic identity which it takes over from the "they." In anxiety Dasein's whole inauthentic mode of being-in-the-world breaks down, thus throwing Dasein into the crisis of self-recognition. As Being-free Dasein experiences anxiety as

> the mood of recognition of the open-ended-ness and personal responsibility for one's own possibilities. Dread [anxiety] is the fear of Being-in-the-world as such. What is dreadful is the utter meaninglessness of human life, the lack of given directions, given standards and values, and a given conception of oneself. It is to escape this nothingness that Dasein tends to retreat into inauthenticity. Dread makes everything insignificant, for it sees that one can always simply choose to make anything significant. This seeing everything as insignificant but by one's own choice is equivalent to the recognition of one's Existenz, and therefore seeing the possibility for authentic Existenz. Dread shows us that we do not derive our meaning from the world (there is no human nature), but rather that the world derives its meaning from us.[97]

As a distinctive and privileged mood anxiety is that primordial experience present in Dasein's pre-ontological awareness, which in being made ontologically explicit, facilitates Dasein's ontological self-recognition. Anxiety explains Dasein's tendency to flee into the world of everyday meanings, thus losing itself, and that from which it flees. As Heidegger has summarized his analysis of anxiety:

> anxiousness as a state-of-mind is a way of Being-in-the-world; that in the face of which we have anxiety is thrown Being-in-the-world; that which we have anxiety about is our potentiality-for-Being-in-the-world. Thus the entire phenomenon of anxiety shows Dasein as factically existing Being-in-the-world. The fundamental ontological characteristics of this entity are existentiality, facticity, and Being-fallen.[98]

We have seen that that in the face of which Dasein is anxious is Being-in-the-world as such. The nothingness of which Dasein is aware in the experience of anxiety is its own existential possibilities, especially the possibility of authentic existence, where that possibility tears Dasein away from its fallen pseudo-identity in the "they." Anxiety, then, discloses the fundamental temporality of Dasein, since it is the state-of-mind in which Dasein's understanding apprehends the future.[99] Dasein is anxious in the first place about its *Existenz*, i.e., about itself as open-ended possibilities, which, when these possibilities are projected into the future, force Dasein into an awareness of its irreducible uniqueness and individuality, thereby disrupting its flight away from itself. However, Dasein is not only anxious about its *Existenz*. It is also anxious about that future event which is its ultimate, "ownmost" possibility, "the possibility of its impossibility," namely, death. Death provides, for Heidegger, the possibility of authentic existence, which anxiety itself cannot provide. It is, therefore, not only that about which Dasein is ultimately anxious, but it is that event in relation to which Dasein's "wholeness" is achieved.

Heidegger begins his analysis of death by posing the question as to the ontological task of explicating Dasein's being as a totality. Once Dasein has been understood as possibility or an openness to the future, then Dasein's incompleteness comes radically into view. Dasein's facticity does not exhaust its being, since Dasein is a constant orientation toward the future into which it projects itself as the "not yet." Dasein is, then, that which it is not. If as long as it is, Dasein is incomplete, how can its totality be understood?

On the one hand, we can say that death is the end of Dasein's possibilities. However, for Heidegger, this does not bring the meaning of death for Dasein into view. Heidegger states:

> just as Dasein is already its "not-yet," and is its "not-yet" constantly as long as it is, it *is* already its end too. The "ending" which we have in view when we speak of death, does not signify Dasein's Being-at-an-end [*Zu-Ende-sein*], but a Being-towards-the-end [*Sein-zum-Ende*] of this entity. Death is a way to be, which Dasein takes over as soon as it is.[100]

Heidegger's point here is that if we see death simply as the termination of Dasein's life, or if we understand Death as that which "happens to others and will someday happen to me," we fail to see the ontologico-existential significance of death for Dasein's being as Care. Death is Dasein's being-towards-the-end, which is to say that death possesses, again, ontological meaning for Dasein, a meaning which it may appropriate prior to its physical death and from which its "totality" or "wholeness" is derived. This ontological meaning Heidegger describes thus:

> Death is a possibility-of-Being which Dasein itself has to take over in every case. With death, Dasein stands before itself in its ownmost potentiality-for-Being. This is a possibility in which the issue is nothing less than Dasein's Being-in-the-world. Its death is the possibility of no-longer-being-able-to-be-there. If Dasein stands before itself as this possibility, it has been fully assigned to its ownmost potentiality-for-Being. When it stands before itself in this way, all its relations to any other Dasein have been undone. This ownmost non-relational possibility is at the same time the uttermost one.

> As potentiality-for-Being, Dasein cannot outstrip the possibility of death. Death is the possibility of the absolute impossibility of Dasein. Thus death reveals itself as that possibility which is one's ownmost, which is non-relational, and which is not to be out-stripped. As such, death is something distinctively impending. Its existential possibility is based on the fact that Dasein is essentially disclosed to itself, and disclosed, indeed, as ahead-of-itself. This item in the structure of care has its most primordial concretion in Being-towards-death.[101]

The ontological meaning of death is that it is Dasein's ownmost possibility (rather than the end of Dasein's possibilities), it is non-relational, that is, no amount of absorption in the "they" can save Dasein from its having to die, and it is not to be outstripped, that is, there is no other possibility open to Dasein which has the power of individuating Dasein as does death. Death is Dasein's final possibility and it pervades everything Dasein thinks about itself and everything it does. Since death is grounded in Care, it is both that distinctive possibility in which Dasein's authenticity can be achieved and it is at the same time that reality which Dasein in its everyday fallenness seeks to evade. Again, it is anxiety as Dasein's awareness of its impending end which can drive Dasein out of its evasive fallenness toward an authentic recognition of itself and, therefore, a lucid affirmation of its own death. Heidegger recognizes that "proximally and for the most part," Dasein exists inauthentically towards its own death.   However, inauthenticity presupposes the possibility of an authentic Being-towards-death. Heidegger writes:

> Can Dasein also understand authentically its ownmost possibility, which is non-relational and not to be outstripped, which is certain and, as such, indefinite? That is, can Dasein maintain itself in an authentic Being-towards-its-end? . . .
>
> Authentic Being-towards-death signifies an existentiell possibility of Dasein. This ontical potentiality-for-Being must, in turn, be ontologically possible.[102]

The ontological possibility, on the basis of which Dasein can achieve its authentic wholeness concretely, i.e., ontically in relation to death, is given in the first place by Dasein's capacity to "anticipate" death, which is both certain and indefinite. Through anticipating death, Dasein brings its death near, that is, Dasein defines itself as having to die. Thus:

> Being-towards-death is the anticipation of a potentiality-for-Being of that entity whose kind of Being is anticipation itself. In the anticipatory revealing of this potentiality-for-Being, Dasein discloses itself to itself as regards its uttermost possibility. But to project itself on its ownmost potentiality-for-Being means to be able to understand itself in the Being so revealed — namely, to exist. Anticipation turns out to be the possibility of understanding one's ownmost and uttermost potentiality-for-Being — that is to say the possibility of *authentic existence*.[103]

The anticipation of Dasein's death brings with it the awareness of the non-relational character of this ownmost possibility of Dasein. Here Dasein comes to understand that:

> Death does not just 'belong' to one's own Dasein in an undifferentiated way; death *lays claim* to it as an *individual* Dasein. The non-relational character of death, as understood in anticipation, individualizing is a way in which the 'there' is disclosed for existence. It makes manifest that all Being-alongside the things with which we concern ourselves, and all Being-with Others, will fail us when our own most potentiality-for-Being is the issue. Dasein can be *authentically itself* only if it makes this possible for itself of its own accord. . . . Dasein is authentically itself only to the extent that, as concernful Being-along-side and solicitous Being-with, it projects itself upon its ownmost potentiality-for-Being rather than upon the possibility of the they-self.[104]

Simultaneously, anticipation of its death allows Dasein to accept its death as the which is "not to be outstripped." Heidegger's language becomes almost religious:

> When, by anticipation, one becomes free *for* one's own death, one is liberated from one's lostness in those possibilities which may accidentally thrust themselves upon one; and one is liberated in such a way that for the first time one can authentically understand and choose among the factical possibilities lying ahead of that possibility which is not to be outstripped. Anticipation discloses to existence that its uttermost possibility lies in giving itself up, and thus it shatters all one's tenaciousness to whatever existence one has reached. In anticipation, Dasein guards itself against falling back behind itself, or behind the potentiality-for-Being which it has understood.[105]

Death is *certain* and yet it is *indefinite*; however, the certainty of death is not the formal certainty of the proposition, "All men are mortal." Neither is it the certainty of statistical probability, and, therefore, to anticipate one's death and the truth it discloses to Dasein is not to transform it into a universal truth or an empirical fact of the present-at-hand, since

> when something present-at-hand has been uncovered, it is encountered most purely if we just look at the entity and let it be encountered in itself. Dasein must first have lost itself in the factual circumstances . . . if it is to obtain the pure objectivity − that is to say, the indifference − of apodictic evidence.[106]

To anticipate one's death is rather to relate to the certainty of its appearance in one's life (its inevitability i.e., an objective necessity) and the indefiniteness of the <u>time</u> of its appearance, not as an item of objective knowledge toward which one should cultivate one's own objectivity, but as a matter of the most personal urgency. As Heidegger has formulated this issue:

> The ownmost, non-relational possibility, which is not to be outstripped, is *certain*. The way to be certain of it is determined by the kind of truth which corresponds to it (disclosedness). The certain possibility of death, however, discloses Dasein as a possibility, but does so only in such a way that, in anticipating this possibility, Dasein *makes* this possibility possible for itself as its ownmost potentiality-for-Being. The possibility is disclosed because it is made possible in anticipation. To maintain oneself in this truth − that is, to be certain of what has been disclosed − demands all the more that one should anticipate.[107]

This passage is reminiscent of Kierkegaard. Heidegger is asserting here that we transform what is, indeed, a universal truth about man, i.e., his mortality, into our most personal truth, (our most subjective truth, for Kierkegaard) by constantly anticipating our own death. When the reality of our own death becomes our most definitive truth, our lives, Heidegger argues, achieve a totality or wholeness which is very much like the wholeness Kierkegaard asserts devolves to the knight of faith in his love for the princess. Heidegger builds upon Kierkegaard's insight as follows:

> Since anticipation of the possibility which is not to be outstripped discloses also all the possibilities which lie ahead of that possibility, this anticipation includes the possibility of taking the whole of Dasein in advance . . . in an existentiell manner; that is to say, it includes the possibility of existing as a *whole potentiality*-for-Being.[108]

It is here that Heidegger's existentialism most clearly asserts itself. There can indeed be an ontological analysis of human being, and even though that analysis can delineate the possibility of Dasein's authentic existence, it is not ontological truth through which Dasein achieves that existence. That can be done only at the ontic-existentiell level. Death discloses to Dasein the possibility of a radically personal relationship to itself in which it achieves the concrete content of its life and thus the personal truth through which Dasein can see itself as a whole. This personal truth (disclosure) of Dasein's death is not, in the first instance, the ontological fact that Dasein dies, but rather the *way* in which Dasein chooses to face its death. Heidegger writes:

> How does the anticipatory understanding project itself upon a potentiality-for-Being which is certain and which is constantly possible in such a way that the "when" in which the utter impossibility of existence becomes possible remains constantly indefinite? In anticipating the indefinite certainty of death, Dasein opens itself to a constant threat arising out of its own "there." In this very threat Being-towards-the-end must maintain itself. So little can it tone this down that it must rather cultivate the indefiniteness of the certainty. How is it existentially possible for this constant threat to be genuinely disclosed? All understanding is accompanied by a state-of-mind. . . . *But the state-of-mind which can hold open the utter and constant threat to itself arising from Dasein's ownmost individualized Being, is anxiety.* . . . Anticipation

utterly individualizes Dasein, and allows it, in this individualization of itself, to become certain of the totality of its potentiality-for-Being. . . . Being-towards-death is essentially anxiety.[109]

The possibility of an existentiell Being-towards-death, then, is Dasein's lucidly and courageously facing and enduring its own death by constantly remaining open to the threat which it casts over Dasein's whole existence. Death provides the possibility for authentic existence in which Dasein (1) becomes aware of its essential finitude; (2) becomes aware that it cannot complete the project of its self-dispersal in the pseudo-identity of the "they," since death individualizes Dasein by forcing it to see that no one else can die Dasein's death for it; (3) extricates itself from its dependency upon the pseudo-identity of the "they"; and (4) begins to choose its possibilities as a whole, integrated, autonomous agent, taking upon itself both the anxiety which is given in the threat of death over all its choices and the anxiety that there are no grounds, reasons, or purposes, and there is no justification for its choices beyond its own acts of choosing, thereby seeing who it really is and taking full responsibility for its own existence.

Facing the threat of its death authentically, then, is the unifying truth of individual Dasein. Insofar as Dasein takes its own death upon itself, choosing every possibility which lies before it with the resolute consciousness of death, it is "in the truth" as disclosedness. However, insofar as Dasein flees its individuation and evades its death in the solicitude of the "they," it is "in untruth."[110] Truth and Being are relative to Dasein, more specifically to the authentic existence of Dasein, and it is disclosed to itself that the philosophical or ontological explication of Dasein is possible.

As we have seen Dasein's original relationship to itself and the world is a "practical" rather than a "theoretical" relationship, and for Heidegger, all theoretical perspectives are grounded in the more primordial structure of Dasein's concern and care. Thus, if a theoretical perspective is rooted in Dasein's ontical inauthenticity, then that theoretical perspective will itself be inauthentic. It is Heidegger's assertion that the mistakes of traditional philosophy are not merely cognitive errors, but rather arise out of Dasein's fundamental project of evading a genuine encounter with itself. Heidegger argues, as did Nietzsche and Kierkegaard before him, that most of traditional philosophy it an expression of the *cowardice* of the philosophers who created it, the latter purposefully deceiving themselves as to the deliverances of their own existential understanding of who they really are.

It should be clear that the philosophy of *Being and Time* does not conform to what we have called the classical philosophical tradition. In the first place, Heidegger's whole argument is that while philosophy seeks ontological knowledge, it is, however, totally grounded in Dasein's pre-ontological structure, and rather than attempting to extricate itself from that structure it wishes to illuminate Dasein's everyday Being-in-the-world. It does not begin with the abstract "knowing subject or substance" but with the concretely existing self. Secondly, it is also clear that philosophy's task is not to liberate man from his concreteness, his finitude, and his contingent existence by driving him toward the detachment and indifference of the theoretical life on the one hand and, therefore, toward his absorption in the quest for the eternal, necessary, universal, and immutable structure of truth with which he is to become as identified as possible on the other.

Quite the contrary: philosophy's task is to intensify Dasein's awareness of itself as concrete, finite and contingent thereby providing the conceptual occasion in which Dasein can take hold of itself and gain itself precisely on the basis of its *Existenz* as concrete, thrown and anxious freedom, in relation to a truth which can be ontologically delimited but must be gained in Dasein's decisionality and which is therefore utterly personal and individuating. It is the case for the Heidegger of *Being and Time* that Dasein cannot gain itself, that is, become authentic through philosophy; however, it is also the case that philosophy should not contribute to Dasein's self-deception and self-evasion by conceiving of Dasein as an object present-to-hand or luring Dasein to seek that truth which is ultimately irrelevant to its own concrete existence on the other. In Kierkegaard's language Dasein's task is not to become "objective" but rather to become "subjective" by individuating and unifying itself passionately around its most personal and concrete truth.

This concludes our analysis of the existentialist movement as it is exemplified in the thought of Soren Kierkegaard and Martin Heidegger. While these two figures obviously do not exhaust the philosophy of existentialism, it is our assumption that the basic concerns of that philosophy are contained in their thought, even though they have undergone criticism and development by other philosophers who belong within this philosophical perspective, especially Jean-Paul Sartre and the French existentialists.

Our task now is to examine Tillich's critique of existentialism, as both an historical and cultural phenomenon as well as a philosophical school. After we have examined Tillich's views on the existentialist movement, we shall address ourselves to our final task, the evaluation of Tillich's conception of the relationship of philosophy and theology.

Part Three

Tillich's Critique of Existentialism

Tillich has made a number of attempts in his writings to assess the significance of existentialism as a philosophy and to evaluate its impact upon his own thinking. Characteristically, his analysis moves between the two poles of the historical antecedents of existentialist thought and the cultural context in which existentialism as a specific philosophical alternative is to be understood. Thus, TIllich argues, existentialism first appears as an *element* within the history of western philosophy; it takes definite shape as a *revolt* against the spirit of the western culture of the last three centuries and, finally, in the 20th century it has become a concrete cultural *style*, which manifests itself in the major forms of 20th century western culture — philosophy, art, literature, the theater, religion, education, politics.[1] As a cultural phenomenon, then, existentialism as a philosophy must be seen in the context of a much larger spiritual development. Consequently, Tillich distinguishes between the existential *attitude*, which he believes defines the cultural *Geist* of the 20th century and that special existential content, which is the philosophy of existentialism.[2]

The distinction between the existential attitude or what Tillich also calls *existential* thinking (ST, II, 26ff.) and existentialism as a content is an extremely important one for Tillich, and we shall return to it below. One of the implications of this distinction is that it allows Tillich to see greater continuity between the history of philosophy and existentialism than the most seminal existentialist thinkers are inclined to see. Tillich, in a way which is already familiar to us, formulates the distinction thus:

> For the sake of further philological clarification, it is useful to distinguish between existential and existentialist. The former refers to a human attitude, the latter to a philosophical school. The opposite of existential is detached; the opposite of existentialist is essentialist. In existential thinking, the object is involved. In non-existential thinking the object is detached. By its very nature, theology is existential; by its very nature, science is non-existential. Philosophy unites elements of both. In intention, it is non-existential; in reality, it is an ever changing combination of elements of involvement and detachment. This makes futile all attempts to create a so-called "scientific philosophy" (ST, II: 26).

Existential thinking is not identical with existentialist thinking, although they both have a common root, which is existence itself, and as we have seen in Part One, since existence presupposes essence from which it has "fallen," both existential and existentialist thought presupposes the distinction between essence and existence. In principle, one can say that existential thinking, for Tillich, is the analysis of the existential predicament of man in which one's own existence is *involved* (as opposed to detached) in the analysis, on the one hand, and in which attention is given to the condition of actualized human existence rather than to its essential structure on the other. Existentialist thinking certainly shares this orientation but as an historical phenomenon of the last two centuries, Tillich claims, it is more self-consciously in revolt against essentialism both in its philosophical and social expressions.

Involvement as the defining characteristic of existential thinking, however, is not a contradictory alternative to the detached attitude of non-existential thinking. Rather involvement and detachment are polar contrasts. Thus, in general one can say the essential structures of reality are accessible to *detached* cognition while the existential predicament is most adequately described through *involved* cognition. In actuality, however, there can be no *purely* involved or *purely* detached cognition, since the involved perspective needs some detachment in order to move beyond the "irrelevant subjectivity" of one's own involvement, while the most detached thinker sustains some minimal existential interest or involvement in the essential structures he cognizes. Thus, there can be no existential analysis without some cognitive detachment and there can be no essential analysis without some cognitive involvement.

Existential thinking, then, is that cognitive enterprise in which the element of involvement is dominant, and existential knowledge is that knowledge which results from the knower's

participating in a situation, especially a cognitive situation, with the whole of one's existence. This includes temporal, spatial, historical, psychological, sociological, biological conditions. And it includes the finite freedom which reacts to these conditions and changes them. An existential knowledge is a knowledge in which these elements, and therefore the whole existence of him who knows, participate . . . Existential knowledge is based on an encounter in which a new meaning is created and recognized. The knowledge of another person, the knowledge of history, the knowledge of a spiritual creation, religious knowledge — all have existential character. This does not exclude theoretical objectivity on the basis of detachment. But it restricts detachment to one element within the embracing act of cognitive participation. You may have a precise, detached knowledge of another person, his psychological type and his calculable reactions, but in knowing this you do not know the person, his centered self, his knowledge of himself. Only in participating in his self, in performing an existential break-through into the center of his being, will you know him in the situation of your break-through to him. This is the first meaning of "existential," namely existential as the attitude of participating with one's own existence in some other existence.[3]

Tillich's claim, then, is that the existential attitude has been operative as an element throughout the history of western thought and that genuine existential knowledge has been achieved in the philosophical, artistic, literary and religious traditions of the West.

The existential attitude can be seen most characteristically and most decisively for the development of existentialism in the thought of Plato. Plato taught

> the separation of the human soul from its "home" in the realm of pure essences. Man is estranged from what he essentially is. His existence in a transitory world contradicts his essential participation in the eternal world of ideas. This is expressed in mythological terms, because existence resists conceptualization. Only the realm of essences admits of structural analysis. Wherever Plato uses a myth he describes the transition from one's essential being to one's existential estrangement, and the return from the latter to the former. The Platonic distinction between the essential and the existential realms is fundamental for all later developments. It lies in the background even of present-day Existentialism.[4]

The platonic distinction between essence and existence and the existential attitude to which it gave birth was carried forward in classical Christian doctrine, especially the doctrines of creation, the fall, sin, and salvation. Classical Christian thought affirmed with Plato the ontological goodness of man and the world in their essential structures, while at the same time asserting that the essential goodness of man and world has been lost in that act of freedom which is thematized in the myth of Adam's temptation and revolt against God. However, in a way analogous to Plato's doctrine of memory, classical Christian thought maintained that the ontological unity between essence and existence obtained after the fall, even though it was disrupted. The essential structure of man and world is preserved by the "sustaining and directing creativity of God, which makes not only some goodness but also some truth possible."[5]

The existential attitude is present, then, both in the thought of Plato and Augustine, but it is present merely as an element within their predominantly essentialist ontologies. It has not yet broken the essentialist framework of classical thought. The existential attitude continues into the Middle Ages in the insights into the existential predicament of man, (which anticipates much of the work of depth psychology) to be found in monastic and mystical self-scrutiny, and in the medieval conception of the demonic and the role it played in confession, especially in the monasteries. It can be found also in the Reformation, quite clearly in Luther's "dialectical descriptions of the ambiguities of goodness, of demonic despair and of the necessity for Divine forgiveness."[6]

Both the Middle Ages and the Renaissance contain literary and artistic expressions of the existential attitude. Dante's *Divina Comedia* develops in poetic symbols "an all-embracing existential doctrine of man," while such artists as Bosch, Breughel, and Grunewald adumbrated the existentialist understanding of the human condition in their art. However, in none of these aesthetic achievements is the power of the medieval tradition and its tacit essentialism broken.

The essentialist orientation of the classical mind and its continuation into the Middle Ages and the Renaissance receives its first major challenge, Tillich argues, in the rise of nominalism in the late Middle Ages. He writes:

> There is a side in nominalism which anticipates motifs of recent Existentialism. This is, for example, its irrationalism, rooted in the breakdown of the philosophy of essences under the attacks of Duns Scotus and Ockham. The emphasis on the contingency of everything that exists makes both the will of God and the being of man equally contingent. It gives to man the feeling of a definite lack of ultimate necessity, with respect not only to himself but also to his world. And it gives him a corresponding anxiety. Another motif of recent Existentialism anticipated by nominalism is the escape into authority, which is a consequence of the dissolution of universals and the inability of the isolated individual to develop the courage to be as oneself. . . . Even so nominalism was not Existentialism although it was one of the most important forerunners of the Existentialist courage to be as oneself. It did not take this step, because even nominalism did not intend to break away from the medieval tradition.[7]

It is in the modern period in the history of philosophy that the existential attitude begins to disappear. The early Renaissance, embodied in the figure of Nicholas of Cusa, the academy of Florence, and early Renaissance painting, continued to exemplify the Augustinian tradition "and created a new scientific essentialism." It is in Descartes' thought that

> the anti-Existential bias is most conspicuous. The existence of man and his world is put into "brackets" — as Husserl, who derives his "phenome-

nological" method from Descartes, has formulated it. Man becomes pure consciousness, a naked epistemological subject; the world (including man's psychosomatic being) becomes an object of scientific inquiry and technical management. Man in his existential predicament disappears.[8]

The development of Protestant scholasticism in the 17th and 18th centuries also lost the existential attitude. Under the impact of Calvinism and sectarianism

man became more and more transformed into an abstract moral subject, as in Descartes he was considered an epistemological subject. And when in the 18th century the content of Protestant ethics became adjusted to the demands of the rising industrial society which called for a reasonable management of oneself and one's world, anti-Existentialist philosophy and anti-Existentialist theology merged. The rational subject, moral and scientific, replaced the existential subject, his conflicts and despairs.[9]

The Enlightenment of the 18th century saw not only the increasing celebration of science as the normative mode of knowing and doing and its consequent objectification of man as rational subject, but it also saw a growing conviction that man's perfection as a rational and moral subject stands on the threshold of completion as a corollary of the inevitable victory of science over ignorance and superstition. Immanuel Kant, who, perhaps more than any other philosopher of his age, contributed to the victory of the rationalism of the Enlightenment, nonetheless exemplified the existential attitude at two points in his critical philosophy, namely, in his doctrine of the distance between finite man and noumenal reality and in his assertion of the perversion of man's rationality by radical evil.[10]

Both these existentialist notions in Kant, however, were rejected by other spokesmen of the anti-existentialist mood which had emerged from the Renaissance, especially Goethe and Hegel. In Hegel, in fact, the essentialist vision achieves its definitive victory, and it is Hegel's philosophy more than any other which transformed the existential attitude into the existentialist revolt. Hegel, then, is a watershed in the career of existentialist thinking, for the essentialist thrust of the classical mind and its modern transformations comes to its final formulation in him. Thus, Hegel's philosophy potentiates the transition from the existential attitude to the existentialist content or expression, i.e., existentialism itself, by powerfully articulating the essentialist vision against which the existentialist thinkers revolted.   There is simply no way of understanding existentialism without grasping the utterly central significance of Hegel's thought for the existentialist development.[11]

In Tillich's interpretation of Hegel, one can see genuine appreciation.   One can also see that Tillich's own thought has been deeply influenced by Hegel.   He has certainly learned from the critique of Hegel's thought, but at least in Tillich's interpretation of Hegel, one can see remarkable parallels between the two men. The tragedy of Hegel's system, Tillich argues, is precisely the self-elevation (*hybris*) of the finite knower to the level of the infinite, thus attributing a finality to the system of thought which it cannot sustain.   This

> does not have primarily to do with the personal character of Hegel. There are others who have much more of this *hybris*, Schelling, for instance. It is in his fundamental idea itself in which the *hybris* is expressed, the idea that world history can possibly come to an end with one's own existence. The reason that Hegel was attacked from all sides and removed from the throne of providence on which he had placed himself was that the finished system cut off openness to the future. Only God is on that throne and only God is able to understand the past and to create the future. When Hegel tried to do both, then he was in the state of *hybris*, and this *hybris* was followed by the tragedy of his system.[12]

Tillich finds Hegel's basic essentialism in his doctrine of God.   In the Hegelian conception of spirit (*Geist*), we find the following meaning:

> Spirit is the creator of man as personality and of everything which through man as person can be created in culture, religion, and morality. This human spirit is the self-manifestation of the divine Spirit, and God is the absolute Spirit which is present and works through every finite spirit. . . . God actualizes his own potentialities in time and space, through nature, through history, and through men. God finds himself in his personal character in man and his history, in different forms of his historical actualization. . . . Hegel sees God as the bearer of the essential structures of all things. This makes him the great representative of essentialist philosophy, a philosophy which tries to understand the essences in all things as expressions of the divine self-

manifestation in time and space. . . . God in himself is the essence of every species of plants and animals, of the structures of the atoms and stars, of the nature of man in which his inner-most center is manifest. All these are manifestations of the divine life as it is manifest in time and space.[13]

Hegel's essentialism expresses itself in the crucial doctrines of his system. One of the most important of these doctrines is Hegel's assertion of the "point of identity between God and man insofar as God comes to self-consciousness in man, and insofar as man in his essential nature is contained together with everything in the inner life of God as potentiality."[14] The principle of identity in Hegel's thought leads him

to attempt to absorb the whole of reality not only in its essential but also in its historical aspect, into the dialectical movement of "pure thought." The logical expression of this attempt is found in statements like these concerning essence and existence: 'Essence necessarily appears.' It transforms itself into existence. Existence is the being of essence, and therefore existence can be called "essential being." Essence is existence, it is not distinguished from its existence.[15]

In denying a real distinction between essence and existence, or more precisely, in asserting that existence is essential being, Hegel presses his essentialism even more relentlessly in the doctrine "that reason is real and reality is rational." The task of philosophy, then, is to reconcile man with reality through the dynamic unfolding of thought itself.[16] The rationality of the real does not mean that everything real is rational, a charge Hegel's critics have made, which Tillich dismisses. Rather it means that the concrete, the particular, and the historical are subsumed into the universal process of absolute Spirit which is the ultimate rationality within the realm of space and time. Thus, Hegel's doctrine that the real is the rational

must first of all be thought of as a paradox. It is the paradox that in spite of the immense irrationality in reality, of which he could speak again and again, there is nevertheless a hidden providential activity, namely, the self-manifestation of the absolute Spirit through the irrational attitudes of all creatures and especially of people. This providential power in history works behind activity, willing, and planning, and through man's rationality and irrationality.[17]

When one sees reality from the point of view of absolute Spirit, and here the *hybris* of Hegel's system is most evident, then one participates in a conceptual reconciliation of man with reality in which existence as essential being's estrangement from itself is lifted to a higher synthesis and all partial, limited, individual perspectives are gathered up into the total, universal, all-encompassing vision of the absolute Spirit itself. The philosopher, who sees things *sub specie aeternitatus*, i.e., who grasps the essential structure of reality by virtue of his identity with it, achieves the absolute standpoint from which he derives absolute knowledge. He is literally post-historical man.[18] Tillich writes:

> But while the paradoxical element in Hegel's statement is obviously there, Hegel did no accept the mystery in the way in which Christianity has always accepted it. Hegel *knew* why things happened as they did. He knew how the process of history unfolds. Therefore, he missed the one element in the Christian affirmation of the paradox of providence, the mystery about the particulars. He did not even discuss the particulars, but he believed he knew the general process as such. He constructed history as the actualization of the eternal essences or potentialities which are the divine life in their inner dialectical movement. . . . These eternal essences are actualized in the historical process in time and space.[19]

One can see the essentialism of Hegel's perspective in his theory of knowledge, his logic, the syntheses he asserted between God and Man, religion and culture, state and church and especially in his philosophy of history.

In spite of his fundamental essentialism, however, there are, Tillich argues, existentialist elements in Hegel's thought just as these elements can be found in Plato, Augustine, and Kant. The first existentialist element Tillich sees in Hegel's consciousness of the ontology of nonbeing. "Negation," Tillich asserts,

> is the dynamic power of his system, driving the absolute idea (the essential realm) toward existence and driving existence back toward the absolute idea (which in the process actualizes itself as the absolute mind or spirit). Hegel knows of the mystery and anxiety of nonbeing; but he takes it into the self-affirmation of being.[20]

One can see a second existentialist element in Hegel's "doctrine that within existence nothing great is achieved without passion and interest. This formula of his introduction to the *Philosophy of History* shows that Hegel was aware of . . . the nonrational levels of human nature."

Finally, Hegel's philosophy of history reveals a third existentialist element where the human predicament within the process of history is evaluated realistically. "History, [Hegel] says, in the same introduction, is not a place where the individual can reach happiness." The implication of Hegel's analysis of man's plight in history is

> either the individual must elevate himself above the universal process to the situation of the intuiting philosopher or that the existential problem of the individual is not solved. And this was the basis for the Existentialist protest against Hegel and the world which is mirrored in his philosophy.[21]

There is no doubt that for Tillich, Hegel's synthesis constitutes one of the great achievements of the human spirit. However, its very greatness and its dominating power in the first half of the 19th century provoked a profound revolt against it. The revolt took many forms and yet its commonality was its attempt to regain the reality of man as am existing subject, and thus to prevent his unique personhood and its predicament from being subsumed into the essentialist vision of the classical mind. As the precursor of existentialism as expression or content, the revolt Tillich argues, was not merely against Hegel. It was a revolt against the very spirit of that cultural attitude and content which emerged from this essentialist thinking and its concrete expressions in science and technology. This thinking has been operative in the West since the Renaissance and is characterized by the increasing loss of the existential attitude and thus the loss of the conception and valuation of man's concrete, particular existence.

The existentialist revolt was anticipated by Pascal in the 17th century in his attack upon the mathematical rationality of Descartes, and in the Romantics' attack in the 18th century upon the rule of moral rationality. However, it takes decisive form in the decade between 1840 and 1850, especially in Germany in which the conception of "existence" received a new formulation. This new conception of existence was self-consciously worked out against Hegel, and it was initiated first by the work of Schelling (1775-1854), Hegel's former friend and colleague, who after Hegel's death developed a new sensitivity to the existential point of view. In 1841, Schelling delivered his famous Berlin lectures before such figures as Kierkegaard, Burckhardt, Engels, and Bakunin.[22]   In these lectures Schelling traced the transition in his own thought from "negative" to "positive" philosophy.   The former, Schelling argues, defined his early position, but Hegel never transcended the "negative" philosophy.   Tillich interprets the meaning Schelling attributes to these two terms thus:

> Negative philosophy is philosophy of identity or essentialism. He called it negative because it abstracts from the concrete situation as all science has to do. It does not imply a negative evaluation of this philosophy, but refers to the method of abstraction. You abstract from the concrete situation until you come to the essential structures of reality, the essence of man, the essence of animals, the essence of mind, etc. Negative philosophy deals with the realm, of ideas, as Plato called it. But negative philosophy does not say anything about what is positively given. The essence of man does not say anything about the fact that man does exist in time and space. The term "positive philosophy" expresses the same thing that we call existentialism today. It deals with the positive, the actual situation in time and space.[23]

Tillich goes on to make the point, which he stresses not only in relation to Schelling's distinction between positive and negative philosophy, but in relation to existentialism itself, that existentialist thinking presupposes essentialist thought.   A philosophy of the concrete givenness of things, Tillich argues,

> is not possible without the negative side, the essential structure of reality. There could not be a tree if there were not the structure of treehood eternally even before trees existed, and even after trees go out of existence on earth altogether. The same is true of man. The essence of man is eternally given, but it is not actually or existentially given. So here we are at a great turning point of philosophical thinking. Now Schelling as a philosopher described man's existential situation. . . .Thus he arrives at all these categories now current in existentialist literature. We have the problem of anxiety dealt with, the problem of the relation between the unconscious and the conscious, the problem of guilt, the problem of the demonic, etc. Here the observation of things, and not the development of their rational structure, becomes decisive.[24]

In working out this distinction both on the methodological level and within the structure of philosophy itself, Schelling, then openly challenged the adequacy of Hegel's project and thereby denied that existence and essence are identical on the level of thought or that the concreteness of existence is comprehended in the delineation of the essence of an entity. The claim of Hegel's rational system to embrace not only the real, the What, but its reality as well is, therefore, a "deception," for, as Schelling puts it, no "merely logical process is also a process of real becoming."[25] By calling attention to the unique character of actualized existence and by showing that a unique philosophical conceptuality is necessary to understand it, Schelling laid the groundwork for the full flowering of the revolt against the Hegelian philosophy.

But Schelling was not alone in his attack upon Hegel. In 1840 Trandelenburg published his *Logische Untersuchungen*, and it was followed in 1843 by Ludwig Feuerbach's critique in *Grundsätze der Philosophie der Zukunft*. In 1884 three extremely important statement were formulated. Marx developed his own critique of Hegel in his *Nationalökonomie und Philosophie*, while the notion of "the individual" came into focus in Max Stirner's *Der Einzige und sein Eigentum*. Kierkegaard in the same year attacked implicitly the Hegelian synthesis between religion and culture, faith and philosophy by drawing his famous contrast between the Greek conception of truth embodied in the figure of Socrates and the Christian paradox in his book, *Philosophical Fragments*. 1844 also saw the second edition of Schopenhauer's *The World as Will and Idea*.

Marx continued to explore an alternative to an essentialist analysis when in 1845-46 he wrote with Engels *Die Deutsche Ideologie* and *Thesen über Feuerbach*, and in 1846 Kierkegaard published the classical expression of existentialist thinking, *The Concluding Unscientific Postscript*. The existentialist revolt had gained, by this time, striking momentum and the rudiments of the existentialist philosophy had been established.[26]

Like most creative movements in thought, however, this extremely fertile period between 1840 and 1850 was followed by a period of dormancy in which Neo-Kantian idealism superseded the

existentialist movement, Schelling was dismissed, Marx and Feuerbach were designated dogmatic materialists, and Kierkegaard was
forgotten. This dormancy period was not broken open until the
1880's   when   existential   thinking   returned   in   the
"Lebensphilosophie" or "Philosophy of Life." During this decade
Nietzsche's most important books had appeared and Dilthey and
Bergson presented the initial results of their own revolutionary
inquiries. While the "Philosophy of Life" is not identical with existentialism, the former is motivated by most of the distinctive concerns of the latter. Tillich further suggests that basic features of
American pragmatism, especially its emphasis upon immediate
experience, correspond to existential philosophy.

By the beginning of the 20th century the vision of existence
which had been adumbrated in the existentialist revolt awaited systematic articulation. Perhaps one can say that the First World War
was the cataclysmic event on the cultural level which precipitated
the movement within philosophical inquiry from the existentialist
revolt to the formulation of a systematic perspective, i.e., existentialism in the proper sense of a philosophical school. Within the
philosophical development itself, existentialism emerged from the
confluence of insights in the "Philosophy of Life" with the basic
work of Husserl, especially his shift from existent objects to the
delineation of a transcendental consciousness which makes them
its objects, as well as the rediscovery of Kierkegaard and the early
Marx. Here the names of Heidegger, Jaspers, Sartre, Marcel,
Merleau-Ponty, Ricoeur, Ortega y Gasset, Miguel Unamuno and
others of lesser stature figure decisively. It is they who have given
the existentialist movement its rigorous formulation as a philosophical perspective. Tillich also finds the existential interpretation of history found in German "Religious Socialism" as representative of this third period in the development of the philosophy of
existence.[27]

As a cultural phenomenon, existentialism in the 20th century is,
for Tillich, the expression of a major spiritual crisis in contemporary western society, which as he has shown, has its roots in the
19th century and has come to full development in our own time.

This crisis is defined fundamentally by the collapse of the traditional patterns of meaning which provided cohesion and purpose to the social world of western man from antiquity. This collapse of meaning was articulated metaphorically in the late 19th century in Nietzsche's image of "the death of God," which means for him the collapse of a whole system of meaning and values within which western man has lived. In attempting to respond to this crisis

existentialism as it appeared in the 20th century represents the most vivid and threatening meaning of "existential." In it the whole development comes to a point beyond which it cannot go. It has become a reality in all the countries of the Western world. It is expressed in all the realms of man's spiritual creativity, it penetrates all educated classes. It is not the invention of a Bohemian philosopher or of a neurotic novelist; it is not a sensational exaggeration made for the sake of profit and fame; it is not a morbid play with negativities. Elements of all these have entered it, but it itself is something else. It is the expression of the anxiety of meaninglessness and of the attempt to take this anxiety into the courage to be as oneself.[28]

In asserting the collapse of traditional meaning, existentialism as the courage to be as oneself places the burden of becoming an authentic self in man's own hands. It is in the thought of Heidegger and Sartre that this theme receives its most radical expression. Writing about Heidegger's thought, Tillich remarks:

Existential philosophy gives the theoretical formulation of what we have found as the courage of despair in art and literature. Heidegger in *Sein und Zeit* . . . analyses a phenomenon which he calls "resolve." The German word for it, *Entschlossenheit*, points to the symbol of unlocking what anxiety, subjection to conformity, and self-seclusion have locked. Once it is unlocked, one can act, but not according to norms given by anybody or anything. Nobody can give directions for the actions of the "resolute" individual — no God, no conventions, no laws of reason, no norms or principles. We must be ourselves, we must decide where to go. Our conscience is the call to ourselves. It does not tell anything concrete, it is neither the voice of God nor the awareness of eternal principles. It calls us to ourselves out of the behavior of the average man, out of daily talk, the daily routine, out of the adjustment which is the main principle of the conformist courage to be as a part. . . . Having the courage to be as ourselves we become guilty, and we are asked to take this existential guilt upon ourselves. Meaninglessness in all its aspects can be faced only by those who resolutely take the anxiety of finitude and guilt upon themselves. There is no norm, no criterion for what is right and wrong. Resoluteness makes right what shall be right. One of

Heidegger's historical functions was to carry through the Existentialist analysis of the courage to be as oneself more fully than anyone else and, historically speaking, more destructively[29]

Tillich sees Sartre as carrying Heidegger's early thought to its logical conclusion, a conclusion that the later Heidegger could not accept because of "the mystical concept of being" which constitutes the background of the latter's thought.   Sartre, however,

carries through the consequences of Heidegger's Existentialist analyses without mystical restrictions. This is the reason he has become the symbol of present-day Existentialism, a position which is deserved not so much by the originality of his basic concepts as by the radicalism, consistency, and psychological adequacy with which he has carried them through. I refer above all to his proposition that "the essence of man is his existence." This sentence is like a flash of light which illuminates the whole Existentialist scene. One could call it the most despairing and the most courageous sentence in all Existentialist literature. What it says is that there is no essential nature of man, except in the one point that he can make of himself what he wants. Man creates what he is. Nothing is given to him to determine his creativity. The essence of his being — the "should-be," "the ought-to-be," — is not something which he finds; he makes it. Man is what he makes of himself. And the courage to be as oneself is the courage to make of oneself what one wants to be.[30]

Because of their radical assertion of the "existence precedes essence" theme, Tillich argues, "Existentialism in philosophy is represented more by Heidegger and Sartre than anybody else."[31]

These rather long interpretative passages on Heidegger and Sartre have been chosen, because they exemplify one of Tillich's major objections to existentialism, namely, its total rejection of the notion of essence. In claiming that man's essence is precisely what he makes of himself, radical existentialism thereby denies that man possesses a "nature" which obtains prior to, and in contrast with, his existence. However, as the above passage on Heidegger's thought makes clear, it is not just the question of "human nature" or man's essence which is at stake in the existentialist attack upon the notion of essence, but the whole question of an intelligible universe in which man lives, whose essential structure is rational and from which human reason can derive those principles or norms

that are indispensable for the conduct of life. We shall examine
what Tillich calls "the loss of the world" in existentialism below, but
clearly his most important objection to the existentialist movement
centers in the question of human nature.

Analysis discloses a

> large group of problems concerning man which have been investigated and
> discussed throughout the history of philosophy in purely essentialist terms.
> They all deal with the question, What is the "nature" of man? What is his
> *ousia*, that which makes him what he is, in every exemplar who deserves the
> name man? Neither nominalism nor process philosophy, neither philosophi-
> cal empiricism nor even existentialism can escape this question. Attempts to
> describe human nature in its essential structures, be it in more static or in
> more dynamic terms, can never cease to be a task of human thought.[32]

Some of the questions regarding the human reality, which can
only be answered adequately through an essentialist analysis
(which presupposes a distinction between essence and existence)
are the following: the question of the *differentia specifica* between
man and nonhuman nature (Aristotle's essentialist answer was that
man is *animal rationale*), the mind-body question, the relation of
man as individuality and man as a community, and man's ethical
structure. Each of these questions is obscured if they are discussed
on the level of man's existence alone, since on the existential level
estrangement has disrupted man's essentialist being. Thus, the
existentialist claim that man's essence is precisely that which
emerges in his existentiality is *ipso facto* an equation of his essence
with the disrupted structures of his existence, and, therefore, a distorted or partial view of man. This can be seen, for example, when
Heidegger identifies man's communal being with the inauthenticity
of "*das Man*" or when Buber "tried to remove the universals from
the encounter between ego and thou, and to make both speechless,
because there are no words for the absolute particular, the other
ego."[33] In both cases we see an invasion of essentialist thinking by
existential analysis. Tillich flatly rejects such invasions.

Existential analysis or existentialism, then, is confined to a
description of the human situation and its subject matter, and is an
expression of "man's anti-essential or estranged predicament."[34] It

cannot, therefore, exist as a *total* philosophical option, since its basic claim that existence precedes or better defines man's essence is fallacious. In rejecting the essential structures of reality as *a priori, necessary, and universal* forms without which there can be no cognitive approach to reality (either essential or existential), existentialism falls into a fundamental self-contradiction.

On the theoretical level, then, existentialism cannot sustain its basic program without essentialist thinking to complement its own inquiry into the human predicament, and its attempt to do so leads to logical contradiction. On the ethical level, as one might call it, the existentialist rejection of essences leads to another seriously vitiating consequence. This is, for Tillich, existentialism's loss of the world by its placing the courage to be as oneself in the radical subjectivity of the self.[35]

It is not altogether clear from Tillich's writings just how he sees the existentialist's loss of the world. He suggests that existentialism articulates within the body of its own thought a larger cultural attitude which began in Europe in the 19th century and continued into the 20th. After 1830 the disintegration of the religious tradition meant the end of a basic component in the definition of the social reality (world) of European man. As the "world of industrial society became more oppressive, existentialism turned to inward experience (*Innerlichkeit*)." The implication seems to be that existentialism in turning from an increasingly intolerable world became an expression of alienated thought, alienated that is, from the whole arena of public reality. Tillich writes:

> In all the Existential philosophers it is this loss of community that has provoked the flight from the objective world. Only in that world — in what Heraclitus called "the common world in which we live our waking lives" — is genuine community between man and man possible. If this common world has disappeared or grown intolerable, the individual turns to his lonely inner experience, where he is forced to spin out dreams which isolate him still further from this world, even though his objective knowledge of it may be very extensive.[36]

There is another way of interpreting Tillich's understanding of the loss of the world in existentialism, that is, that in the experience of anxiety and meaninglessness, as we have seen in Heidegger's thought, the objective world ordered through the categories of space, time, causality and substance actually disappears. In tracing the development of visual art from the beginning of the 20th century (which Tillich sees as predominantly existentialist), the experience of meaninglessness and the courage to be as oneself are decisive. Hence:

> In expressionism and surrealism the surface structures of reality are disrupted. The categories which constitute ordinary experience have lost their power. The category of substance is lost: solid objects are twisted like ropes; the causal interdependence of things is disregarded: things appear in a complete contingency; temporal sequences are without significance, it does not matter whether an event has happened before or after another event; the spatial dimensions are reduced or dissolved into a horrifying infinity. . . . The world of anxiety is a world in which the categories, the structures of reality, have lost their validity. Everybody would be dizzy if causality suddenly ceased to be valid. In Existential art (as I like to call it) causality has lost its validity.[37]

The existentialist insight into the experience of anxiety is that in a radical sense the social reality is reality "for us," that is, that the objective world appears real and substantial or unreal and insubstantial only in correlation with those states of the self in which the latter is experienced as real and substantial or unreal and insubstantial. This is not to suggest, however, that the doctrine of subjectivity in existentialist thought means that the objective world has no reality apart from the self which perceives it. It does mean, especially in the thought of Kierkegaard, Heidegger and Sartre, that the self defines the *character* of the world out of its own subjectivity.

In the state of anxiety, especially the anxiety of meaninglessness, the self experiences the dissolution of its own substantiality, and in effect the dissolution of the life world around it. If, then, the self must reconstitute itself in the face of anxiety out of its own resources, that is, if there is no source for the courage to be as oneself outside the self, as at last the early Heidegger and Sartre insist, then the world will be constituted insofar as the self can gain an adequate sense of its own being. But, on Tillich's terms, this is precisely what the self cannot do without the power of being — itself working in and through it. Consequently, the limits on the courage to be as oneself which the existentialists impose by stressing *autonomy* rather than *theonomy*, and the self as the creator of meaning and value, rather than its participation in a structure of meaning and value it does not create but encounters, cut the self off from that power by which both the self and its world are ultimately constituted. Cut off from the power of being, the self remains problematic and aspiring, in existentialist thought, but the world is lost, since the self is not grounded in that power which ultimately constitutes it and, therefore, enables the self to have a word precisely in the face of the problematic of the self's existence.

As his comment on Heidegger suggests, the loss of the world in existentialist thought and practice also means, for Tillich, the loss of those principles and norms in relation to which the self actualizes its potentiality. Although Tillich does not make this charge explicitly, the loss of the world in existentialism is tantamount to the assertion of a radical relativism, the relativism of a self whose *existential* possibilities are its *only* norm. Cut off from the essential self, in which Tillich roots the moral imperative, the "will of God,"[38] the self is also cut off from the essential structure of reality, the universality of language, moral wisdom, a universal ethical obligation as well as the categories and polarities of being — in short, the whole world as cosmos. The self is thus an empty shell of possibilities.[39]

We may summarize Tillich's critique of existentialism as following two lines of argument. In the first, existentialism is found theoretically inadequate, that is, internally contradictory, by attempting to assert itself as a *pure* form of thinking, which does not need essentialist thought to complete its analysis. This theoretical deficiency leads secondly to an ethical deficiency (ethical in the broadest sense), namely, the isolation of the self from its world or the radical severing of the self-world correlation. The most practical consequence of this second deficiency is the ironic involvement of existentialist thought in the totalitarian movements of the 20th century.[40] In the face of such criticism, the question naturally arises as to Tillich's *positive* evaluation of existentialism.

In spite of the inadequacies Tillich finds in existentialism, his over-all evaluation is positive and sympathetic. In protesting the actual development of a dehumanizing and self-estranged form of life in advanced industrial society, the existentialists rendered the human community an invaluable service. In resisting the ethos of industrial life, they were

> not prevent [ed] . . . from achieving fundamental insights into the sociological structure of modern society and the psychological dynamics of modern man, into the originality and spontaneity of life, into the paradoxical character of religion and the Existential roots of knowledge. They immensely enriched philosophy, if it be taken as man's interpretation of his own existence, and they worked out intellectual tools and spiritual symbols for the European revolution of the twentieth century.[41]

The challenge existentialism presents to the Christian Church and to the Christian theologian is that they leave behind the "safety" of those versions of the courage to be as a part and identify themselves clearly with the existentialist concern to look beneath the "surface" appearances of 20th century culture to the actual condition of man. Too often the Christian Church and Christian theology have been refuges for those who cannot face the human predicament honestly. Theology must not be guilty of the bad "faith" (Sartre) of denying or glossing over the extremities of man's being-in-the-world.[42]

From Tillich's perspective, then, the *theological* significance of existentialism (and psychoanalysis) is its capacity to illuminate the existential predicament of man, and, therefore, its capacity to be utilized within the structure of the method of correlation. Obviously, the theologian's use of existentialism must be dialectical; it must involve a "yes" and a "no." The formal appropriation of existentialism, of course, is controlled by the theological method in which existential analyses help the theologian develop the human question to which the Christian answer can then be applied. Tillich writes:

Existentialism has analyzed the "old eon," namely, the predicament of man and his world in the state of estrangement. In doing so, existentialism is a natural ally of Christianity. Immanuel Kant once said that mathematics is the good luck of human reason. In the same way, one could say that existentialism is the good luck of Christian theology. It has helped to rediscover the classical Christian interpretation of human existence. Any theological attempt to do this would not have had the same effect. This positive use refers not only to existentialist philosophy but also to analytic psychology, literature, poetry, drama and art. In all these realms there is an immense amount of material which the theologian can use and organize in the attempt to present Christ as the answer to the question implied within existence . . . In recovering the elements of man's nature which were suppressed by the psychology of consciousness, existentialism and contemporary theology should become allies and analyze the character of existence in all its manifestations, the unconscious as well as the conscious. The systematic theologian cannot do this alone; he needs the help of creative representatives of existentialism in all realms of culture (ST, II: 27-28).

In confining the scope of existentialism to the "old eon," that is, to an analysis of the existential predicament of man, Tillich has made an important methodical decision both for systematic theology and for existentialism. On the one hand, he has defined existentialism as a species of philosophy whose task is the analysis of existential human being in space and time. The existential thinker is indeed involved in that which he analyses (i.e., he sustains the *existential* attitude toward his subject matter), but his analysis of human existence is nonetheless *objective and universal* in regard to human being, and *neutral* in regard to the answer to the question of human existence, i.e., when his methodology is followed consistently. Theology can, on the other hand, appropriate the insights of existentialism insofar as it, too, must examine the structure of existential being, but the *content* of the answer theology correlates with the problem of human existence is in no way determined by the deliverances of existential analysis, since the former is based upon a vision of essential being about which existentialism cannot speak and remain existential thinking. It is necessary to examine these methodological decisions more carefully.

It will be recalled that one of Tillich's critiques of the existentialist movement is that "pure" existentialism is impossible and that the existentialist attack upon the notion of essence is misinformed, since the existentialist denial of man's essence or the claim that his essence is his existence leads to a basic self-contradiction. In commenting upon Sartre and Heidegger, Tillich states this contradiction clearly:

> Sartre says man's essence is his existence. In saying this he makes it impossible for man to be saved or to be healed. Sartre knows this, and every one of his plays shows this too. But here also we have a happy inconsistency. He calls his existentialism humanism. But if he calls it humanism, that means he has an idea of what man essentially is, and he must consider the possibility that the essential being of man, his freedom, might be lost. And if this is a possibility, then he makes, against his own will, a distinction between man as he essentially is and man as he can be lost: man is to be free and to create himself.[43]

The same problem emerges in Heidegger.

> Heidegger talks also as if there were no norms whatsoever, no essential man, as if man makes himself. On the other hand, he speaks of the difference between authentic existence and unauthentic existence, falling into the average existence of conventional thought and nonsense — into an existence where he has lost himself. This is very interesting, because it shows that even the most radical existentialist, if he wants to say something, necessarily falls back to some essentialist statements because without them he cannot even speak.[44]

Existentialism, then, becomes contradictory when it transgresses its own methodological boundary, that is, when it attacks the notion of essence or when its own utterances contain an implicit distinction between essence and existence, while it denies such a distinction formally. Existentialism is internally consistent when it remains within its methodological boundary, which seems to involve for Tillich two components: on the one hand, the acknowledgement that existential analyses cannot proceed without at least some *essential structures*, e.g., language and the essential nature of man (only in contrast to which the existential predicament can be delineated) and on the other a *neutral* analysis of the actual character of existence as it presents itself in the immediacy of experience. This second methodological component means that existentialism cannot become *ideology* (or theology) in the sense that it is a "faith" or an *answer* to the problem of human existence. It can analyze *Angst* as a phenomenon of existence, but it cannot show men the way out of its crippling power. It can uncover the existentialist structures of estrangement, alienation, meaninglessness, absurdity, contingency, and guilt, but it cannot heal men of these destructive structures.

Tillich has made this second methodological point thus:

> The distinction has been made between atheistic and theistic existentialism. Certainly there are existentialists who could be called "atheistic," at least according to their intention; and there are others who can be called "theistic." But, in reality, there is no atheistic or theistic existentialism. Existentialism gives an analysis of what it means to exist. It shows the contrast between an essentialist description and an existentialist analysis. It develops the question implied in existence, but it does not try to give the answer, wither in atheistic or in theistic terms. Whenever existentialists give answers, they do so in terms of religious or quasi-religious traditions which are not derived from their existentialist analysis. Pascal derives his answers from the Augustinian tradition, Kierkegaard from the Lutheran, Marcel from the Thomist, Dostoievski from the Greek Orthodox. Or the answers are derived from humanistic traditions, as with Marx, Sartre Nietzsche, Heidegger, and Jaspers. None of these men was able to develop answers out of his questions. The answers of the humanists come from hidden religious sources. They are matters of ultimate concern or faith, although garbed in a secular gown. Hence the distinction between atheistic and theistic existentialism fails. Existentialism is an analysis of the human predicament. And the answers to the questions implied in man's predicament are religious, whether open or hidden (ST, II: 25-26).

The contribution, then, existentialism has to make to theology is its clarification of that region of being which is its proper object, namely, human being, *Dasein* as it is actualized in space and time. It is an internally consistent philosophy when it remains within its proper methodological orbit, namely, the delineation of that aspect of the *Logos* of being which is manifest in human existence in time and space. When existentialism remains a consistent philosophy, there can be no conflict between itself and theology. However, it is when the existentialists step outside the methodological boundary of existentialism and make either *self-contradictory* or *ultimate* judgments (e.g., man's essence is his existence or God does not exist) that they come into conflict with theology. Thus as we have seen above, the theologian must argue with the existentialists as a philosopher in conflict with other philosophers (as Tillich has done in regard to the doctrine of essence) or as a theologian in conflict with the "hidden theologian" in the existentialists (e.g., in regard to the question of God or salvation). Tillich's interpretation, criticism, and appropriation of existentialism embodies quite clearly his conception of the relationship between philosophy and theology.

The method of correlation permits a *theological* critique of existentialism, but it does not allow an *existentialist* critique of the basic content of the Christian message, which the theologian interprets. Tillich has developed this theological critique in the following terms. The theologian must stand in judgement upon the *partiality* of the existentialist vision and protest the tendency among the existentialists to absolutize their partial vision. In the name of the essential nature of man, the theologian must sort out what is true from what is fallacious in existentialism. In making this judgement the theologian is guided, of course, by the way the essential nature of man is interpreted within the Christian tradition.

As we have seen, there are three fundamental concepts in Christian thought which must be brought to bear upon a theological evaluation of existentialism. The first is the doctrine *Esse qua esse bonum est*, that is, "Being as being is good." Christian thought thereby affirms the unity of being (there is no dualism between good and evil) and its created goodness. The second conception is that of the universal fall from the created or essential goodness of being into existential estrangement or disruption. The third conception is the notion of salvation, that is, the possibility of *healing* or *wholeness* within the estranged condition of actual being. "These three considerations of human nature," Tillich asserts:

> are present in all genuine theological thinking: essential goodness, existential estrangement, and the possibility of something, a "third," beyond essence and existence, through which the cleavage is overcome and healed. Now, in philosophical terms, this means that man's essential and existential nature points to his teleological nature (derived from *telos*, aim, that for which and toward which his life drives).[45]

Existentialism is the philosophical doctrine of actualized human existence or in terms of the conceptions above, the doctrine of the human predicament after the fall: existentialism deals with the existential nature of man, the state of disruption and estrangement. Not only is existentialism fallacious when it denies the essential nature of man as we have seen, but it is also fallacious when it denies the teleological nature of man by confining the possibilities open to him to the state of existential disruption. It is one thing to describe the human predicament (which is existentialism's exhaustive task) and it is quite another to maintain that there is either no essential nature to which man can be reconciled or that the possibilities of being-in-the-world are subsumed within man's existential predicament, that is, that there is no teleological nature in man because there is no power of being at work in him by which the split between his essence and his existence can be overcome. From Tillich's perspective, when the existentialists make this latter claim, they are no longer speaking as existentialists, but as poor informed or confused theologians, who must be criticized on the basis of a more adequate theological conceptuality.

The methodological consideration in this critique of existentialism is significant. In construing it as a philosophical development within a larger philosophical whole, the task of which is the analysis of the existentialist predicament of man and *only* that analysis (and therefore having nothing to say about the content of the Christian message, but only the clarification of the existentialist situation to which the Christian message is addressed), Tillich has been able to appropriate existentialism within the structure of his thought in spite of the atheistic tendencies in the major existentialist spokesmen. He is not open to the charge, as has been made against Bultmann, for example, that he has simply dissolved the Christian message into the concepts of the philosophy of existence. Although, as we shall see below, serious questions remain in regard to Tillich's use of existentialism, they are not comparable to the questions which have ordinarily been raised in the larger theological discussion of the relationship of existentialism to Christian thought.

Once having developed his critique of existentialism as well as having made the methodological decision described above, Tillich goes on to develop the positive contribution of existentialism to his own theological system. This contribution is adumbrated in a remark Tillich makes about Heidegger's thought in the course of his autobiographical reflections.

When existential philosophy was introduced into Germany, I came to a new understanding of the relationship between theology and philosophy. Heidegger's lectures at Marburg, the publication of his *Sein und Zeit* . . ., and also his interpretation of Kant were significant in this connection. Both to the followers and to the opponents of existential philosophy, Heidegger's work is more important than anything since Husserl's *Logische Untersuchungen*. . . . Three factors prepared the ground for my acceptance of existential philosophy. The first was my close knowledge of Schelling's final period, in which he outlined his philosophy of existence in response to Hegel's philosophy of essence. The second was my knowledge, however limited, of Kierkegaard, the real founder of existential philosophy. The final factor was my enthusiasm for Nietzsche's "philosophy of life." These three elements are also present in Heidegger. Their function into a kind of mysticism tinged with Augustinianism accounts for the fascination of Heidegger's philosophy. Much of its terminology is found in the sermon literature of German Pietism. His interpretation of human existence implies and develops, however unintentionally, a doctrine of man that is one of human freedom and finitude. It is so closely related to the Christian interpretation of human existence that one is forced to describe it as "Theonomous philosophy" in spite of Heidegger's emphatic atheism. To be sure, it is not a philosophy which presupposes the theological answer to the question of human finitude and then explains it in philosophical terms. That would be a variant of idealism and the opposite of a philosophy of existence. Existential philosophy asks in a new and radical way the question whose answer is given to faith in theology.[46]

The theological significance, then, of existential philosophy is that it is "theonomous" and for this reason it can be used in a creative theological correlation in spite of its internal inconsistencies, its atheism and its emphasis upon autonomy. The theonomous character of existentialism can be seen as manifesting itself in two important directions. In the first place, as we have seen, existentialism protests the "self-sufficient finitude"[47] of industrial society by pointing to the depth dimension of existence. In doing so it disrupts the subject-object structure of reality and therefore provokes men to experience the problematic of finitude and to see that finitude is not self-sufficient. Thus, existentialism prepares men for the reception of the Christian message. In the second place, as

Tillich' remark on Heidegger indicates, existentialism has achieved a doctrine of man in contemporary terms which largely corresponds to the classical Christian view of man. Consequently, existentialism has provided an interpretative structure in relation to which the Christian symbols can be made intelligible to 20th century man. It is for these reasons that existentialism lends itself to theological correlation in a way, for example, that idealism and naturalism do not, but this correlation must be achieved in terms of the dialectical character of the method of correlation. Thus:

> Theology must use the immense and profound material of the existential analysis in all cultural realms, including therapeutic psychology. But theology cannot use it by simply accepting it. Theology must confront it with the answer implied in the Christian message. The confrontation of the essential analysis with the symbols in which Christianity has expressed its ultimate concern is the method which is adequate both to the message of Jesus as the Christ and to the human predicament as rediscovered in contemporary culture. The answer cannot be derived from the question. It is said *to* him who asks, but it is not taken from him. Existentialism cannot give answers. It can determine the form of the answer, but whenever an existentialist artist or philosopher answers, he does so through the power of another tradition which has revelatory sources. To give such answers is the function of the Church not only to itself, but also to those outside the Church.[48]

In challenging the self-sufficient finitude of capitalistic culture, Tillich argues, existentialism points to the dimension of depth beyond the subject-object structure. It does so in its full doctrine of man. In existentialist thought, as we have seen, human existence is defined by its *finitude*, but the finitude of human existence, rather than making man self-sufficient, opens him in principle to threat. As Kierkegaard and Heidegger have shown, anxiety is the existential correlate in awareness of human finitude. Anxiety is thus the disclosure to man in immediate awareness that he is subject to that which is not contained within the subject-object structure. Tillich builds upon Heidegger's distinction between anxiety and fear. Fear, we are reminded, is an affective response to threat, but the source of the threat is located among the external stimuli of the world. When man experiences fear, therefore, he does not transcend the subject-object structure, and even though he is under threat, he does not experience himself as *in principle* threatened. Fear is thus contextual, energizing the self to take appropriate actions toward that which provokes the fear. Because fear locates man in the subject-object structure, it does not have the potentiality of opening him to that which lies beyond that structure. As long as man is aware only of fear, he is not driven to question the illusion of self-sufficient finitude.

Anxiety, on the other hand, because it has no object, has the power of making man aware that his finitude is not self-sufficient. Tillich writes:

Anxiety is the more fundamental affection because the fear of something special is ultimately rooted in the fact that as finite beings we are exposed to annihilation, to the victory of non-being in us. In this sense, anxiety is the foundation of fear. Their ontological relation is different; for anxiety has an ontological precedence; it reveals the human predicament in its fundamental quality, as finitude.[49]

Anxiety is thus the disclosure of nothingness, non-being, the abyss that lies at the base of finitude. In taking man out of the subject-object structure anxiety opens man, negatively, to the depth dimension of existence.

Finitude is not only subject to a fundamental ontological anxiety, but it is also subject to estrangement, loneliness, insecurity, guilt, existential doubt, and meaninglessness. It is these structures within finitude which existentialist analysis has uncovered for contemporary man, thus opening the possibility to him that he will raise the basic question which his finite existence implies. In opening man to his own depth in terms of the radical question, Tillich argues, existentialism can be used apologetically to confront man with the problematic of his own existence, thus creating the possibility that he will receive the Christian answer to the question of the meaning of existence which existentialism articulates.

There seem to be two major aspects to Tillich's appropriation of existentialism. The first is to join theology in the existentialist attempt to "shake" contemporary man into considering more seriously than the spirit of capitalist culture will allow the problematic of his existence. The theologian, then, builds on the existentialist's work in laying bare the nature of the question which man's existence puts to him. However, theology, unlike existentialism, is not limited merely to asking the question of existence, and the second aspect of the theological appropriation of existentialism consists in developing the Christian answer to the question which existentialist analysis has explicated for contemporary man. This can be done, of course, only by correlating the symbols of the Christian faith with the questions which existentialism has formally delineated, or to put it somewhat differently, to interpret the Christian symbols in relation to the understanding of existence which the existentialists have developed.

The presupposition which informs this second aspect of Tillich's appropriation of existentialism is stated by him. He writes:

> Existential analyses express conceptually what the religious myth has always said about the human predicament. And in doing so they make all of those symbols understandable in which the answer to the question implied in the human predicament is given: the symbols and myths which center around the idea of God.[50]

The task, then, is to show how the religious symbol thematizes or symbolizes these same structures in existence which existentialism has clarified conceptually in order to persuade contemporary man that the religious symbol is not as irrelevant to his existence as the secular character of western culture might suggest.

Existential analysis has shown that anxiety is a necessary experience for finite man. The religious symbol which thematizes this experience is the symbol of man as *creature*. While this symbol can be found in every major religious tradition,

> the consequence of the Western attitude is that creation has a positive side, answering the question implied in the experience of creatureliness. The answer is not a story according to which once upon a time divine or half-divine beings decided to produce other things. But creation expresses symbolically the participation of the finite in its own infinite ground; or more existentially expressed, the symbol of creation shows the source of the courage to affirm one's own being in terms of power and meaning in spite of the ever present threat of non-being. In this courage, the anxiety of creatureliness is not removed but taken into the courage.[51]

So, too, the symbol of man as creature, as one whose existence is derived from and sustained by the power of the all-inclusive reality of being-itself comprehends and *answers* the question implied in man's finitude as loneliness and existential insecurity. Thus,

> symbols like omnipotence, omnipresence, and providence . . . become absurdities and contradictions if taken literally. They radiate existential truth if opened up with the key of existential analysis.[52]

The notion of existential estrangement is also symbolized by a large group of symbols, which before existential analysis clarified man's passage from potentiality to actuality, from innocence to guilt in the decisions he must make, were not only unintelligible but repugnant to the contemporary consciousness. However, when understood in relation to the existential structures of estrangement and guilt, symbols like temptation, sin, judgment, condemnation, punishment, and hell take on new significance, especially when it is our estrangement from our essential being which is expressed in these symbols. From this perspective, for example, symbols of

> condemnation and punishment are obviously not things which judge us from above, but symbols of the judgement we inescapably make against ourselves, of the painful split within ourselves, of the moments of despair in which we want to get rid of ourselves without being able to, of the feeling of being possessed by structures of self-destruction, in short, of all that which the myth calls demonic.[53]

In the same way, the symbols of salvation, redemption, regeneration, justification and the personal symbols of savior, mediator, Messiah, and Christ are all illuminated by existential analysis. The symbol of salvation, for example, symbolizes "the act in which the cleavage between man's essential being and his existential situation is overcome." The existentialist insight that "the situation of existence cannot be overcome in the power of this situation" also illuminates man's quest, out of his existential estrangement, "for that which transcends existence although it appears within it, creating a new being," and a third existential insight, namely, the power of self-acceptance, radically clarifies the symbols of reconciliation and justification by faith.[54]

Existential analysis can also provide the key for the understanding of the eschatological symbols of Christianity.   In existential doubt, man experiences despair about his own meaning, that is, hopelessness. The eschatological symbols seek to answer the question which existential doubt and despair raise for man. Thus

> Taken as highly symbolical, they express the conviction that in the realities of our daily experience, in spite of their seemingly meaningless transitoriness and ultimate emptiness, there is a dimension of meaning which points to an ultimate or eternal meaning in which they participate here and now. This is the key to the symbol of eternal life which . . . is less open to literalism than more dramatic but dangerously inadequate symbols such as life after death, immortality, reincarnation, heaven. Eternal life means that the joy of today has a dimension which gives it trans-temporal meaning.[55]

In all these symbols and their explication by the method of existential analysis, the central and all-embracing symbol of religion is presupposed, namely, the symbol of God. Each of the existential analyses and their symbolic thematizations in a cluster of religious symbols, converges in the explication of the symbol of God.[56] In following this method, Tillich states:

> We lead from different points and with different keys to the central symbol. But we do not start with it. This is an implication of the existential method, which, I believe is adequate to religion, because religion is a matter of man's existential situation. We must start from below and not from above. We must start with man's experienced predicament and the questions implied in it; and we must proceed to the symbols which claim to contain the answer.[57]

The apologetic weight which Tillich places upon the correlative use of existentialism within the structure of his systematic theology can be seen in the following statement. "My task," he says (in interpreting religious symbols existentially),

> was to show that existential analysis has made it more difficult for the modern mind to dispose of religious symbols by first taking them literally and then properly rejecting them as absurd.[58]

It is clear, then, that, for Tillich, the existentialist movement constitutes a moment in 20th century culture in which the possibility of

interpreting the Christian message is greatly enhanced by the former's impact upon the self-interpretation of contemporary man.

In Tillich's appropriating the insights found in existentialism,
however, one can see the concrete embodiment of the method of
correlation and the formal relationship between philosophy and
theology as Tillich has defined it. Consequently, Tillich's critique
of existentialism is informed both by philosophical and theological
analysis. His philosophical critique is that existentialism or existentialist thinking (in contrast to existential thinking) is internally
inconsistent insofar as it fails to acknowledge its own methodological boundary, i.e., human existence in time and space, which its own
intuitive-experimental method is uniquely appropriate to analyze.
Thus, in making negative judgments about the notion of essence,
and in cutting itself off from the philosophy of essence, existentialism falls into contradiction.

Tillich's theological critique of existentialism, i.e., that existentialism cannot give answers, but articulates the question of existence, follows consistently from his definition of the relationship
between philosophy and theology. Philosophy cannot become theology even though the existential concerns of the philosopher may
drive him to become a theologian. Philosophy is not soteriological
thinking; rather it describes conceptually the *logos* of being. Thus,
while existentialism is a unique form of philosophy, it nonetheless
shares in the general character of all philosophical activity at least
insofar as it shares the *intention* of discovering the truth *vis-a-vis*
the structure or *logos* of being.

It is in terms of these two critiques of existentialism that the
answer to the question of Tillich's relationship to existentialism can
be fully understood. Tillich himself has defined that relationship
thus:

> Often I have been asked if I am an existentialist theologian, and my answer is
> always short. I say, fifty-fifty. This means that for me essentialism and exis-
> tentialism belong together. It is impossible to be a pure essentialist if one is
> personally in the human situation and not sitting on the throne of God as
> Hegel implied he was doing when he construed world history as coming to an
> end in principle in his philosophy. This is the metaphysical arrogance of pure
> essentialism. For the world is still open to the future, and we are not on the

throne of God, as Karl Barth has said in his famous statement: "God is in heaven and man is on earth."

On the other hand, a pure existentialism is impossible because to describe existence one must use language. Now language deals with universals. In using universals, language is by its very nature essentialist, and cannot escape it. All attempts to reduce language to mere noises or utterances would bring man back to the animal level on which universals do not exist. Animals cannot express universals. But man can and must express his encounter with the world in terms of universals. Therefore, there is an essentialist framework in his mind. Existentialism is possible only as an element in a larger whole, as an element in a vision of the structure of being in its created goodness, and then as a description of man's existence within that framework. The conflicts between his essential goodness and his existential estrangement cannot be seen at all without keeping essentialism and existentialism together. Theology must see both sides, man's essential nature, wonderfully and symbolically expressed in the paradise story, and man's existential condition, under sin, guilt, and death.[59]

We have now come to the conclusion of our analysis of Tillich's conception of philosophy, theology and their relationship. We have chosen to analyze Tillich's relationship to existentialism, because it functions as a concrete example of the way the formal definitions and methodological principles actually function within his systematic theology on the one hand and it allows us to clarify the meaning of the claim that theology is existential thinking on the other. Our final task, to be accomplished in the next chapter, is to explore critically the issues which Tillich's thought raises *vis-a-vis* the question of the relationship of philosophy and theology.

Notes

Part One

1 Werner Jaeger, *Paideia*, tr. Gilbert Highet (Oxford University Press, N.Y., 1945), Vol. 1, pp. 153-154.

2 *Ibid.*, p. 453.

3 *The Dialogues of Plato*, tr. B. Jowett (Random House, N.Y., 1937), Vol. 1, p. 740ff.

4 *Ibid.*

5 The notion of the philosopher as the "friend of God" can be found throughout Plato's dialogues. For example, in *The Symposium*, the man who learns to love beauty "which is everlasting, not growing and decaying, or waxing and waning, . . . beauty absolute, separate, simple, and everlasting, which without diminution and without increase, or any change, is imparted to the evergrowing and perishing beauties of all other things" — such a man — "beholding beauty with the eye of the mind, . . . will be enabled to bring forth, not images of beauty, but realities . . . to become the friend of God and be immortal, if mortal man may" (*Ibid.*, pp. 334-335).

6 *Ibid.*, p. 761.

7 Cf. Jaeger's claim that Plato's conception of *Paideia* is based upon the two ancient Greek ideas of the model (*Paradeigma*) and its imitation (*Mimesis*). Jaeger, *op. cit.*, p. 259ff.

8 These themes can be seen in the following comment by Copleston on Plato's theory of knowledge. "Plato has assumed from the outset that knowledge is attainable, and that knowledge must be (i) infallible and (ii) of the *real*. True knowledge must possess both these characteristics, and any state of mind that cannot indicate its claim to both these characteristics cannot be true knowledge. In the *Theaetetus* he shows that neither sense-perception nor true belief are possessed of both these marks; neither, then, can be equated with true knowledge. Plato accepts from Protagoras the belief in the relativity of sense and sense-perception, but he will not accept a universal relativism; on the contrary, knowledge, absolute and infallible knowledge, is attainable, but it cannot be the same as sense-perception, which is relative, elusive and sub-

ject to the influence of all sorts of temporary influences on the part of both subject and object. Plato accepts, too, from Heraclitus the view that the objects of sense-perception, individual and sensible particular objects, are always in a state of becoming, of flux, and so are unfit to be the objects of true knowledge. They come into being and pass away, they are indefinite in number, cannot be clearly grasped in definition and cannot become the objects of scientific knowledge. But Plato does not draw the conclusion that there are no objects that are fitted to be the objects of true knowledge, but only that sensible particulars cannot be the objects sought. The object of true knowledge must be stable and abiding, fixed, capable of being grasped in clear and scientific definition, which is of the *universal*, as Socrates saw. . . . If we examine these judgments in which we think we attain knowledge of the essentially stable and abiding, we find that they are judgments concerning *universals* . . . Scientific knowledge, as Socrates saw, aims at the definition. . . . A scientific knowledge of goodness, for instance, must be enshrined in the definition "Goodness is . . . ," . . . But definition concerns the universal. Hence true knowledge is knowledge of the universal. Particular constitutions change, but the concept of goodness remains the same, and it is in reference to this stable concept that we judge of particular constitutions in respect of goodness. It follows, then, that it is the universal that fulfills the requirements for being an object of knowledge. Knowledge of the highest universal will be the highest kind of knowledge, while knowledge of the particular will be the lowest kind of 'knowledge.'" Frederick Copleston, *A History of Philosophy* (Doubleday, N.Y., 1962), Vol. I, Part I, 173-175. Our thesis is that the state of mind in which the philosopher achieves genuine knowledge must conform as nearly as possible to the object of knowledge itself, that is, the philosopher must become detached, objective, and universal himself.

9   Cf. Frederick Copleston, *A History of Philosophy, op. cit.*, Vol. I, Part II, p. 35ff. Cf. also Rex Warner, *The Greek Philosophers* (The New American Library, N.Y., 1958), pp. 108-110.

10 Werner Marx, *Heidegger and the Tradition*, tr. T. Kisiel & M. Greene (Northwestern University Press, 1971).

11 John H. Randall, Jr., *Aristotle* (Columbia University Press, 1960), p. 32ff.

12 Marx, *op. cit.*, pp. 18-19.

13 It is not adequate to say that being is simply changeless for Aristotle. Randall, for example, asserts that "for Aristotle, who since he gave the technical meaning to the term *ousia* rendered into Latin as *substantia*, ought to know, *ousia*, or *substantia* is defined precisely as that which undergoes change in change, what is at the end of any process different from what it was at the outset. And in the most important and fundamental change of all, *genesis kai phthora*, "generation" and "corruption," a new *ousia* or substance is present at the end that was not there at all in the beginning, or a substance has disap-

peared completely. Thus it is clear, Aristotle's pattern of motion and change is a pattern of novelty that emerges in process." (Randall, *op. cit.*, pp. 112-113). Randall, however, fails to grasp the distinction between the "first ousia" and the "second ousia," which Marx's discussion of the selfsameness of being presupposes. It is Marx's awareness of this distinction which constitutes the superiority of his treatment of this issue over Randall's. Marx argues that in dealing with the question of change in the "first ousia" or essence (*genesis haplos*) Aristotle asserted "that there must be a substratum, a something always already present, a hypokeimenon, so that something can become at all. . . . Looked at in this way, all coming to be would be only a remodeling, an augmenting, or a compounding of the substrate, which as such purdures. The treatise *De Generatione et Corruptione* goes beyond this crass position; in this work it is acknowledged that the substrate need not at all be only something perceivable by the senses. Rather the substrate is understood as that which is already present in potentiality and purdures, as, for example, the Being of the living being in the animal-human genesis. This Being is consistent with the Eleatic principle 'beyond all coming to be and passing away.' It is that which in relation to the many qua a sequence of generations, remains the same. But insofar as, in the *genesis haplos*, the matter has to do with the becoming of 'determinate being' into 'determinate Being,' two additional structural elements belong to the occurrence as a whole: the form (*eidos*), the whereto of the movement of the *genesis*; interrelated determinations, together with the substrate as *hypokeimenon*, have always extensively pre-structured the process of genesis, so that the Aristotelian ideal of an 'order' moving within itself is in no way endangered by the possibility of a 'transformation.' Herein lies the consequence, so decisive for the history of the problem, that even the transforming of the essence does not permit the origin of something *new*, something never there before" (Marx, *op. cit.*, p. 36).

14 Cf. Randall's thesis that for Aristotle, science is "right talking." Randall, *op. cit.*, Chapter III.

15 Marx, *op. cit.*, pp. 38-39.

16 *The Basic Works of Aristotle*, ed. R. McKeon (Random House, N.Y., 1941), pp. 1104-1115.

17 Marx, *op. cit.*, p. 40.

18 *Aristotle, op. cit.*, p. 880.

Part Two

1 This interpretation can be found, for example, in Walter Lowrie's and David Swenson's work on Kierkegaard.

2   With proper qualifications, Hegel, too, as Tillich himself recognizes, stands clearly within the philosophical tradition we have delineated. Perhaps this can be most easily seen in Hegel's profound commitment to Reason, which, in spite of the dialectical and dynamic way in which it is conceived, is realized through the individual thinker, who becomes the vehicle for the Absolute's actualization of itself in the world-historical process. In this transmutation of the notion of the objectification or divinization of the thinker, Hegel is even more radical than the tradition, for his argument is, as Quentin Lauer has written, the "contention that throughout the process of thought (throughout philosophy's history) there is one subject — i.e., Spirit — thinking. In saying this," Lauer continues, "Hegel is certainly not denying that each subject — each philosopher — down through the ages does his own thinking. If nothing else, the writing of a history of philosophy demands that he name names. What he is saying, however, is that in thinking his own thoughts each philosopher is participating in universal thought — and universal thinking — and that the universality of thought must be objective, if logic is to have any meaning whatever." Quentin Lauer, S. J., *Hegel's Idea of Philosophy* (Fordham University Press, N.Y., 1971), p. 40. Truth is still understood by Hegel as universal and objective, but the philosopher is not so much required to divest himself of his particularity and concreteness for truth to be achieved, since Spirit, "the cunning of Reason" will use the subjectivity of the thinker for its own needs. For a fuller discussion of Hegel's relationship to Greek philosophy, Cf. J. Glenn Gray, *Hegel and Greek Thought* (Harper, N.Y., 1968).

3   S. Kierkegaard, *Fear and Trembling*, tr. W. Lowrie (Doubleday, N.Y., 1954), p. 24.

4   *Ibid.*, pp. 47-48.

5   *Ibid.*, p. 46.

6   *Ibid.*, p. 46-47.

7   *Ibid.*, pp. 43-44. James Collins has written of Hegel's philosophy of religion: "What enters into the Hegelian philosophy through the gateway of phenomenology is not simply religion, but religion insofar as it is completely phenomenologized. Filtered and reinterpreted in this way, religion becomes a thoroughly domesticated member of the household of the philosophy of spirit. Tamed and deprived of its potentiality, it can furnish us with no independent basis for making the religious meaning and disposition of human life ultimately decisive on questions of truth and certainty. Hegel can now proceed confidently to reconstruct God and religion entirely in terms of his own categories, because the meanings permitted entrance into his systematic philosophy of religion have been phenomenologized well in advance. . . . This total control in principle over human religiousness is quite compatible with an acknowledgment of the nonrational and mystical aspects of religious life.

Hegel grants the presence and importance of these aspects, but views them as moments in the self-estranging life of living reason itself. . . . Religion pure and unstained is present only after man's religious life has been strenuously purified by being swept into, and completely dominated by, this dance of the absolute spirit. In thus submitting, religion furnishes philosophy with crowning evidence that the world is indeed a process with a purpose aiming at rationality, and that its purpose is properly achieved in the rational self-awareness of the philosophical spirit." James Collins, *The Emergence of Philosophy of Religion* (Yale University Press, New Haven, 1967), pp. 277-278.

8 *Fear and Trembling, op. cit.*, pp. 48-51.

9 *Ibid.*, p. 52.

10 *Ibid.*

11 *Ibid*, pp. 52-53.

12 *Ibid.*, pp. 53-54.

13 Cf. S. Kierkegaard, *Either/Or*, tr. W. Lowrie (Doubleday, N.Y., 1959).

14 *Ibid.*, p. 54.

15 *Ibid.*

16 *The Confessions of St. Augustine*, tr. E. B. Pusey (The Modern Library, N.Y., 1949), p. 62.

17 *Fear and Trembling, op. cit.*, p. 54.

18 *Ibid.*, p. 55. The motion picture, *Hiroshima, Mon Amour* by Alain Resnais is a brilliant analysis of this strategy of resignation.

19 Cf. Martin Heidegger, *Being and Time, op. cit.*, for this distinction. Kierkegaard tells us that "any other instance whatsoever in which the individual finds that for him the whole reality of actual existence is concentrated, may, when it is seen to be unrealizable, be an occasion for the movement of resignation." *Fear and Trembling, op. cit.*, p. 52.

20 I am indebted to Prof. H. L. Dreyfus, University of California, Berkeley, for the concept of the defining relationship.

21 *Fear and Trembling, op. cit.*, p. 59.

22 *Ibid.*, p. 57.

23 *Ibid.*, pp. 60-61.

24 *Ibid.*, pp. 64-65.

25 *Ibid.*, p. 65.

26 *Ibid.*, p. 67.

27 *Ibid.*, p. 70.

28 *Ibid.*

29 *Ibid.*, pp. 70-71.

30 Martin Buber, *Eclipse of God* (Harper and Brothers, N.Y., 1952), pp. 149-150.

31 *Fear and Trembling, op. cit.*, pp. 80-82.

32 *Ibid.*, p. 89.

33 *Ibid.*, pp. 89-90.

34 *Ibid.*, p. 90.

35 Huston Smith has called Kierkegaard's solution to the problem of human existence "this-worldly Transcendence." He writes: "The clearest instance of this-worldly Transcendence is occasioned by love. Kierkegaard better than anyone else has explained the dynamics of this solution to the human problem. The self, being dichotomous (composed of two halves, finite and infinite, temporal and eternal) is incapable of uniting itself by itself. Only when something outside the self takes possession of it, causing it to become fully absorbed with this outside something, can the self's two parts be aligned. In living with the princess day by day, the swain fulfills the temporal half of his being; at the same time she fulfills his need for eternity, for something that doesn't change and isn't in flux, by "gestalting" all the time in his life. This gestalt is experienced as constant and is in this sense eternal: the time before he encountered the princess was prelude, her entry into his life was decisive climax and everything subsequent has been consummation."

"The dynamics are similar with respect to finitude and infinity. The princess fulfills the swain's finite yearning; he can touch her and delight in her beauty which is concrete and particular. But she fills equally his infinite need. She provides him with something (herself) to which he can give himself infinitely (totally, completely)." Huston Smith, "The Reach and the Grasp: Transcendence Today" in *Transcendence*, ed. Richardson and Cutler, (Beacon Press, Boston, 1969), pp. 6-7.

36 S. Kierkegaard, *The Sickness Unto Death*, tr. Walter Lowrie (Doubleday, Inc., N.Y., 1954), p. 146ff.

37 S. Kierkegaard, *Concluding Unscientific Postscript*, tr. W. Lowrie (Princeton University Press, Princeton, N.J., 1941), p. 173.

38 Robert C. Solomon, *From Rationalism to Existentialism: The Existentialists and their Nineteenth-Century Backgrounds* (Harper & Row, N.Y., 1972), p. 79.

39 *Concluding Unscientific Postscript, op. cit.*, pp. 279-281.

40 Solomon, *op. cit.*, p. 81.

41 *Ibid.*, pp. 88-89.

42 *Concluding Unscientific Postscript, op. cit.*, p. 306.

43 *Ibid.*, pp. 116-117.

44 *Ibid.*, p. 318.

45 *Ibid.*, p. 182.

46 Solomon, *op. cit.*, pp. 79, 84-85.

47 For a suggestive effort to build on the Kierkegaardian revolution, see Roger Poole, *Towards Deep Subjectivity* (Harper, N.Y., 1972).

48 *Concluding Unscientific Postscript, op. cit.*, pp. 176-177.

49 This move in Kierkegaard's career is, of course, related to his personal biography. The real inconsistency in Kierkegaard's thought, I submit, is between the position of *Fear and Trembling* and his mature view of the Christian faith. There is, for example, no way "the God-man," the Christian paradox can satisfy the temporal, concrete and finite needs of the contemporary believer. Kierkegaard's attempt to resolve this issue through memory fails, and reduces the Christian, whose life necessity is the Christian paradox to a form of the knight of resignation.

50 Solomon has traced the following changes in emphasis in Heidegger's work since *Being and Time*. "First, and most famously the discussion turns from a heavy emphasis on *Dasein* back to the problem of Being itself. (This since it was announced in *Sein und Zeit* that the investigation of *Dasein* was only a preliminary to the problem of Being.) Secondly, Heidegger's views on language and philosophy become increasingly radical: in *Sein und Zeit*, traditional language was insufficient; in later writings, only Greek is truly adequate to the task (for example in *What is Philosophy?*) and ultimately all conceptual language is incapable of grasping Being and Truth (for example in *What is Thinking?*) Philosophy moves from creating new ('ideal') languages to ancient Greek etymology to poetry to mysticism. Thirdly, there is the transi-

tion from the disclosure of Being as a function of human (*Dasein*) understanding to the reception of this disclosure of Being in a special non-conceptual insight. (Thus 'ontology', which plays so great a role in *Sein und Zeit*,
gradually fades in importance in later writings.)   Fourthly, there is an
increased emphasis on the role of *nothing* in the analysis of Being. This
notion of 'nothing' and the 'not' appears in *Sein und Zeit*, but becomes central to philosophy in the essay on Kant and in "What is Metaphysics?" With
this emphasis, an increased Kierkegaardian development of an attack on reason and logic occurs." Solomon, *op. cit.*, p. 233.

51   One of the peculiar ambivalences in Heidegger's later thought is his repudia-
tion of value theory on the grounds that values are the outcome of human
subjectivity, that is, values are "the objectifications of individual wants." This
position suggests the strange paradox that Heidegger has moved toward
objectivity in his later thought and thus much closer to the tradition he sees
himself dismantling in *Being and Time*. Cf. "Plato's Doctrine of Truth with a
Letter on Humanism," tr. J. Barlow & E. Lohner in *Philosophy in the Twentieth Century*, ed. H. Aiken & W. Barrett, Vol. II (Random House, N.Y.,
1962), pp. 292-293.

52   Heidegger, *Being and Time, op. cit.*, p. 32.

53   *Ibid.*, p. 33.

54   *Ibid.*, pp. 33-34.

55   *Ibid.*, p. 34.

56   Solomon, *op. cit.*, p. 199.

57   *Ibid.*, p. 200.

58   Calvin O. Schrag, "Phenomenology, Ontology, and History in the Philosophy
of Heidegger" in *Phenomenology*, ed. Joseph J. Kockelmans (Doubleday,
N.Y., 1967), pp. 288-289.

59   *Ibid.*, pp. 289-290.

60   *Ibid.*, p. 291.

61   Jean-Paul Sartre, "Existentialism is a Humanism," ed. W. Kaufmann, *loc. cit.*,
p. 289ff.

62   Heidegger, "Letter on Humanism," *loc. cit.*, p. 290; Cf. *Being and Time, op.
cit.*, p. 67.

63   *Being and Time, op. cit.*, pp. 67-69.

64 *Ibid.*, pp. 79-80.

65 *Ibid.*, pp. 81; 83.

66 Solomon, *op. cit.*, pp. 201; 202.

67 Peter L. Berger, *The Sacred Canopy* (Doubleday & Co., Garden City, N.Y., 1969), p. 11.

68 Solomon, *op. cit.*, pp. 202-203.

69 *Being and Time, op. cit.*, p. 85.

70 *Ibid.*, p. 86.

71 *Ibid.*, pp. 83-84.

72 *Ibid.*, pp. 88-89.

73 *Ibid.*, p. 95.

74 *Ibid.*, p. 95.

75 *Ibid.*, pp. 97-98.

76 *Ibid.*, p. 98.

77 *Ibid.*, p. 99.

78 *Ibid.*, p. 102.

79 *Ibid.*, p. 249.

80 *Ibid.*, pp. 103-105.

81 *Ibid.*, p. 105.

82 Solomon, *op. cit.*, p. 207.

83 *Ibid.*, pp. 207-208.

84 *Ibid.*, pp. 212-213.

85 *Being and Time, op. cit.*, p. 33.

86 *Ibid.*, p. 68.

87 *Ibid.*, p. 176.

88 *Ibid.*

89   *Ibid.*, p. 175.

90   *Ibid.*, p. 155.

91   *Ibid.*, p. 157.

92   *Ibid.*, p. 164.

93   Solomon, *op. cit.*, pp. 217-218.

94   *Being and Time, op. cit.*., p. 230.

95   *Ibid.*, p. 241.

96   *Ibid.*, p. 232.

97   Solomon, *op. cit.*, pp. 222-223.

98   *Being and Time, op. cit.*, p. 235.

99   Division Two of *Being and Time* is an analysis of "Dasein and Temporality." Dasein's character as *care* is here developed in terms of the three temporal modes of past, present, and future. Dasein's *facticity* is its past, its *fallenness* is its present and its *Existenz* is its projection into the future.

100 *Being and Time, op. cit.*, p. 289.

101 *Ibid.*, p. 294.

102 *Ibid.*, p. 304.

103 *Ibid.*, p. 307.

104 *Ibid.*, p. 308.

105 *Ibid.*

106 *Ibid.*, p. 309.

107 *Ibid.*

108 *Ibid.*, p. 309.

109 *Ibid.*, p. 310.

110 *Ibid.*, p. 263ff.

Part Three

1 Paul Tillich, *A History of Christian Thought, op. cit.*, pp. 539-541. Tillich also uses the schema: existentialism as point of view, protest and expression. *The Courage to Be, op. cit.*, p. 126ff.

2 Paul Tillich, *The Courage to Be, op. cit.*, p. 123ff.

3 *Ibid.*, pp. 124-125.

4 *Ibid.*, p. 127.

5 *Ibid.*; Cf. ST, I: 252ff.

6 *Ibid.*, p. 128.

7 *Ibid.*, pp. 129-130.

8 *Ibid.*, p. 131. It should be pointed out here that Tillich's conception of "the two lines" of development in modern philosophy corresponds to the distinction between the existentialist and non-existentialist points of view.

9 *Ibid.*, p. 133.

10 *Ibid.* p. 133. It is interesting to note that Tillich fails to mention a third element in Kant's thought, which is probably more decisive for the development of existentialism than the two mentioned, namely his emphasis upon the legitimate domain of practical reason and its postulates. Cf. F. Ferre, *A Basic Modern Philosophy of Religion* (Charles Scribners, N.Y., 1968), Chs. 8 and 9 for a critical analysis of Kant's view of practical reason and its influence on Kierkegaard and the subsequent course of existentialism itself.

11 "Neither Marx, nor Nietzsche, nor Kierkegaard, nor existentialism, nor the revolutionary movements, are understandable apart from seeing their direct or indirect dependence on Hegel. Even those who opposed him used his categories in their attacks on him. So Hegel is in some sense the center and the turning point, not of an inner-philosophical school or an inner-theological way of thinking about religion, but of a world-historical movement which has directly or indirectly influenced our whole century." *A History of Christian Thought, op. cit.*, p. 411.

12 *Ibid.*, p. 414.

13 *Ibid.*, p. 417-418.

14 *Ibid.*, p. 418.

15 *Theology of Culture, op. cit.*, p. 82.

16 *Ibid.*, pp. 82-83.

17 *A History of Christian Thought, op. cit.*, p. 427.

18 Cf. Robert P. Scharlemann, *Reflection and Doubt in the Thought of Paul Tillich* (Yale University Press, New Haven, 1969), pp. 184-186.

19 *A History of Christian Thought, op. cit.*, pp. 427-428.

20 *The Courage to Be, op. cit.*, p. 134.

21 *Ibid.*, pp. 133-135.

22 For a brief discussion of the historical context of Schelling's Berlin lectures, Cf. Walter Kaufmann, *Hegel: A Reinterpretation* (Anchor Books, Doubleday & Co., N.Y., 1966), pp. 288-290; 294-297. Kaufmann claims that Schelling, out of personal jealousy, developed a mere caricature of Hegel's thought in these lectures, thus contributing to a major misunderstanding of Hegel, which he (Kaufmann) is seeking to correct.

23 *A History of Christian Thought, op. cit.*, pp. 447-448.

24 *Ibid.*, p. 448.

25 *Theology of Culture, op. cit.*, p. 84.

26 *Ibid.*, pp. 77-78.

27 *Ibid.*, p. 79.

28 *The Courage to Be, op. cit.*, p. 139.

29 *Ibid.*, pp. 148-149.

30 *Ibid.*, pp. 149-150.

31 *Ibid.*, p. 150.

32 P. Tillich, "Existential Analyses and Religious Symbols," *Contemporary Problems in Religion*, H.A. Basilius, ed. (Wayne University Press, Detroit, 1956), pp. 38-39.

33 *Ibid.*, p. 40.

34 *Ibid.*, p. 41.

35 *The Courage to Be, op. cit.*, p. 154.

36 *Theology of Culture, op. cit.*, p. 105. Harvey Cox has offered a similar analysis of the sociology of existentialism. Cf. Harvey Cox, *The Secular City, op. cit.*, pp. 251ff. For a critique of Cox's thesis, Cf. Don Ihde, *"The Secular City* and The Existentialists," *Andover Newton Quarterly*, March, 1967, pp. 188-198.

37 *The Courage to Be, op. cit.*, pp. 146-147.

38 Cf. P. Tillich, *Morality and Beyond* (Harper, N.Y., 1963). p. 17ff.; Cf. also *My Search for Absolutes, op. cit.*, p. 92ff.

39 *The Courage to Be, op. cit.*, p. 151.

40 Marx's protest against objectification and dehumanization led to Marxism, "which had been conceived as a movement for the liberation of everyone," but which "has been transformed into a system of enslavement of everyone, even those who enslave the others." Nietzsche and Heidegger's conceptions of the courage to be as oneself have been transformed "into the Fascist-Nazi forms of neocollectivism," that is, "the totalitarian machines which these movements produced embodied almost everything against which the courage to be as oneself stands. They used all possible means in order to make such courage impossible." *Ibid.*, pp.152-153. Cf. also *Morality and Beyond, op. cit.*, pp. 80-81. Having sensitized men to the actual condition of human existence, Tillich implies that existentialism prepared the way for the creation of those totalitarian worlds which were desperate attempts to protect man from the very situation the existentialists describe.

41 *Theology of Culture, op. cit.*, p. 106.

42 *The Courage to Be, op. cit.*, p. 141.

43 *Theology of Culture, op. cit.*, p. 121.

44 *Ibid.*

45 *Ibid.*, p. 119.

46 *On the Boundary, op. cit.*, pp. 56-57.

47 P. Tillich, *The Religious Situation*, tr. H. Richard Niebuhr (Meridan Books, Inc., N.Y., 1956).

48 *Theology of Culture, op. cit.*, p. 49; Cf. ST III: 202-204.

49 "Existential Analyses and Religious Symbols," *op. cit.*, p. 44.

50 *Ibid.*, p. 48.

51 *Ibid.*, p. 49.

52 *Ibid.*

53 *Ibid.*, p. 52.

54 *Ibid.*, pp. 52-52.

55 *Ibid.*, pp. 53-54.

56 "In relation to creation, He is the creator, in relation to salvation, He is savior, in relation to fulfillment, He is the eternal." *Ibid.*, p. 54.

57 *Ibid.*

58 *Ibid.*, p. 55.

59 *A History of Christian Theology, op. cit.*, p. 541.

Chapter Eleven

The Relationship of Philosophy
and Theology:
An Evaluation of Tillich's Solution

In our exploration of Tillich's thought we have seen that the conceptual and methodological ideal which controlled his entire career was that of synthesis. Perhaps the most significant attempt at synthesis in Tillich's work is that between the classical philosophical and theological heritage and the contemporary world. The theologian, he insisted, must stand in history and move between past intellectual achievements and contemporary developments with both a "yes" and a "no." Thus, while Tillich had a profound appreciation for the classical tradition, he was not a "classicist" in the strict sense of the term; and while he participated fully in the *Weltanschauung* of 20th Century Western civilization, he refused to grant an unqualified affirmation to the assumptions and presuppositions of that *Weltanschauung*. On the one hand, he drew upon the insights of the classical tradition to criticize and interrogate the positivism of the scientific culture of the modern world and the revolt against the classical consensus found in such thinkers as Feuerbach, Marx, Freud, Neitzsche, Kierkegaard, Heidegger, Sartre, Whitehead, and the pragmatic-analytic tradition of Anglo-American philosophy. At the same time he drew upon that which he considered valid in these thinkers and movements to distinguish himself from a naive, uncritical relationship to classical thought.

It is his attempt to create a system of thought firmly rooted in the classical tradition and at the same time open to the intellectual currents of the modern world which accounts for the complexity and uniqueness of Tillich's achievement. However, it is this same attempt which raises the most serious questions as to the adequacy of Tillich's synthesis. Since Tillich, himself, recognized that every significant intellectual synthesis must undergo its own dissolution as the historical process moves against it and away from it, we are clearly within the orbit of his own spirit if we attempt to suggest the points at which Tillich's enterprise is at least questionable. We shall, of course, direct our attention to Tillich's resolution of the problem of the relationship between philosophy and theology.[1]

We have seen that Tillich's mature reflections drew him to conclude that the relationship between philosophy and theology is one of convergence and divergence, which is to say that the relationship is one of *complementarity* in that the integrity of neither discipline is encroached upon by the other and neither is completely dependent nor totally independent of the other. In this complementary relationship, however, philosophy is predominantly theoretical thinking and theology is predominantly existential thinking.

That theology is existential thinking is the basic reason for its divergence from philosophy, since the latter intends to be detached or objective thinking. Even though philosophy can never fully extricate itself from its existential basis, there is no doubt that for Tillich philosophy *does* and *should* seek such objectivity. Its ideal is the detached thinker. It is at this point that Tillich's understanding of philosophy raises a fundamental question, which we shall formulate thus: given that the existential component is an inescapable datum in the philosophical enterprise, the transcendence of which can only be approximately achieved in philosophical activity, and the presence of which is necessary if philosophy is to have power and historical significance, that is, if it is to be relevant to human life,[2] why should philosophy commit itself to the ideal of objectivity in the first place?

The question we are raising here does not rest upon the problem of the impossibility of fully achieving the ideal of objectivity. Ideals are useful even though they may not be fully realized in human conduct. Rather we are using the question to focus our attention upon the considerations which have been raised in our analysis of Kierkegaard and Heidegger, namely, that the classical tradition in its search for the absolute standpoint and that universal, necessary, eternal, and objective structure of truth, which is the highest, most significant truth open to man, has, in fact, perpetuated a subtle form of self-deception within Western man, which it is the task of authentic philosophy itself to overcome.

Whether or not one agrees with the existentialist tradition that the search for objective truth and the detached and disinterested epistemological stance it presupposes is a matter of self-deception, Tillich's understanding of philosophy is clearly within that historical consensus which the existentialists have challenged. As a result, we shall argue in what follows that rather than establishing the complementary relationship between philosophy and theology which Tillich claims, the contrary is the case in his thought, namely, that his conception of philosophy is determinative for his conception of theology and thus controls the theological task in the Tillichian system. We shall further argue that Tillich's claim that theology is existential thinking, which therefore distinguishes it from philosophy, is so ambiguous that it is, in effect, vacuous.

In examining the foundational notions of Tillich's thought in Part One of this study, we concluded that finitude and Tillich's resolution of the problem of finitude through the assertion of the unconditionedness of being-itself were among the constitutive notions of his thought. Both the classical and existentialist traditions place the reality of human finitude at the center of their analyses; however, these traditions diverge in their conceptions of the resolution of the problem of finitude. For the classical philosophical tradition in general, the problematic of man's finitude is resolved in relation to the eternal, universal and objective structure of being which man can imitate by seeking to divest himself as much as possible of his own particularity and concreteness.

Tillich shares this classical assumption. The ultimate, eternal, universal and objective truth in which all men share is being-itself, and being-itself is the unconditioned power through which the problematic of man's finitude is overcome. There can be no finite or existential truth for Tillich, which can paradoxically establish man's "eternal happiness" (Kierkegaard), authenticity (Heidegger) or salvation (Tillich). As we have seen in discussing the ontological categories, Tillich finds man "between" being and nonbeing. The categories express both positive and negative features of finitude, the reality that man "is" but that he is also subject to "non-being." The categories reveal that man requires a basic courage to affirm himself and maintain himself in spite of the threat of nonbeing. But, Tillich asks, how is this courage possible? "How can a being," for example,

> who is dependent on the casual nexus and its contingencies accept this dependence and, at the same time, attribute to himself a necessity and self-reliance which contradict this dependence (ST, I: 197)?

Or:

> Man attributes substantiality to something which proves ultimately to be accidental — a creative work, a love relation, a concrete situation, himself. This is . . . the courage of affirming the finite, of taking one's anxiety upon himself. The question is how such a courage is possible. How can a finite being, aware of the inescapable loss of substance, accept this loss (ST, I: 198)?

One can see the influence of existentialism in Tillich's analysis of the categories. As we have shown, for the early Kierkegaard and Heidegger, man does experience ultimacy in relation to a finite (accidental) reality, and he does this by becoming aware that the ultimate meaning of his life is finite (there is no self-deception), while passionately maintaining his relationship to that truth, including the anxiety which is an inevitable component of the relationship. The courage is possible for both Kierkegaard and Heidegger on the basis of a consciousness which has become lucid about itself and at the same time is grounded in a definitive experience of meaning, which if one does not appropriate, results in his losing his personal identity. In short the courage for such self-affirmation, when it is expressed, emerges out of man's own resources, activated by his finding himself between the realities of self-definition and self-possession or self-loss.

For Tillich, on the other hand, this is not an adequate under-standing of the source of such courage. The courage to be is rooted in being-itself. Tillich writes:

> Only because being-itself has the character of self-affirmation in spite of non-being is courage possible. Courage participates in the self-affirmation of being-itself, it participates in the power of being which prevails against non-being. . . . Man is not necessarily aware of this source. In situations of cyni-cism and indifference he is not aware of it. But it works in him as long as he maintains the courage to take this anxiety upon himself. In the act of the courage to be the power of being is effective in us, whether we recognize it or not. Every act of courage is a manifestation of the ground of being, however questionable the content of the act may be. The content may hide or distort true being, the courage in it reveals true being.[3]

There is, then, in the very foundational notions of Tillich's thought an ontological commitment, which in our view, clearly ties him to the classical tradition, a tradition which arose initially on Greek soil and which is mediated in Tillich's system through his understanding of philosophy and philosophical truth. This onto-logical commitment requires that the ultimate structure of meaning and reality, and thus that which is most "truthful" or the ultimate referent of truth, is universal, eternal, necessary, and essentially unchanging. It is because of this ontological commitment that Tillich can define philosophy as the objective search for this struc-ture of meaning, and it is this ontological commitment which becomes normative for his conception of theology, i.e., Tillich's philosophical orientation establishes the model of truth and reality in relation to which the theological enterprise is understood.

Even though Tillich struggled hard to open his predominantly classical vision to the modern critique of that vision as can be seen in his doctrine of fate, the ambiguity of the idea, the historical and decisional elements in all knowledge, the *Kairos*, and his insistence that there is an inescapable existential component in every philo-sophical system, in all philosophical truth, we are claiming that Tillich did not allow these notions to alter in any fundamental or substantial way the classical philosophical assumptions on the basis of which they were incorporated into his thought. Theology, too, is brought under the controlling power of his classical philosophical vision.

If only that which transcends finite being and its essential and existential modes can be a matter of ultimate concern and therefore the object of theology, it follows that, while God as being-itself is not a universal essence (ST, I: 236), yet every theological proposition, if it is true at all, must be universally true, because being-itself, the ground and aim of all finite being, is the universal structure of meaning and, therefore, the universal meaning (truth) of every theological statement. As we have seen from Tillich's earliest writings onward, theology, to have validity and relevance to human culture, must speak about that which is and should be the ultimate concern of all men everywhere, and it does so in propositions which must have universal validity.

The demand that theology must articulate universal and objective truth derives from Tillich's philosophical orientation. Philosophy achieves the ontological delineation of the structure of being through the philosophical concept, and while the concepts and categories must be continuously criticized and reformulated, that they have universal validity is, for Tillich, beyond question. Since the claims of theology cannot contradict the rational structure of mind and reality, and since rationality is grounded in the *Logos* structure of self and world, which means that in which all men share (hence, the rational is intersubjective, thus objective and therefore capable of articulation through the universality of philosophical language), the truth of theology must conform to the criterion of universality as a constitutive element in the conception of rationality itself.

One can see Tillich executing the theological task in terms of the demands of the classical philosophical conception of the universality of truth in every part of the theological system. The doctrine of God is worked out in relation to the concept of being: the doctrine of the Christ is worked out as the universal power of being, fully present in a concrete life, which restores man fragmentarily under the conditions of existence to his essential nature; the doctrine of the Spirit is worked out as the universal process of the divine life overcoming the ambiguities of finite life; and the doctrine of the

Kingdom of God is worked out as the universal process of the divine life overcoming the ambiguities of historical existence and achieving the ultimate "essentialization" of man at the "end" of history. For Tillich, as John Cooper[4] has pointed out, there are universal principles of meaning, an objective reality, behind the words "being," "God," "the Christ," "Spirit," and "the Kingdom of God," which bestow upon the theological symbols their universal validity.

In discussing, for example, the theology of the early Christian apologist, Justin Martyr, Tillich states:

Justin taught that this Christian philosophy is universal; it is the all-embracing truth about the meaning of existence. From this it follows that whatever truth appears, it belongs to the Christians. Truth concerning existence, wherever it appears, is Christian truth. . . . This is not sheer arrogance. He does not mean Christians now possess all the truth, or that they alone discovered it. He means, in terms of the Logos doctrine, that there cannot be truth anywhere which is not in principle included in Christian truth. . . . Justin said what I think is absolutely necessary to say. If anywhere in the world there were an existential truth which could not be received by Christianity as an element of its own thinking, Jesus would not be the Christ. He would be merely one teacher alongside other teachers, all of whom are limited and partly in error. But that is not what the early Christians said. They said — and we should say — that if we call Jesus the Christ, or the Logos as the apologists called him, this means that by definition there cannot be any truth which cannot in principle be taken into Christianity. . . . [This] mean[s] that the fundamental truth which has appeared in [Jesus as the Christ or Logos] is essentially universal, and therefore can take in every other truth.[5]

As final revelation:

The revelation in Jesus as the Christ, is universally valid, because it includes the criterion of every revelation and is the *finis* or *telos* (intrinsic aim) of all of them. The final revelation is the criterion of every religion and of every culture, not only of the culture and religion in and through which it has appeared. It is valid for the social existence of every human group and for the personal existence of every human individual. It is valid for mankind as such, and, in an indescribable way, it has meaning for the universe also. Nothing less than this should be asserted by Christian theology (ST, I: 137).

Christian theology can claim to be based upon final revelation, and as we have seen, can claim for itself the status of *the* theology, i.e., the completion of all forms of theology, because it is grounded in the *Logos*, which does not mean for Tillich, an abstract principle of meaning exemplified in the particulars, but rather the universal in the concrete. Thus, that upon which Christian theology is based is the "concrete universal," which is at once the most universal and the most concrete of meanings.

It is not our intention here to analyze the internal consistency of Tillich's conceptions of universality and concreteness, the *Logos*, or his Christological assertions. Rather we wish to make the point, again, that theology, in his understanding, must be based upon universal and objective truth, even though the concreteness of the personal life of Jesus makes an existential relationship to the universal truth of Christian theology necessary. The universality of the truth of Jesus as the Christ is an ontological requirement, which in turn is construed on the basis of the classical philosophical tradition in which not only the *structure of being* can be specified in universal concepts and categories, but that the *truth* (i.e., that which true propositions delineate as well as what is given in true propositions) in which the structure of being is grounded must itself be universal. Tillich's theology clearly conforms to the ontological demands mediated through his understanding of philosophical truth.[6]

Granted that theology is based upon universal and objective truth, and that its own statements have, for Tillich, universal validity, this does not, in itself, confirm the claim made above that Tillich's conception of philosophy controls his conception of theology. Tillich has claimed that there is a divergence between philosophy and theology precisely because theology is predominantly existential thinking while philosophy is predominantly theoretical, or one might say, essentialist thinking. Is not this claim carried through within the structure of Tillich's theology such that it clearly vitiates the thesis asserted above that theology is subordinated to and modeled after Tillilch's conception of philosophical truth? We must now examine this problem in detail.

It will be helpful to attempt to summarize the meanings Tillich attributes to the words "existential thinking." Existential thinking, first, is *involved* thinking. The existential thinker is *concerned* personally with that about which he thinks. In the case of the theological thinker, his concern or involvement is ultimate, i.e., that about which he thinks is a matter of life and death, being or not being. The theologian risks the meaning of his existence upon that about which he thinks: the object of his thought *matters* to him; he cannot be indifferent or detached toward it.

The second meaning of existential thinking is that it is intrinsically circular thinking, i.e., one cannot "establish" the validity of the object of existential thinking apart from one's being grasped by it, and one's being grasped by it means that it then becomes normative for one's thought. In relation to the question of final revelation Tillich says:

> In accord with the circular character of systematic theology, the criterion of final revelation is derived from what Christianity considers to be the final revelation, the appearance of Jesus as the Christ. Theologians should not be afraid to admit this circle. It is not a shortcoming; rather it is the necessary expression of the existential character of theology (ST, I: 135).

Existential thinking proceeds from a foundation which it does not establish but presupposes. This is why, for Tillich, all knowledge of God is existential knowledge, since "God is the presupposition of the question of God," and that which concerns man ultimately.

The existential thinker, thirdly, "participates," through his own existence in that which he knows. Consequently, existential knowledge strives for a kind of "communion" with that which is known in which the knower "shares" in the reality of the known and thus his own existence is qualified by that which is known. In seeking to participate in that which he knows, the existential thinker seeks to overcome the separation between himself and the known and seeks further, in knowing the "other," to transcend the "objectification" of the other in "controlling knowledge." Controlling knowledge essentially objectifies the other, requiring the knower to assume the attitude of detached observation. The existential thinker, therefore, seeks those notions which are minimally "objectivating"; hence, the use of psychological notions with ontological significance in existentialist thought.[7] Existential knowledge is clearly in contrast with controlling knowledge, with science as the most pure example of the latter.

Theology is existential thinking insofar as the existence of the theologian is involved with the Christian message, insofar as he stands within the theological circle, and insofar as he participates within the meaning of the Christian truth with his whole being. These are the criteria which distinguish theology as existential thinking from philosophy.

Existential thinking, however, is identifiable on the basis of one further feature, which has been fulfilled in existentialism, namely, its analysis of human existence as it has been actualized in time and space in contrast with the essential being of man. Theology, because it must interpret the meaning of the Christian symbols to the existential predicament of man, needs the analysis of existentialism, and consequently, it does not necessarily carry out this analysis itself. This has been done for it by existentialism. Theology, then, is *existential* thinking in the senses described above, but it is not *existentialist* thinking. Theology cannot dispense with an essentialist ontology. In commenting upon Kierkegaard as a theologian, Tillich states:

> With respect to the content [of theology] we must say that not much can be found of it in Kierkegaard. He was not a constructive theologian, and he could not be, because one can be a constructive theologian only if he is not only existentially interested and passionate, but also has an essentialist vision of the structure of reality. Without this, systematic theology is impossible.[8]

Tillich's claim, then, is that theology is existential-essential thinking and philosophy is essential-existential thinking. In theology, the existential component is predominant and in philosophy the essentialist component is predominant. However, theology cannot dispense with essentialist thinking and maintain its identity as constructive or systematic theology, and philosophy cannot dispense with the existential component and remain vital and relevant to human life. A distinction between theology and philosophy is possible on the basis of the emphasis given by the two disciplines to these polar components in all thought. However, the distinction is a relative one only.

At the risk of oversimplifying we will assert that what Tillich means basically by theology as existential thinking is its concern to relate the essential truth of the Christian message to the structure of human existence and the concerns which emerge from that structure. The existential significance of the truth of the Christian faith is that it is *saving* truth, i.e., it contains the answers to the questions of human existence; however, it is saving truth because it is concrete-universal or existential-essential, where both "concrete" and "existential" mean not "fallen from essential being," as they ordinarily do in Tillich's system, but rather essential truth manifest within the concrete and the existential, i.e., in a personal life. The ultimate truth of the Christian message, essential God-manhood, is an exception to the universality of Tillich's ontological categories, for there is one human life in which existence was not separated from nor a distortion of essential being.

One of the basic meanings of Tillich's claim that philosophy is predominantly essentialist thinking is that the philosopher can seek to conceptualize the essential structure of reality without being concerned to show how his vision relates to his own existential concerns or those of other human persons. He may even achieve a theory of man and his place in the cosmos and be utterly indifferent to the question of the way it meets man's most urgent existential needs. In fact, as we have seen, in Tillich's view the more detached he is from this question the more successful he is as philosopher *qua* philosopher.

Apart from this basic content it is difficult to distinguish theology from philosophy with the criteria Tillich uses to define theology as existential thinking. Let us consider this problem in more detail.

Given Tillich's understanding of knowledge, it is impossible for the philosopher, as he admits, to be totally uninvolved in that about which he thinks, or what is the same thing, to eliminate his existence from his thought project. If the philosopher, for example, accepts the task of becoming as objective as possible, he becomes existentially *involved* in that task and therefore *decides* not to admit into his search for truth a rich and complex field of subjectivity. In other words, his involvement is precisely to remove his own involvement with the object he seeks to know. However, there are profound existential motivations which have led to the model of truth as objectivity and the concomitant detachment of the objective knower. As Michael Gelven has written:

> Logic, for example, ultimately presupposes the disposition of the logician to attend only to the formal concepts and relations of propositions. Logic further presupposes the willingness of the logician to sacrifice the wealth of probable knowledge for the paucity of certain knowledge, because one of the ways in which a man exists is to long for the assurance of certainty in *some* of his knowledge. Would logic be of any value unless it carried with it the assurance of *a priori* and necessary inference? It seems not. Therefore, the interest of those who develop logic itself *determines* to some extent what it is that logic is going to be.[9]

Since on Tillich's own terms the existence of the philosopher inescapably intrudes, to some extent, upon his project of achieving the *Bios Theoretikos*, then it cannot be the case that the theologian is involved in his thought and the philosopher is not; rather Tillich is pointing to the relative degrees of involvement of the two types of thinkers. But on what grounds can Tillich say that the theologian is more involved than the philosopher in that about which he thinks? Is not the philosopher's involvement in excluding the existential needs of the knower from that which is known as radical and ultimate as the theologian's involvement in relating his truth to the structure of human existence?

The answer to this question in Tillich's analysis seems to be that involvement is correlated with *two* types of truth, the objective philosophical truth of being as it is in itself and the personal, saving truth of the meaning of being for us, which theology explicates. The theologian is more involved because his whole sense of meaning and identity is posited in the truth he thinks about, whereas the ultimate meaning of the philosopher's existence is not posited in the philosophical truth he achieves (ST, I: 22-23). The philosophical *eros*, the philosopher's passion, is for objective, non-soteriological truth; the theologian's passion and love is for personal, soteriological truth. These two types of truth account for the degree of existential involvement in the philosopher and the theologian.

The question we are raising, given Tillich's epistemology and his conception of ultimate concern, is whether it is meaningful and consistent for him to make this distinction in terms of involvement, and if it is not, can involvement be a meaningful criterion by which theology is distinguished from philosophy on the ground that it is in principle existential thinking, while philosophy in principle is not?

Every profound philosophy, for Tillich, is an expression of ultimate concern, because the philosopher sees himself serving the ultimate truth about the world, at least as it is given to philosophical inquiry. Thus, while he may not be "saved" by the truth he knows, his existential involvement itself in the search for truth is not thereby diminished, unless Tillich is prepared to say that involvement in the pure sense is possible only with the truth of the Christian message. If Tillich were to say that, his whole conception of ultimate concern would be disqualified, since he explicitly admits that men can have idolatrous ultimate concerns, i.e., that they can be ultimately concerned about that which is not ultimate.

Now the philosopher may deny his existential involvement with the truth he seeks, (he *intends* not to be a theologian) or he may not be aware of it, but for Tillich's notion of ultimate concern to work every human enterprise is implicated in a context of ultimacy which becomes explicit upon analysis. This means that the stance a man takes toward himself and the world involves him inevitably in an existential commitment (faith commitment) which is *logically* ultimate in the senses that (1) the person whose commitment it is believes it to be the most adequate of the options available and thus (2) it excludes other options, thus committing the person to a decisive position in which the ultimate meaning of his own existence is included. These are adequate grounds for establishing logically the full existential involvement of the person in the sense that, for him the ultimate meaning of his life is posited in whatever decision about himself he makes. He may be ultimately committed to the wrong structure of meaning; he may be unaware of his existential involvement or wish to exclude it or deny it, but it does not follow that he is not fully involved, as fully involved as any existential commitment presupposes.

Suppose a philosopher were to say that that which he knows philosophically has nothing to do with his life. Then on Tillich's terms he is ultimately committed to, what is for him, the ultimate presupposition that philosophical truth and human life have nothing to do with each other, and he has risked at least the ultimate meaning of himself as philosopher upon this proposition, and the meaning of his existence upon the claim that his life cannot be illuminated by philosophical knowledge. He is fully involved (committed) existentially to that truth. At this one point in his existence as a philosopher it becomes a matter of ultimate concern to maintain and defend his view against all counterviews, and in that one point in his existence he is fully involved existentially in the decision he has made, just as involved, we are asserting, as the theologian who asserts the meaning of existence in the truth that Jesus is the Christ. By extension, any philosophical commitment involves the philosopher existentially.

We are not questioning here the validity of Tillich's distinction between two types of truth. What we are challenging is his attempt to distinguish theology as existential thinking from philosophy through the criterion of involvement, for it turns out on Tillich's own terms that the philosopher is as fully involved existentially in his thought project as is the theologian, unless Tillich means by involvement *only* that relationship which the Christian sustains to Christian truth. If he does not mean that, and there is convincing evidence in his thought that he does not, then, as we have seen, the criterion of involvement by which theology as existential thinking is distinguished from philosophy breaks down.

If Tillich's conception of ultimate concern is to be consistently employed, he cannot avoid this problem by insisting that this is a relative distinction only and that as a relative distinction he means merely that the theologian is *more* involved than the philosopher. This will not do because the notion of ultimate concern asserts that we can push any philosophical commitment to its foundational assumptions, thus disclosing the ultimate commitment of the philosopher. At best the criterion of involvement asserts that the theologian may be more conscious than his philosophical counterpart of his existential commitment, but it does not follow that a *formal* distinction between philosophy and theology can be made on the basis of an ontical state of affairs within the thinker.

The criterion of circularity is also employed by Tillich to distinguish theology as existential thinking from philosophy. The theologian stands in and thinks from the "theological circle," which is to say that he is brought into the circle of the concrete *Logos* through "believing commitment" and not through "rational detachment," which is the stance in which the philosopher receives the universal *Logos* (ST, I: 24).

When one examines Tillich's claims that existential thinking is circular and that theology is distinguished from philosophy by virtue of the theologian's thought project proceeding from believing commitment rather than rational detachment, again it is seen that we are dealing with a relative distinction between philosophy and theology, because all great philosophies, for Tillich, arise from an awareness of that which can be neither inductively nor deductively established nor confirmed nor denied by any purely scientific or empirical pattern of verification. A comprehensive philosophical vision of the essential structure of reality emerges, for Tillich, from an ultimate certainty given in the structure of reason itself (the identity of thought and being), the certainty of which is given because it is the presupposition of cognition and not its result. As we have seen, Tillich calls this the "mystical a priori."

The philosophies of naturalism and idealism, Tillich asserts:

differ very little in their starting point when they develop theological concepts. Both are dependent on a point of identity between the experiencing subject and the ultimate which appears in religious experience or in the experience of the world as "religious." The theological concepts of both idealists and naturalists are rooted in a 'mystical a priori,' an awareness of something that transcends the cleavage between subject and object. And if in the course of a 'scientific' procedure this a priori is discovered, its discovery is possible only because it was present from the very beginning. This is the circle which no religious philosopher can escape. And it is by no means a vicious one. Every understanding of spiritual things (*Geisteswissenschaft*) is circular (ST, I: 9).

Tillich also sees that the great philosophical systems of the past endure because they have the power to draw out of man a response to their meaning, which is efficacious beyond their empirical or rational verification (ST, I: 105). They have the capacity to grasp men's minds on the intuitive level because they point to that which is beyond dispute in human consciousness whenever men reflect upon their experience, and they became normative for thought because the mind is first grasped by their intuitive certitude. Thus, the truth of philosophical systems is "existential" to the extent that they compel human assent beyond the level of the strict cannons of evidence and verification by illuminating the structure of human existence, and thus philosophical thinking is circular to the extent that the ultimate ground in relation to which philosophical inquiry is possible is not established by philosophical reason, but rather philosophical reason presupposes it.

Theology, however, is the definitive paradigm of circular thinking, because it adds to the mystical a priori (in which it too is grounded) the criterion of the theological message, which criterion establishes its identity as systematic theology and consequently becomes normative for its thinking. The circularity of theology thus further establishes its character as existential thinking. The argument, then, would seem to be that there is an existential component in philosophy as seen in its circularity, but theology is *more* existential because it is grounded in the concrete content of the Christian message, which adds to the circularity of the mystical a priori the even more radical circularity of the concrete-universal truth of the Christian faith.

The question is: what makes the concrete-universal truth of the Christian faith "more" circular than the circularity of the mystical a priori such that a distinction between theology and philosophy can be drawn on this basis and theology established as "more" existential than philosophy? The answer seems to be that the theologian is committed to a truth which cannot be "proved" logically or empirically (including historically) and its very concreteness demands that the theologian do his thinking within a radically more delimited context than the philosopher; at the same time the theologian's commitment to this truth is more "final" than the philosopher's commitment to a particular perspective, since philosophical truth has an "open, infinite, and changeable character" (ST, I: 23). It would seem that since the universal *Logos* is inexhaustible in meaning the philosopher is free to abandon those specific conceptualities to which he may have been committed in his theoretical task when he becomes convinced that they are no longer adequate; however, the theologian cannot abandon the central symbols in which Christian truth is expressed, especially the symbol of Jesus as the Christ, and remain a Christian theologian. He is free to be critical of these symbols and to reinterpret them, but as long as he stands within the theological circle, he cannot abandon them.

The conclusion of our analysis of the criterion of involvement by which theology is identified as existential thinking and distinguished from philosophy was that the "existential" element in Tillich's thought makes the philosopher as involved as the theologian in that about which he thinks thus undercutting the meaning of the distinction. In regard to the criterion of circularity, we shall argue that it is precisely the classical element in Tillich's thought which renders this notion meaningless as a distinction between philosophy and theology, again seriously qualifying Tillich's claim that theology is existential thinking.

We shall base our argument upon the following considerations: if the universal *Logos* is the manifestation of being-itself within the rational structure of mind and reality (thus making philosophy possible) as well as within the personal life of Jesus of Nazareth (thus making theology possible), and if being-itself is the presupposition of thought and not its consequent, then it follows that both philosophy and theology are equally circular insofar as the foundation of their enterprises are concerned. Secondly, if the concrete *logos* upon which Christian theology is based is itself universally valid and if its universal validity means that, as Tillich asserts, there can be no existential truth that is incompatible with it, than the very inclusiveness of the Christian truth makes the theologian's commitment as "open" as the philosopher's, since no amount of evidence could require the theologian to abandon his commitment. Tillich cannot define the theological circle as a more existential response from the theologian, if the circumference of the circle does not, in fact, exclude competing perspectives from the theologian's truth claims. We conclude again that, given the classical assumptions of Tillich's thought, his attempt to establish the existential character of theology and distinguish it from philosophy as predominantly existential thinking fails.

The ontological polarity of individualization and participation expresses itself in human knowledge. Individualization expresses itself in the separation of subject from object and accounts for the emergence of technical reason from ontological reason and the controlling knowledge of technical reason. As we said science is, for Tillich, the paradigm of technical reason and controlling knowledge. The ambiguity of this kind of knowledge under the conditions of existence is that it tends to deprive the object known of its "subjectivity," completely "objectifying" it. Controlling knowledge demands the detachment of the knower from the known; consequently, this necessary detachment can lead to the "estrangement" of knower from that which is known and thus the complete disregard of the subjectivity of the object by the knowing subject (ST, I: 97ff).

The polar ontological element of participation accounts for the component of union in knowledge. It asserts that just as there is an essential identity between thought and being so there is an essential identity or unity between subject and object. It is the component of union in the epistemological situation which makes "receiving knowledge" possible. In receiving knowledge the element of separation and the stance of cognitive detachment is reduced (it is not removed, since all knowledge is a dialectical relationship in which separation and union are always present in varying degrees), and the knower "participates" in that which is known. "Receiving knowledge," says Tillich, "takes the object into itself, into union with the subject" (ST, I: 98).

From the pole of individualization, then, comes separation and the cognitive stance of detachment. From the pole of participation comes union and the cognitive stance of involvement. Thus, existential knowledge arises from participation, union, and involvement. Theology is existential thinking (even though the theologian becomes detached toward all concrete expressions of his ultimate concern), science is non-existential thinking (stressing cognitive detachment in a pure way), while philosophy unites both existential and nonexistential elements in its cognitive attitude (ST, II: 26). It *intends* to be non-existential thinking, but it is a mixture of existential passion (union) and rational detachment (separation); thus, it is possible to distinguish theology and philosophy as existential and non-existential thinking in a relative way, using in this case the criterion of participation by which theology as existential thinking is identified and distinguished from philosophy; however, it is quite difficult if not impossible to know how to distinguish what Tillich means by participation and what he means by involvement. At best perhaps one can say that involvement refers to the impact of the object upon the existence of the subject while participation refers to the subject's desire to know the object in such a way that the "essence" of the object is not violated nor distorted by the conceptuality one uses to know it. As an ontological element, however, participation refers to the essential unity between subject and object, knower and known, which obtains for both controlling and receiving knowledge and for both theology and philosophy.

Let us say then that existential knowledge as participation *intends* not to objectify that which it knows. Theology as existential thinking intends not to objectify its object (it denies that God is *a* being or that he exists), but it inevitably does so if it is to make any cognitive claims at all. Tillich does not want to say, however, that philosophy *intends* to objectify that which it knows. This is his claim regarding the scientific enterprise. Certainly, the philosopher seeks that cognitive distance by which he can know objectively, but he seeks precisely those concepts and categories which adequately describe the essence of things. The philosopher, too, seeks to participate in that which he knows, i.e., he seeks to penetrate to the essence of the known and he inevitably allows the known to penetrate his own existence (note the classical philosopher's desire to become universal by knowing the universal.) If it were the case that philosophy *intentionally* does distort that about which it thinks, then Tillich would be much more hard-pressed to show why theology should use philosophical categories in its interpretation of the Christian message. In fact, it would seem that to say that God is being-itself (both a philosophical and a theological statement) is far less objectifying than to say that God is "heavenly father," "shepherd," or "creator of the world."

Tillich may be asserting that all reality is intrinsically distorted by the objectification of thought, but in insisting that theology is a form of thought, carried out in correlation with philosophy, and that the theologian, in order to theologize, must exercise rational detachment toward the concrete expressions of ultimate concern to show the universal validity of the Christian message, he has implicated theology as much as philosophy in such cognitive distortions. It becomes difficult, in the face of these considerations, to know how to distinguish theology from philosophy using the criterion of existential thinking as participation.

In terms of the three criteria by which Tillich identifies theology as existential thinking and thereby distinguishes it from philosophy, our argument has reached the following conclusions: (1) that the basic distinction between philosophy and theology based upon the claim that theology is existential thinking while philosophy is non-existential thinking is a relative rather than an absolute distinction, because both disciplines include within themselves existential and essential components.

Thus what Tillich's claim comes to, in the final analysis, is that a distinction between the two disciplines, at the level of their basic cognitive attitudes, is possible on the basis of their *intentions*: theology intends to be existential thinking while philosophy intends to be non-existential thinking; however, these intentions cannot be consistently carried out in either discipline, because as *thought* theology must conform to the demands of ontological reason and the structure of cognition, i.e., it must express its truth in objective, universal and essentialist terms.

The theologian, then, must exercise the rational detachment characteristic of philosophy to accomplish this task; and because philosophy originates within human existence, it cannot fully extricate itself from the existential concerns of the philosopher nor can it pursue its essentialist vision independently of the question of its relation to the structure of existence without losing its profundity and relevance to human life; (2) that if one tries to give this distinction meaning in relation to the structure of the two disciplines, i.e., beyond the intention of either the theologian or the philosopher, the very attempt to include both existential and essential components within the two disciplines renders this meaning highly problematic even as a relative distinction, and (3) that consequently a serious question emerges as to the existential character of theology if the theologian cannot carry out his intention to be an existential thinker in a way that is *distinctively* in contrast with the way the philosopher carries out his task.

As Tillich's analysis stands the philosopher's thinking is no less involved, circular or participatory than the theologian's and the theologian's thought is no less essentialist than the philosopher's. The distinction, we conclude, rests upon a possibility alone (the intention of the thinker), but cannot be supported in actuality, i.e., in the actual character of the two disciplines.

It is clear that for Tillich existential thinking is not in opposition to or incompatible with essentialist thinking. Existential thinking is present, for Tillich, throughout the history of philosophy wherever philosophers have sought to relate philosophical truth to the concrete issues of human existence. On this criterion, Plato was, as Tillich points out, an outstanding existential philosopher. In fact, Michael Gelven, commenting upon Heidegger's relationship to Plato, says:

> ... among all the great thinkers, Plato is unique in relating the problems of the individual human being to the immensely speculative reaches of abstract metaphysics. ... Plato's theory of Forms arose out of such immediately existential needs as love, death, and justice. It may well be that Heidegger wishes to achieve a similar kind of unity between his own ontological description and the immediate and existential awareness of everyday life. Perhaps no thinker

since Plato has relied for his metaphysics (sic) so heavily upon the concerns of
the individual man as Heidegger does n *Being and Time*.[10]

As we have seen, however, it is not *necessary* for philosophy
explicitly to relate its essentialist vision to the immediate existential
concerns of man. But the fourth criterion by which Tillich identifies theology as existential thinking is that it *must* relate the universal truth of its own essential vision to the profound and urgent
questions of human existence. The method of correlation requires
this; in fact, this is theology's reason for being. Theology as a cognitive enterprise is existentially relevant, because the truth in which
it is grounded is the ultimate answer to the questions of existence.

Existentialism as a philosophy, for Tillich, takes as its explicit
task the analysis of existence. Theology, as existential thinking,
therefore, uses the analysis of existentialism in its task of relating
the truth of the Christian message to the existential questions of
man, but it does so only after it has criticized existentialism both
philosophically and theologically.

If the three criteria discussed above ultimately fail to establish
the identity of theology as existential thinking and to distinguish
theology from philosophy as a distinctive way of thinking, then the
question emerges as to whether Tillich has been able to establish a
more secure basis by which to distinguish the two disciplines in this
fourth criterion. Theology cannot repudiate essentialist thinking,
but unlike philosophy, it *must* relate its essential truth to man's
existential questions. This criterion, however, has the consequences of making all thought existential (including Plato and
Hegel) if it seeks to relate its cognitive inquiries to existential concerns. Thus, the demand that the philosopher seek objective truth
does not, for Tillich, in principle, *exclude* his relating that truth to
existence, but neither is he under the demand that he do so. The
extent that he does so, however, is the extent to which his thought
may be characterized as existential thinking. Obviously, this criterion is no more decisive than the others in distinguishing theology
from philosophy, since philosophical truth (knowledge of being) is
profoundly relevant to human existence and there are neither cognitive nor methodological constraints on relating that truth to exis-

tence. If the philosopher chooses to undertake this task, his thought is as existential as theology, even though his truth may not have the efficacy to heal the human spirit as does theology's. This latter consideration, however, is a distinction in the nature of truth and not in the character of the disciplines of philosophy and theology. What, then, does it mean for Tillich to say that theology is existential thinking and philosophy is nonexistential thinking?

The difficulty with giving decisive content to Tillich's claim such that a *real* distinction between philosophy and theology is possible on the basis of this claim is that Tillich's conception of theology is determined by his classical understanding of philosophy, and, therefore, he attempts to appropriate the existentialist revolution into the structure of his thought without fundamentally rethinking the classical assumptions upon which his thought is based. He thereby removes what is distinctive about existential thinking as it was formulated in the existentialist movement, extrapolating from that movement some general criteria which apply, upon analysis, as equally to philosophy as they do to theology. We shall draw this essay to a close by briefly developing this assertion.

We have argued, in our discussion of Kierkegaard and Heidegger, that what is *distinctive* in the existentialist movement is the attempt to achieve a "new" conception of truth, which has explicit implications for the nature of the philosophical task. Both Kierkegaard and Heidegger assert that existence is the *source* of truth and therefore the source of philosophical inquiry and that philosophy itself is existential in its very essence. Thus, both thinkers consider the efforts of philosophers to "transcend" their existence toward objective truth a tragically self-deceiving and cowardice enterprise. Philosophy should not even *intend* to be nonexistential thinking, because on their terms, such an attempt is impossible, i.e., the project of becoming objective is itself an existential undertaking; it is one of the ways a person may exist; consequently, so-called objective truth is a derivative from a more fundamental structure, that is, the truth of existence itself. Furthermore, objective truth (which is for both thinkers clearly possible, although for Kierkegaard it is possible only for God) is neither the most fundamental nor the most significant truth open to man, and putting the matter rather simply, since philosophy historically has pursued that which it thought most fundamental and most significant, it should under no circumstances compromise or abandon its existential calling, even though to pursue its calling it does have to abandon certain traditional definitions of itself and the "object" it seeks.

Heidegger's development of the Kierkegaardian revolution has shown that the existentialist movement does not construe existential truth as mere "subjectivism." Truth is not whatever one happens to believe or wants to believe. Further, we have argued that Heidegger has overcome the inconsistencies in Kierkegaard's view by showing that fundamental ontology is possible and that the ontological analysis of human existence is universal, objective, and necessary (its results are applicable to all men, they are not merely "personal," idiosyncratic or autobiographical, and they disclose the conditions which are intrinsic to what it means to be); however, what is unique in Heidegger's ontology (shaped as it is by Kierkegaard's insights) is (1) it is self-consciously rooted in the existential need of man to know who he is and thus it establishes the radical priority and circularity of existence as the presupposition of all thought and (2) it establishes through the very rationality and universal objectivity of its analysis how a finite, personal, subjective truth is ontologically *possible* on the one hand and how such truth is *necessary* for the individuation and integration of personal existence on the other.

It is this truth which arises from the finitude of being itself and which is not universal, objective, or eternal, but rather radically personal (unique for the person whose truth it is), radically subjective (it is the truth which defines, beyond the definition of existence given in ontological terms, the *meaning* and *identity* of the individual; it is therefore *ontic* or *existentielle*), radically temporal (it can change as the individual changes and it will pass out of existence with his death), and it has an existential priority over the universal and objective truth of ontological analysis (philosophy); therefore, it cannot be given to the individual by philosophy, but is rather a matter of personal decision (freedom), even though philosophy, remaining faithful to its existential calling, may *prepare* one to receive this truth by enhancing one's awareness of one's self as existing.

The Kierkegaardian-Heideggerian revolution in philosophy, then, as it was formulated in Kierkegaard's early writings and developed by Heidegger (as well as others) moves around two basic assertions, which cut it off from the classical tradition (with which it is to some extent continuous), and we shall assert, it is these two considerations which define, in the rigorous sense, the meaning of existentialist thinking.

The first assertion is as Heidegger has developed it in *Being and Time*, that "Being is finite." This is obviously not a new insight in the history of Western philosophy; however, the existentialist movement does not work within the classical ontology in which the finite is contrasted with the infinite order of being, the contingent with the necessary, the relative with the absolute, the temporal with the eternal, the mutable with the immutable, the ultimately unreal with the ultimately real. It does not attempt to refute the classical vision that "beyond" the contingency, relativity, and ultimate impermanence of the finite world there is the ontological order of perfection characterized as absolute, permanent, and eternal, in relation to which the finite world is ultimately meaningful; rather it asserts that *if* such an order of eternal truth exists, it cannot be the source of man's authentic existence of "eternal happiness," because man is *essentially* temporal and concrete and he can be "healed" only by that truth which itself is *essentially* temporal and concrete.

This affirmation of the finitude of human existence means that philosophy must abandon all attempts to construct a theory of knowledge and a theory of ultimate human felicity based upon the "divine perspective."

Gelven's analysis of Heidegger's relationship to Nietzsche captures this assertion well:

> In the works of Friedrich Nietzsche we find another step in the attempt to explain the transcendental perspective of philosophy. In one of the most

troublesome and exciting works in all philosophy, *Thus Spoke Zarathustra*, Nietzsche argues that the transcendental perspective necessary to philosophy and indeed to a worthwhile existence can no longer be the *infinite* perspective taken by previous thinkers, for "God is dead," having been murdered by "the people." In a rather dramatic style that offends the more refined and cautious, Nietzsche nonetheless hammers home his central point: The over-man is finite. Having "killed God," man no longer could either believe in Him as the source of values and hence the perspective of philosophy, or even imagine Him under such pseudonyms as the Absolute Spirit or History. Nietzsche's insistence upon the finitude of philosophical perspective did not keep him from uttering very absolutistic and even eternal claims: e.g., his theory of the eternal recurrence of the same. Nietzsche's point, then, is not that there can be no logical possibility of infinity, but that the values and functions of human activity and reason cannot be formulated from an infinite and hence "other" perspective. Transcendence is still necessary; but the stepping beyond is *not* from the finite human perspective to the infinite of God, but from the finite perspective of man to the still finite but transcendent view of the overman . . .

Heidegger was much influenced by Nietzsche, and although he did not follow the latter's exorbitant use of language, nor his focus on value, he did follow Nietzsche in establishing the basis of transcendence in finite man. Indeed, Heidegger goes further than Nietzsche by arguing that the very ontological ground of transcendence is man's finitude.[11]

No doubt Tillich would agree with Heidegger that the capacity for and the drive toward transcendence is based upon man's finitude. Where they disagree, however, is in the existentialist's claim that the content of transcendence is also finite. For Tillich man transcends himself toward that which is infinite and eternal, being-itself, whereas for early Kierkegaard, Nietzsche, and the early Heidegger man transcends himself by relating passionately and lucidly to the predicament his own finitude imposes upon him through affirming a finite structure of meaning in which he establishes his identity, exercises his courage and integrity, and takes full responsibility for himself as "finite freedom" (Tillich), i.e., one who defines his ultimate meaning in terms of finitude.

The second assertion found within the existentialist movement, which establishes its distinctiveness as a philosophical alternative, is what we shall call the *existentiality* of truth and essence. In relation to the question of truth, both Kierkegaard and Heidegger insist, as we have seen, that existence itself is normative for the meaning of truth, i.e., since existence is the presupposition of thought, then all truth, no matter how abstract or universal, is existential and that, therefore, that truth which directly establishes the existentiality of the self (as opposed to Kierkegaard's "so-called" existing self) to the self is the ultimate truth for which man longs, even though it places upon him the burden of choosing his own authentic existence. Most forms of abstract or universal truth are relegated to a *derivative* and thus *secondary* position under the existentialist critique precisely because they fail to confront the self with its own concrete existence.

Not only does the existentialist movement seek a new conception of truth; it also seeks a new conception of man in which the essential-existential bifurcation is overcome. It is not the case, then, as Tillich asserts, that existentialism rejects the notion of essence and, therefore, essentialist thinking. It does, to be sure, reject one historical formulation of the doctrine of essence, a formulation which has its inception with Plato and is continued in Tillich's thought in which it is posited that what man *is* in space and time is somehow a distortion or "fall" from what he essentially is, and consequently his ultimate ethical task is to become reunited with that which he has lost in his concrete existence.

In seeking a new conception of essence, the existentialist movement, especially in the thought of the early Heidegger, does not seek the "pure" existentialism of Tillich's interpretation in which it would seek to describe existence without the universality of language.[12] Heidegger explicitly and Kierkegaard implicitly accepts the capacity of thought to generalize, to abstract, and to develop formal conceptual constructs by means of which its own cognitive function can be fulfilled. Insofar as the conception of essence includes the notions of universals, ideas, and conceptual norms (ST, I: 202), the existentialist movement may be said to work with such a conception, even though it denies the centrality the classical philosophical tradition has given to the essential structure of *cognition* in the search for authentic existence.

It is the valuational meaning of essence (*Ibid.*), in which a distinction is made at the ontological level between what man *actually* is and what he *essentially* is, that the existentialist movement rejects. In trying to develop a conception of man's essence, however, there is significant disagreement among those thinkers who can be appropriately related to the existentialist movement. Tillich, for example, links Heidegger and Sartre together on this issue, even though Heidegger has specifically rejected Sartre's formulation that "existence precedes essence" on the grounds that it is merely another metaphysical statement, the inversion of the classical claim that essence precedes existence.[13] Again, we shall take Heidegger's as the most representative view within the existentialist movement.

Heidegger argues in *Being and Time* that his conception of man's essence breaks with the tradition in which *existentia* means actuality as opposed to *essentia* understood as possibility. The basic reason that Heidegger introduces the term *Existenz* to distinguish it from *existentia* in its traditional usage is that the latter term has been used fundamentally to designate something which merely occurs in the universe, something "present-at hand." The crucial passage is as follows:

> The 'essence' ["*Wesen*"] of this entity lies in its "to be" [*Zu-sein*]. Its Being-what-it-is [*Was-sein*] (essentia) must, so far as we can speak of it at all, be conceived in terms of its Being (existentia). But here our ontological task is to show that when we choose to designate the Being of this entity as "existence" [*Existenz*], this term does not and cannot have the ontological signification of the traditional term "existentia"; ontologically, *existentia* is tantamount to *Being-present-at-hand*, a kind of Being which is essentially inappropriate to entities of Dasein's character. ... The essence of Dasein lies in its existence. Accordingly those characteristics which can be exhibited in this entity are not 'properties' present-at-hand of some entity which 'looks' so and so and is itself present-at-hand; they are in each case possible ways for it to be, and no more than that.[14]

For Heidegger, then, Dasein's essence is its existence, where existence (*Existenz*) is not the individual instantiations of some objective, abstract human nature, but rather where existence refers to those characteristics which make Dasein what it is. Gelven has explicated Heidegger's assertion with helpful clarity. He says:

> The very *meaning* of Dasein is one who reflects on one's existence. This means that I cannot think of Dasein except in terms of possible ways of existing. . . . A look at the etymology of *Existenz* may prove beneficial. The term comes from the Latin *existere*, which, in its root meaning, signifies a "standing out." In later works Heidegger has drawn attention to this etymology by hyphenating the term (*Ex-sistenz*). The point being that only Dasein can stand back from or "out" from its own occurrence in the world and observe itself. Indeed, it is the ability of Dasein to consider and be aware of its own occurrence that is uniquely characteristic of it, and hence is its essence. Thus Existenz does not refer to Dasein's being alive or functioning, but rather to its awareness that it is.[15]

To say that Dasein's essence is its existence is to say that Dasein is essentially that which is expressed in its existence, namely, its being aware of and reflecting upon itself (Dasein's being is an issue for it) and its reflecting upon itself (understanding itself) through that which its existence discloses to it, i.e., its possibilities. It is this we have in mind when claiming that the existentialist movement is based upon the "existentializing" of the notion of essence. Apart from Dasein's existence it has no essence.

Tillich's interpretation of Heidegger (and the existentialist movement in general) is that he, as a "radical" existentialist, wishes to be free of the notion of essence, but his very thought betrays the impossibility of doing so. Heidegger must use language to express himself, and his distinction between inauthentic and authentic existence implies a distinction between what man is essentially (authentic) and what he is existentially (inauthentic). Furthermore, Tillich asserts, Heidegger speaks as if there were no norms, principles, or laws of reason in relation to which Dasein can achieve authentic existence; however, to make the distinction between authentic and inauthentic existence implies a norm and Dasein's capacity to use reason to distinguish between them; hence, Heidegger is inevitably involved in essentialist thought. He cannot consistently carry out his own thought project.[16]

This critique of Heidegger loses much of its force when it is seen that he is not trying to think without essentialist statements, but rather that he is challenging an historical doctrine of essence on the grounds that an existential-ontological analysis of Dasein reveals that its ontological character is not compatible with that historical doctrine. If Dasein's essence is self-aware being-toward-possibility, then both inauthentic and authentic existence are *ways* or *modes* of Dasein's being, and therefore equally expressions of its essentiality, since, for Heidegger, inauthenticity is never a matter of the complete unawareness of one's "mineness." Neither is inauthenticity a matter of the distortion of or fall from one's essence, since one of Dasein's essential possibilities is to be as inauthentic.

Is it the case that Heidegger's thought is, as Tillich charges, *relativistic*, i. e., that it lacks essential and objective norms, principles, laws or reasons which become the teleological content of the self's authenticity?[17] It is true that Being, that is, what it means to be is relative to Dasein's existence; however it does not follow that Heidegger understands Dasein as normless or that his thought's without absolute principles, but it is clear that Dasein must project its own norms from among its own possibilities and *essentially* it can relate to these norms either authentically or inauthentically. The norms are not there as the eternal principles of an essential reality overagainst Dasein; rather they emerge out of the existentiality of Dasein and thus Dasein must assume full responsibility for what it makes of itself. In this regard Tillich is right: no god or conventions "can give directions for the actions of the 'resolute' individual."[18] However, Dasein does have norms and principles, 'laws' of reason which are rooted in its essential reality, but Heidegger's existentialism rules out that these norms or principles can be determined or derived from a source other than man's existence itself. It is the absoluteness of man's finitude and the centrality of man's existence as the fundamental source for the ultimate meaning of his existence in Heidegger's *Being and Time*, which Tillich wishes radically to deny.

Finitude and the existentiality of truth and essence are absolute principles for existentialist thought and constitute, we are suggesting, the *distinctive* motifs of the existentialist movement. Tillich has been deeply influenced by this movement, but his thought, in its ultimate assumptions, is not compatible with existentialism and his critique of existentialist thought, we believe, misses the mark. We conclude, then, that Tillich's claim that theology is existential thinking cannot be sustained, because the classical philosophical assumptions upon which his theology is based deprive this claim of specific meaning by which theology can be distinguished from philosophy in such a way that the distinctive nature of theology emerges from it. Secondly, Tillich's thought in its foundational notions is so divergent from the principles of existentialist thinking that he cannot be understood as an existentialist theologian or philosopher, not even as one who is "fifty percent" an existentialist as he has described himself.[19] This is not to deny that Tillich's use of existentialism is brilliant and creative, but to use existentialism within a structure of thought which remains fundamentally unaffected by it is a quite different matter from working out a theology grounded fully upon existentialist presuppositions.

How, then, shall we assess Tillich's conception of the relationship between philosophy and theology? Tillich's claim that theology is grounded in a universally valid truth, we are asserting, is based upon the classical philosophical model of truth. Tillich uses this model of truth, ironically, to assert the superiority of the truth of theology to that of philosophy itself, for all philosophical truth is ultimately incomplete and can only ask the question which revelatory truth can answer; hence philosophy is fulfilled in revelation. Marvin Fox has mounted a significant critique of Tillich's position at this point. He writes:

> Now if philosophy, at least when it is serious, finds its fulfillment in revelation, and if revelation means the Christian revelation (in Tillich's version), then it is clearly the case that even when he is explicating specifically Christian doctrine Tillich must believe that he is setting down universal philosophical principles, or at least pointing to the conclusions which all philosophic inquiry must reach.[20]

As reason is the preparation for revelation, and the history of revelation is the preparation for final revelation, so philosophy is ultimately preparation for theology, for philosophy is the cognitive clarification of the *question* of being, which philosophy itself cannot answer, and theology is the cognitive clarification of the *answer* of being in relation to the question, the answer, of course, given in revelation; however, Fox's point is that Tillich, speaking as a theologian about the limits of philosophical truth, on his own terms, is also speaking *philosophically* about the nature of the philosophical enterprise and of philosophical truth, and that two of his basic assumptions here are that every serious philosophical inquiry must, if it thinks rightly, come to understand the *intrinsic* incompleteness of whatever truth it achieves by the most rigorous philosophical methods, and that, in fact, all philosophy has been and is, consciously or unconsciously, the search for that revelation which has been given in its finality in Jesus as the Christ.

A very obvious point emerges here, but it should be articulated nonetheless. Tillich could not define the relationship of philosophy and theology to be that of *question* and *answer* if he were not committed to the classical view that theology is grounded in universally valid truth, which not only conforms to the canons of philosophical rationality but is more existentially efficacious than philosophical truth, since it has the capacity to "save" man. Thus, what Tillich has done is join the classical philosophical model of truth with an ontic or existentiell "form of life" (Wittgenstein), namely, the Christian mode of being in which what it means to be a Christian is to be "saved" by the existential truth, Jesus as the Christ. With the ultimate concern that this form of life grounded in Jesus as the Christ is also the universal truth of all men (which Tillich acknowledges is a philosophical assertion), Tillich interprets the nature of philosophy and its relationship to theology. Fox has stated the problem with Tillich's position succinctly:

> It is the sheerest arbitrariness on Tillich's part to present his own . . . very idiosyncratic reading of the history of philosophy as if it were universal. Only if one approaches philosophy with Tillich's kind of Christian conviction already in hand can one arrive at the conclusion that philosophy fulfills itself in revelation. Tillich claims that all philosophy is concerned to know only that it may finally believe. This is a distortion of most of the history of western philosophy.[21]

The implication of Fox's assertion is that in order to be faithful to his classical ontological assumptions, and thus to establish the *complete* universality of Christian truth (i.e., that it is both the cognitive answer to all existential questions, thus compatible with all forms of knowledge and existential truth, and "the power unto salvation") in contrast to the merely abstract and non-existential universality of philosophical truth, Tillich has defined the relationship between theology and philosophy in such a way that philosophy must either accept its incomplete status in relation to theology or become itself a form of theology in the very act of rejecting theology's claims as to its own status, since it is implicated in an ultimate orientation in negating the ultimate truth of theology; thus, wherever an ultimate concern is explicitly expressed by philosophy it becomes a form of theology. Fox's point is that the autonomy of philosophy is radically violated when Tillich imposes Christian theological limitations upon philosophical inquiry at any point, a situation which philosophy cannot accept in spite of Tillich's doctrine of theonomy. Tillich's insistence upon the unity of truth seems to fly in the face of the very substance of the intellectual culture of the West of the last two hundred years.

The consequence of Tillich's conception of the relationship between philosophy and theology is that only a relative distinction is possible between them, a distinction, we have argued, which finally breaks down because of its very relativity. Since Tillich refused to abandon the classical orientation of his thought, it becomes impossible to establish the distinctive identity of the two disciplines on his terms. If Tillich had allowed the existentialist revolution to become normative for his thought, he could have resolved the ambiguity of his conception of the relationship of philosophy and theology by asserting that philosophy's function is to establish the transcendental reality of the existing self as the presupposition of all thought, and thus to show ontologically how Christian truth is possible as an existentiell form of life. Theology's task would be to work out the cognitive implications of that existentiell truth; however, for theology to be existentialist it could *not* assert that its truth is universally valid and thus normative for all men, cultures, and religions and it could *not* assert philosophy's incompleteness and its fulfillment in the truth of the Christian style of life.

Since Tillich could not work out of a consistently existentialist orientation, but rather attempted to graft existentialist concerns into a substantially classical structure of thought, his conception of philosophy, theology, and their relationship to each other is plagued by an ultimately unsatisfying ambiguity and inconsistency. However, to make this judgment is to be more fully aware of his greatness as a thinker and to appreciate more fully the profundity of the task he set for himself. That he was not able to remove this ambiguity from his thought he himself would have understood only too well.

Notes

1 We have seen that Tillich states that no synthesis between philosophy and theology is possible. However, the context makes clear that Tillich does not use the term in the way it is used here. In that context, Tillich means that no synthesis is possible in terms of the development of a "Christian philosophy." Here the term refers to that mutual interaction between philosophy and theology in which a genuinely philosophical theology emerges on the ground of what are, on the surface, two distinct disciplines.

2 *The Protestant Era, op. cit.*, p. 89.

3 *The Courage to Be, op. cit.*, p. 181.

4 John C. Cooper, *The Roots of the Radical Theology* (Westminster Press, Philadelphia, 1967), p. 91.

5 *A History of Christian Thought, op. cit.*, pp. 27-29.

6 It is illuminating to consider that that which makes Jesus the Christ, namely, his surrendering everything which was concretely himself as Jesus of Nazareth to the presence of God as the ground of being within him is precisely what the classical philosopher wished to do, i.e., to rid himself of his peculiarity and particularity in order to become universal himself, and thus to become "the friend of God." Cf. Chapter 10, Part Two.

7 *Theology of Culture, op. cit.*, p. 94ff; Cf. also P. Tillich, "Participation and Knowledge: Problems of an Ontology of Cognition," *op. cit.*, p. 204ff. 8 *A History of Christian Thought, op. cit.*, pp. 470-471.

9 Michael Gelven, *A Commentary on Heidegger's Being and Time* (Harper and Row, N.Y., 1970), p. 25.

10 *Ibid.*, p. 16.

11 *Ibid.*, pp. 231; 204.

12 Cf. *A History of Christian Thought, op. cit.*, p. 541.

13 Cf. Heidegger, "Letter on Humanism," *op. cit.*, p. 280.

14   *Being and Time, op. cit.*, p. 67.

15   Gelven, *op. cit.*, pp. 44-45.

16   *The Courage to Be, op. cit.*, pp. 148-149; *Theology of Culture, op. cit.*, p. 121.

17   *Theology of Culture, op. cit.*, p. 119.

18   *The Courage to Be, op. cit.*, p. 148.

19   *A History of Christian Thought, op. cit.*, p. 541.

20   Marvin Fox, "Tillich's Ontology and God," in *God, Man, and Religion*, ed. Keith E. Yandell (McGraw-hill, N.Y., 19730, p. 263.

21   *Ibid.*, p. 265.

Bibliography

I. Books by Paul Tillich

Biblical Religion and the Search for Ultimate Reality. Chicago: University of Chicago Press, 1955.

The Courage to Be. New Haven: Yale University Press, 1952.

Dynamics of Faith. New York: Harper and Row, 1957.

Gesammelte Werke. Edited by Renate Albrecht. Stuttgart: Evangelisches Verlags-Werke. Volume I (1959), Volume II (1962), Volume III (1965), Volume IV (1961), Volume V (1964), Volume VI (1963).

A History of Christian Thought. Edited by Carl Braaten. New York: Simon and Schuster, 1967.

The Interpretation of History. Translated by N. A. Rasetzki and Elsa L. Talmey. New York: Charles Scribner's Sons, 1936.

Love, Power, and Justice. New York: Oxford University Press, 1954.

Morality and Beyond. New York: Harper and Row, 1963.

My Search for Absolutes. New York: Simon and Schuster, 1967.

On the Boundary. New York: Charles Scribner's Sons, 1966.

The Protestant Era. Translated by James Luther Adams. Chicago: University of Chicago Press, 1948.

Religiöse Verwirklichung. Berlin: Furche-Verlag, 1930.

The Religious Situation. Translated by H. Richard Niebuhr. New York: Meridian Books, 1962.

Systematic Theology. Three volumes. Chicago: University of Chicago Press. Volume I (1951), Volume II (1957), Volume III (1963).

Theology of Culture. Edited by Robert C. Kimball. New York: Oxford University Press, 1959.

Ultimate Concern: Tillich in Dialogue, Edited by D. Mackenzie Brown. New York: Harper and Row, 1965.

What is Religion? Translated with an introduction by James Luther Adams. New York: Harper and Row, 1969.

II. Articles by Paul Tillich

"Existential Analyses and Religious Symbols". *Contemporary Problems in Religion*. Edited by H. A. Basilius. Detroit: Wayne University Press, 1956.

"Kritisches und Positives Paradox; Ein Auseinandersetzung mit Karl Barth und Friedrich Gogarten". *Theologische Blätter*, Vol. II, No. 11, November, 1923. Reprinted in *The Beginnings of Dialectical Theology*. Edited by James M. Robinson. Richmond: John Knox Press, 1968.

"The Meaning and Justification of Religious Symbols". *Religious Experience and Truth*, Edited by Sidney Hook. New York: New York University Press, 1961.

"Mystik und Schuldbewusstsein in Schelling's Philosophischer Entwicklung". *Gesammelte Werke*, Vol. I. Edited by Renate Albrecht. Stuttgart: Evangelisches Verlagswerk, 1959.

"Nietzsche and the Bourgeois Spirit". *Journal of the History of Ideas*, Vol. 6 (1945).

"Participation and Knowledge: Problems of an Ontology of Cognition". *Sociologica. Aufsätze Max Horkheimer zum sechzigste Geburtstag gewidmet*, Vol. I. Edited by Theodor W. Adorno and Walter Dicks. Frankfurt: Europâîsche Verlagsastalt, a. M., 1955.

"Philosophical Background of My Theology". Lecture, Tokyo, Japan: St. Paul's University (May 12, 1960). Unpublished.

"Philosophie: Begriff und Wesen". *Die Religion in Geschichte und Gegenwart*, Tübingen: J.C.B. Mohr, 1930. Reprinted in *Gesammelte Werke*, Vol. IV, Edited by Renate Albrecht. Stuttgart: Evangelisches Verlagswerke, 1961.

"The Problem of Theological Method". *Four Existentialist Theologians*. Edited by Will Herberg. Garden City, N. Y.: Doubleday and Co., 1958.

"Rechtfertigung und Zweifel". *Vorträge der theologischen Konferenz zu Giessen*, No. 39, 1924.

"A Reinterpretation of the Doctrine of Incarnation". *Church Quarterly Review*, Vol. CXLVII, 1949.

"Das religióse Symbol". *Blätter für deutsche Philosophie*, Vol. I, No. 4, 1928. Reprinted in *Religiose Verwirklichung*. Berlin Furche-Verlag, 1930. Translated into English by J. L. Adams and Ernest Fraenkel, *Journal of Liberal Religion*, Vol. 2, 1940. Reprinted in *Daedalus*, Summer, 1958 and *Religious Experi-*

ence and Truth. Edited by Sidney Hook. New York: New York University Press, 1961.

"The Struggle Between Time and Space", *Theology of Culture.* Edited by Robert Kimball. New York: Oxford University Press, 1959.

"Das System Der Wissenschaften nach Gegenständen und Methoden". *Gesammelte Werke*, Vol. I. Edited by Renate Albrecht. Stuttgart: Evangelisches Verlagswerk, 1959.

"The Two Types of Philosophy of Religion". In *Theology of Culture.* Edited by Robert Kimball. New York: Oxford University Press, 1959. "What is Wrong with the 'Dialectical' Theology?". *The Journal of Religion*, Vol. XV, No. 2 (1935).

III. Other Works Cited.

Books

Adams, James L. *Paul Tillich's Philosophy of Culture, Science, and Religion.* New York: Harper and Row, 1965.

Berger, Peter L. *The Sacred Canopy.* Garden City, New York: Doubleday and Co., 1969.

Brown, James. *Subject and Object in Modern Theology.* London: SCM Press Ltd., 1955.

Buber, Martin. *Eclipse of God.* New York: Harper and Brothers, 1952.

Christian, William S. *Meaning and Truth in Religion.* Princeton, N. J.: Princeton University Press, 1962.

Cobb, John B., Jr. *Living Options in Protestant Theology.* Philadelphia: The Westminister Press, 1962.

Collingwood, R. G. *An Essay on Philosophical Method.* London: Oxford University Press, 1933.

Collins, James. *The Emergence of Philosophy of Religion.* New Haven: Yale University Press, 1967.

Copleston, Fredrick. *A History of Philosophy.* Garden City, N.Y.: Doubleday & Co.., Inc.

Cooper, John C. *The Roots of the Radical Theology.* Philadelphia: Westminister Press, 1967.

Cox, Harvey. *The Secular City.* New York: Macmillan Company, 1965.

Dilley, Frank B. *Metaphysics and Religious Language.* New York and London: Columbia University Press, 1964.

Emmet, Dorothy. *The Nature of Metaphysical Thinking.* New York: Macmillan and Co., 1966.

Ferré, Frederick. *A Basic Modern Philosophy of Religion.* New York: Charles Scribners, 1968.

_____. *Language, Logic, and God.* New York: Harper and Row, 1961.

Gelven, Michael. *A Commentary on Heidegger's Being and Time.* New York: Harper and Row, 1970.

Gilkey, Langdon. *Religion and the Scientific Future.* New York: Harper and Row, 1960.

Gray, J. Glenn. *Hegel and Greek Thought.* New York: Harper and Row, 1968.

Hamilton, Kenneth. *The System and the Gospel.* New York: Macmillan and Co., 1962.

Hartshorne, Charles. *The Divine Relativity.* New Haven: Yale University Press, 1948.

Hegel, G. W. F. *Phenomenology of Mind.* Translated by J. B. Baille. London: George Allen and Unwin, 1961.

Heidegger, Martin. *Being and Time.* Translated by John Macquarrie and Edward Robinson. New York: Harper and Row, 1962.

Hick, John. *Philosophy of Religion.* Englewood Cliffs, New York: Prentice-Hall, 1963.

Hook, Sidney, Editor. *Religious Experience and Truth.* New York: New York University Press, 1961.

Hopper, David. *Tillich, A Theological Portrait.* Philadelphia and New York: J. B. Lippincott, 1968.

Jaeger, Werner. *Paideia.* Translated by Gilbert Highet. New York: Oxford University Press, 1945.

Johnson, Robert C. *Authority in Protestant Theology.* Philadelphia: The Westminister Press, 1959.

Jowett, Benjamin, Translator. *The Dialogues of Plato.* New York: Random House, 1937.

Kaufmann, Walter. *Hegel: A Reinterpretation.* New York: Doubleday and Co., Anchor Books, 1966.

Kantonen, T. A. *Paul Tillich: Retrospect and Future.* Nashville and New York: Abingdon Press, 1966.

Kelsey, David H. *The Fabric of Paul Tillich's Theology.* New Haven and London: Yale University Press, 1967.

Kierkegaard, Soren. *Concluding Unscientific Postscript.* Translated by W. Lowrie. Princeton, N. J.: Princeton University Press, 1941.

_____. *Either/Or.* Translated by W. Lowrie. New York: Doubleday, 1959.

_____. *Fear and Trembling.* Translated by W. Lowrie. New York: Doubleday, 1954.

_____. *The Sickness Unto Death.* Translated by W. Lowrie. New York: Doubleday, 1954.

Lauer, Quentin, S. J. *Hegel's Idea of Philosophy.* New York: Fordham University Press, 1971.

Magee, John. *Religion and Modern Man.* New York: Harper and Row, 1969.

Marcuse, Herbert. *One Dimensional Man.* Boston: Beacon Press, 1941.

_____. *Reason and Revolution.* Boston: Beacon Press, 1941.

Martin, Bernard. *Paul Tillich's Doctrine of Man.* London: James Nisbet, 1966.

Marx, Werner. *Heidegger and the Tradition.* Translated by T. Kisiel and M. Green. Evanston, Illinois: Northwestern University Press, 1971.

May, Rollo, Angel, Ernest, and Ellenberger, Henri F., Editors. *Existence.* New York: Basic Books, 1958.

Mckelway, Alexander J. *The Systematic Theology of Paul Tillich.* Richmond: John Knox Press, 1964.

McKeon, Richard, Editor. *The Basic Works of Aristotle.* New York: Randon House, 1941.

Nietzsche, Frederick. *Beyond Good and Evil.* Translated by Walter Kaufmann. New York: Vintage Books, 1966.

Norenberg, Klaus-Dieter. *Analogia Imaginis.* Gutersloh: Gütersloher Verlagshaus Gerd Mohn, 1966.

Nygren, Anders. *Agape and Eros.* Translated by Philip S. Watson. Philadelphia: The Westminister Press, 1953.

Poole, Roger. *Towards Deep Subjectivity.* New York: Harper, 1972.

Pusey, E. B., Translator. *The Confessions of St. Augustine.* New York: The Modern Library, 1949.

Randall, John H., Jr. *Aristotle.* New York: Columbia University Press, 1960.

_____. *The Theology of Paul Tillich.* Edited by Charles W. Kegley and Robert W. Bretall. New York: Macmillan Co., 1952.

Robinson, James M. *The Beginnings of Dialectical Theology.* Vol. I. Richmond, Virginia: John Knox Press, 1968.

Rome, Beatrice and Sydney, Editors. *Philosophical Interrogations.* New York: Holt, Rinehart, and Winston, 1964.

Rowe, William. *Religious Symbols and God.* Chicago: The University of Chicago Press, 1968.

Sartre, Jean-Paul. *Being and Nothingness*. Translated by Hazel E. Barnes. New York: Philosophical Library, 1956.

Scharlemann, Robert P. *Reflection and Doubt in the Thought of Paul Tillich*. New Haven: Yale University Press, 1969.

Shwayder, David S. *The Stratification of Behaviour*. New York: The Humanities Press, 1965.

Smith, John E. *Reason and God*. New Haven: Yale University Press, 1961.

Snell, Bruno. *The Discovery of the Mind*. Translated by T. G. Rosenmeyer. New York: Harper and Row, 1960.

Solomon, Robert C. *From Rationalism to Existentialism: The Existentialists and their Nineteenth-Century Backgrounds*. New York: Harper and Row, 1972.

Towne, Edgar E. "Ontological and Theological Dimensions of God in the Thought of Paul Tillich and Charles Hartshorne." Unpublished Ph. D. dissertation, University of Chicago, 1967.

Warner, Rex. *The Greek Philosophers*. New York: The New American Library, 1958.

Whitehead, Alfred North. *Process and Reality*. New York: The Macmillan Co., 1929.

Wieman, Henry N. *Intellectual Foundations of Faith*. New York: Philosophical Library, 1961.

_____. *The Source of Human Good*. Carbondale: Southern Illinois University Press, 1946.

Williams, Daniel D. *The Spirit and Forms of Love*. New York: Harper and Row, 1968.

Articles

Adams, James L. "What Kind of Religion Has a Place in Higher Education?". *Journal of Bible and Religion*, Vol. XIII (1945).

Dillenberger, John. "Paul Tillich: Theologian of Culture". *Paul Tillich, Retrospect and Prospect*. Nashville and New York: Abingdon Press, 1966.

Driver, Tom. *Union Seminary Quarterly Review*, Vol. XX, No. 1 (Nov. 1965).

Edwards, Paul. "Professor Tillich's Confusions". *Mind*, Vol. 74, No. 294 (1965).

Fenton, John Y. "Being-itself and Religious Symbolism". *The Journal of Religion*, Vol. XV, No. 2 (April, 1965).

Ford, Lewis S. "The Three Strands of Tillich's Theory of Religious Symbols". *The Journal of Religion*, Vol. 46, No. I, I (1966).

_____. "Tillich and Thomas: The Analogy of Being", *The Journal of Religion*, Vol. 46, No. 2 (April, 1966).

Fox, Marvin. "Tillich's Ontology and God". *God, Man, and Religion*. Edited by Keith E. Yandell. New York: McGraw-Hill, 1973.

Hartshorne, Charles. "Tillich and the Nontheological Meanings". *Paul Tillich: Retrospect and Future*. Nashville and New York: Abingdon Press, 1966.

Harvey, Van A. "Review of *Systematic Theology*, Volume III". *Theology Today*, Vol. XXI, No. 3 (October, 1964).

Heidegger, Martin. "Plato's Doctrine of Truth with a Letter on Humanism". Translated by J. Barlow and E. Lohner. *Philos-*

ophy in the Twentieth Century, Vol. II. Edited by H. Aiken and W. Barrett. New York: Random House, 1962.

Hick, John. *Scottish Journal of Theology,* Vol. 12, No. 3 (1959).

Howe, LeRoy T. "Tillich on the Trinity". *The Christian Scholar,* Vol. XLIX, No. 3 (Fall, 1966).

Kaufman, Gordon. "Can a Man Serve Two Masters?". *Theology Today,* Vol. 15.

Livingston, James. "Tillich's Christology and Historical Research". *Paul Tillich: Retrospect and Future.* Nashville and New York: Abingdon Press, 1966.

Loomer, Bernard M. "Tillich's Theology of Correlation". *The Journal of Religion,* Vol. XXVI, No. 3 (July, 1956).

Macquarrie, John. "How is Theology Possible?". *Union Seminary Quarterly Review,* Vol. XVIII, No. 2 (Winter 1963).

Novak, Michael. "Philosophy for the New Generation". *American Philosophy and the Future.* Edited by Michael Novak. New York: Charles Scribner's Sons, 1968.

Ogden, Schubert M. "Theology and Objectivity". *The Reality of God and Other Essays.* New York: Harper and Row, 1966.

Pepper, Stephen. "The Root Metaphor Theory of Metaphysics". *The Journal of Philosophy,* Vol. XXXII, No. 14 (July, 1935).

Peters, Eugene H. "Tillich's Doctrine of Essence, Existence, and the Christ". *The Journal of Religion,* Vol. 43, No. 4 (Oct. 1963).

Pruyser, Paul W. "Anxiety: Affect or Cognitive State?". *Constructive Aspects of Anxiety.* Edited by S. Hiltner and K. Menninger. New York: Abingdon Press, 1963.

Ross, James. "On the Relationships of Philosophy and Theology". *Union Seminary Quarterly Review*, Vol. XXVI, No. I (Fall, 1970).

Rowe, William L. "The Meaning of 'God' in Tillich's Theology". *The Journal of Religion*, Vol. 42, No. 4 (1962).

Scharlemann, Robert. "Tillich's Method of Correlation: Two Proposed Revisions". *The Journal of Religion*, Vol. 46, No. 1, I (1966).

Schrag, Calvin O. "Phenomenology, Ontology, and History in the Philosophy of Heidegger". *Phenomenology*. Edited by Joseph J. Kockelmans. New York: Doubleday, 1967.

Smith, D. Moody, Jr. "The Historical Jesus in Paul Tillich's Christology". *The Journal of Religion*, Vol. 46, No. 1, I (1966).

Smith, Huston. "The Reach and the Grasp: Transcendence Today". *Transcendence*. Edited by Herbert W. Richardson and Donald R. Cutler. Boston: Beacon Press, 1969.

Urban, William. "Critique of Tillich's 'The Religious Symbol'". *The Journal of Liberal Religion*, Vol. 2 (1940).

Williams, Daniel D. "Barth and Brunner on Philosophy". *The Journal of Religion*, Vol. 27, No. 4 (1947).

_____. "Review of *Systematic Theology*, Vol. II." *The Journal of Religion*, Vol. 46, No. 1, II (1966).

Williamson, Clark. "Review of *Systematic Theology*, Vol. III". *The Journal of Religion*, Vol. 46, No. 2 (1966).

Index

A

Abraham
  Kierkegaard on, 316-318
  teleological suspension of the
    ethical and, Kierkegaard on,
    329-330
Absolute standpoint, 177
Actus purus, doctrine of, rejection of,
  101
Alston, William, on Tillich's
  conception of God, 91
Analogia entis, participation and,
  120-121
Analysis, method of, 3-10
Answer and question, correlation of,
  in system, 19
Anxiety
  change and, 61-62
  in existentialism, 410-411, 412
  and fear, Heidegger's distinction
    between, 374-375, 410-411
  finitude and, 57
  mood of, Dasein's response to,
    374-377
  of nonbeing, 62-63
Apologetic method, theological,
  243-244
Aristotle
  on nature of being, 309-311
  on philosopher, 312-313
  on rationality, 311-312
Augustine
  existential attitude in, 387
  ontological way with, 124
Autonomy, reason and, 166-167

B

Barth, Karl
  on divine-human relationship in
    Tillich, 269

on independence of theology
    from philosophy, 286
  Tillich's criticism of, 127-128
Becoming, form-dynamics polarity
    and, 45
Being
  analogical doctrine of, essence
    and existence and, 70-72
  concept of, 21, 23
  of equipment as readiness-to-
    hand, 363-365
  Heidegger on, 350-384
  is finite, existentialist movement
    and, 455
  meanings of, 55
  philosophy and, 289
  power of, Tillich's Christology
    and, 130-132
  states of, 66-67
  structure of. See Structure of
    being
  theology and, 289
  Tillich's conception of, distinction
    between essence and
    existence and, 70-72
  unconditioned and conditioned,
    unity of, 119-143. See also
    Unity of unconditioned and
    conditioned being
Being and Time (Heidegger), 349-
  384. *See also* Heidegger, Martin
"Being as such," Tillich's use of,
    Randall on, 29-30
Being-in-the-world
  as concern, Dasein as, 361-366
  Dasein as, 357-360
Being-itself
  and God, conceptual-linguistic
    distinction between, 93-94
  God as, 95-96
  as nonentity, 96-97
  structure of being and, 30-31

DATE DUE

AUG 15 2005			
JAN 3 2006			
JAN 3 2006			
JUL 1 2006			
FEB 0 2016			
JUN 1 2 2016			